Personal Autonomy in Plural Societies

This volume addresses the exercise of personal autonomy in contemporary situations of normative pluralism. In the Western liberal tradition, from a strictly legal and theoretical perspective the social individual has the right to exercise the autonomy of his or her will. In a context of legal plurality, however, personal autonomy becomes more complicated. Can and should personal autonomy be recognized as a legal foundation for protecting a person's freedom to renounce what others view as his or her fundamental 'human rights'? This collection develops an interdisciplinary conceptual framework to address these questions and presents empirical studies examining the gap between the principle of personal autonomy and its implementation. In a context of cultural diversity, this gap manifests itself in two particular ways. First, not every culture gives the same pre-eminence to personal autonomy when examining the legal effects of an individual's acts. Second, in a society characterized by 'weak pluralism', the legal assessment of personal autonomy often favours the views of the dominant majority. In highlighting these diverse perspectives and problematizing the so-called 'guardian function' of human rights, i.e., purporting to protect weaker parties by limiting their personal autonomy in the name of gender equality, fair trial, etc., this book offers a nuanced approach to the principle of autonomy and addresses the questions of whether it can effectively be deployed in situations of internormativity and what conditions must be met in order to ensure that it is not rendered devoid of all meaning.

Marie-Claire Foblets is Director of the Department of Law and Anthropology at the Max Planck Institute for Social Anthropology in Halle, Germany, and Professor of Law at the Catholic University of Leuven, Belgium.

Michele Graziadei is Professor of Comparative Law at the University of Turin, Italy, and President of the Italian Society for Research on Comparative Law (SIRD).

Alison Dundes Renteln is Professor of Political Science, Anthropology, Law, and Public Policy at the University of Southern California, where she teaches International Law and Human Rights.

Law and Anthropology Series
Series Editor: Marie-Claire Foblets,
Max Planck Institute for Social Anthropology, Germany

The series is intended as a forum for the publication of outstanding scholarly contributions that strive systematically to involve legal practitioners in the research, thinking, and theorizing about the search for justice and the accommodation of diversity in contemporary pluralistic societies. It focuses on applied legal anthropology, giving equal weight both to an anthropologically informed understanding of diversity of normative orders (often existing side-by-side within a single state system) and to the practical, pragmatic experience and concerns of legal practitioners (judges, lawyers, legal services representatives, etc.) who, in their daily practice, confront the phenomenon of 'internormativity' – situations where different normative logics come into contact (and often conflict) with one another – and the resulting need for state legal systems to accommodate this diversity.

www.routledge.com/Law-and-Anthropology/book-series/LAWANTH

Personal Autonomy in Plural Societies

A Principle and its Paradoxes

Edited by
Marie-Claire Foblets,
Michele Graziadei, and
Alison Dundes Renteln

Routledge
Taylor & Francis Group
LONDON AND NEW YORK

First published 2018 by Routledge

2 Park Square, Milton Park, Abingdon, Oxfordshire OX14 4RN
52 Vanderbilt Avenue, New York, NY 10017

Routledge is an imprint of the Taylor & Francis Group, an informa business

First issued in paperback 2019

British Library Cataloguing-in-Publication Data
A catalogue record for this book is available from the British Library

Library of Congress Cataloging-in-Publication Data
Names: Foblets, Marie-Claire, 1959– editor. | Graziadei, Michele, editor. | Renteln, Alison Dundes, editor.
Title: Personal autonomy in plural societies: a principle and its paradoxes / edited by Marie-Claire Foblets, Michele Graziadei, Alison Dundes Renteln.
Description: Abingdon, Oxon ; N.Y., NY : Routledge, 2018. | Series: Law and anthropology | Includes bibliographical references and index.
Identifiers: LCCN 2017027829 | ISBN 9781138220218 (hardback)
Subjects: LCSH: Human rights. | Religious minorities—Legal status, laws, etc. | Legal polycentricity. | Autonomy (Psychology)—Social aspects. | Law and anthropology.
Classification: LCC K3242 .P468 2018 | DDC 342.08/5—dc23
LC record available at https://lccn.loc.gov/2017027829

ISBN: 978-1-138-22021-8 (hbk)
ISBN: 978-0-367-88449-9 (pbk)

DOI: 10.4324/9781315413617

Contents

Contributors

Toon Agten is a PhD Candidate and teaching assistant at the Leuven Institute for Human Rights and Critical Studies (LIHRICS) within the Law Faculty at the Katholieke Universiteit (KU) Leuven. He received a Master of Law from the KU Leuven (2011) and a Bachelor of Arts in Philosophy (2013). He is currently preparing his PhD dissertation on the principle of autonomy in the European Convention on Human Rights as applied to reproductive autonomy and pre-implantation genetic diagnosis (PGD).

Rajnaara Akhtar is currently a Lecturer in Law at De Montfort University, Leicester, UK. She received her doctorate in 2013 from the University of Warwick, for which she focused on legal pluralism, dispute resolution, sharia councils, British Muslims, and Islamic family law. She is professionally trained as a solicitor.

Shaheen Sardar Ali is Professor of Law, University of Warwick, UK, and a former vice chair of the United Nations Working Group on Arbitrary Detention. She has taught and published extensively on Islamic law, gender, human rights, and international law, and served in an advisory role for a number of international organizations. Professor Ali has received a number of national and international awards, and was named one of the 100 most influential women of Pakistan in 2012.

Katayoun Alidadi is an Assistant Professor of Legal Studies at Bryant University (Smithfield, RI, USA) and a Research Associate at the Max Planck Institute for Social Anthropology (Halle, Germany). She holds a PhD in law from the KULeuven (Leuven, Belgium) and an LL.M. from Harvard Law School (Cambridge, MA, USA). She has written extensively on human rights and anti-discrimination law, private international law, employment law, and the intersections of law and religion. She is the author of *Religion, Equality and Employment in Europe: The Case for Reasonable Accommodation* (Hart 2017).

Lucia Bellucci is an Assistant Professor in the Law School at the University of Milan. She holds a PhD in Sociology of Law from the University of Milan as well as a PhD in Law from the University of Paris 1-Panthéon Sorbonne. She taught International and European Media Regulation at the International Master's in Sociology of Law at the Oñati International Institute for the Sociology of Law (2011–2013), and has lectured at Italian and Canadian universities. She has published widely on media law in context and law and anthropology.

Keebet von Benda-Beckmann is an honorary Professor Emeritus of Legal Pluralism at Martin Luther University Halle-Wittenberg. She headed the project group Legal Pluralism at the Max Planck Institute for Social Anthropology (Halle, Germany) until the end of 2012, and since then has been an associate researcher at the MPI. She has conducted research in West Sumatra and the Moluccas in Indonesia and among Moluccan migrants in the Netherlands. She is co-author (with Franz von Benda-Beckmann) of *Political and Legal Transformations of an Indonesian Polity* (Cambridge, 2013).

John Christman is Professor of Philosophy, Political Science, and Women's Studies at Pennsylvania State University. His work covers agency and autonomy, freedom, social identity, the nature of the self, human rights and human trafficking, and related issues in moral and political philosophy. He is author or editor of a number of volumes including *The Politics of Person: Individual Autonomy and Socio-historical Selves* (Cambridge, 2009) and *Autonomy and the Challenges to Liberalism* (Cambridge, 2005, co-edited with Joel Anderson).

Monique Deveaux is Professor of Philosophy at the University of Guelph, where she holds the Canada Research Chair in Ethics and Global Social Change. She is the author of the books *Gender and Justice in Multicultural Liberal States* (Oxford 2006) and *Cultural Pluralism in Liberal and Democratic Thought* (Cornell 2000), and co-editor of the volumes *Exploitation: From Practice to Theory* (Rowman & Littlefield 2017), *Introduction to Social and Political Philosophy* (Oxford 2014), *Reading Onora O'Neill* (Routledge 2013), and *Sexual Justice/Cultural Justice* (Routledge 2007). Deveaux's current research focuses on the problem of social and political agency in the context of global inequality and poverty.

Avigail Eisenberg is Professor and Chair of the Department of Political Science at the University of Victoria. Her research focuses on political pluralism and democratic theory, with a particular interest in minorities and identity politics. Her recent publications include *Reasons of Identity* (Oxford 2009), *Identity Politics in the Public Realm* (co-edited, UBC Press 2011), and *Recognition versus Self-Determination* (co-edited, UBC Press 2014).

Marie-Claire Foblets is Director of the Department of Law & Anthropology at the Max Planck Institute for Social Anthropology in Halle, Germany, and Professor of Law and Anthropology at the Katholieke Universiteit (KU) Leuven and the Martin Luther University in Halle. She has published widely on, among other topics, migration law, citizenship/nationality laws, and compulsory integration. In the field of anthropology of law, her research focuses on cultural diversity and legal practice and the accommodation of cultural and religious diversity under state law. Her publications on these topics include the co-edited volumes *Cultural Diversity and the Law* (Bruylant 2010) and *Legal Approaches to Cultural Diversity* (Martinus Nijhoff 2013).

Michele Graziadei is Professor of Comparative Law at the University of Torino and also teaches at the Faculté internationale de droit comparé, Strasbourg. His research focuses on the methodology of comparative law, legal pluralism, law and language, and other theoretical problems relating to the comparison of laws. He is President of the Italian Society for Research on Comparative Law (SIRD). His publications include 'Children's Rights: The Law's Uncertain Search For Principle and the Relevance of Cross-Cultural Thinking', in G. Cortese (ed.), *Reflections on Children's Rights – Marginalised Identities in the Discourse(s) of Justice* (Polimetrica 2011), and *Comparative Property Law: Global Perspectives* (Edgar Elgar 2017, with L. Smith).

Jessica Johnson completed her PhD at the University of Cambridge in 2013 and is currently a Lecturer in the Anthropology of Africa at the University of Birmingham, UK. Dr Johnson's research concentrates on issues of gender and law in the southern African country of Malawi, where she has carried out extensive participant observation research in a police victim support unit, magistrates' courts, and village settings. She is author of 'After the Mines: The Changing Social and Economic Landscape of Malawi-South Africa

Migration' (*Review of African Political Economy* 2017). She is currently working on a monograph based on her doctoral thesis, which focuses on ideas of justice as they pertain to gender and marital relations.

Ian Kalman is a postdoctoral fellow of Indigenous-Local Intergovernmental Relations in the Department of Political Science at Western University (London, Ontario). He holds a doctorate in anthropology from McGill University. Since 2012 he has engaged in ethnographic research with Canadian border officers and residents of Akwesasne, an indigenous community straddling the border of Canada and the United States. His research juxtaposes phenomenological approaches to place and space – how the border is experienced by different actors – with questions of legal pluralism – how those actors understand, interpret, and articulate border crossing.

Arjumand Bano Kazmi is currently a PhD Candidate in Law at the University of Warwick, UK. She has extensive experience working with non-governmental organizations in Pakistan and the United Kingdom, with a focus on women's and minority rights, constitutionalism, and the promotion of democracy in fragile states. She holds a Master's in Law in Development from the University of Warwick.

Kalindi Kokal holds an LLM degree from the University of London and completed her PhD dissertation in law at the Martin Luther University, Halle, Germany (in conjunction with the Law and Anthropology Department of the Max Planck Institute for Social Anthropology) in 2017. Her research interests include legal pluralism, legal ethnography, non-state dispute processing, and translations of state law in everyday life in India and in South Asia generally. Her PhD research focused on understanding the manner in which non-state forums and actors of dispute processing engage with state law in two rural communities in India.

Geoffrey Brahm Levey is an Australian Research Council Future Fellow and Associate Professor in Political Science at the University of New South Wales, Sydney. He was the Founding Director of UNSW's Program in Jewish Studies. He has published extensively on issues in contemporary political theory (with special reference to cultural rights and multiculturalism), the philosophy of social science, and Jewish politics and society. He is editor of *Authenticity, Autonomy and Multiculturalism* (Routledge 2015) and *Political Theory and Australian Multiculturalism* (Berghahn 2012, 2008), and co-editor of *The Politics of Citizenship in Immigrant Democracies* (Routledge 2015, with Ayelet Shachar) and *Secularism, Religion and Multicultural Citizenship* (Cambridge 2008, with Tariq Modood). He is currently completing a book on autonomy and the right to culture.

Annelies Moors is Professor of Contemporary Muslim Societies in the Department of Anthropology, University of Amsterdam. From 2001 to 2008 she was the chair of the International Institute for the Study of Islam in the Modern World (ISIM), directing the programme on Muslim cultural politics. She has conducted ethnographic fieldwork in Palestine, Yemen, and the Netherlands and has published widely on gender, nation, and religion as they relate to topics such as Muslim family law, wearing gold, the visual media, migrant domestic labour, Islamic fashion and anti-fashion, face veiling, and Islamic marriages. She is the PI of an ERC-funded project, 'Problematizing "Muslim marriages": Ambiguities and Contestations' and of a project on Muslim activism funded by the Netherlands Organisation for Scientific Research (NWO).

Alberto H. Neidhardt holds a master's degree in International Comparative Legal Studies from SOAS (University of London), where he focused on intercultural human rights, comparative family law, and ethnic minority studies. His interest in cultural diversity and legal pluralism also grew out of formative experiences at the Centre for Ethnic Minority Studies in London and in the RELIGARE project, a Europe-wide research project on religious diversity and innovative approaches to law and policy. In 2013 he was awarded an LLM in Comparative, European, and International Laws by the European University Institute (EUI) in Florence, Italy, where he is now working on his PhD on the relationship between the evolution of the nation-state, models of private international law, and the protection of normative diversity and equality in the European context.

Chiara Quagliariello is currently Research Associate at the European University Institute (EUI) in Florence, Italy, where she is working within the ERC-funded project 'Intimate Encounters in EU Borderlands: Migrant Maternity, Sovereignty, and the Politics of Care on Europe's Periphery'. She holds a PhD in Anthropology from the University of Siena, Italy, and a PhD in Sociology from the University of Paris VIII, France. She has extensive field research experience in Italy, France, and Senegal. Her research interests include medical anthropology with a particular focus on childbirth models; women's reproductive rights; social and health inequalities; health democracy; intercultural medicine; and medical challenges in migrant patients' health care and assistance.

Alison Dundes Renteln is Professor of Political Science, Anthropology, Law, and Public Policy at the University of Southern California, where she teaches International Law and Human Rights. A graduate of Harvard (History and Literature), she has a PhD in Jurisprudence and Social Policy from the University of California, Berkeley, and a JD from the USC Gould School of Law. Her publications include *The Cultural Defense* (Oxford 2004), *Folk Law* (University of Wisconsin 1995), *Multicultural Jurisprudence* (Hart 2009), and *Cultural Law* (Cambridge 2010). She has collaborated with the UN on the implementation of the Convention on the Rights of Persons with Disabilities and served on several California civil rights commissions and the California committee of Human Rights Watch. In spring 2014 she was Human Rights Fellow at the School of Advanced Study at the University of London.

Jinske Verhellen studied law (1994, Ghent University, Belgium) and anthropology (1995, KULeuven, Belgium). She worked at the Ghent University Institute of Private International Law (1996–2000), during which time she participated in a research project on family disputes involving Moroccan women in Belgium. In 1998 she started to practise law, specializing in international family law and migration law. In 2006 Verhellen helped develop the Private International Law Centre in Brussels, which gives advice and engages in policy work in the field of private international law in family matters. In 2012 Verhellen obtained her PhD from Ghent University and since 2014 has been Professor of Law at Ghent University, lecturing on private international law and international family law.

Olaf Zenker is Professor of Social Anthropology at the University of Fribourg, Switzerland. He received his Ph.D. from the Martin Luther University in Halle, Germany (in conjunction with the Max Planck Institute for Social Anthropology) and his *habilitation* from the University of Bern, Switzerland. His research has dealt with politico-legal issues such as statehood, the rule of law, modernity, and conflict and identity formations, as well as sociolinguistics and anthropological epistemologies. His recent co-edited and authored books include: *South African Homelands as Frontiers: Apartheid's Loose Ends in the Postcolonial Era* (2016); *Transition and Justice: Negotiating the Terms of New Beginnings in Africa (2015); Irish/ness Is All Around Us: Language Revivalism and the Culture of Ethnic Identity in Northern Ireland (2013);* and *Beyond Writing Culture: Current Intersections of Epistemologies and Representational Practices* (2010).

Acknowledgements

This volume represents the first publication in the series *Law & Anthropology*, which will be the flagship series of the Law & Anthropology Department of the Max Planck Institute for Social Anthropology in Halle, Germany.

Most of the contributions presented in this collective volume were first presented at the conference *(Not) Outside My Culture: The Paradoxes of Personal Autonomy in a Plural Society*, sponsored by the Law & Anthropology Department and held at the Max Planck Institute for Social Anthropology in Halle, Germany, 26–28 May 2014. In the course of developing the volume some authors dropped out, while others were invited to contribute pieces that were not originally presented at the conference.

The volume has also benefitted greatly from conference participants who served as discussants, chairs, and presenters, but whose contributions are not represented here as individual chapters, including Julie Billaud, John Bowen, Clémence Désiré, Ute Frevert, Armando Guevara Gil, Anthony Good, Armin Höland, Matthias Lehmann, Werner Menski, Ralf Michaels, Mathias Rohe, Bertram Turner, Geert Vervaeke, and Nadjma Yassari.

One unique aspect of the conference was the concluding roundtable of judges. These six judges from five different European countries – Giacinto Bisogni (Italy), Esther de Rooij (Netherlands), Horatius Dumbrava (Romania), Carlos Gómez (Spain), Sir Peter Singer (UK), and John Thornhill (UK) – provided the 'view from the bench', so to speak, on many of the thorny issues discussed in these chapters. Their perspectives are formed by years of practical experience in hearing such cases and having to reach immediate decisions without the luxury of research and interdisciplinary discussions, trying to balance the needs and desires of people from minority backgrounds with the demands of a majority society while working within the strictures of state and international law. Their comments throughout the conference and especially during the roundtable greatly enriched the discussions and, while not represented directly, have found their way into the introduction to this volume and informed the writing of many of the contributing authors.

Special thanks go to Dr Brian Donahoe, the Senior Scientific Editor at the Max Planck Institute for Social Anthropology, for his meticulous work on this volume. His contribution goes far beyond language editing and management of the publication. We would also like to thank Ute Gradmann and Kateřina Marencakova for making sure the chapters and especially the footnotes are all uniformly formatted.

Finally, the editors would like to thank Ashgate Publishers for issuing the initial contract and Routledge for honouring the contract following its purchase of Ashgate. Alison Kirk, the Commissioning Editor, has provided invaluable advice, support, and encouragement and has exhibited extraordinary patience in her dealings with us throughout this entire process. She has been a joy to work with, and we look forward to years of productive cooperation with her and Routledge as this series moves forward.

Marie-Claire Foblets
Michele Graziadei
Alison Dundes Renteln

Introduction

Individual autonomy in contemporary plural societies: how to reconcile competing normative standards?

Marie-Claire Foblets, Michele Graziadei, and Alison Dundes Renteln

Introduction: autonomy in the context of contemporary plural societies

The autonomy of the person, understood in law as the capacity of a person to make his or her own decisions on legal matters, including the choice of rules that apply to a given situation, has been the subject of extensive debate in recent years.[1] At a conference convened by the Department of Law & Anthropology at the Max Planck Institute for Social Anthropology in Halle, Germany, in late May 2014, some 30 participants – legal scholars and practitioners as well as scholars in the social sciences – grappled with a range of issues concerning the paradoxical nature of autonomous decision-making in situations where individuals are confronted with competing claims reflecting different normative standards. In this volume, contributors tackle hard questions – both theoretical and practical – that arise when individuals immersed in a pluralistic setting are faced with multiple normative options and often experience deep ambivalence about their own identity and relationship(s) to law.

From a liberal point of view, the principle of autonomy seems relatively simple to put into practice: the individual in society – the subject of the law, as jurists put it – has certain rights that the contemporary legal order recognizes and protects. In this conception, the legal subject is able to assert subjective rights thanks to the autonomy of his or her will. This capacity allows individuals to weave social relationships with other subjects (individual or collective) as they see fit. In law, the instrument that gives these relationships their normative force is the contract: a contractual arrangement is legally binding on the parties involved. In international law, individual choice is mentioned in various articles of human rights treaties, for example, the right to freely choose one's partner and the right to decide on the number and spacing of children.[2] An approach that focuses on the individual privileges personal choice. Yet, at the same time, international law to a certain extent also safeguards decisions by families, religions, cultural communities, and linguistic groups, enabling them to preserve their cherished traditions. How, then, are we to balance the decisions made by autonomous individuals and those made by groups, especially when they collide?

Careful observation of empirical reality and its increasing complexity from the perspective of individuals' lived experience suggests that the principle of the person's autonomy

1 See, e.g., M Kühler and N Jelinek (eds), *Autonomy and the Self* (Springer 2013); K-P Köpping, M Welker, and R Wiehl (eds), *Die autonome Person – eine europäische Erfindung?* (Wilhelm Fink Verlag 2002).

2 See, e.g., SB Boyd, 'Autonomy for Mothers? Relational Theory and Parenting Apart' (2010) 18 *Feminist Legal Studies* 137.

DOI: 10.4324/9781315413617-1

and the resulting ability to choose freely among the normative regimes that could possibly apply to his or her situation is often merely a *legal fiction*.[3] 'This is a conception of subjectivity grounded in secular modernity,' observes Sally Merry.[4] What guarantees that a person's consent is *free*? Can autonomy serve as the foundation for the obligations a person assumes towards a community or organization and its rules and, if so, under what conditions? In practice, this is where things become complicated and difficult to implement. Some reject the proposition that groups should be empowered to make decisions, and insist that individuals who disagree with community standards be entitled to exercise a right of exit.[5] But even if such an exit option exists, not all individuals who wish to deviate from one or another tradition within their own cultural communities want to deploy an exit option and make a complete break from their communities. The empirical evidence presented in a number of the chapters in this volume shows that a strong sense of belonging on the part of members of various communities often takes precedence over the desire to assert one's individuality by bucking a custom. In other words, people can make an autonomous choice to forgo their individual interests in the name of group or community interests.

Traditionally, scholarship has tended to concentrate on abstract interpretations of the concept of personal autonomy in political theory.[6] Emphasis is placed on the elusive nature of this notion, what it means in liberal theory, and how it is flawed from an individual perspective.[7] The purpose of this book is to show that a commitment to personal autonomy, if it is to be effective and serve its ends in the context of contemporary plural societies, needs

3 In applying the principle of individual freedom and personal autonomy, individuals are entitled to make choices ostensibly on the basis of free will. This means they have legal capacity to enter into various types of agreements. Transactions are documented in the form of contracts (business, prenuptial, and marital), advance directives, and consent protocols that document subjects' willingness to participate in clinical trials. From a legal perspective, it is sometimes challenging to determine whether individuals do, in fact, have the legal capacity to enter into legal agreements. Insofar as individuals live within communities, their choices may be limited in significant ways, which raises the question of whether their decisions are made autonomously. Sometimes the issue is a matter of 'informed consent', sometimes it is whether an individual consented under duress or coercion, and sometimes it is a matter of whether the individual is capable of making a choice independent of family, religion, or community.

4 SE Merry, 'Relating to the Subjects of Human Rights: The Culture of Agency in Human Rights Discourse' in M Freeman and D Napier (eds), *Law and Anthropology: Current Legal Issues*, vol 12 (Oxford University Press 2008) 384, 386; see also D Copp, 'Rationality, Autonomy and Basic Needs' in N Roughley (ed), *Being Humans: Anthropological Universality and Particularity in Transdisciplinary Perspectives* (Walter de Gruyter 2000) 334.

5 For an analysis of this particular question, see, e.g., A Eisenberg and J Spinner-Halev (eds), *Minorities Within Minorities: Equality, Rights and Diversity* (Cambridge University Press 2005).

6 See, e.g., J Nedelsky, 'Reconceiving Autonomy: Sources, Thoughts and Possibilities' (1989) 1 *Yale Journal of Law and Feminism* 7; W Kymlicka, *Multicultural Odysseys: Navigating the New International Politics of Diversity* (Oxford University Press 2007); S Conly, *Against Autonomy: Justifying Coercive Paternalism* (Cambridge University Press 2012).

7 Some feminists propose an alternative formulation. For instance, Jennifer Nedelsky (n 6) first proposed the concept of relational autonomy, a concept that is also addressed explicitly by Monique Deveaux, Jessica Johnson, Keebet von Benda-Beckmann, Alison Dundes Renteln, and Shaheen Ali and Arjumand Kazmi in this volume. Others use it as well; see, e.g., SB Boyd, 'Motherhood and Law: Constructing and Challenging Normativity' in M Davies and VE Munro (eds), *The Ashgate Research Companion to Feminist Legal Theory* (Ashgate 2013) 267; M Deckha, 'Gender, Difference, and Anti-Essentialism: Towards a Feminist Response to Cultural Claims in Law' in A Eisenberg (ed), *Diversity and Equality: The Changing Framework of Freedom in Canada* (University of British Columbia Press 2006) 118.

to be critically assessed.[8] In the face of the complexity of the debate surrounding certain minority practices and traditions seen as problematic from the point of view of human rights, and given the overall lack of consensus on the position legislators should take in many such cases, one may wonder whether the principle of autonomy, even if accompanied by certain solid guarantees, is indeed the best guide to finding a middle ground between respect for diversity – cultural, ethnic, religious – and for other values, while also avoiding ideological rifts.[9]

The chapters in this volume do not offer a single answer to this question; rather, they address it in three different ways. The six analyses in Part I, *Autonomy in the Face of Cultural Diversity: Disciplinary Perspectives*, explore the liberal principles of individual freedom and personal autonomy, their historical background, and some of the questions that come with the attempt to validate them in various contemporary settings that are marked by diversity and complexity. **Michele Graziadei's** contribution (Chapter 1), for example, concentrates on the historical roots of autonomy in political philosophy, while others highlight the contemporary significance of the concept. In 'Confronting Autonomy in Liberal Practice' (Chapter 2), **Geoffrey Brahm Levey** provides an overview of the standard interpretations of autonomy in political theory. After outlining the difficulties associated with autonomy, he suggests that 'liberal practice provides the arena where the tensions within the concept of autonomy itself are played out' (p. 43) and that a 'liberal' approach to autonomy 'genuinely opens up the debate about the limits of cultural diversity in liberal societies' (p. 50). Other contributors show how autonomy is conceptualized in sociology and cultural studies. **Olaf Zenker** (Chapter 6) challenges the critical and often dismissive approach to 'methodological individualism' in anthropology, concluding that the only way to understand autonomy is to start from the individual.

In Part II, *Autonomy in Context: Empirical Illustrations*, one finds ample evidence of the tensions that come with advancing individual freedom and personal autonomy in the context of contemporary plural societies, showing that in order to be effective and sustainable, these (liberal) principles must reflect the concrete circumstances of each case, that is, the context of their application. The contributions grouped under section A (*The Majoritarian Assessment of Personal Autonomy*) show that it does not suffice to define the

8 For a solid critique of applying the autonomy perspective to debates about cultural diversity, see AE Galeotti, 'Autonomy and Multiculturalism' in GB Levey (ed), *Authenticity, Autonomy and Multiculturalism* (Routledge 2015) 45. See also A Phillips, *Multiculturalism Without Culture* (Princeton University Press 2007).

9 While the authors in this volume usually refer to the concept of autonomy, in some instances they conflate this idea with agency. What is the difference between autonomy and agency? For some theorists, autonomy concerns the frame of mind or the capacity to make decisions without undue influence. Agency is usually used to refer to acting on the decisions. Authors do not always make a sharp distinction between these two terms. While recognizing that these concepts are closely linked, for the most part we use autonomy rather than agency when referring to individuals' capacity to make independent decisions and exercise choice. When members of ethnic or religious communities make choices that to members of the mainstream culture seem contrary to their own self-interest, some would describe their decision-making as based on 'false consciousness' (a phrase that has historically been associated with Marxist approaches to the politics of culture), which demonstrates a lack of personal autonomy. This line of reasoning is based on an assumption on the part of non-members of communities that the decision-making processes of members of minority groups are flawed and overly influenced by external factors; if individuals were presumably subject to overwhelming social pressure or some form of mind control or 'brainwashing', it is not necessary to accept the choices they appear to have made as genuinely autonomous.

expectations about what 'solution' best fits the prevailing normative order of a society, as that prevailing order is invariably biased. For an accurate exploration of what are, in daily life, *realistic* options for individuals when it comes to taking a position on certain situations of normative plurality, one needs to assess the situation from the point of view of the actors as well. This actor-centred approach is the common distinguishing feature of all six contributions brought together under section B of Part II (*Individual Agency In Situ*): what are the actual practices of the individuals involved; what are the systems of religious, customary, or indigenous law that they consider binding on them; what logics of power, respectability, and/or solidarity are playing in the background; and is there room for individual manoeuvring? The illustrations show that, when exploring a wide range of case studies from around the world, one finds often surprising creativity on the part of individuals who manage to create space for some form of self-government and, if needed, to resist the rules of one or more of the normative order(s) with which they interact. At the same time, they need to ensure that this does not result in the loss of the social support upon which they depend for their future lives, either within or outside their own community or group.

The role of human rights: setting the bar too high?

We are certainly not the first to discuss the complex dimensions of autonomy, agency, and consent in the contemporary context of plural societies. In recent years, authors of various disciplines have studied the issue of autonomy with a particular interest in situations that require one to take account of cultural diversity. They have proposed innovative concepts and approaches such as 'strategic essentialism', 'asymmetric anti-essentialism', 'cultural voluntarism', 'multicultural jurisprudence', and 'multiculturalism without culture', to cite but a few.[10] These concepts were often developed in light of the question of how to balance women's rights against culture.[11]

10 See esp. A Eisenberg, 'Identity, Multiculturalism and Religious Arbitration: The Debate Over Shari'a Law in Canada' in B Arneil et al. (eds), *Sexual Justice/Cultural Justice: Critical Perspectives in Political Theory and Practice* (Routledge 2007) 211; C Mackenzie, 'Relational Autonomy, Sexual Justice and Cultural Pluralism' ibid. 103; C Kukathas, 'Is Feminism Bad for Multiculturalism?' (2001) 15(2) *Public Affairs Quarterly* 83; S Mahmood, 'Agency, Performativity, and the Feminist Subject' in L Sjørup and H Rømer Christensen (eds), *Pieties and Gender* (Brill 2009) 13; S Mahmood, *Politics of Piety: The Islamic Revival and the Feminist Subject* (Princeton University Press 2005); U Narayan, 'Essence of Culture and a Sense of History: A Feminist Critique of Cultural Essentialism' (1998) 13(2) *Hypatia* 86; U Narayan, 'Minds of Their Own: Choices, Cultural Practices, and Other Women' in L Antony and C Witt (eds), *A Mind of One's Own: Feminist Essays on Reason and Objectivity* (Westview Press 2002) 418; A Phillips, 'It's My Body and I'll Do What I Like With It: Bodies as Objects and Property' (2011) 39(6) *Political Theory* 724; Phillips (n 8).

11 See esp. S Conly, *Against Autonomy: Justifying Coercive Paternalism* (Cambridge University Press 2012); S Conly, 'Seduction, Rape and Coercion' (2012) 115(1) *Ethics* 96; M Friedman, 'Women's Rights, Oppressed Minorities and the Liberal State' in B Arneil et al. (eds) (n 10) 96; M Friedman, *Autonomy, Gender, Politics* (Oxford University Press 2003); M Malik, 'Progressive Multiculturalism: Minority Women and Cultural Diversity' (2010) 17(3) *International Journal on Minority and Group Rights* 447; J Marshall, 'Freedom of Religious Expression and Gender Equality: Sahin v Turkey' (2006) 69(3) *The Modern Law Review* 452; S Saharso, 'Feminist Ethics, Autonomy and the Politics of Multiculturalism' (2003) 4 *Feminist Theory* 199; S Saharso, 'Female Autonomy and Cultural Imperative: Two Hearts Beating Together' in W Kymlicka and W Norman (eds), *Citizenship in Diverse Societies* (Oxford University Press 2000) 224; A Shachar, 'Demystifying Culture' (2012) 10(2) *International Journal of*

For example, in an article devoted to the widespread practice of 'arranged marriage' and the question of what distinguishes it from 'forced marriage', Monique Deveaux argued in favour of 'an alternative understanding of agency'.[12] The topic addressed in her analysis is not limited to cases of engagement to be married; rather, its significance extends to any person whose culture or community follows certain traditions or practices that are seen as violating or at least not meeting the protections prescribed by the guarantees enshrined in human rights legislation. Such persons are therefore left with the dilemma that they have to decide for themselves whether they wish to stick to the tradition of their group or emancipate themselves from those traditions by abandoning the practice in question. Both options in fact involve the exercise of autonomy.

One should not underestimate the number of cases today that present themselves, not only for women, as in the research conducted by Deveaux, but for anyone whose cultural, ethnic, or religious group maintains a normative system (self-regulation) that deprives some of its members of certain protections or liberties that human rights law aims at guaranteeing, if not effectively, then at least formally (that is, on paper). There is no shortage of illustrations, ranging from inheritance rights that discriminate against certain family members (especially women) to marriage practices stemming from patriarchal values and 'restrictive' dress codes, to mention but a few. The critical question is: can the principle of personal autonomy also serve as the basis for justifying why a person may decide freely to renounce the rights and freedoms guaranteed by human rights law?

Deveaux issues a warning to those who, perhaps due to their zeal for human rights, are not willing to acknowledge that a person can genuinely consent to certain controversial (from a human rights point of view) traditions or practices because, they assert, the effect of such consent is to uphold traditions that are oppressive and quash the very possibility of individual emancipation:

> Both the idealized conception of autonomy as free will and the more moderate conceptions of autonomy as requiring self-determination or the capacity for self-definition and authenticity in the context of a socialized existence obscure the context of important decisions that people may make . . . [I]n overlooking the complexity of individuals' own relationships to tradition, it would appear that the liberal autonomy framework would dispose the liberal state towards regulating or even censuring too wide a range of social customs that arguably should be accommodated.[13]

The types of situations to which this warning applies have been multiplying in recent years. Professionals in plural societies (whether legal practitioners or others such as surgeons, midwives, school principals, etc.) come across situations in their daily practice where persons have agreed to renounce certain 'protective' (human) rights in favour of the requirements of their culture or religion. These professionals are faced with the dilemma of how to reconcile their professional ethics with that person's 'autonomy'. One could speak of situations

---

Constitutional Law 429; A Shachar, 'Feminism and Multiculturalism: Mapping the Terrain' in D Owen and A Laden (eds), *Multiculturalism and Political Theory* (Cambridge University Press 2007) 115.

12 M Deveaux, 'Personal Autonomy and Cultural Tradition: The Arranged Marriage Debate in Britain' in B Arneil et al. (eds) (n 10) 139, 157.

13 Ibid. 145.

of 'inter-normativity',[14] which often give rise to a veritable 'power struggle' between diverging systems of rules in which several mechanisms are available for legal practitioners to coordinate the different sets of norms at play.[15] One such mechanism is to invoke respect for human rights as an aspect of public reason: in recent years, the argument regarding the respect ultimately due to public reason has been playing an important – and ever-increasing – role in laying down the criteria for what constitutes (legally) valid autonomous action. Public reason,[16] however, as several contributors in this volume illustrate, is obviously majority driven.

In practice, invoking public reason means that the freedom of the individual to exercise his or her autonomy is subject to severe restrictions: under this approach, autonomy will not be granted any effect in law wherever doing so would encourage the continuation of a practice or tradition that is considered incompatible with human rights law. A general principle in human rights is that a person cannot voluntarily renounce his or her fundamental rights. In this sense, one could speak of human rights as a form of 'imposed protection'.

One example of this 'guardian function' of human rights, and one that is generally perceived as perfectly justified, is the protection of a contracting party who is unable to read and hence cannot validly consent to the text of a contract. Other limitations are placed on personal autonomy with a view to safeguarding, for example, the best interests of the child,[17] fair trial, or gender equality. In practice, however, such limitations risk producing the opposite effect to the one intended: they introduce a 'filter' system into the lives of persons. In the name of human rights certain practices are considered 'deviant' or 'contentious' and are therefore either prohibited by or not granted recognition under state law.[18] An all too rigid human rights approach, therefore, not only prevents individual actors from following their

14 E Bernheim, 'Le "pluralisme normative": un nouveau paradigme pour appréhender les mutations sociales et juridiques?' (2011) 2 *Revue Interdisciplinaires d'Etudes Juridiques* 1.

15 At least three types of mechanisms can be distinguished. The first is that of subordination, or 'weak pluralism': in their relations with the state (as well as with international law), alternative or parallel systems remain subordinate. Second, and at the other end of the spectrum, is the mechanism of self-regulation, whereby groups, communities, or social organizations successfully continue to apply their own regulations within their given sphere of activity or competence. These groups to some extent rival the state, which in turn must tolerate this competition from parallel normative systems that are often better adapted to the social relations that they govern. The scholarly literature speaks of this as 'strong pluralism' See esp. J-G Belley, 'Le droit comme "terra incognita": Conquérir et construire le pluralisme' (1997) 12(2) *Canadian Journal of Law & Society/La Revue Canadienne Droit et Société* 1. A third coordination mechanism is one that allows individuals to *choose* between the competing normative systems and to decide for themselves to which set of norms they will adhere. See also J Levy, 'Three Modes of Incorporating Indigenous Law' in W Kymlicka and W Norman (eds) (n 11) 297.

16 See, e.g., N Bernard-Maugiron (ed), *Ordre public et droit musulman de la famille en Europe et en Afrique du Nord* (Bruylant 2012); J-M Ducomte, 'Entre respect des libertés publiques et garantie de l'ordre public: l'évolution de la normativité en matière de laïcité' in J Baubérot, M Milot, and P Portier (eds), *Laicité, laicités: reconfigurations et nouveau défis* (Editions de la Maison des sciences de l'homme 2014) 319.

17 See, e.g., P Alston (ed), *The Best Interests of the Child: Reconciling Culture and Human Rights* (Clarendon Press 1994); UNICEF (ed), *Protecting the World's Children: Impact of the Convention on the Rights of the Child in Diverse Legal Systems* (Cambridge University Press 2007).

18 In practice, much will depend on the extent to which institutional actors are prepared to take an active role in giving a person genuine support. We could take the example here of shelters for women fleeing an intolerable family situation. The shelter is only a first step, and must be followed by a more lasting and comprehensive form of support to help the woman out of the crisis from which she was escaping. This is often a complex and highly delicate task for the support staff.

traditions, but in certain cases may even deny them capacity to seek, *from within*, renewal and adaptation of certain traditions or practices of the group or community in question. Such an approach makes the exercise of autonomy depend on so many external conditions that *in effect* it results in a denial of autonomy. Minority cultures are often accused of patriarchy and paternalism, but the limitations imposed by majority opinion, 'public interest', and the law may at times turn out to be just as restrictive. Setting the bar high by insisting on conformity to human rights criteria can itself give rise to marginalization: people stay away from courts or refrain from registering (religious) marriages, 'divorces of convenience' are entered into, and limping situations arise in private international law, to name but a few examples well known to practitioners.

The ethnographic lens: not all cultures value personal autonomy

Anthropologists who have done ethnographic field research in various parts of the world have shown that the space for choice left to the individual, in terms of his or her free consent, varies considerably depending on the culture, tradition, and social context. Anthropology thus offers ample illustrations of the complex dimensions of autonomy, agency, and consent. Anthropological studies convincingly demonstrate that the model of individual autonomy in which the criterion for judging the validity of a (legal) act is the individual's free and informed consent is far from prevalent throughout the world. As David Copp has put it, 'There presumably are cultures that do not value personal autonomy.'[19] This observation – which should be weighed against the complexity of the notion of culture and the fact that all cultures must balance opposing tensions – in turn may help explain why, when tensions arise between cultural (minority) traditions and the requirements of state law, individuals are not automatically prepared to align themselves with human rights criteria. In certain situations, freedom may consist in wanting at the appropriate time what the group also wants, even when that entails abstaining from making one's own 'autonomous' choice.

By scrutinizing human behaviour ethnographically – that is, by using an in-depth, long-term, field-based approach – anthropologists have observed that certain practices that are perceived as clashing with human rights criteria of protection of the autonomous individual go far back in history and are part of the complex processes of creating and re-creating personal and social identities. They regulate people's belonging and have a role to play in maintaining the social structures of groups and societies.[20]

In assessing motivations and various forms of behaviour in human societies, anthropologists have come across a wide variety of practices that regulate identities, yet they are careful to locate these practices *within the subjects' own context*. For the anthropologist, there is no other scientifically valid, empirically based way to apprehend these practices. It is understandable that some feel discomfort with those ethnographic writings that offer 'mere' description. Yet an anthropologist will in the first place scrutinize the normative logic at play according to which certain practices meet the standards of acceptability by the group that continues to observe it, while other practices do not. Why, in the perception of the outside world, are some practices considered banal and unproblematic, while others are deemed

19 Copp (n 4) 348.

20 See, e.g., O Harris (ed), *Inside and Outside the Law: Anthropological Studies of Authority and Ambiguity* (Routledge 1997).

*un*acceptable, although the group's pressure on its members to abide by a practice may be very similar in each case?[21] These are questions addressed by anthropologists.

Moreover, empirical observations show that perceptions of what sorts of procedures a community may or may not impose on a person (with or without that person's consent) – whether a child or an adult, a man or a woman, an insider or an outsider to a particular group – not only vary with the cultural context but also change over time, often to a considerable extent.[22] In Western legal thinking, for example, the *age of consent* has now become the ultimate precondition of the legal validity of a person's actions or decisions.[23] Yet if that line of demarcation is applied without taking into account sufficiently accurately the full context of a concrete situation, it risks not only emptying the principle of autonomy of much of its meaning, but also being applied more harshly to some than to others. One could thus speak of the risk of invoking a double standard in the invocation of human rights.

The risks of a double standard

An illustration of the consequences of ignoring such a risk is provided by the heated discussion in Germany concerning the practice of circumcision.[24] It followed a court decision handed down in 2012 by the Cologne Regional Court (*Landgericht*) stating that the right of a child to his bodily integrity must take precedence over his parents' right to circumcise him as an expression of their religious faith.[25] The court did not go so far as to find the

21 The practice of human body modification serves well as an example. From a human rights point of view, modifications of the human body for *medical/therapeutic* reasons are considered perfectly justifiable; as we explain later, modifications for *aesthetic* or other *personal reasons* are considered with ever more leniency to be acceptable, at least when the person concerned is a consenting adult and sufficiently well informed of the risks he or she takes. By contrast, modifications on *penal grounds* are generally considered (in Western legal thinking) to be repugnant and thus totally unacceptable. One such practice is the cutting off of a hand (as punishment for, e.g., theft). While rare, it offers the illustration of a culturally grounded bodily mutilation for penal reasons (see, e.g., K Vogt (ed), *New Directions in Islamic Thought: Exploring Reform and Muslim Tradition* [Tauris 2011]). Another illustration is the principle of 'an eye for an eye', or the law of retaliation: it is the principle that a person who has injured another person is to be penalized to a similar degree. In softer interpretations, the victim receives the (estimated) value of the injury in compensation. The principle is sometimes referred to by the Latin term *lex talionis*.

22 For the anthropologist, appropriate child care practices are – like any standards or values – appraised and interpreted in relation to the cultural context in which they apply.

23 See, e.g., M Waites, *The Age of Consent: Young People, Sexuality and Citizenship* (Palgrave Macmillan 2009); C Breen, *Age Discrimination and Children's Rights: Ensuring Equality and Acknowledging Difference* (Martinus Nijhoff 2006).

24 The discussion that follows draws heavily on a more detailed analysis of this debate in M-C Foblets, 'The Body as Identity Maker: Circumcision of Boys Caught Between Contrasting Views on the Best Interests of the Child' in M Jantera-Jareborg (ed), *The Child's Interests in Conflict: The Intersections Between Society, Family, Faith and Culture* (Intersentia 2016) 125.

25 Landgericht Köln, Judgment of Monday 7 May 2012, No. 151 Ns 169/11; English translation by the ILM Website at Durham University Law School <www.dur.ac.uk/resources/ilm/CircumcisionJudgmentLGCologne7May20121.pdf> accessed 26 April 2017. A family physician had circumcised a four-year-old boy at the request of his parents, who were religious Muslims. A few days after the procedure, the boy had to be taken to the emergency room because of secondary bleeding. From what the mother said there, the doctor inferred that she had not fully consented to the procedure and informed the police. Based on this information, the public prosecutor of the city of Cologne launched proceedings against the physician who had performed the circumcision. The Cologne District Court (*Amtsgericht*) acquitted the doctor of the charge of grievous bodily harm. But on appeal, the Cologne Regional Court reviewed

physician who had circumcised the boy guilty, as he had acted to the best of his knowledge within the law and could not have known that what he was doing was punishable by law. Nevertheless, the decision of the appellate judge was alarming for other physicians who performed (or might perform) circumcisions and gave rise to a veritable clash of values in the debate regarding the relationship between religion and society.

From the discussion that followed the Cologne Court ruling, it appears that the practice of circumcising young boys triggered emotions that are very similar to those previously induced by other 'contentious' minority practices such as the ritual slaughtering of animals[26] and religious dress codes.[27] The judgment outraged Muslims and Jews in the country. The Central Council of Jews in Germany responded vigorously, considering that it was 'an unprecedented and dramatic interference into the right of self-determination of religious communities' in Germany.[28] For Jews, circumcision is more than just a pious custom: 'Circumcision of newborn boys is an inherent part of the Jewish religion and has been practiced worldwide for centuries,' noted the council's president, Dieter Graumann, in an interview published in the daily *Frankfurter Allgemeine Zeitung*.[29]

Some commentators, expressing what they saw as a general feeling shared by Jews and Muslims in Germany, regarded the ruling as an illustration not so much of the importance of physical integrity to the individual development of children, but of a more general tendency to restrict the personal autonomy of members of religious minorities.[30] As such, the ruling runs the risk of applying a double standard. Moreover, they were of the opinion that treating the circumcision of infants and young boys in isolation is a highly selective – and thus unfair – way to address the overall question of how to achieve the right balance between protecting freedom of religion (in this case of the parents) and concern for the best interests of children. Parents are constantly confronted with the need to make decisions and consent to practices that have an irreversible impact on their children's souls and bodies, whether through the choice of schooling, vaccination, or orthodontic work. The Cologne Regional Court's ruling on circumcision was therefore perceived to be an arbitrary and misguided application of the principles of individual freedom of religion and the right to control one's physical integrity.[31]

---

the grounds for acquitting the doctor and reversed the decision (without, however, charging the doctor), ultimately deciding that the protection of the physical integrity of minors precedes the rights of parents to choose in which religion they raise their children.

26 See, e.g., F Bergeaud-Blackler, 'New Challenges for Islamic Ritual Slaughter: A European Perspective' (2007) 33(6) *Journal of Ethnic and Migration Studies* 965.

27 See, e.g., J Grigo, *Religiöse Kleidung: vestimentäre Praxis zwischen Identität und Differenz* (Transcript Verlag 2015); E Howard, *Law and the Wearing of Religious Symbols: European Bans on the Wearing of Religious Symbols in Education* (Routledge 2013).

28 'Graumann: Ein unerhörter und unsensibler Akt' *Frankfurter Allgemeine Zeitung* (Frankfurt 26 June 2012) <www.faz.net/aktuell/politik/urteil-zu-beschneidung-von-jungen-graumann-ein-unerhoerter-und-unsensibler-akt-11799759.html> accessed 26 April 2017.

29 'On the Decision of the District Court of Cologne Concerning Circumcision of Boys' *Central Council of Jews in Germany* (Frankfurt/Berlin 26 June 2012) <www.zentralratdjuden.de/en/article/3706.on-the-decision-of-the-district-court-of-cologne-concerning-circumcision-of-boys.html> accessed 26 April 2017.

30 For an earlier critique of this tendency, see AM Viens, 'Value Judgement, Harm and Religious Liberty' (2004) 3 *Journal of Medical Ethics* 242; more recently: A Bodenheimer, *Haut Ab! Die Juden in der Beschneidungsdebatte* (Wallstein Verlag 2012).

31 On this inconsistency, see GB Levey, 'Thinking About Infant Male Circumcision After the Cologne Court Decision' (2013) 3(2) *Global Discourse: An Interdisciplinary Journal of Current Affairs and Applied Contemporary Thought* 326; RA Shweder, 'The Goose and the Gander: The Genital Wars' ibid. 348.

This is no minor accusation, as it echoes a reproach already voiced on several occasions in recent years in other European countries as well: certain minority groups (mainly religious minorities) protest against what they perceive to be a selective policy of intrusion into their religious norms and practices.[32] To them, an intrusion that is grounded in the concern that human rights and fundamental liberties should be respected in effect – and somewhat paradoxically – restricts their personal autonomy while ignoring the fact that this autonomy had historically been guaranteed by states precisely in the name of religious freedom.[33] In their perception, these intrusions, whether in the form of court decisions or of legislation, have more to do with an increasing uneasiness in Europe about the presence of Jewish and more recently Muslim communities and their continued practices than with views about how to consistently protect individuals and their personal autonomy against infringements of their basic rights.

It is a basic tenet of human rights protection that one right may conflict with another. In practice, therefore, the autonomy of a person to freely choose his or her religion or belief or, conversely, to claim protection *from* any religion and belief (which also falls within the scope of freedom of religion) may very well clash with other rights.[34] As regards the circumcision of young boys, the debate in Germany showed how complex – not least because of its extreme sensitivity – is the question of what to prioritize: the (autonomous) choice of the parents to raise their children in a particular religious community and according to the tenets of their faith *or* the autonomy of the child and the requirement to safeguard his physical integrity by every possible means until he has reached the age of consent.

Disputes like the one brought before the Cologne courts are likely to become more frequent in societies where different groups and communities disagree among one another about answers to such basic questions as 'how best to give . . . expression to one's identity, if at all'.[35] Practices such as the circumcision of young boys are perceived by large portions of Jewish and Muslim communities to be constitutive of the person and to 'build on deeply personal beliefs about . . . the human condition'.[36] These are not convictions that people discuss easily or openly, let alone are prepared to compromise on. The subject is

32 See, e.g., C Durham (ed), *Islam, Europe and Emerging Legal Issues* (Ashgate 2012); M Adrian (ed), *Religious Freedom at Risk: The EU, French Schools and Why the Veil Was Banned* (Springer 2016). Note that the Committee on the Rights of the Child, which monitors the implementation of the Convention on the Rights of the Child, has only taken a stance against unsafe conditions during the circumcision procedure, but not against the practice per se; see S Schmahl, 'The Rights of the Child in Germany: The UN Convention on the Rights of the Child and Its Implementation in National Law' in O Cvejić-Jančić (ed), *The Rights of the Child in a Changing World 25 Years After the UN Convention on the Rights of the Child* (Springer 2016) 123.

33 Recent attempts both in the courts and in the national legislation of various European countries (e.g., the Netherlands, Belgium, and Denmark) have also targeted the Jewish method of slaughtering animals known as *shechita*; see M-C Foblets and J Velaers, 'Recent Discussions in Belgium and the Netherlands on Religious Freedom and the Slaughter of Animals Without Prior Stunning' in B Schinkele et al. (eds), *Recht, Religion, Kultur. Festschrift für Richard Potz zum 70. Geburtstag* (Facultas 2013) 67.

34 See, e.g., A Scolnicov, *The Right to Religious Freedom in International Law: Between Group Rights and Individual Rights* (Routledge 2011).

35 Shweder (n 31).

36 M Kristiansen and A Sheikh, 'Legislation on Male Infant Circumcision in Europe: A Call to Avoid Paternalism and to Promote Evidence-Based Patient-Centred Care' (2013) 3(2) *Global Discourse: An Interdisciplinary Journal of Current Affairs and Applied Contemporary Thought* 342, 345.

highly sensitive and, as history demonstrates, can often prove inflammatory.[37] The interesting point is that, as a consequence of this controversial court ruling, the German legislature swiftly agreed upon a legislative solution in the autumn of 2012. The new law (20 December 2012)[38] protects non-therapeutic circumcisions as an expression of the care exercised through parental rights, provided that the procedure is carried out in conformity with the *lex artis*. In general, circumcision ought to be performed by certified doctors, but if a boy is less than six months old, the procedure can also be performed by another qualified person, who may be designated by a religious body. Concern for the respect of the rights of the child in the new law is expressed in the provision that parents can have the boy circumcised only on the condition that it does not endanger the child's welfare. Furthermore, in order to give appropriate weight to possible health risks associated with the procedure, the parents must be fully informed of the possible adverse consequences associated with circumcision through an informed consent procedure.[39]

The ruling in the Cologne case reflects ongoing debates concerning circumcision among constitutional and human rights scholars and medical professionals, but what was considered untenable by the German Parliament and in public opinion was precisely the risk of applying a double standard that targeted, albeit indirectly, norms that specific religious minorities uphold.

The complex dimensions of autonomy, agency, and consent: what role for legislators?

As mentioned earlier, societies worldwide that commit themselves to modern liberalism by leaving wide scope for the personal autonomy and freedom of competent adults offer just one model of how to conceive of identity and social cohesion. The view that legislators or any other public authorities should not interfere with the conduct of a competent adult citizen unless and until that conduct harms or seriously threatens to harm third parties[40] clearly clashes with other views that disapprove of the focus on individual freedom and are instead

37 See esp. JT Levy, 'Cruelty and Conflict in Multiethnic Politics' in JT Levy (ed), *The Multiculturalism of Fear* (Oxford University Press 2004); S Hall, 'Political Belonging in a World of Multiple Identities' in G Baumann and S Vertovec (eds), *Multiculturalism* (Routledge 2011) 151. As Robert Wheeler and Pat Malone note, 'The European reluctance to circumcise boys becomes even more apparent when requested for religious or cultural indications'; R Wheeler and P Malone, 'Male Circumcision: Risk Versus Benefit' (2013) 98(5) *Archives of Disease in Childhood* 321.

38 Now incorporated into article 1631d of the German Civil Code (BGB) (see <http://last-conformer.net/2012/12/28/its-official/> accessed 21 April 2017). For more detailed comments, see esp. M Germann, 'Die Verfassungsmässigkeit des Gesetzes über den Umfang der Personensorge bei einer Beschneidung des männliches Kindes vom 20.12.2012' (2013) 7 *Medizinrecht* 412; T Walter, 'Der Gesetzentwurf zur Beschneidung – Kritik und strafrechtliche Alternative' (2012) *JuristenZeitung* 110; J Isensee, 'Grundrechtliche Konsequenz wider geheiligte Tradition' (2013) *JuristenZeitung* 317; T Hörnle and S Huster, 'Wie weit reicht das Erziehungsrecht der Eltern?' (2013) *JuristenZeitung* 328.

39 B Breig, 'Law and Religion in Germany: The Case of Circumcision of Boys' in J Gerlach and J Töpfer (eds), *The Role of Religion in Eastern Europe Today: Interdisciplinary Perspectives* (Springer 2015) 83.

40 The aforementioned debate in Germany on circumcision illustrates a move towards a more protective approach to the relationship between human beings and their bodies: only the fullest possible respect for the physical integrity of a child will make it possible to preserve the young man's autonomy until he has reached the age of consent, i.e., the age at which, by law, he has the autonomy to make decisions on his own, including any act that might violate his bodily integrity but which concerns no one but himself.

more preoccupied with the perpetuation of particular patterns of behaviour (grounded in tradition, religion, or culture) and therefore require that specific restraints be imposed on individual conduct.

How, then, on a practical level, can these divergences in views be overcome?[41] To what extent can law assist in finding the right balance between an approach that demonizes certain practices and 'rushes to dark judgments about . . . others', as Richard Shweder puts it,[42] and a hands-off policy that would allow minority groups and communities to continue following traditions and activities that seem incompatible with the values of the majority society? And what role could the principle of personal autonomy and its protection play here? Can it, in the short term, offer a compromise that would satisfy everyone? As things stand, the answer cannot but be a nuanced one.

The aforementioned debate surrounding the circumcision of infants and young boys and the issue of the respect due to the integrity of children's bodies is just one illustration of a discussion that has in the past already taken place with regard to other contentious practices and traditions. With regard to Europe, it is very likely that other discussions will follow in the years to come. In the absence of consensus and in light of the particularly delicate nature of some of these debates about practices reflecting profound values and touching on human rights, one wonders to what extent respect for the principle of individual freedom and personal autonomy, accompanied by some caveats, could lay down the signposts for a middle way and fulfil the aspirations of certain members of minority communities, without having to fear a complete abdication of human rights and fundamental freedoms. Such a way forward could perhaps help avoid face-to-face confrontations exacerbated by emotions and further whipped up by the media and the intolerant populisms of both sides.

Assessing choice: what makes for a truly 'autonomous' individual?

In this volume, several authors question the presumption that choices that seem 'illiberal' necessarily indicate a lack of personal autonomy. There are indeed several reasons to reject such a position. The fact that every person's choices reflect a certain degree of social pressure does not automatically invalidate them. Everyone, whether a member of the majority or the minority community, is indeed subject to enculturation or socialization, and these processes necessarily influence decision-making.

41 The challenge of how to effectively transpose ethnographic knowledge into legal reasoning is an issue in legal anthropological circles today: can anthropologists be there at the moment when a decision-maker (courts, legislatures, or any other corporate or non-governmental organization) could benefit from ethnographic expertise, and how would it impact on the decisions to be taken? See, e.g., PJ Stewart and A Strathern (eds), *Anthropology and Consultancy: Issues and Debates* (Berghahn 2005); B Morris and R Bastin (eds), *Expert Knowledge, First World Peoples, Consultancy and Anthropology* (Berghahn 2004); RJ Currie, 'The Bounds of the Permissible: Using "Cultural Evidence" in Civil Jury Cases' (2005) 20(1) *Canadian Journal of Law and Society* 75; E Oring, 'Folklore and Advocacy' (2004) 41(2) *Journal of Folklore Research* 259; V Sanford and A Angel-Ajani (eds), *Engaged Observer: Anthropology, Advocacy and Activism* (Rutgers University Press 2008).

42 Shweder (n 31) 364.

Contributors to this volume come from anthropology, law, political science, and philosophy. Each of them grapples with the coexistence of multiple normative orders and with policies that involve debates about how to reconcile competing claims regarding the standards that apply. Their conceptual frameworks differ, as will be seen in their approaches to autonomy and the difference it makes in interpreting the normative underpinnings of the claims and positions they encounter in the disputes they have chosen to analyse. While many disputes concerning cultural diversity arise within courts, these inter-normative debates also occur in other institutional settings. For instance, we observe them in situations where employers, school principals, public administrators, and others must reconcile professional ethics with the personal autonomy of those with whom they interact: pupils, employees, citizens, and so forth.

Several chapters deal with medical procedures, such as **Lucia Bellucci's** consideration of personal autonomy in French female genital cutting cases (Chapter 13) and **Alison Dundes Renteln's** analysis of hymen reconstruction surgery (Chapter 14). **Kalindi Kokal's** study of sex-selective abortion in India (Chapter 17) also shows that autonomy cannot be assumed, especially in situations where families and communities exert strong pressures on women to make decisions that some may question. In a number of highly publicized controversies, the issue is how legal actors regulate the right to refuse medical treatments such as inoculations (as in Chapter 12 by **Toon Agten**) or blood transfusions. What sorts of arguments are invoked to defend such refusal, and what limits can be put on the need to secure principles that are specific to a group's religious normative system? **Chiara Quagliariello** (Chapter 18) offers an incisive analysis of the use of contraception in contemporary Senegal. She identifies three main responses to what is socially acceptable recourse to contraception for women who want to have some degree of control over the number and spacing of their children. What lurks behind Senegalese society's resistance to the use of contraceptives is only partly to be explained by the concern to protect cultural values; it is also linked to power relations and the sense that women should refrain from challenging the reigning patriarchy.

But opposition does not necessarily come only from within one's community. **Alison Dundes Renteln's** chapter (Chapter 14) shows how women seeking hymenoplasty (revirgination surgery) are sometimes met with resistance from their own physicians. Even though these are adults asking for a reconstructive procedure, often in order to avoid honour-related violence within their own community, their surgeons express concern that the desired procedure would reinforce sexist attitudes and misogynistic tendencies. Renteln argues that if women have to navigate in a world where they risk honour-related violence, surgeons should accede to their requests for revirgination procedures. Considering that, in accordance with a liberal understanding of self-determination today, women can have much more drastic cosmetic surgery on highly visible parts of their bodies, it is odd that requests for revirgination have been questioned in European and North American countries. To Renteln, this reflects a double standard.

Yet another concern that makes it difficult to balance respect for individual autonomy, on the one hand, with the struggle against oppression *within* groups and communities on the other is the question of how one should ascertain whether a choice was made autonomously. For example, in recent years visible religious symbols have often sparked controversy, as some members of the majority society assume that women who don religious garb must be lacking autonomy. **Monique Deveaux's** chapter (Chapter 5) considers debates over the *hijab* and *niqab* to examine what model of equality Canadian law supports. Finding inspiration in the work of Uma Narayan, Deveaux rejects simplistic binary interpretations of the religious garb debate. In her nuanced interpretation of this conflict, she suggests that 'procedural and relational accounts of autonomy are not mutually exclusive. Both offer resources for rethinking autonomy in ways that do not depend upon binaries (such as coercion and agency, or coercion and equality) or privilege idealized versions of independence and choice' (p. 90). **Katayoun Alidadi** (Chapter 7), focusing on anti-discrimination law as it applies throughout the European Union, also examines headscarf debates in an attempt to elucidate the challenges associated with enforcing existing legal standards. As she puts it, her chapter 'aptly illustrates the paradoxes of personal autonomy encountered by projects of culturally sensitive law' (p. 115).

Political scientist **Avigail Eisenberg** (Chapter 4) offers a more expansive approach to categorizing disputes about autonomy. Her chapter suggests that choice is only one way of framing the debate, and she advances her persuasive argument by applying her analysis to the case law of the European Court of Human Rights. In her view, there has been a shift from choice-based autonomy arguments to claims linked to identity and interests.

In this volume authors delve into a wide range of complex situations. In all of the case studies gathered in Part II of this volume, the central question is whether individuals acted on the basis of genuinely autonomous decision-making and, indeed, how genuine autonomy can even be determined. For those outside the cultures involved, it seems easy to question their choices, if only because the issues at stake are not of immediate relevance to them. The risk is, as we have mentioned, the existence of a double standard; when individuals in the dominant culture act in ways that are self-destructive, their autonomous decision-making is not questioned, or at least not to the same extent.

The term 'relational autonomy' has been invoked in no fewer than five papers in this volume (Deveaux, Chapter 5; Renteln, Chapter 14; Johnson, Chapter 15; Benda-Beckmann, Chapter 16; Ali and Kazmi, Chapter 19) to characterize the situation of women making choices that appear to be incompatible with gender equality.[43] According to this view, when women make 'bad' or illiberal choices primarily because of their affiliations and membership in certain social networks, their decision-making is not considered to be truly autonomous. Consequently, some infer that their choices need not be respected. Some chapters in this volume draw on the notion of relational autonomy in an effort to challenge the standard Western legal notion of the autonomy of the individual. For example, in her consideration of Moluccan women in the Netherlands, **Keebet von Benda-Beckman** (Chapter 16) calls for a more complex understanding of autonomy when studied in the context of plural societies: 'Personal autonomy is constituted in many different but interdependent relationships, each with its own combination of normative demands and possibilities, based on a mix of different and at times contradictory normative orders of which state law is only one' (pp. 242–43). Likewise, **Jessica Johnson's** (Chapter 15) discussion of the institution of ***unkhoswe*** (marriage guardianship) in mediating marriage disputes in Malawi shows how the work of settling marital disputes can be distributed among family members without sacrificing autonomy in a situation where 'two people do not make a marriage' (p. 225).

The elusive concept of autonomy is part of many public debates about the need to limit some cultural traditions. As contributors show in both the theoretical essays and the case

43 See (n 7).

studies in this volume, this concept is extremely malleable and can lead to a paradoxical double (though variable) standard by which majority society attributes a lack of personal autonomy to those whose decisions are viewed as unacceptable.

Discarding or accompanying personal autonomy?

How should the law ensure that individuals in pluralistic societies have the ability to make their own life plans? And is it the role of the law to do so? To what extent should it continue to privilege choice or, in the final analysis, should we discard the principle of autonomy as a way of judging the legitimacy of particular decisions and instead seek alternative methods of evaluating these disputes?

An introduction to a collective volume is probably not the place to try to systematically engage in an extended effort to answer these questions. Perhaps the best we can hope for is to draw some lessons from the contributions selected for this publication. They are intended to allow the reader to form a more specific idea of the many pitfalls and difficulties of seeking to maintain respect for individual free will as a guiding principle of life in increasingly diverse contemporary societies. We have referred to a few of these already: the risk of imposing double standards, the difficulty of identifying what constitutes unacceptable social pressure, and not least the complications involved in trying to put matters in context *not* by looking at social phenomena from the outside, but by considering what truly has meaning for the persons who will be most affected by the choices to be made.

In light of these difficulties, need one abandon the idea of retaining the ideal of individual autonomy altogether? Does it follow that the vulnerability of certain individuals has become so problematic that we need in certain cases to adopt constraints that significantly curtail their autonomy or even deprive them of it by legal means in order to protect them from the risks associated with certain situations? To do so would be to short-circuit the problem. Even if that approach may have its appeal, allowing legislative authorities to simply adopt laws that prohibit or even criminalize certain controversial practices without having to worry about the reasons why those practices continue to survive among certain groups or communities does not, in our view, offer an appropriate solution. We have seen in Europe the adoption of numerous laws intended to eradicate certain practices such as the ritual slaughter of animals, the wearing of visible symbols expressing religious or philosophical convictions, or so-called religious marriages (those that are never registered with the state authorities).

More recently, the Court of Justice of the European Union issued two rulings that caused some uproar among commentators.[44] It ruled that a private enterprise's internal regulations prohibiting the wearing of certain types of clothing (e.g., a headscarf) or other visible displays of political, philosophical, or religious symbols do not constitute direct discrimination. In the court's view, the protection of freedom of enterprise within the private sector may justify the adoption of a neutral dress code policy as long as it does not introduce any differential treatment among employees on the basis of their religion or belief. The neutral image of a business towards its customers or clients thus takes precedence over the freedom of religion and belief of the employees. While one can easily understand that certain jobs may

44 Judgments of the Court of Justice in Cases C-157/15,C-188/15 (No 30/2017: 14 March 2017) <http://curia.europa.eu/jcms/upload/docs/application/pdf/2017-03/cp170030en.pdf> accessed 26 April 2017.

require a strictly regulated dress code, the acceptance of the legitimacy of a ban on certain forms of dress in the name of neutrality risks leading to the exclusion of a not insignificant group of jobseekers, in this case Muslim women.[45] In giving priority to neutrality while also accepting the principle of labour market regulation in the private sector, it seems the court is circumventing the very principle of individual freedom of religion and philosophy that is a core element of a policy that is both inclusive (i.e., concerned with the effective participation of minorities in society) and respectful of the individual autonomy of all members of society.

A basic premise in law is that prohibition and criminalization can only be the last resort, and must not target some practices and traditions more harshly than other comparable ones. If there exist more constructive and equally effective ways to deal with practices that are considered – by majority society and perhaps even from a strict human rights perspective – abusive and therefore unacceptable, they should be given preference whenever possible. Recourse to the principle of respect for and protection of individual autonomy needs to be embedded in a broader policy approach and supplemented by forms of support that can serve as important tools for any person who has to decide what course of action to take in a concrete situation. Education and institutions such as faith-based organizations, trade unions, and sport and recreation programmes, to name but a few, could prove more effective in this regard than punitive laws could possibly be.[46] Ultimately, the aim is to find solutions that maintain a balance between respect for a person's wishes and the concern that, in the medium and long run, the consequences of his or her choices do not increase his or her vulnerability in society, even if these consequences are difficult to foresee. Experience shows that a supportive approach is far more effective than a punitive approach that considers the matter only in terms of violations; the latter approach rarely proves useful as a proactive

45 In 2015, the United Nations Special Rapporteur on freedom of religion and belief, Prof. Heiner Bielefeldt, deemed it necessary to devote his annual report to the problem of exclusion from the labour market precisely on religious and philosophical grounds, warning against a marginalization that may threaten social cohesion in all Western societies. The 2015 *Eurobarometer*, as well as the report titled 'Forgotten Women: The Impact of Islamophobia on Muslim Women' published by the European Network against Racism in 2016, shared the same concern and provided statistics to back it up.

46 For an argument in the same vein, see D Peacock et al., 'Men, HIV/AIDS, and Human Rights' (2009) 51(suppl 3) *Journal of Acquired Immune Deficiency Syndrome* 119, 122. In the case of female genital mutilation, another approach may be to ensure the availability of symbolic scarification, as was proposed in the Netherlands (K Bartels and I Haaijer, *'s Lands wijs, 's lands eer? Vrouwenbesnijdenis en Somalische vrouwen in Nederland* [A Country's way, a country's honour? Female excision and Somali women in the Netherlands] [Pharos 1992]) and in Italy by Omar Abdulcadir, a Somali gynaecologist who heads the centre for the prevention and therapy of female genital mutilation at the Careggi Hospital, Florence. In 2003 he submitted a proposal to the Ethics Committee in Florence to perform a symbolic *sunna*, which would involve pricking the clitoris – under medical supervision and with an anaesthetic cream – in order to draw a symbolic 'drop of blood'. The principle was rather simple: a symbolic rite, without physical harm, as an alternative to FGM. The proposal was adopted unanimously first by the Florence Ethics Committee in December 2003 and then by the Regional Bioethics Committee in 2004. The proposal elicited a massive reaction in the media and gave rise to much debate. However, the proposal was opposed by the Regional Council of Tuscany in 2004 and by several feminist organizations in Italy. See M La Barbera, *Multicentered Feminism: Revisiting the 'Female Genital Mutilation' Discourse* (Compostampa 2009) 184–187; E Bottini, 'Is Juridicization of Female Genital Mutilation an Effective Way of Eliminating It? Western Democracies Facing the Violation of Female Integrity and Dignity: Illegal FGM as an Integration Problem' *Jura Gentium* (2009) <www.juragentium.org/forum/mg/sunna/en/bottini.htm> accessed 26 April 2017.

instrument against contentious practices. Specific repressive legal provisions often turn out to be primarily symbolic, having hardly any real impact. For example, in countries that have criminalized female genital mutilation (FGM), the excision of young girls is still an ongoing practice.[47] There is indeed evidence that an exclusively punitive approach that singles out particular practices and imposes serious constraints upon specific minority groups and communities adds to the stigmatization of those who continue to abide by their practices and traditions. In effect, criminalization comes down to 'blaming the victim'.[48]

The path of offering guidance is far from easy; on the contrary, it demands a change in mentalities and greater openness to the reality of the normative pluralism that such persons must face, especially members of cultural and religious minorities who truly take an interest in the values and traditions to which they remain attached and in the deeper reasons for that attachment. We know from experience how difficult it is to bring about such a change in approach. By way of example, **Jinske Verhellen** (Chapter 11) shows how in private international law, the introduction of the choice of the law applicable in certain matters of personal status (*optio iuris*) has thus far met with only moderate success. Its implementation requires investing in supporting professionals whose task is to accompany the individuals and couples who might benefit from it. This in turn requires that professionals be sufficiently familiar with the different rules (i.e., legal systems) that might be applicable and from which persons can 'choose', so as to be able to inform them of the legal consequences of their choice. As long as conditions are not met for an effective implementation of a rule that allows persons to choose from among various legal regimes for certain aspects of their personal status, it is foreseeable that such a choice will remain largely an abstraction.

There is no lack of good will on the part of legal professionals. Ten judges from across Europe also took part in the conference. These are people who, in their daily practice, have to deal with questions associated directly or indirectly with the growing plurality of European society. They are called upon to find solutions when that diversity gives rise to tensions or conflicts. Their testimonies were poignant and quite revealing: without exception the judges attending the conference were interested in our discussions, but they confided that their legal training had not prepared them adequately to face certain types of situations and that even if they had been better prepared, they lacked the time to undertake in-depth examinations of the cultural contexts of the questions they had to decide. This was a striking observation, and if it proved to be representative for the judiciary in Europe (something yet to be tested), it would mean that judicial authorities are ill-equipped to offer effective practical support to a policy encouraging respect for the principle of personal autonomy in situations where a person is required to choose between divergent legal regimes.

To address the difficulty, some judges told us that, given their current working conditions and the fact that their task is ultimately to hand down decisions within a relatively short time frame, they prefer to be able to resort to legislative solutions that are clear and leave no doubt, even if these solutions are restrictive or even punitive vis-à-vis personal autonomy.

47 This is the case for Belgium; see M Dieleman, *Excision et migration en Belgique francophone: Rapport de recherche de l'Observatoire du sida et des sexualités pour le GAMS, Belgique* (GAMS 2012).

48 The latter effect may explain why there is some hesitation on the part of prosecutors to take action against practices such as FGM, which would likely drive the practices underground. Very few cases have thus far been brought before the courts in Europe, with the exception of France; see F Lionnet, 'Women's Rights, Bodies and Identities: The Limits of Universalism and the Legal Debate About Excision in France' in O Nnaemeka (ed), *Female Circumcision and the Politics of Knowledge: African Women in Imperialist Discourses* (Praeger 2005) 97.

In fact, some of them actually welcome the proliferation of criminal laws relating to certain cultural practices. This may be regrettable, of course, but given the context, it is perfectly understandable.

Responsibility should not rest entirely with the judges. Any policy that really seeks to tackle the question of how to maintain the principle of individual autonomy in an ever more diverse context must work on several fronts at once. On the one hand, it must ensure that every person called upon to manage a specific situation (for example, school administrators, health care givers, civil servants, educators) feels sufficiently well informed and prepared to guide persons who must make choices, without falling into paternalism. On the other hand, the persons directly concerned find themselves having to function in the most diverse conditions, without necessarily knowing how matters will evolve over time. Trusting them – that is to say, granting them the legal right to make their own choice of which regime should take precedence – presupposes that they are also in a position of being adequately informed of the consequences of their choices. Often this is not possible, given how complex certain situations can be and the unpredictable effects of certain choices. In the years to come, we will probably see developments in diverging directions: some communities will over time grow more flexible with regard to the degree of control they can exert over their cultural and religious practices, while others will move in the opposite direction. Education and the way in which young people from minority communities adapt to the normative diversity of the society in which they have grown up will also play a role. The best way to guarantee that the young people of tomorrow are duly prepared to assume the consequences of their choices in a plural social context is to educate them in that diversity. To do so successfully, civic education should have as its goal enabling each person to know what sort of protection and what options are available to them under the laws of the state in which they live, as well as to be aware of what those laws do not guarantee, so as to be in a better position to evaluate the pros and cons of the options open to them. There is probably no other way to ensure that the principle of personal autonomy is applied in an even-handed way to all, within so complex and unpredictable a context as that of contemporary plural societies. But this cannot be expected to happen overnight. The path is easier to outline in the abstract than to achieve in concrete terms.

Part I

Autonomy in the face of cultural diversity

Disciplinary perspectives

1 The fault in our stars

Personal autonomy, philosophy, and the law

Michele Graziadei

Introduction

Personal autonomy has a prominent place in the legal landscape of contemporary democracies. In a liberal democracy, individual rights rest on the recognition and protection of the individual's entitlement to free, unconstrained decision-making over matters concerning oneself and one's relationships with others. Many rules of public law aim to secure personal autonomy either at the individual or at the collective level. With respect to private law, personal autonomy is often presented as an overarching theme of the law of persons, contracts, property, torts, and so on. Personal autonomy in the private sphere thus mirrors the ideal of a liberal government in the public sphere. This general approach makes the legitimacy of a given government conditional upon its capacity to secure the protection of personal autonomy.[1]

Even under liberal democratic regimes, however, personal autonomy is not the sole organizing principle of the law of the state. Policymaking is often grounded as well on considerations of utility, expediency, security, and solidarity. Furthermore, when human beings lack autonomy – think of an unconscious patient whose will cannot be ascertained – other principles take over, such as the beneficial principle that obliges doctors to act for that patient's good.[2]

From a philosophical point of view, in the nineteenth century idealism made personal autonomy a central concern for the law, thus providing it with new ethical foundations. Nevertheless, whether personal autonomy can universally be recognized as a concept and a norm that truly has cross-cultural meaning and value or not remains a troubling question that is often debated by commentators without directly consulting the available empirical evidence.[3]

Even within as the Western legal tradition, personal autonomy has gained the reputation of an *enfant terrible*: brilliant, but unsettling, to say the least. The various meanings associated with the term are a good illustration of the variety of views that the notion of personal autonomy elicits among contemporary legal thinkers;[4] the doubts surrounding the subject, however, go beyond the purely terminological, as I will show.

1 See, e.g., J Habermas, *Between Facts and Norms: Contributions to a Discourse Theory of Law and Democracy* (William Rehg tr, MIT Press 1998); J Rawls, *Political Liberalism* (expanded edn, Columbia University Press 2005).

2 See, e.g., ED Pellegrino, DC Thomasma, 'The Conflict Between Autonomy and Beneficence in Medical Ethics: Proposal for a Resolution' (1987) 23 *Journal of Contemporary Health Law and Policy* 27.

3 See CC Helwig, MD Ruck, and M Peterson-Badali, 'Rights, Civil Liberties and Democracy' in M Killen and JG Smetana (eds), *Handbook of Moral Development* (2nd edn, Psychology Press 2014) 46.

4 For a survey of the various concepts associated to the term, see G Dworkin, *The Theory and Practice of Autonomy* (Cambridge University Press 1998) 10; TE Hill Jr, 'Kantian Autonomy and Contemporary Ideas of Autonomy' in O Sensen (ed), *Kant on Moral Autonomy* (Cambridge University Press 2015) 15.

DOI: 10.4324/9781315413617-3

To discuss these doubts in an orderly way, the various interpretations that come together under the heading of 'personal autonomy' need to be untangled. They reflect different lines of research into human agency and highlight the varied concerns and outlooks on it. My coverage of these interpretations will be unapologetically selective, as space does not allow for a more comprehensive overview, yet I still hope that this cursory attempt to trace their genealogies will help readers appreciate why the notion is both productive and problematic and, in my view, is bound to remain so.

In the first sections of this chapter I will therefore briefly consider the philosophical tradition closely associated with Kant and Hegel to show how that tradition has pushed for the recognition of personal autonomy as an organizing principle of Western law. By focusing on this philosophical tradition, I shall explore what I know best, but that is not to suggest that I dismiss other philosophical traditions or systems of thought that have reflected on and make room for this idea.[5]

I will first show how Kant's notion of autonomy was borrowed by some nineteenth-century jurists influenced by idealism to model the law as a system of rights. Following Kant, those jurists believed that the law could guarantee maximum freedom to all through the ascription of individual rights. This approach distanced the law not only from a status-based system of rights, but also from a prior utilitarian tradition that adopted an interest-based theory of human actions as well as an empirical concept of individual will. In contrast to the approach advanced by Kant, Hegel objected that rights, which are the mechanism whereby law guarantees personal autonomy, do not necessarily coexist peacefully; in fact, they may clash with one another, sometimes with tragic consequences.

In the Romantic period, the critique of the philosophical ideas of the Enlightenment brought with it the demise of faith in abstract reason as the foundation of autonomy, which the Kantian project both upheld and required. As will be shown, this offered the possibility to rethink autonomy and conceive of it as an individualized experience of the subject acting in the world from a personal point of view. For Hegel, morality can still be experienced in the form of shared moral commitments that have their centre of gravity in the institution of the state. As commentators have noted, this possibility is obviously more difficult to achieve today, both for reasons that are linked to the diminishing weight of the state in a globalized world and for the increasing individualization that characterizes life in advanced economies. Nevertheless, Hegel's reconstruction of autonomy as an individualized experience comes much closer to our understanding of autonomy today than does Kant's understanding of it.

A number of academic disciplines now employ empirical methods to conduct research on personal autonomy. These disciplines have taken up the most important question that was set aside by philosophers like Kant and Hegel, namely, how to measure personal autonomy in operational terms, both in a particular cultural context and across different cultures. As part of the psychological constitution of human beings, personal autonomy plays out very differently in different cultures. The remaining sections of this chapter briefly touch upon the need to provide concrete opportunities to exercise autonomy as an essential means to foster human development. Suffice it here to say that social inclusion, which is a vital part of

5 On autonomy in other philosophical traditions and systems of thought, see, e.g., J Sias, 'Buddhism, Confucianism, and Western Conceptions of Personal Autonomy' (2015) 1 *The Downtown Review* 1, 5; J Chan, 'Moral Autonomy, Civil Liberties, and Confucianism' (2002) 52 *Philosophy East and West* 281; A Sen, *Human Rights and Asian Values* (Carnegie Council on Ethics and International Affairs 1997); KG Dastidar, 'Individual Autonomy in Traditional Indian Thought' (1987) 15 *Journal of Indian Philosophy* 99.

the mandate of democratic governments, requires more than the recognition of the personal competence for autonomous choice. It requires making opportunities to exercise autonomy concretely available for the entire political community. In a globalized world, that community is constantly expanding, as are the corresponding moral, political, and legal obligations.

The birth of a philosophical tradition and its alternatives

The idea that the law should protect personal autonomy is relatively recent in the history of Western law. For this breakthrough, legal thought is indebted to ideas first fully developed by eighteenth- and nineteenth-century Western philosophy.[6] A quick review of the genesis of the idea of personal autonomy singles out two leading themes.

The first is the shift from morality conceived in terms of prompt obedience to authority to morality conceived in terms of self-governance. Immanuel Kant's famous answer to the question 'What is Enlightenment?', published in 1784, is explicit in this respect: 'Enlightenment is the human being's emergence from his self-incurred minority. Minority is inability to make use of one's own understanding without direction from another.'[7]

The second major theme is related to the idea of equality, an idea that can be connected to the notion that all human beings have equal moral competence. They do not need instruction from above to understand the moral law, and they all are capable of taking responsibility for their own self-governance, assuming they are mentally competent. The idea that all persons have equal moral competence comes into the picture in a variety of ways through both religious and non-religious thinkers.[8] Before turning to the reconstruction of personal autonomy advanced by thinkers as different as Kant and Hegel, here I must at least consider how a particular line of thought maintained that the foundations of social order rest on individual choice, but failed to provide idealistic grounds for it.

In the sixteenth century the idea of the equal moral competence of humanity was first advanced in the name of a realistic view of the nature of humankind, which made sense in a world divided by religious controversies and wars. As shown by Albert O. Hirschman,[9] this view rebelled against the reigning philosophical tradition, which extolled an ethics of virtues as the foundation of social order. The notion of 'interest' was then introduced as a key to understanding how society can exist and possibly thrive, despite all the moral shortcomings of human beings. In the sixteenth century, and even more so in the seventeenth century, a number of thinkers started insisting that the world is not governed by virtue, but rather by the personal drive to satisfy various appetites.[10]

6 The whole story is told in the superb study by JB Schneewind, *The Invention of Autonomy: A History of Modern Moral Philosophy* (Cambridge University Press 1998).

7 I Kant, 'An Answer to the Question: What Is Enlightenment?' in *Kant's Practical Philosophy* (MJ Gregor tr, Cambridge University Press 1996) 16. This has not spared Kant the reproach that the categorical imperative reflects an authoritarian, patriarchal, religious tradition that should have been abandoned rather than reconstructed; see R Rorty, 'Trapped Between Kant and Dewey: The Current Situation of Moral Philosophy' in N Brender and L Krasnoff (eds), *New Essays on the History of Autonomy: A Collection Honoring J. B. Schneewind* (Cambridge University Press 2004) 198.

8 See (n 6).

9 AO Hirschman, *The Passions and the Interests: Political Arguments for Capitalism Before Its Triumph* (Princeton University Press 1977).

10 See also P Force, *Self-Interest Before Adam Smith: A Geneology of Economic Science* (Cambridge University Press 2003).

This current of thought turned vices such as avarice and greed into psychological features that are intrinsic to human nature, but which can nonetheless be turned to good social purposes. Many moral shortcomings of humans were thus newly appraised; rather than denouncing them, it was argued that they should be exploited to lay the foundations of a new order. A new science of man, established on realistic premises, was built during these centuries. The first principle of this new science was that it was necessary 'to take humankind as it is' because it is futile to try to go against human nature.

According to this analysis, which abandoned both the status-based and the virtue-based views of morality, conformity to outward standards of behaviour sanctioned by legislation was enough to satisfy the requirements of civic conduct. In the eighteenth century, Giovan Battista Vico's *New Science* echoed this view:

> Philosophy considers man as he ought to be and is therefore useful only to the very few who want to live in Plato's republic and not to throw themselves into the dregs of Romulus. Legislation considers man as he is and attempts to put him to good uses in human society.[11]

Accordingly, subjects who entertain different spiritual inclinations can all participate in civic life. The consequence of this analysis is that anybody can be a good subject, no matter what his or her inner religious or moral beliefs are. Civic life thus turns out to be possible under less stringent conditions than those required by the predicaments of virtue.[12]

This philosophy did not put much faith in the exercise of individual will as an element of a philosophical system centred on the notion of reason as extolled by thinkers like Kant and Hegel. Consider, for example, what David Hume wrote in his *Treatise of Human Nature* about the concept of individual will: '[B]y the *will*, I mean nothing but the internal impression we feel and are conscious of, when we knowingly give rise to any new motion of our body, or a new perception of our mind.'[13] This is an experimental notion of what individual will is, and it cannot ground a theory of personal autonomy such as that inaugurated by Kant. Nonetheless, as explained below, this experimental notion opens up new ways of understanding how human capabilities work and how autonomy can be fostered.

Autonomy and conflicts among rights: the unravelling of a canon

The architects of personal autonomy as a principle of the legal order, who were influenced by the philosophy of Immanuel Kant, intended to recognize personal autonomy by reconstructing the law as an abstract system of rights assigned to each individual in accordance

11 G Vico, 'La scienza nuova' in F Nicolini (ed), *G Vico, Opere* (Ricciardi 1953) paras 132–133 (quoted in Hirschman [n 9], 14).

12 Ibid., para 132–133: 'Out of ferocity, avarice and ambition, the three vices which lead all mankind astray, society makes national defence, commerce and politics, and thereby causes the strength, the wealth, and the wisdom of the republics; out of these three vices which would certainly destroy man on earth society thus causes the civil happines to emerge. This principle proves the existence of divine providence' (quoted in Hirschman [n 9], 16–17). Similar ideas were anticipated by prominent Jansenists like Pierre Nicole (1625–1695) and Jean Domat (1625–1696).

13 D Hume, *A Treatise of Human Nature, Being an Attempt to Introduce the Experimental Method of Reasoning Into Moral Subjects, 1739–1740* (DF Norton and MJ Norton eds, Oxford University Press 2000) b. II, 3.1. This tradition goes back to Hobbes. For a succint, lucid reconstruction of it, see L Krasnoff, 'Pythagoras Enlightened' in Brender and Krasnoff (eds), (n 7) 133, 137–138.

with the law of the state. The project thus pursued was an inclusive one. Up to the middle of the nineteenth century, more than a few European states were still organized through the division of society into separate estates, such as the nobility, the clergy, the bourgeoisie, and so on. In many parts of Europe, religious faith could still mark a fundamental difference in the civic condition of subjects. In that epoch, as Hegel showed, the notion that an individual could have rights as such, simply by virtue of being an autonomous individual under the law of the state, was novel and, indeed, even revolutionary.[14]

This philosophical approach shaped the jurisprudential definition of a right, which was elaborated to serve this project.[15] In the words of Savigny, perhaps the most distinguished German jurist of the nineteenth century, this is to be conceptualized as the sphere in which individual will 'rules independently of every foreign will'.[16]

The specific function of the law in general was, in Savigny's view, to establish 'an invisible boundary within which the existence and the activity of each individual gains a secure, free space' so that the human desire for sociability can be achieved in the world.[17] Once rights are ascribed by the law to each individual – this is the message – the conditions for the existence of peaceful social life are established. Under this approach, the law assists morality 'not by performing its bidding but by securing the free development of its power indwelling in each individual will'.[18]

Kant's famous proclamation – that the law is simply the whole of the conditions under which 'the voluntary actions of any one person can be harmonised in reality with the voluntary actions of every other person, according to a universal law of freedom'[19] – is the immediate philosophical precedent of this view of the function of the law as a system of rights.

It is impossible to overestimate how influential this reconstruction of the role of personal autonomy in the law was throughout the nineteenth century.[20] Nonetheless, as the industrial age developed, a gap between Kant and Savigny's ideal model of the law and the everyday working of the legal system soon became apparent.

According to Kant and Savigny, rights are assigned to individuals in such a way that their initial attribution establishes *ex ante* who is entitled to what in every circumstance. The possibility of a clash between two rights is simply not conceivable under this approach.[21] In their

14 GWF Hegel, *The Elements of the Philosophy of Right* (AW Wood ed, HB Nisbet tr, Cambridge University Press 1991) 240, § 209: 'It is part of education [*Bildung*], of thinking as consciousness of the individual [*des Einzelnen*] in the form of universality, that I am apprehended as a universal person, in which [respect] *all* are identical. *A human being counts as such because he is a human being*, not because he is a Jew, Catholic, Protestant, German, Italian, etc.' (italics in original). But see K Marx, 'On the Jewish Question' in K Marx, *Selected Writings* (2nd edn by D McLellan, Oxford University Press 2001).

15 M Graziadei, 'Rights in the European Landscape: A Historical and Comparative Profile' in S Prechal and B van Roemund (eds), *The Coherence of European Law: The Search for Unity in Divergent Concepts* (Oxford University Press 2008) 63ff.

16 FC von Savigny, *System of the Modern Roman Law*, I, (1840, J Holloway tr, Higgibotham 1867) § 52.

17 Ibid.

18 Ibid.

19 I Kant, *The Metaphysics of Morals* (1797, tr and ed by Mary J Gregory, Cambridge University Press 1996), 24, [230].

20 From a classical natural law perspective, the Kantian notion of autonomy suffers a serious flaw, namely its lack of substantive criteria to choose among alternative courses of action; cf. J Gordley, *Foundations of Private Law* (Oxford University Press 2002).

21 J Timmermann, 'Kantian Dilemmas? Moral Conflict in Kant's Ethical Theory' (2013) 95 *Archiv für Geschichte der Philosophie* 36–64 (the only explicit discussion of the topic in Kant's published writings confirms that there is no room in his philosophy for moral dilemmas generated by conflicting claims).

account of the law, however, something important is missing. Take, for example, the right of property, a cornerstone of the nineteenth-century system of rights. The image of an owner as an isolated rights holder who can exercise despotic powers over property occurs over and over in the literature of this period. And yet, no matter how enthralling that vision was, material resources and individual actions are not completely separable through the simple allocation of individual rights. Idealized models of property rights stop short of capturing the complex reality of actual conflicts involving, for example, incompatible land uses.[22]

What is true of property and of the regulation of conflicting land uses is also true of rights in general. Rights can and often do conflict, and yet the law does not cast much light on how these conflicts should be resolved. What happens when rights are in conflict was thus bound to become a major philosophical and jurisprudential challenge for the idea of personal autonomy. Ongoing debates over balancing and proportionality show that it was also a lasting one.[23]

Hegel was the first of the nineteenth-century philosophers to dedicate attention to the problems raised by the conflict of rights. Commenting on the German Constitution, young Hegel noted that the most intractable conflicts were not those that originated in the clash between right and wrong, but rather those generated by the opposition between right and right.[24] More than 20 years later, in his lectures on aesthetics, Hegel analysed the structure of the Greek tragedy – in particular Sophocles's *Antigone* – as characterized by the unfolding of this type of conflict:

> [W]ithin such a conflict each of the opposed sides, if taken by itself, has *justification* while each can establish the true and positive content of its own aim and character only by denying and infringing the equally justified power of the other.[25]

Hegel's remarks on this topic are a prelude to our plight, namely the difficulty of dealing with conflicts of this kind.

It is not by chance that twentieth-century legal thought was confronted with the challenge of providing ways to balance rights to an unprecedented extent and having to resort to techniques such as proportionality to govern conflicts among rights. To many, this is the most salient feature of twentieth-century jurisprudence, as highlighted by the practice of the highest courts.[26]

22 The point was elegantly made in the classic article by CM Rose, 'Crystals and Mud in Property Law' (1987) 40 *Stanford Law Review* 577.

23 See (n 26).

24 Hegel's analysis focused on war among nations; see GWF Hegel, 'The German Constitution' in GWF Hegel, *Political Writings* (1798–1802 ed Lawrence Dickey and HB Nisbet, Cambridge University Press 1999) 6ff, 68–70: 'In this way . . . an unresolved contradiction is set up . . . although the characters have a purpose which is valid in itself, they can carry it out in tragedy only by pursuing it one-sidedly and so contradicting and infringing someone else's purpose.'

25 GWF Hegel, *Aesthetics: Lectures on Fine Arts* (1835–1842, TM Knox tr, Oxford University Press 1998) II, 1196. For more on this, see RR Williams, *Tragedy, Recognition, and the Death of God: Studies in Hegel and Nietzsche* (Oxford University Press 2012).

26 J Bomhoff, *Balancing Constitutional Rights: The Origins and Meanings of Postwar Legal Discourse* (Cambridge University Press 2013); M Cohen-Eliya and I Porat, *Proportionality and Constitutional Culture* (Cambridge University Press 2013); AM Yetano, *La dynamique du principe de proportionnalité* (LGDJ 2014); A Barack, *Proportionality: Constitutional Rights and Their Limitations* (Cambridge University Press 2012); D Kennedy, 'A Transnational Genealogy of Proportionality in Private Law' in

Balancing does not intervene at the level of constitutional adjudication only. It has its grip on ordinary legislation and case law as well. This is why the law of torts in the twentieth century has become a major field of theoretical enquiry in every jurisdiction. Tort law is the arena where conflicting rights constantly confront each other: my right to privacy against your right to freedom of expression, to pick a familiar example of this type of conflict.[27] Beyond property and torts, contract law also presents a similar problematique: the need and the necessity to balance competing normative claims.[28]

Being outside the Kantian canon, utilitarianism holds that only an unflinching commitment to the cardinal rule – 'maximize happiness' – can avoid similar problems. Nonetheless, if the maximization of happiness does not lead to the betterment of all but requires the sacrifice of some, that rule is hard to keep, especially when the lives of human beings enter the calculus as instruments of collective happiness.[29] The rejection of utility maximization in such hard cases makes sense for utilitarian legal philosophers as well,[30] and is supported by common sense, especially when lives are visibly traded for money. Corporate defendants relying on utility maximizing calculations of this kind thus risk having to pay punitive damages.[31]

The possibility of a true conflict of rights is denied by the philosophical view that comes under the rubric 'specificationism'.[32] Specificationism holds that each right is defined by an elaborate set of qualifications concerning its scope. Once these qualifications are properly considered, rights never clash. According to this view, one can determine the scope of rights in such a way that conflicts among them do not actually occur. For instance, the content of the right to privacy can be specified so as to avoid conflict with the right to free speech by providing, for example, that under certain conditions the right in question is limited. This approach is not truly convincing, however. Hegel himself noted that the attempt to specify the rights attributed to each subject would have multiplied – rather than reduced – the occasion of friction among them: 'Because of the indeterminacy of rights, conflict *may* arise, and because of their determinacy, contradictions between them *must* arise'.[33] To this, one may add that fully specified rights are unknowable in practice: to explicitly set out all

---

R Brownsword et al. (eds), *The Foundations of European Private Law* (Hart 2011); A Stone Sweet and J Mathews, 'Proportionality Balancing and Global Constitutionalism' (2008) 47 *Columbia Journal of Transnational Law* 72; E Brems (ed), *Conflicts Between Fundamental Rights* (Intersentia 2008); L Zucca, *Constitutional Dilemmas: Conflicts of Fundamental Legal Rights in Europe and the USA* (Oxford University Press 2007).

27 This conflict is subdued where arguments based on rights are not prominent, like in England, but even there it is present. See, e.g., N Jansen, 'Duties and Rights in Negligence: A Comparative and Historical Perspective on the European Law of Extracontractual Liability' (2004) 24 *Oxford Journal of Legal Studies* 443, and more generally, R Stevens, *Torts and Rights* (Oxford University Press 2007).

28 See, e.g., D Kennedy, 'From the Will Theory to the Principle of Private Autonomy: Lon Fuller's Consideration and Form' (2000) 100 *Columbia Law Review* 94.

29 J Waldron, 'Rights in Conflict' (1989) 99 *Ethics* 503.

30 See, e.g., J Coleman, *Markets, Morals and the Law* (Yale University Press 2003).

31 Grappling with this point is problematic from the economic analysis of law perspective: G Calabresi, 'The Complexity of Torts: The Case of Punitive Damages' in MS Madden (ed), *Exploring Tort Law* (Cambridge University Press 2005) 333, 340–343 (on punitive damages in the *Pinto* case).

32 See, e.g., CH Wellman, 'On Conflicts Between Rights' (1995) 14 *Law and Philosophy* 271; R Shafer-Landau, 'Specifying Absolute Rights' (1995) 37 *Arizona Law Review* 209; H Steiner, *An Essay on Rights* (Blackwell 1994).

33 Hegel, 'German Constitution' (n 25) 69–70.

the qualifications that would precisely define even the simplest right is too daunting a task.[34] Furthermore, specificationism does not account for the moral residue of a 'defeated' right, namely of the right that succumbed to an opposing right. This residue – the moral conviction that the claim based on that right, although defeated, had strong merits – highlights the psychologically and socially 'tragic' nature of the conflict between opposing rights because it leads the prevailing party to experience guilt, even though that party presumably followed a rightful course of action, as Hegel's comments on *Antigone* reveal. This is, in other words, a conflict that does not and will not go away. *Roe v Wade*,[35] the most famous decision on abortion ever rendered by the US Supreme Court, provides an unsettling example of arguments that generate this type of conflict. Guido Calabresi considers this decision 'a disaster' precisely because the Court was unprepared to meet the theoretical and discursive challenge posed by a tragic conflict between personal autonomy and the right to life.[36]

A second general point to consider is that personal autonomy can be self-defeating. Autonomy is prone to becoming illusory unless limits to it are set in order to restrict, for example, the possibility of totally relinquishing one's autonomy by consent. Kant, for example, held that a contract by which a person gives up his or her freedom in order to become a slave cannot be binding because it fundamentally contradicts autonomy.[37]

One of the functions of the law in contemporary societies is thus to design the contours of the freedom of contract (or indeed of any other institution of private law) in such a way that it does not become a means to belittle or sacrifice salient aspects of personal autonomy.

Wide-ranging restrictions on the freedom of contract to protect health and safety are generally justified on this ground. Employment contracts cannot oblige workers to give up fundamental rights that are protected at the workplace, such as the right not to be discriminated against on the basis of gender, religion, or personal, philosophical, or political opinions.[38] Legislation targeting unfair contractual terms in consumer contracts is likewise justified by making the point that freedom of contract should not end up destroying itself. Market competition cannot by itself iron out unfair contract terms because the ability of consumers to shop around for the best possible terms is limited or non-existent. Hence the necessity of legislation to curb an abuse of legal techniques. Market competition itself also requires rules to police contracts, agreements, and practices that are a threat to it. Legislation to this effect was passed in the United States with the Sherman Act of 1890, and is now in force in one version or another in most industrialized countries.

Difficult cases remain controversial and open for discussion, however. Surrogacy contracts are among the best examples of this point. Arguments based on commodification, exploitation, gender inequality, and children's interests are regularly invoked against the validity of these contracts. All of these arguments drive home the conclusion that surrogacy

34 J Feinberg, *Rights, Justice, and the Bounds of Liberty* (Princeton University Press 1980) 221–251.

35 *Roe v Wade* (1973) 410 US 113.

36 See G Calabresi, *Ideals, Attitudes, Beliefs, and the Law* (Syracuse University Press 1985) 91.

37 I Kant, *Observations on the Feeling of the Beautiful and Sublime* (JT Goldthwait tr, University of California Press 1991).

38 On this point, see S Deakin, 'Contracts and Capabilities: An Evolutionary Perspective on the Autonomy-Paternalism Debate' (2014) 2 *Erasmus Law Review* 141; S Deakin and A Supiot (eds), *Capacitas: Contract Law and the Institutional Foundations of a Market Economy* (Hart 2009). The difficult cases are usually those in which accepting a job means entering an organization that is ideologically coloured or that proclaims adherence to a particular set of beliefs. Even in these cases, certain basic safeguards must be upheld: *Lombardi Vallauri v Italy* (ECHR, 20 October 2009).

contracts are not a legitimate exercise of autonomy. The opposite view holds that they are legitimate manifestations of personal autonomy, although they surely pose some difficult questions concerning the commodification of the human body, the unequal exploitation of reproductive sexuality, and so on.[39]

Some social relationships – such as those based on love or friendship – are the source of both very gratifying and very onerous moral obligations and claims and thereby contribute to the development of personality. These are excluded from the realm in which the law governs, possibly because their legal regulation would pervert the exercise of autonomy with respect to them. Therefore, although a person seeking a job may enter into a contract of employment, an employment contract cannot oblige an employee to be the employer's friend. Even though creating or maintaining friendship is an important expression of personal autonomy, it still cannot be the object of a legal obligation. It is tempting to say that autonomy in these matters is too serious a thing to have it governed by the law except in the negative, that is, by providing that the law cannot regulate these relationships.[40] Autonomy can also be exercised to decide that a certain business transaction shall be binding in honour only, and therefore shall not be governed by the law.[41]

A romantic, individualized notion of autonomy

As shown in the previous section, philosophers like Kant and jurists like Savigny believed that through the ascription of rights one could establish *ex ante* the proper ambit for the legitimate exercise of autonomy, under general rules that would have guaranteed maximum liberty for all. A major problem with this approach was that it did not consider the possibility of a conflict among rights. Hegel was the first philosopher to systematically pursue this point. He demonstrated that rights do conflict, and that these conflicts are very difficult to manage because each party to the dispute can ground his or her claim on a justification. Personal autonomy could then still be conceived as one of the pillars of the moral and legal orders, but hardly as a means to avoid conflicts involving competing claims such as those occurring in society. Jurists like Jhering first drew upon and elaborated on this insight, and in the twentieth century techniques such as balancing and proportionality were developed by leading lights to try to manage the problem in its most general terms.[42]

In this section I will discuss a second type of criticism levelled against the notion of autonomy that Kant supported. Kant's version of autonomy was the expression of a universal, impersonal, and cosmopolitan type of reason. For Kant, autonomy was based on the necessity to consider the humanity of persons as an end in itself. The fundamental precept

39 C Fabre, *Whose Body Is It Anyway? Justice and the Integrity of the Person* (Oxford University Press 2006) 186ff.

40 Consider, for example, what FC von Savigny, *System of the Modern Roman Law* (William Holloway tr, Hyperion Press 1979 [1867]) 282 says about family law: '[R]elations of family only partly carry in them a juridical nature; indeed we must add that the juridical side of its nature is plainly the smaller for the most important belongs to a province quite other than that of law.' Some civil codes (e.g., the Italian Civil Code, art. 1321) stipulate that contracts can only regulate *patrimonial* relationships. This means that contracts cannot be concluded to regulate relationships such as friendship, which are to be governed by social rather than legal rules.

41 See, e.g., *Edwards v Skyways Ltd* [1964] 1 WLR 349 (QBD). But this choice is not to be too easily inferred; see *Edmonds v Lawson* [2000] 2 WLR 1091 (CA).

42 See (n 27).

he endorsed was: 'So act that you use humanity, whether in your own person or in the person of any others, always at the same time as an end, never merely as a means'.[43] The term 'humanity' in this context had a technical meaning: it denoted the rational capacity of individuals, and posited a requirement about how that capacity must be applied. This implied the capacity and willingness of individuals to give the demands of morality priority over their personal pursuits. According to Kant, then, personal autonomy is a concept grounded in the notion of rationality as a general criterion to judge what is an autonomous act.

Precisely this point was called into question in the Romantic age. Hegel and the German Romantics intended to realize freedom by grounding personal subjectivity in terms of the existing, concrete subjectivity of particular individuals, rather than in the form of an impersonal rational subjectivity along the lines elaborated by Kant.

According to Terry Pinkard, the Romantics

> thus shift the conception of modern freedom away from the idea of rational, anonymous self-determination toward something more like the ideas of authenticity, irony, and true feeling. In particular, they shift moral consciousness away from the idea of obedience to a self-imposed *law* toward the idea of being 'true to oneself'.[44]

For the first time autonomy thus meant acting from the personal point of view, pursuing one's deepest personal convictions, realizing one's own concrete conceptions of the good life, and so on. Utilitarians like John Stuart Mill showed sympathy for this approach when commenting upon the cultivation of character:

> A person whose desires and impulses are his own – are the expression of his own nature, as it has been developed and modified by his own culture – is said to have a character. One whose desires and impulses are not his own has no character, no more than a steam engine has a character.[45]

Personal autonomy and the law: between universalism and particularism

The Romantics' attack on the idea of a universal law based on reason as a source of morality unearthed a fault line running deep below the surface of the Western legal tradition. Since antiquity, the law in the West has been conceived as a universal measure of human relationships established by nature, by divine will, or by human authority, and at the same time as a particular rule grounded in a specific social and material context. It can be either the rule of a particular locality or group (most often associated with the notion of custom), or the rule that is specifically appropriate to the circumstances (most often associated with the notion of equity).[46]

43 I Kant, *Groundwork of the Metaphysics of Morals* (MJ Gregor, rev J Timmermann, Cambridge University Press 2011 [1785]) 4:429.

44 T Pinkard, *Hegel's Phenomenology: The Sociality of Reason* (Cambridge University Press 1996) 207, 209; HE Alison, 'Autonomy in Kant and German Idealism' in Sensen (n 4) 129ff.

45 JS Mill, *On Liberty* (Liberal Arts Press 1956 [1859]) 73.

46 M Graziadei, 'Natural Law in the Story of Comparative Law' (2013) 8 *Journal of Comparative Law* 13.

Comparative law scholars are quick to note that even where law as a principle of social organization prevails – a circumstance not to be taken for granted for every place on earth – there is a great deal of variation among the laws of the different nations or communities, a phenomenon long observed by philosophers and ethnologists. Philosophers from Aristotle to Hegel concur that positive laws are not determined by pure philosophical concepts. Since antiquity, ethnologists have noted how customs vary from locality to locality. As early as the fifth century BC, Herodotus made the point that cultural relativists would pick up later in history: what is right for one group may horrify the members of another group, and vice versa.[47]

There are ways to bring all these cultural manifestations under the umbrella of general principles – usually working in the shadow of classical natural law – by showing that human beings around the world share a notion of 'the good life' that may be interpreted differently but still responds to certain common human needs (although the experience of living under one or the other of these various regimes may be very different indeed).[48] Nonetheless, what is proclaimed as a universal rule must still be accommodated to govern the particularity of a single case. The notion of equity, as mentioned earlier, was coined precisely to think about how to adapt the law to the particular case at hand.[49] This adaptation shows once more that certain universal principles give way to different practices in different circumstances.

Lastly, despite the modern tendency to consider the law as a body of rules to be applied uniformly across society, society is not an undifferentiated totality for many purposes, even under the conditions of modernity. Equality under the law has erased neither the need to establish one's own social identity nor the need to maintain social relations and bonds that reflect particular commitments, arrangements, ideals, and interests. The notion that, to advance personal autonomy, the state should strip individuals of their particular social affiliations and identities and get them to conform to an abstract model of citizenship that the state itself defines for its own purposes is bound to raise the strong objection that the state is modelling citizenship on the dominant culture and the values of a section of society only.[50]

Hegel and the Romantics, as well as later critics of the Enlightenment, had a point when they criticized the universalizing tendency underpinning the Enlightenment's project of modernity, and in particular Kant's approach to personal autonomy. Hegel's way of overcoming it moved in the direction of interiorizing moral judgements, which involved acquiring a practical skill, namely, the ability to discern the moral salience of individual actions in particular contexts. This meant that there could not be a cardinal rule such as Kant's

47 Herodotus, *The Histories* (A De Sélincourt tr, rev J Marincola, Harmondsworth 1972) 219–220: 'One might recall, in particular, an anecdote of Darius. When he was king of Persia, he summoned the Greeks who happened to be present at his court, and asked them what they would take to eat the dead bodies of their fathers. They replied that they would not do it for any money in the world. Later, in the presence of the Greeks, and through an interpreter, so they could understand what was said, he asked some Indians, of the tribe called Callatiae, who do in fact eat their parents' dead bodies, what they would take to burn them. They uttered a cry of horror and forbade him to mention such a dreadful thing. One can see by this what custom can do, and Pindar, in my opinion, was right when he called it "king of all".'

48 J Gordley, *Foundations of Private Law* (Oxford University Press 2006).

49 'Equity' in this sense has foundations that go back to antiquity; see Aristotle, *Nichomachean Ethics*, V.10.1137b13–14; V.10.1137b34–1138; Aristotle, *Rhetoric*, I.13.1364a33 – b1. See also FD Miller Jr, 'Aristotle's Philosophy of Law' in FD Miller Jr, in association with C-A Biondi (eds), *A Treatise of Legal Philosophy and General Jurisprudence. Volume 6: A History of the Philosophy of Law From the Ancient Greeks to the Scholastics* (Springer 2007).

50 RA Macdonald, 'Legal Republicanism and Legal Pluralism: Two Takes on Identity and Diversity' in M Bussani and M Graziadei (eds), *Human Diversity and the Law* (Bruylant 2005) 43ff.

categorical imperative from which all moral maxims can be derived. Hegel thus argued that the individual can be 'at home with himself' in that he can 'find his own ***particular*** way of being ethical ("universal"), his own particular *way* of orienting himself in "social space" in the light of a determinately structured "whole" that nonetheless embodies within itself reasons that can be shared by all'.[51]

A form of collective morality thus emerges that is not dependent on the application of a universal law, but rather on the specification of what a community holds as most sacred. As one commentator has noted, this model largely followed Kant's view of aesthetic judgements: 'One learns to make such judgements by having one's eye trained in certain ways, and one learns moral judgements by having one's moral sensibilities trained in the right way.'[52] At the same time, Hegel's notion of morality (*Sittlichkeit*) was anchored to the institutions of the state; he contemplated the state as the 'actuality of the ethical Idea'.[53] This is what makes his philosophy unappealing to most people today. Any sentiment of ethical order of the kind that Hegel had in mind when he wrote that line is by now a relic of the past. It has been buried by the process of individualization – that is, placing individuals at the centre of social life – and the pervasive loss of faith in traditional or preordained social order as well as in the moral authority of the state. Sociologists like Beck, Giddens, and Baumann have shown that the erosion of state sovereignty in the age of globalization has brought about even more pressing demands of individual self-sufficiency: the state is not an answer to such demands, as the weakening of traditional bonds continues and the normativity of traditional lifestyles is constantly challenged.[54]

Under these conditions, tradition itself is something that is now elaborated as a hallmark of identity.[55] This explains why contemporary societies exhibit simultaneous tendencies towards greater individualization and greater emphasis on tradition, not necessarily mediated by irony or by a shared sense of community such as that cherished by the Romantics. Yet in this fragmented, divided world, the question of whether personal autonomy should be the ultimate standard by which to regulate controversial issues remains more urgent than ever. The rest of this chapter shows how research across several disciplines supports the view that autonomy has a strong cross-cultural dimension that is shared by all of humankind.

The various dimensions of autonomy beyond idealism

In the previous sections I have shown how idealism succeeded in making personal autonomy a central concern for the law. In exploring the idea of autonomy, the proponents of this current of thought never considered how to measure autonomy in operational terms. This question was beyond the horizon of idealism.

51 T Pinkard, 'Virtues, Morality, and *Sittlichkeit*: From Maxims to Practices' (1999) 7 *European Journal of Philosophy* 217, 227 (italics in original).

52 Ibid. This approach still captures aspects of the contemporary legal consciousness: see P Schlag, 'The Aesthetics of American Law' (2002) 115 *Harvard Law Review* 1047.

53 Hegel (n 14) 275. Compare M Shuster, *Autonomy After Auschwitz: Adorno, German Idealism, and Modernity* (University of Chicago Press 2014).

54 K Lõhmus, *Caring Autonomy* (Cambridge University Press 2015) 115ff. The author notes that this brings about a crisis of trust. To counter it, she advances the notion of *caring autonomy* based on a relational concept of the self.

55 See B Anderson, *Imagined Communities: Reflections on the Origin and Spread of Nationalism* (revised and extended edn, Verso 1991).

Even though the law sometimes draws a bright line to establish whether a person has the competence to take autonomous decisions, as it does, for example, when it sets the age of majority, autonomy is not an abstract, all-or-nothing capacity of human beings. This is an important point to consider, as the law may hinder or facilitate the exercise of autonomy, understood as the capacity to set goals for oneself and to pursue them in motivationally autonomous terms.

Research reveals, for example, that people with dementia can react in nuanced ways to social situations even at an advanced stage of their illness, and hence can exercise autonomy if their personal condition is properly taken into account.[56] Health institutions that try to accommodate people who object to blood transfusions on religious grounds can manage to avoid destructive conflicts over what is an autonomous decision better than institutions that resist such objections on the grounds that they presumably indicate a lack of autonomy on the part of the patients who articulate them.[57]

How to measure autonomy is, therefore, no banal question. Actually, it is a question riddled with epistemological issues. Even a superficial examination of this aspect highlights a number of problems. A first methodological pitfall is the adoption of double standards to measure autonomy. Criteria to evaluate the capacity for autonomy that discriminate among various ways of exercising autonomy in different cultural contexts are suspect.[58] They speak of the not-so-innocent expectation that, as a result of the diffusion of modernization, Western cultural models and lifestyles must be considered acceptable and even preferable across the world. By now, however, it has become clear that modernization does not bring about cultural uniformity, as modernity comes in multiple varieties in different places.[59] As a consequence, the message of human rights, and the notion of personal autonomy that comes along with it, must be understood in the vernacular of other traditions, cultural expressions, systems of thought, and philosophical and religious beliefs.[60] These produce different constellations of hybridity, which are all part of modernity. The tension between the law of the state, personal autonomy, and religious claims is evident in this context.[61] Yet even phenomena that are frequently labelled revolts against modernity paradoxically adopt aspects of it, as some features of recent fundamentalist movements show, such as their use of the media.[62]

56 R Harding, 'Legal Constructions of Dementia: Discourses of Autonomy at the Margins of Capacity' (2012) 34 *Journal of Social Welfare and Family Law* 425.

57 DB Hughes, BW Ullery, and PS Barie, 'The Contemporary Approach to the Care of Jehovah's Witnesses' (2008) 65 *Journal of Trauma-Injury Infection & Critical Care* 237–247 (the rejection of transfusions does not affect medical outcomes if hopitals are ready to cater to the needs of patients adhering to this religion).

58 AE Galeotti, 'Autonomy and Cultural Practices: The Risk of Double Standards' (2015) 14 *European Journal of Political Theory* 277 (arguing for a political notion of autonomy).

59 L Ronigen, 'Multiple Modernities, "East" and "West", and the Quest for Universal Human Rights' in G Preyer and M Sussman (eds), *Varieties of Modernity* (Brill 2016).

60 SE Merry and S Wood, 'Quantification and the Paradox of Measurement: Translating Children's Rights in Tanzania' (2015) 56 *Current Anthropology* 217–218; T Destrooper, 'Linking Discourse and Practice: The Human Rights-Based Approach to Development in the Village Assaini Program in the Kongo Central' (2016) 38 *Human Rights Quarterly* 787–813; cf. H Yang, 'Editor's Reflections: Academic Indigenization' (2004) 11 *Peace and Conflict Studies* 96.

61 See, e.g., F Ahmed, 'Personal Autonomy and the Option of Religious Law' (2010) 24 *International Journal of Law, Policy and the Family* 222.

62 A Aly et al. (eds), *Violent Extremism Online: New Perspectives on Terrorism and the Internet* (Routledge 2016).

The rejection of the claim that, as a lived experience and as a norm, personal autonomy is inextricably bound up with the cultural traits of Western societies opens up the possibility of exploring in empirical terms these dimensions in cross-cultural perspective. Among the disciplines that have embarked on this study, psychology is perhaps the one that has the most extensive body of research on this issue.[63] Psychologists have expressed widely differing views on personal autonomy, ranging from Skinner's denial of it (because the real determining causes of human behaviour are neither the will nor autonomy)[64] to theories that give great weight to autonomy in the making of personality, such as the self-determination theory elaborated by Deci and others.[65] To be sure, these opposing views reflect older disagreements among philosophers; in fact, they mirror the debates that divided philosophers into incompatibilists and compatibilists. The first group maintained that in a deterministic world free will has no place; the second argued there is room for both constraint and flexibility in human action, and thus defended a view of human beings that allows for personal autonomy.[66]

The turn towards the use of experimental methodologies in these fields has pushed both philosophers and psychologists in new directions. For the first time, philosophers are using empirical methods to ask whether people's intuitions are closer to the compatibilist or the incompatibilist vision of the free will problem.[67] Psychological research, on the other hand, investigates how to obtain empirical measures of autonomy.[68] Pursuing this goal, such research has shown that the experience of autonomy is transcultural. The exercise of autonomy (as experienced by human beings) satisfies universal psychological needs pertaining to agency and identity formation,[69] and should be understood as an adaptative response with a biological basis.[70]

This refutes the idea that autonomy is instantiated only in individualistic societies where the self is construed as independent from the social order, a view that leads to an emphasis on individual rights as a means to develop the law. Collectivistic cultures that have developed a morality of duty based on conforming to social role obligations, upholding hierarchy, and

63 Other disciplines have now taken up the same challenge as well; see S Navetta and P Navarra, *The Economics of Freedom, Theory, Measurement, and Policy Implications* (Cambridge University Press 2015).

64 As a reaction to this, current research investigates willed behaviour rather than the question of whether free will exists or not; see M Brass et al., 'Imaging Volition: What the Brain Can Tell Us About the Will' (2013) 229 *Experimental Brain Research* 301.

65 RM Ryan and EL Deci, 'Self-Regulation and the Problem of Human Autonomy: Does Psychology Need Choice, Self-Determination, and Will?' (2006) 74 *Journal of Personality* 1557.

66 M McKenna and JD Coates, 'Compatibilism' in EN Zalta (ed), *The Stanford Encyclopedia of Philosophy* (Summer 2015 edn). Anthropologists have flirted with similar ideas; see KM Murphy and CJ Throop, 'Willing Contours: Locating Volition in Anthropological Theory' in KM Murphy and CJ Throop (eds), *Toward an Anthropology of the Will* (Stanford University Press 2010) 1.

67 N Schaun, 'Experimental Philosophy and the Problem of Free Will' (2011) 331 *Science* 1401.

68 N Weinstein, AK Przybylski, and RM Ryan, 'The Index of Autonomous Functioning: Development of a Scale of Human Autonomy' (2012) 46 *Journal of Research in Personality* 397.

69 CC Helwig, 'The Development of Personal Autonomy Throughout Cultures' (2006) 21 *Cognitive Development* 458; VI Chirkov, RM Ryan, and KM Sheldon (eds), *Human Autonomy in Cross-Cultural Context, Perspectives on the Psychology of Agency, Freedom, and Well-Being* (Springer 2011); VI Chirkov, 'The Universality of Psychological Autonomy Across Cultures: Arguments From Developmental and Social Psychology' in N Weinstein (ed), *Human Motivation and Interpersonal Relationships* (Springer 2014) 27.

70 LA Leotti, SS Iyengar, and KN Ochsner, 'Born to Choose: The Origins and Value of the Need for Control' (2010) 14 *Trends in Cognitive Sciences* 457.

maintaining social harmony also provide evidence of the role that personal autonomy plays in certain contexts.[71] Both autonomy and relatedness are important universal human needs; autonomy is, therefore, compatible with relatedness, contrary to what previous psychological research held.[72]

These important findings help overcome the confusion that results from the failure to distinguish between cultural models of self and the experiential selves of particular members of a community. The best known cultural models of self are individualism and collectivism,[73] which reflect independent and interdependent cultural construals of personal selves.[74] But individualism should not be conflated with autonomy, nor collectivism with the lack of it, because social and ideological constructs of autonomy must not be confounded with experiential autonomy.[75]

Anthropologists have contributed to this line of research by criticizing the idea of 'a one-to-one correspondence between cultural models and the experiential self' that dominated cultural psychology.[76] This observation leads to the conclusion that 'one cannot assume that the individual's experiential self can be reduced to the concepts and terms which are used to talk about it.'[77]

Autonomy as a personal and an institutional practice

Assessing the discourse of autonomy with the benefit of hindsight, one can see why it cuts both ways. The flipside of the notion of autonomous conduct and personality is the notion of non-autonomous conduct and personality.

Throughout the nineteenth century personal autonomy gained wider recognition in legal thought and in the making of the law than in previous times. Nonetheless, during the same century and well into the last century, authoritarian and paternalistic discourses undermined personal autonomy by denying it wholly or in part to certain segments of society on various grounds.

This is what happened, for example, to the mentally ill in many countries as a consequence of the trend towards institutionalized care. Diagnoses that certified the incapacity for autonomous action and therefore the need for internment filled madhouses to an unprecedented extent just when autonomy became law's guiding light.[78] Wide-ranging discrimination based on gender or race limited autonomy on a large scale as well until it was prohibited in the 1960s, usually on constitutional grounds. Prior to decolonization and independence, autonomy was widely limited among the exoticized, subjugated 'other'

71 CC Helwig, 'The Development of Personal Autonomy' (n 69).

72 Ibid.

73 HC Triandis, *Indvidualism and Collectivism* (Westview Press 1995).

74 HR Markus and S Kitayama, 'Culture and the Self: Implications for Cognition, Emotion, and Motivation' (1991) 98 *Psychological Review* 224.

75 Chirkov, 'The Universality of Psychological Autonomy Across Cultures' (n 69).

76 Helwig, Ruck, and Peterson-Badali (n 3).

77 D Hollan, 'Cross-Cultural Differences in the Self' (1992) 48 *Journal of Anthropological Research* 283; this applies as well to the concept of legal culture; see F von Benda-Beckmann and K von Benda-Beckmann, 'Why Not "Legal Culture"?' (2010) 5 *Journal of Comparative Law* 104.

78 D Wright, 'Getting Out of the Asylum: Understanding the Confinement of the Insane in the Nineteenth Century' (1997) 10 *Social History of Medicine* 137; R Porter and D Wright (eds), *The Confinement of the Insane: International Perspectives, 1800–1965* (Cambridge University Press 2003).

oppressed by colonial regimes, as well as among minority groups and other marginalized people closer to home in Europe and other Western countries.

Beyond constitutional proclamations defending autonomy, international conventions framing general and regional regimes of human rights, protecting the rights of the disabled, women, children, patients, and so forth have set the international agenda in these matters since the end of the Second World War. These instruments are framed to enhance autonomy, but they also tend to show how autonomy is to be understood as promoting self-development across different cultures. These instruments attest to the growth of personal autonomy as a universally recognized faculty. Their implementation is uneven and fraught with problems, including translation problems,[79] but their adoption is not meaningless, as it indicates a trend in thinking about how to frame general social goals. Under human rights regimes, personal autonomy is to be protected independently of citizenship; it is a prerogative of all subjects within the jurisdiction of a given state. Personal autonomy thus finds its ways by navigating across frontiers.[80]

Considering the practice of autonomy in everyday life, it is by now clear that there are various psychological components, including emotions, that are inextricably involved in making autonomous choices; these are elements that reason alone does not control and cannot explain.[81]

Parents, teachers, lawyers, psychologists, medical practitioners, and so on – in short, those who are in a position to assist persons in difficulty – know that there are ways to enhance or undermine personal autonomy in every phase of the decision-making process involving the interests of the people they attend to.[82] Institutional practices can likewise be organized to support (or discourage) the exercise of autonomy. The evolution of medical law in the twentieth century thus speaks of an increased recognition of patients' autonomy.

Quite often, the most intractable conundrums relating to personal autonomy arise when one asks who owns, so to speak, a certain institution.[83] The obvious contemporary example is marriage. Who owns the concept of marriage? The state? A religion? Conceiving of marriage as an institution governed by unbending rules, defined by a single authority, no matter how members of society consider it, is to uphold an idealized version of its legal regime. The reforms that have introduced same-sex marriage Canada, the United States, and several European countries show the limits of such a conception. But even before these reforms, putative marriages were recognized by the law of the state and by the canon law to protect reasonable expectations or favour desirable social outcomes in special cases where no valid marriage existed. There have always been variations in the legal definition of marriage. Nowadays, advancements in science, technology, and medicine pose new challenges in this respect. Countries that have not recognized same-sex marriages must now adjudicate disputes about the continuing validity of a marriage when one of the spouses changes his or her sex. If the couple does not divorce, a conflict arises between the legal

79 See, e.g., Merry and Wood (n 60).

80 M-C Foblets, 'Moroccan Women in Europe: Bargaining for Autonomy' (2007) 64 *Washington and Lee Law Review* 1385.

81 P Livet, 'Rational Choice, Neuroeconomy and Mixed Emotions' (2010) 365 *Philosophical Transactions of the Royal Society B: Biological Sciences* 259.

82 For instance, inducing people not to believe in free will reduces their self-control and increases anti-social behaviour; see D Rigoni et al., 'Reducing Self-Control by Weakening Belief in Free Will' (2012) 21 *Conscious Cognition* 1482.

83 Macdonald (n 50).

recognition of transsexualism and the regulation of marriage as an exclusively heterosexual union. Confronted with this case, the German Constitutional Court held that the country's legislation on the matter was unconstitutional because it required post-operative transsexuals to choose between two protected rights: individual integrity and marriage. The Court held that nobody should be forced to make this choice.[84] The Italian Constitutional Court handed down a similar decision: although at the time there was no adequate legislation protecting the union of same-sex couples, the Court nevertheless decided that the state could not force a couple to dissolve their marriage simply because one of the spouses had changed sex.[85] In Europe, Germany now allows parents to register babies who do not have clear gender-determining physical characteristics without having to designate a gender.[86] The Supreme Court of India validated the same regime, noting that both Hinduism and Jainism recognize this possibility.[87]

Conclusions

When discussing personal autonomy as a norm-setting agenda in the contemporary world, one should be mindful of the genealogy of the concept. Both as a philosophical ideal and as a foundational principle of the law, personal autonomy was first conceived to expand personal freedom according to a project that made that freedom dependent on the freedom of other human beings.

This social aspect of autonomy should not be understood as a later addition to its original constitution. On the contrary, that constitution implies that autonomy grows together with the capacity for communication and interaction, which is an essential, primeval constituent of social life. Autonomy, therefore, does not pertain exclusively to the individual dimension of personal life; it also belongs to the social nature of human beings, which is written in the species. This is why any society that subscribes to a solipsistic view of personal autonomy undermines the concept's foundations.

84 Bundesverfassungsgericht [BVerfGE] [Federal Constitutional Court] 27 May 2008, 1 BvL 10/05, § 72.

85 Corte Costituzionale, 11 June 2014, n. 170. See Corte di Cassazione, 21 April 2015, n. 8097.

86 Personenstandsgesetz (PStG) § 22.

87 Supreme Court of India, 15 April 2014, *National Legal Services Authority v Union of India*, Writ Petition (Civil) NO.400 of 2012. See R Sampath, 'India Has Outlawed Homosexuality. But It's Better to Be Transgender There Than in the U.S.' *Washington Post* (29 January 2015).

2 Confronting autonomy in liberal practice

Geoffrey Brahm Levey

When discussion turns to the actual or theoretical clash between liberal values and minority practices, the liberal value typically cited is individual autonomy. It is not equality or fraternity or toleration or even liberty. This is not surprising. For one thing, autonomy is commonly understood as a foundational value, that is, a principle which itself explains and justifies why people should be treated as equals, be tolerated and accorded liberty, and so on. But the focus on autonomy also reflects its pervasive influence as a governing value in contemporary liberal societies. Whether one looks to human rights protocols, legislation and judicial review, public policy and its attendant debates, or even patterns of interpersonal relations, the autonomy of the individual – the idea that individuals, as rational agents, are best left to make their own decisions and to chart their own course in life – figures prominently and, oftentimes, decisively.

Yet despite or because of this influence, autonomy's critics are numerous and appear to be growing, even, and perhaps especially, among liberals. The latter's concerns about autonomy tend to oscillate between two somewhat conflicting charges. One is that the meaning of autonomy is too vague or contested for it to be useful as a principle of political morality.[1] The second is that its meaning and normative implications, while clear, are simply too controversial and not neutral enough.[2] Not all cultural minorities share the value liberals place on individual choice and self-direction. So individual autonomy, on this view, establishes a liberalism that is actually intolerant, illiberal, and unjust.

There are certainly many vying conceptions of autonomy. However, autonomy is little different in this regard from most political values and concepts. Liberty, equality, justice, the state, power, you name it, are all essentially contested concepts.[3] It is the stuff of politics that they should be so. The more serious criticism is that autonomy is too demanding a value and too inhospitable to non-liberal groups to be a just basis for culturally diverse societies. This is the current challenge that all of us who dwell in multicultural democracies must face squarely.

1 See, for example, B Parekh, *Rethinking Multiculturalism: Cultural Diversity and Political Theory* (Macmillan 2000).

2 See, for example, IM Young, *Justice and the Politics of Difference* (Princeton University Press 1990); A Margalit and M Halbertal, 'Liberalism and the Right to Culture' (1994) 61 *Social Research* 491; WA Galston, *Liberal Pluralism* (Cambridge University Press 2002); C Kukathas, *The Liberal Archipelago: A Theory of Diversity and Freedom* (Oxford University Press 2003); L Swaine, *The Liberal Conscience: Politics and Principle in a World of Religious Pluralism* (Columbia University Press 2006); T Modood, *Multiculturalism: A Civic Idea* (Polity Press 2007).

3 WB Gallie, 'Essentially Contested Concepts' (1955) 56 *Proceedings of the Aristotelian Society* 167.

DOI: 10.4324/9781315413617-4

In this chapter, I want to focus on three of the issues raised by the editors of this volume in their introduction: the problem of the gap between the principle of autonomy and its implementation; what guarantees that a person's consent is truly free and fully informed; and whether the principle of personal autonomy supports an individual's voluntary renunciation of the rights and freedoms guaranteed by state law and human rights protocols. In addressing these three questions I will venture a view on a fourth – and arguably the central – issue raised: namely, the 'degree to which the principle of autonomy effectively serves as a coordinating mechanism within the context of internormativity in today's plural legal societies'.[4] My argument is that autonomy does effectively serve this role in practice, but also could be made to do it better.

Before tackling these questions, however, it is worth considering some standard responses to autonomy's alleged inhospitality to cultural diversity.

Standard responses to autonomy's 'inhospitality'

There have been three standard responses to the criticism that autonomy is too demanding and intolerant to serve as a governing value for multicultural democracies. One is to reject autonomy altogether for such a role. Another seeks to limit its scope. And a third defines or reformulates it so that it might be more accommodating of cultural diversity.[5] Let me say a few words about each of these strategies.

Liberals who reject autonomy as a foundational liberal value have proposed a range of other justificatory values in its stead, including neutrality,[6] freedom of conscience,[7] equality based on authenticity or identity,[8] identity *simpliciter*,[9] and diversity.[10] These are powerful responses to a genuine conundrum related to pluralism and the limits of liberal toleration. They are, I think, unfeasible nevertheless. The rise of autonomy as a public value in the twentieth century and beyond constitutes something of a world historical transformation. It runs like a single thread through the fabric of liberal institutions and practices. It is not easily wished away and, unsurprisingly, is often let in through a back door by those liberal theorists who claim to be rid of it.[11]

Of course, non-liberals are not similarly beholden to liberal values. Indeed, they tend to see the claimed universality of such values as a Western conceit that refuses to take cultural

4 Call for papers for the conference *(Not) Outside My Culture: The Paradoxes of Personal Autonomy in a Plural Society*, Department of Law and Anthropology, Max Planck Institute for Social Anthropology, Halle/Saale, Germany, 2014; see <http://intra1:8080/mpi-eth/idatDownload.eth?subDir=3605&FileName=2014_CfP_Personal_Autonomy_140117.pdf&saveMode=true> accessed 25 April 2017.

5 A fourth position, if not response, might be identified as ignoring the issue and insisting on autonomy as a foundational liberal value regardless. See, for example, S Macedo, *Liberal Virtues: Citizenship, Virtue and Community in Liberal Constitutionalism* (Oxford University Press 1990).

6 C Larmore, *Patterns of Moral Complexity* (Cambridge University Press 1987); B Barry, *Justice as Impartiality: A Treatise on Social Justice*, vol 2 (Oxford University Press 1995).

7 Kukathas (n 2).

8 C Taylor, 'The Politics of Recognition' in A Gutmann (ed), *Multiculturalism and "The Politics of Recognition"* (Princeton University Press 1992); Young (n 2); Modood (n 2).

9 Margalit and Halbertal (n 2).

10 Galston (n 2).

11 GB Levey, 'Identity and Rational Revisability' in I Primoratz and A Pavković (eds), *Identity, Self-Determination and Secession* (Ashgate 2006).

difference seriously enough. They have a point. Sophisticated arguments seeking to prove the neutrality of liberal values rarely convince fellow liberals, let alone those outside the camp.[12] And yet arguments built on a supposition that Western states must refrain from privileging Western values, including autonomy, are as unrealistic, it seems to me, as liberals who think autonomy can be dethroned by proclamation. For all their intellectual interest and importance, both approaches are unlikely solutions to the practical problem.

In contrast, the strategy of seeking to delimit autonomy's scope is unavoidable if one works with this value. That is, unless one believes – along with Kant, Mill, and other so-called ethical or comprehensive liberals – that autonomy is so important that it prescribes how individuals should live in every aspect of their lives, whether public or nonpublic.[13] For the rest of us, the pertinent question is *where* autonomy's limits should be drawn.

The best-known attempt to narrow the scope of autonomy as a governing norm is so-called political liberalism, most prominently associated with John Rawls's reworked theory of justice. 'Political' liberals argue that autonomy serves to determine only individuals' *public* rights and obligations, while leaving them and their groups free to pursue their own conceptions of the good in their personal, familial, and associational life.[14] The trouble with this proposal is that the capacities of autonomy required in the political sphere are likely to transform the nature of individuals' agency and relationships also in other spheres.[15] Some scholars downplay this liberalizing effect because they read Rawls's political conception of the person as simply a normative postulate or ideal. That is, they take the argument to be that the state treats citizens *as if* they were autonomous agents rather than that they must actually be autonomous or act autonomously. This 'third-person' perspective is an important consideration, and I will return to it. But the critical point here is that this way of thinking about Rawlsian autonomy does not stop political liberalism from intruding into the lives of citizens. As Will Kymlicka notes, even a political conception of the person will generate rights and obligations at odds with the traditions of nonliberal minorities.[16] He cites the example of liberal rights ruling out attempts by religious minorities to prohibit apostasy or to prevent children from receiving some general education and exposure to other ways of life. The examples could be multiplied. In such cases, it might be said that the force of autonomy is not breaching the political sphere; it is just that the political sphere extends into areas that some believe should be 'non-political'. Either way, the scope for cultural diversity is narrowed.

What, then, of the third strategy for making autonomy more accommodating of cultural diversity – reformulating the concept? As with delimiting scope, defining autonomy

12 Jeremy Waldron, for example, rejects the complaint that autonomy is not a neutral value on the grounds that 'basing one's neutrality on a commitment to autonomy is not basing it on a commitment drawn from the domain of options among which neutrality is enjoined.' See J Waldron, 'Autonomy and Perfectionism in Raz's *Morality of Freedom*' (1989) 62 *Southern California Law Review* 1097, 1136.

13 I Kant, *Groundwork of the Metaphysic of Morals* (HJ Paton tr, Harper and Row 1964); *Perpetual Peace and Other Essays on Politics, History, and Morals* (T Humphrey tr, Hackett 1983); JS Mill, *On Liberty* (Macmillan 1959).

14 J Rawls, *Political Liberalism* (Columbia University Press 1993); JD Moon, *Constructing Community: Moral Pluralism and Tragic Conflict* (Princeton University Press 1993); C Larmore, *The Morals of Modernity* (Cambridge University Press 1996); NC Nussbaum, 'Perfectionist Liberalism and Political Liberalism' (2011) 39 *Philosophy & Public Affairs* 3.

15 E Callan, *Creating Citizens* (Oxford University Press 1997).

16 W Kymlicka, *Multicultural Citizenship: A Liberal Theory of Minority Rights* (Oxford University Press 1995) 160–162.

is unavoidable. If it is to be a core political value then obviously we need some clarity on what it means and entails. Beyond this elementary point, quests to reformulate autonomy are strung between two poles. On the one hand, there is no shortage of liberal accounts of autonomy that are perfectly unserviceable for practical politics. Take, for example, the highly intellectualized accounts of rational self-direction in which agents are charged with critically assessing just about everything that comes their way. As Gerald Dworkin observes, autonomy here would seem to be the preserve mainly of professors of philosophy.[17] Then there are the definitions that so emphasize the individual's independence that autonomy is deemed incompatible with any authority beyond oneself or even with binding relationships or commitments.[18] As John Christman and Monique Deveaux (Chapters 3 and 5 in this volume) both argue, faced with such accounts the reformulation of autonomy is imperative.

On the other hand, there is the temptation, in the face of diversity, to define autonomy so minimally that its normative value is effectively neutered. Autonomy becomes, for example, merely volition, agency, or project pursuit, with none of the depth or complexity typically invested in the concept. Happily, most of the philosophical analyses of the concept of autonomy today avoid both of these definitional tendencies. Yet they tend to proceed at such a high level of abstraction that they often bear only a passing relation to how the value on autonomy operates, or even could operate, in liberal practice.

Turning to liberal practice

Appealing to practice for insights into a normative principle may seem like a category mistake. Why would one defer to 'what is' in pursuit of what should be? Isn't this just to endorse the status quo? The volume editors, as noted, refer to the problem of the gap between the principle of autonomy and its implementation.[19] However, if the interest is in trying to get a grip on a serviceable notion of autonomy, looking to liberal practice is instructive.

For a start, liberal practice provides a basis for addressing the criticism that autonomy is invoked as a 'double standard'. Anna Elisabetta Galeotti, for example, notes how cultural minorities are usually judged against the full force of the autonomy ideal, whereas those in the majority culture are assumed to be autonomous unless they are subject to outright coercion.[20] This problem reflects a deeper one of disparate power. As the editors put it in the conference's call for papers, 'in situations of "weak pluralism" (where there is one dominant majority with several minorities and the dominant law has, in principle, the last say), personal autonomy is often assessed in a way that favours the majority.'[21] Denying cultural majorities and the established institutions the 'last say' is, however, immensely difficult. Some years ago, Bhikhu Parekh – a critic of liberal autonomy – set out a protocol by which a meaningful intercommunal dialogue between minorities and the majority over contested practices could proceed.[22] Yet even Parekh's proposal ultimately rested on what

17 G Dworkin, *The Theory and Practice of Autonomy* (Cambridge University Press 1988) 17.
18 See, for example, RP Wolff, *In Defense of Anarchism* (Harper & Row 1970).
19 Call for papers (n 4).
20 AE Galeotti, 'Authenticity and Multiculturalism' in GB Levey (ed), *Authenticity, Autonomy and Multiculturalism* (Routledge 2015).
21 Call for papers (n 4).
22 Parekh (n 1).

he called the 'operative public values' of a society, which gave the dominant majority (and autonomy) the upper hand.

If denying the established institutions and dominant majority the role of final arbiter is unrealistic, at least the arbitration based on societal values should be fair. A close examination of how autonomy operates in political practice is important here. Revealing the way in which autonomy operates in *mainstream* practice enables minorities (and others) to hold the majority to its own often loose and variable standards.

Political practice also has the virtue of short-circuiting conundrums that plague the theoretical elaboration of autonomy. Take, for example, the so-called infinite regress problem,[23] to wit: Why is autonomy realized when one's second-order (or reflective) preferences endorse one's first-order or immediate preferences? Should there not also be a check on and endorsement of one's second-order preferences by a yet higher-order preference? And so on *ad infinitum*. Like Descartes's question of how one can tell one is not now dreaming, every anchor one reaches for can be made subject to the same challenge.

In contrast, consider a real-world political analogy. The argument for bicameral legislatures is that a 'house of review' is needed as a check on the laws proposed by the other or lower house. About half of the world's sovereign states implicitly accept this argument and have bicameral legislatures, and about half have unicameral legislatures. Only a couple of states have ever had tricameral legislatures, a third chamber to check the other two. That is, even among the large number of states that accept the need for a separate chamber to scrutinize proposed legislation, almost all reject a third chamber to scrutinize the scrutinizers. Why is this? It is certainly not because the deliberations of the 'upper' chamber are unassailable. Rather, it is a pragmatic arrangement that marries the need for some scrutiny with timely lawmaking. And in democracies, at least, additional 'checks and balances' are left to other mechanisms, notably, the media, legal challenges, and the electoral cycle.

Something of the same pragmatic arrangement, I submit, applies to how individual autonomy is treated in liberal practice. Considered and informed choices are generally deemed superior to impulsive, whimsical, or uninformed ones, but the process of information gathering and reflection is not expected to continue indefinitely lest a decision never be made. Autonomous citizens are supposed to be active and not only contemplative. Second-order 'preferencing' acts as a cautionary check on rash choices, but otherwise individuals' preferences are further tested precisely by submitting them, in discourse and in practice, to the 'marketplace of ideas'. In practice, rational self-direction is as much the process and product of engaging with one's fellows as it is of the inner life of the lone individual imagined in theory.

A third reason to consider liberal practice is that some of the standard dimensions of autonomy in theory do not and, indeed, cannot operate nearly so demandingly at this level. For example, critically reflecting on one's preferences figures centrally in many and varied models of autonomy. Yet, clearly, liberal states cannot routinely monitor their citizens' decision-making nor compel them to make critically reflective choices without ceasing to be *liberal* states.[24] This underscores one of the paradoxes of autonomy as a political principle: as demanding as it might be or seem as a character ideal for the individual, it also checks

23 See, for example, JS Taylor, 'Introduction' in JS Taylor (ed), *Personal Autonomy: New Essays on Personal Autonomy and Its Role in Contemporary Moral Philosophy* (Cambridge University Press 2005) 6.

24 S Wall, 'Freedom as a Political Ideal' in EF Paul, FD Miller Jr, and J Paul (eds), *Autonomy* (Cambridge University Press 2003) 380.

state interference in how individuals conduct their lives. Critical capacities are inculcated in young citizens through mandatory general education (though homeschooling and various exemptions, such as in the famous 1972 *Wisconsin v Yoder* case in the United States, apply in some jurisdictions).[25] Liberal states also legally require evidence of critical decision-making in some areas. Consider the informed consent protocols we are now required to sign before undergoing a medical operation or taking out a mortgage, in which we must certify that we fully understand and accept the implications of the proposed action. However, more often, liberal states seek only to encourage informed choices by providing relevant information or guidance. For the greater part of their lives, liberal citizens today are perfectly free to operate on impulse, behave like sheep, and ignore the information or assistance that may be available. Even so-called informed consent protocols can easily be circumvented in many cases. How many mobile phone plans or software download agreements have you 'signed' without reading or fully understanding their terms and conditions?

Much the same is true of another standard dimension in conceptualizations of autonomy, namely, what Dworkin calls 'procedural independence'.[26] This is the idea that an individual's critical reflections are free of 'external' distortions such as manipulative or undue pressure from others, whether through coercion, threats, bribes, drug inducement, or misinformation and the like. Liberal states obviously regulate the most egregious of these cases, from coercion to false advertising. However, again, they are usually reluctant to intervene where individuals are simply induced or implored to do things by others or allow themselves to be misled, such as believing in conspiracy theories or joining crazy sects. And all of us are subject to relentless subliminal advertising and product pushing, a pressure now being co-opted for paternalistic purposes under the buzzword of 'nudging'.[27]

Finally, liberal practice provides the arena where the tensions within the concept of autonomy itself are played out. Liberal autonomy is a complex value of multiple dimensions. The individual's volition and consent are important, but so too are critical reflection and *rational* self-direction, as well as the background conditions in which individuals' consent and reflective preferences are made. Respecting autonomy also entails reciprocity among individuals, and thus a basic equality. More controversially, respecting autonomy seems to preclude individuals' alienating or surrendering their future autonomy. Not all conceptions of autonomy endorse all of these dimensions or emphasize each to the same extent. And even where they converge on a dimension they often disagree about its content. For example, 'proceduralists' tend to be satisfied with preference formation where it is free of coercion, threats, or deceptive forms of manipulation.[28] 'Substantivists', on the other hand, tend to judge the authenticity of individuals' preferences according to their content, or else insist on their background conditions having a particular character, such as exhibiting relations of equality, nurturance, love, or recognition.[29]

25 *Wisconsin v Yoder* (1972) 406 US 205.

26 Dworkin (n 17) 18–19.

27 RH Thaler and CR Sunstein, *Nudge* (Penguin 2009).

28 See, for example, Dworkin (n 17); DT Meyers, *Self, Society, and Personal Choice* (Columbia University Press 1989); M Friedman, *Autonomy, Gender, Politics* (Oxford University Press 2002).

29 See, for example, C Mackenzie and N Stoljar (eds), *Relational Autonomy: Feminist Perspectives on Autonomy, Agency, and the Social Self* (Oxford University Press 2000); J Anderson and A Honneth, 'Autonomy, Vulnerability, Recognition, and Justice' in J Christman and J Anderson (eds), *Autonomy and the Challenges to Liberalism: New Essays* (Cambridge University Press 2005); M Oshana, *Personal Autonomy in Society* (Ashgate 2006).

Nevertheless, multiple dimensions and their inner tensions are features of most renderings of autonomy. This conceptual complexity is what grants autonomy its power and utility. On most proceduralist and substantivist accounts, autonomy encapsulates a *set* of moral intuitions about freedom of the individual; it identifies the kinds of issues we should worry about. But for this very reason autonomy is far from a precise instrument for deciding cases. The dimensions of autonomy are often fulfilled to varying degrees in particular cases, and this presents both dilemmas and latitude for policymakers and those directly concerned.[30] To cite a general medical example, patients requesting (active) euthanasia might well be doing so on their own volition and even after critical reflection. Yet autonomists rightly worry whether the decision is truly authentic and not unduly influenced by the pain experienced at a particular point, or a sense of being a burden on family members. Moreover, since euthanasia is irrevocable, there is also a concern about individuals alienating their future autonomy. Such tensions in honouring the component dimensions of autonomy underscore the need for argument, judgement, and 'balancing' even where there is agreement on autonomy as the relevant decision principle. In recent times, we have witnessed a reassessment of active euthanasia in some jurisdictions, with greater emphasis being placed on the individual's volition and the rationality of a decision to terminate one's life in unbearable circumstances. Public recalibration of the dimensions of autonomy is an ongoing process.

Taken together, the preceding several points address the second question that I noted in my introduction: what 'guarantees that a person's consent is truly free and fully informed?' Taken literally, it is unclear what 'truly free' and 'fully informed' might even be. If, however, the question is what guarantees that a person's consent meets the conditions of authenticity, the short answer is that nothing does. There is no such *guarantee* in liberal practice. Again, liberal practice differs from liberal theory in this regard, where simple tests are proposed and hypothetical assumptions are made. For example, Christman proposes a test for authenticity according to which the individual would not be alienated from her values were she to critically reflect on their genesis, and where her hypothetical reflections are 'not constrained by reflection-distorting factors'.[31] In practice, however, reflection-distorting factors cannot simply be assumed away and must be reckoned with.

That there is no guarantee that consent is 'truly free and fully informed' in liberal practice is, to my mind, a good thing. Instead, liberal practice puts in place some conditions and protections and creates a certain environment. Liberal states equip their citizens for autonomous agency by inculcating the critical skills necessary to process information and assess options (via a general education), protecting the free flow of information (a free press, etc.), and offering a range of meaningful options (a diverse and open society). The expectation or presumption is that citizens will then lead autonomous lives. While the presumption becomes a legal requirement where various rights and misdemeanours are at issue, for much of civil and public life it remains no more than a presumption.

Hence the significance of the third-person perspective I considered earlier. Liberal states do indeed treat their citizens *as if* they were autonomous agents in the sense that autonomy is *largely* ascribed to them. However, contrary to Rawlsian and other 'political' liberalisms, this presumption cuts across the public-nonpublic divide and applies to an array of places where autonomy is required or protected under force of law, and places, both public and

30 GB Levey, 'Liberal Autonomy as a Pluralistic Value' (2012) 95 *The Monist* 103.

31 Chapter 3 in this volume and J Christman, *The Politics of Persons: Individual Autonomy and Socio-historical Selves* (Cambridge University Press 2009) 155.

nonpublic, where it is neither presumed nor required. As I have suggested elsewhere, the picture that emerges of autonomy's scope thus resembles more a web with interwoven threads and gaps than it does a simple dichotomy between public and nonpublic domains.[32]

Autonomy and minority cultural practices

Autonomy has been invoked in *defence* of minority cultural rights or recognition in three distinct ways. Two of these efforts have figured mainly in the theoretical literature, while the third is discernible also in liberal practice.

Kymlicka's autonomy-based theory of cultural rights contends that cultures provide a 'context of choice' that enables members to exercise their autonomy and which constitutes a primary good. Thus, citizens who are disadvantaged, through no fault of their own, in realizing this good of cultural membership are entitled to some state support or accommodation.[33] Another theoretical approach holds that not recognizing or misrecognizing individuals' identities damages their sense of self-respect and self-worth and so cripples their capacity to act autonomously. Appropriate recognition of individuals' identities is therefore a precondition of autonomous agency.[34] A third approach follows the model of other liberal rights such as freedom of expression and freedom of religion. Here, cultural commitments are construed as the expression of individuals' autonomy, and so respecting autonomy entails accommodating these commitments.

The two more theoretical approaches have the seeming advantage of offering an account of why cultural rights might trump others' interests or claims, depending on the circumstances. Kymlicka, for example, builds an egalitarian element into his theory by targeting *unchosen* disadvantage in relation to a primary good (cultural membership or access to a 'societal culture'). Honneth's recognition approach is based on the psychological-cum-social harm that is alleged to follow from non- or misrecognition, the avoidance of which may well override other, more routine interests. In contrast, cultural rights as universal rights based on the expression of individual autonomy seem to lack such overriding weight. This is because, first, individuals are generally thought to be responsible for the costs associated with their choices and, second, because the free expression of culture must compete with other individual rights similarly based on respecting autonomy.[35]

Closer inspection upsets this commonly accepted picture, however. For example, since Kymlicka assumes that most immigrant and ethnic minorities have chosen to leave their homelands to join a new societal culture, thus waiving their rights to actualize their former

32 GB Levey, *The Web of Autonomy* (Midwest Political Science Association conference, Chicago, April 2013).

33 W Kymlicka, *Liberalism, Community and Culture* (Oxford University Press 1989); Kymlicka (n 16). George Crowder has argued in support of autonomy from an acceptance of value pluralism; that is, autonomy is to be prized insofar as it enables individuals to choose among multiple and incommensurable values. Since the value of autonomy, on this argument, is contingent and not foundational, I do not discuss it among the autonomy-based defences of minority cultural rights. See G Crowder, *Theories of Multiculturalism: An Introduction* (Polity Press 2013).

34 A Honneth, *The Struggle for Recognition: The Moral Grammar of Social Conflicts* (MIT Press 1996); Anderson and Honneth (n 29).

35 Some theorists try to rectify this weakness by referring to 'constitutive choices' that are connected to one's identity, and which are claimed to have greater weight than other sorts of choices. See, for example, Y Tamir, *Liberal Nationalism* (Princeton University Press 1993).

societal culture, it is unclear why, even on his own theory's terms, they are entitled to any remedial cultural rights.[36] Honneth's theory suffers from the opposite problem of being too powerful. Like Charles Taylor's recognition theory based on individual and group authenticity, Honneth's recognition argument implies that the state is obliged to recognize and accommodate individuals and groups in just the way they seek lest their self-respect be undermined.[37] At the same time, cultural rights construed as universal rights based on individual autonomy are nowhere near as limited or inconsequential as the conventional picture suggests.

For one thing, there are many cultural rights claims that do not impose any substantive costs on others or entail circumscribing others' rights. A prominent example is the wish of some Muslim girls and women to wear the *hijab* or other Islamic clothing, which case provides the focus for Deveaux's analysis in this volume (Chapter 5). While there may be other grounds for restricting such practices – as Deveaux discusses and which I'll come to – there is no cost to the state or other citizens involved in some citizens choosing to wear such clothing. There are also minority cultural claims that may involve a modest cost on the broader community but which ordinarily would be considered and absorbed as a routine public expense.

Take the case of Sunday closing laws. Such laws neither prohibit nor hinder the observance of minority customs. Rather, the issue involves the commercial disadvantage that observant Jews, Muslims, and some other religious minorities might suffer in having to close their business on two days a week rather than only on their own Sabbath, typically, Saturday or Friday. Avigail Eisenberg discusses the case in Canada to illustrate how a 'choice' approach (she does not use the term 'autonomy') to minority accommodation is unpersuasive. As she puts it,

> In a religiously diverse society, freedom to choose one's faith often involves costs and, unless these costs are covert obstacles to prohibit people from practising their religions, citizens should not expect the public purse to subsidize the choices they make with respect to the religious beliefs and practices they follow.[38]

These strictures may apply if the challenge or accommodation involved abolishing Sunday closing laws. However, abolition is not the only way minority interests might be accommodated here. As occurred in the United States in the late nineteenth and early twentieth centuries, exemptions from the closing laws might be entertained for religious minorities that observe a different Sabbath.[39] Instituting such exemptions carries minimal administrative costs and does not entail denying the majority its established day of rest. A 'choice' model or autonomy-based defence of cultural claims points to how room might be made for minorities without remaking the established institutions.

But perhaps the biggest mistake liberals can make in defending cultural rights or recognition is to suppose that a single liberal value can do all the work. Consider the so-called

36 Kymlicka (n 16) 86, 96; GB Levey, 'Autonomy, Equality and Cultural Rights' (1997) 25 *Political Theory* 215.

37 Taylor (n 8); GB Levey, 'Authenticity and the Multiculturalism Debates' in GB Levey (ed), *Authenticity, Autonomy and Multiculturalism* (Routledge 2015).

38 A Eisenberg, Chapter 4 in this volume.

39 NW Cohen, *Jews in Christian America: The Pursuit of Religious Equality* (Oxford University Press 1992).

identity approach to minority accommodation. Since 1985, this approach, Eisenberg suggests, has become the dominant pitch in Canadian court challenges to perceived discriminatory practices, and has proved far more successful than the earlier 'choice' approach. The 'identity' defence of religious and cultural practices views the latter, she says, as 'non-negotiable features of individual and group-based identities'.

The language of identity here is, I think, a bit misleading. While an identitarian element is present in these cases, the same is true of most so-called choice or autonomy-based arguments for cultural recognition. At the same time, choice and autonomy are often evident in how religious and cultural traditions have been interpreted and practised by group members, and through which they express their identities. Furthermore, liberal courts are not swayed by religious and cultural practices just because they are claimed or even shown to be non-negotiable features of an individual's or a group's identity. Some cultural practices – for example, honour killings, female genital mutilation, and *sati* – are not sanctioned no matter how deep the identification. This fact alerts us to the likelihood that it is not actually 'identity' that is doing the normative work in these legal arguments and court decisions.

Unsurprisingly, it is liberal values that drive and govern even the 'identity' approach. As Eisenberg writes in this volume (Chapter 4):

> Whereas before 1985 the Canadian court adopted an approach to religious freedom that assessed law and policy in terms of their impacts on individual choice, after 1985 the court begins to consider arguments about minority *inclusion*, to use a discourse about *equal respect* for religious minorities, and to display sensitivity to *religious freedom* not only for individuals, but also for collectivities.
>
> (p. 70, italics added)

Inclusion, equal respect, and religious freedom – otherwise and more generally designated by liberalism's revolutionary creed, *Liberté, égalité, fraternité!* The court's increased sensitivity to the culturally loaded and often unfriendly context in which minorities have to operate should not be seen as presenting an alternative to the value of liberal autonomy, but rather as presupposing it. The greater attention to minorities and collectivities as against lone individuals is consistent with the more sophisticated accounts of liberal autonomy – as championed by Christman (Chapter 3) and Deveaux (Chapter 5) in this volume – which recognize individuals as social and cultural beings. After all, when courts find in favour of majority practices or national-cultural traditions, they do not thereby deny the autonomy of the members of the dominant culture or its role in relation to these practices and traditions.

Liberty (including autonomy), equality, and fraternity (or inclusion) supplement each other in the liberal-democratic firmament. While these values may conflict in particular cases, be subject to many interpretations, and be variously emphasized, they nevertheless work in tandem and operate as a package or complex of commitments. Certainly, multicultural accommodation needs each of them.

Autonomously renouncing rights?

The value of autonomy is, however, also raised in opposition to multicultural accommodation and not only in its support. That is, controversial minority practices are often perceived to jeopardize autonomy by violating particular individual or human rights. Yet, as Deveaux notes in this volume (Chapter 5), often the contention turns on different conceptions of autonomy rather than on whether or not autonomy should be valorized.

Deveaux cites the controversy surrounding Muslim women and girls who wear the *niqab* or *burqa*. She points to how substantivist interpretations of autonomy tend to view these forms of Islamic clothing as signifying women's subjugation and a breach of autonomy, whereas proceduralist interpretations, especially those sensitive to the social or relational grounding of individual autonomy, focus on women's choice and agency in deciding to wear these garments. While such a division is certainly evident in the debate, I think that proceduralists also divide on the issue. Objections are often heard to the effect that Muslim women or girls are pressured into wearing this clothing or else have internalized repressive norms, which are concerns that go to the procedural independence of their preferences. Be that as it may, I fully endorse Deveaux's call for protagonists to be more self-conscious and explicit about their conceptions of autonomy in debates over minority practices.

What if we assume that procedural independence has not been compromised? Are liberal citizens then entitled, in the name of proceduralist autonomy, to choose self-abrogation and self-abnegation? Thus we come to the third question mentioned at the outset of this chapter: 'Can the principle of personal autonomy also serve as the basis for justifying an individual's voluntary renunciation of the rights and freedoms guaranteed by state law and enshrined in human rights legislation in order to follow certain traditions or practices?'[40] In other words, might the principle of autonomy itself provide a solution to its own putatively inhospitable implications for many cultural traditions and practices? Two quite different issues are involved here.

One is the question of divided (and dividing) authority between or among different legal codes. Liberal constitutionalism does not tend to brook exceptions to what it regards as universal values. Some jurisdictions recognize minority legal codes in specific cases. For example, for many years, Canada allowed Catholics and Jews to use their respective religious tribunals as alternative dispute resolution avenues; it was only when Muslim Canadians sought the same recognition for sharia institutions that Canada outlawed all such facilities in 2005. In Australia, some banks are authorized to specialize in 'sharia-compliant finance'. Another example concerns Jewish divorce law. The Second New York Get Law authorizes civil courts to impose a higher maintenance/property settlement on the recalcitrant party until a *get* (Jewish bill of divorce) is granted and barriers to remarriage are removed.[41] The Ontario Family Law Act allows the court to set aside any transaction that has been brought about as a result of withholding a *get*, while the Canadian Federal Parliament Divorce Act denies access to the civil courts until the recalcitrant party honours the directive of the Jewish Orthodox court (*Beth Din*).[42] In all these cases, however, the individual's freedom and autonomy are *enhanced* rather than circumscribed, and the provisions remain subject to civil authority. The question posed is whether the principle of personal autonomy can also sanction the *abridgement* of individual rights and freedoms.

Ideas along these lines have been proposed. For example, Jeff Spinner-Halev has advanced the notion of 'partial citizenship', whereby segregationist groups like the Amish may be relieved of some of the burdens and privileges of liberal citizenship in order to follow their own path, as long as they respect freedom of association (and dissociation), are aware that options are available to them beyond their own community, and refrain from

40 Call for papers (n 4).
41 NY Domestic Relations Law § 236 (b) in *McKinney's Consolidated Laws of New York Annotated: Domestic Relations Law* (West Publishing, multiple years).
42 *Family Law Act*, RSO 1990, ch F.3, s 56(5) – 56(7); Divorce Act RSC 1985, § 2(4) (Can.).

harmful practices.[43] Ayelet Shachar proposes a 'joint governance' model between cultural communities and the state based on different areas of law.[44] Because such 'exit' options are presumably available only to members of cultural minorities, the question remains of whether members of the dominant majority would also have an opportunity to 'exit' (short of emigration) and, if so, what that would look like. If the latter is not feasible, then there may be equity issues in granting the opportunity of 'exit' only to some born citizens.

Dividing authority based on consent in this manner raises, however, a second issue as far as autonomy is concerned. As previously noted, alienating one's future autonomy is commonly understood to be outside the bounds of legitimate consent.[45] The classic statement of the principle is Mill's injunction against selling oneself into slavery: 'by selling himself for a slave, [a man] abdicates his liberty; he forgoes any future use of it beyond this single act . . . It is not freedom to be allowed to alienate his freedom.'[46] Dworkin, a proceduralist, initially defended the proposition that inalienability was integral to autonomy, but later changed his mind, arguing that one can legitimately exercise one's autonomy even in alienating it and agreeing to be a slave.[47] Many substantivists disagree, arguing that the very condition of slavery is a travesty of individual autonomy; even if the slave master is benevolent, it entails a relation of subservience.

My view is that proceduralists should also find self-imposed slavery (and like cases) problematic, since the very conditions of autonomy that proceduralists ostensibly value in making a decision to become a slave – volition, critical reflection, and procedural independence – are either absent or precarious once one is a slave. These deficits may impinge on the initial choice to have become a slave, denying the individual the agency to revise that choice, but they also seriously compromise the individual's agency in every other respect as well. Slaves are not their own persons. In liberal practice, the inalienability of autonomy finds considerable protection in international protocols and state legislation. For example, there are protocols and laws prohibiting slavery, servitude, debt bondage, and the like, even where these are consensual.[48]

Of course, forswearing one's rights does not necessarily amount to slavery. Much depends on the fine print. If the 'voluntary renunciation of the rights and freedoms guaranteed by state law and enshrined in human rights legislation in order to follow certain traditions' means the *irrevocable* loss of these rights and freedoms, then the principle of autonomy – whether on a substantivist or practical proceduralist account – is unlikely to sanction them. However, this objection might be overcome by protecting the right of 'cultural objectors'

43 J Spinner, *The Boundaries of Citizenship: Race, Ethnicity, and Nationality in the Liberal State* (Johns Hopkins University Press 1995).

44 A Shachar, *Multicultural Jurisdictions: Cultural Differences and Women's Rights* (Cambridge University Press 2001).

45 I discuss inalienability more fully in Levey (n 30), from which I derive some of the following points.

46 Mill (n 13) 125.

47 See Dworkin (n 17) ch 8.

48 Sometimes slavery is distinguished from servitude on the basis that it lacks any condition of voluntariness. However, the modern tendency is to blur the boundaries between slavery, servitude, debt bondage, forced labour, etc. towards a uniform condemnation, and to widen their indicia. See, for example, the League of Nations' Convention to Suppress the Slave Trade and Slavery (25 September 1926) 60 LNTS 253, Registered No. 1414; and the United Nations' Supplementary Convention on the Abolition of Slavery, the Slave Trade, and Institutions and Practices Similar to Slavery (adopted by a Conference of Plenipotentiaries convened by Economic and Social Council resolution 608(XXI) of 30 April 1956 and done in Geneva on 7 September 1956).

to reclaim their individual rights and freedoms, or at least some of them, at certain junctures. Such a system may be costly and burdensome to administer. It might also depend on making sure that the capacities for autonomous agency of those taking this option are not so atrophied by the minority practices that the right to reverse one's renunciation is rendered ineffectual.

Yet even here autonomy-based liberalism offers considerable latitude. As noted earlier regarding the shift in public sentiment on euthanasia, precisely because autonomy is a complex value involving multiple dimensions, it is possible that meeting the dimensions of volition, critical reflection, and procedural independence will come to be considered more important than the limit of inalienability in a given case. Judgments will depend, therefore, not only on which conception of autonomy, if any, is brought to bear on a case, but also on which dimensions of autonomy are prioritized within a particular conception. Ultimately, the case for renouncing rights in pursuit of cultural observance needs to be publicly made. Far from hosing it down, liberal autonomy genuinely opens up the debate about the limits of cultural diversity in liberal societies.

3 Autonomy and deeply embedded cultural identities

John Christman

It is widely recognized that a deep conflict exists between protecting individual autonomy and protecting cultural practices and identities that seem to eschew the value of individual self-determination. This is largely due to the fact that the rights associated with individual autonomy perforce presuppose an interest in reflectively evaluating one's fundamental value commitments, including elements of one's social identity, while many cultural forms appear to devalue an individual's interest in revising her self-conception or seeing her value commitments as 'up to her' as an individual. Indeed, the very survival of certain social groups is thought to hinge on discouraging, if not restricting, individuals' (equal) right to determine for themselves the nature of their inherited identities and the obligations and values attached to it.

However, I will suggest in what follows that this apparent clash rests on an overly narrow understanding of self-government and hence the relation between autonomy and choice over the nature and meaning of one's social identity. I will argue that autonomy can be understood in a way that is plausible in its own right and does not assume or require that self-governing individuals necessarily have a fundamental interest in reflectively reassessing their deepest commitments, at least not under all conditions. Building on work developed elsewhere, I discuss such a conception of self-government and argue that it significantly lessens the clash between autonomy-based legal protections and the interest in protecting the stability and dignity of entrenched cultural forms. Similarly, such a view minimizes the conflict between individual self-government and a person's interest in maintaining a deeply held identity and cultural location, with or without reflective self-questioning and powers of self-alteration promoted in standard liberal discourse.[1]

The structure of identity-based claims

In the dynamics of political encounters among citizens, we can say that there are different degrees of expression and commitment that citizens exhibit and which they wish to be taken into account. These can be grouped as preferences, interests, and values, listed in increasing

1 This chapter is a revised version of a paper presented at the conference '(Not) Outside My Culture: Personal Autonomy in a Plural Society' Max Planck Institute for Social Anthropology, Halle, Germany, 26–28 May 2014. The author is grateful to the hosts of that conference and to audience members for helpful comments on that presentation. The ideas presented here are developed in more detail in J Christman, *The Politics of Persons: Individual Autonomy and Socio-historical Selves* (Cambridge University Press 2009) ch 9. Some material in the following two sections is taken from that chapter. Reprinted with the permission of Cambridge University Press.

DOI: 10.4324/9781315413617-5

order of weight that such claims can be expected to receive. Such weighting also reflects the relative degree to which people are expected to bear the cost of their satisfaction, so that a mere preference, for example, is something I must negotiate myself, as long as I enjoy a fair share with which to do so. But at the other end of the spectrum, *values*, and more particularly, values based on a person's *identity*, are thought to claim more serious attention from others, and in some cases form the basis of rights that such identity-based groups expect to be protected.

When an indigenous people makes a claim to traditionally sacred ground, for example, say where a real estate firm wants to develop a property, the controversy plays itself out as something more than simply a conflict of preferences or even interests. When such claims are debated, the fact that the claims by the native people are connected to their sense of tradition, culture, and identity gives them special force, even to the point of halting the development, which would otherwise proceed without state intervention.[2]

In a slightly different but related register, women, members of racial or ethnic minorities, and gay people, among others, often couch claims of past and ongoing injustice in terms of attacks on them *as members of such groups*, rather than as individuals. Hate-crime legislation in the United States, for example, is supported in part by the understanding that crimes motivated by opprobrium towards people because of their membership in such groups are especially heinous. Anti-discrimination and equal protection law also rest on the especially grievous harms involved when people suffer disadvantages due to their membership in certain protected groups. The particular weight given to these kinds of claims, when or if they are valid, rests on an assumption of the importance of group membership that the politics of identity (as I am using that term) attempts to capture.[3]

Identity-based claims, then, are said to command greater normative attention than preferences or mere interests. As Daniel Weinstock argues, identity arguments express a connection between identity-related claims and those that are 'rhetorically and symbolically very close to those of integrity and of self-esteem'.[4] 'This would not be true', he goes on to say, 'if [the subject of the claim] were asked merely to sacrifice one of her preferences or only partially realize one of her values'.[5]

For this reason, hateful and denigrating designations of another's group membership expresses a particular kind of harmful treatment. Taylor is surely right that there is a special

2 See, for example, RS Michaelson, 'Dirt in the Court Room: Indian Land Claims and American Property Rights' in D Chidester and ET Linenthal (eds), *American Sacred Space* (Indiana University Press 1995) 43.

3 I use the term 'social group' as a generic phrase to refer to culturally organized groups as well as other identity groupings that lack a cultural commonality, such as women, gay men and lesbians, the disabled, and racial groups. This is not to say, of course, that these latter groups lack common experiences or social position. But for cultural groups, participation in, or at least a tendency to acknowledge the personal importance of, linguistic, religious, or cultural practices is part of what grounds membership. For ascriptive identities, such as sex, race, and physical ability, what determines membership is merely those facts about one (as defined by social classification schemes), independent of whether one's mode of behaviour, social practices, language, way of speaking, and so on are shared with other co-members (see, for example, B Barry, *Culture and Equality* [Harvard University Press 2001] for an argument that ascriptive identities share no common culture).

4 D Weinstock, 'Is "Identity" a Danger to Democracy?' in I Primoratz and A Pavković (eds), *Identity, Self-Determination and Secession* (Ashgate 2006) 15, 21. It should be noted, however, that Weinstock identifies this special character of identity arguments in order to claim that such arguments are damaging to democratic deliberation. I do not agree with that conclusion, but the point I am making, which Weinstock endorses, is that identity-based claims have this special character.

5 Ibid.

sort of unjust damage that people suffer when others mirror back to them a 'confining or demeaning or contemptible picture of themselves'.[6] But such treatment is not merely an expression of contempt, full stop, for then an adequate defence against such assaults would be, 'But I'm not like that person you're describing so contemptibly.' Demands for (respectful) recognition, on the other hand, must imply that the damage is deeper and the response must be, 'I *am* that kind of person, but such identities are not to be denigrated in that way.' Control over the language of public valuation must be reclaimed by the offended groups so that the terms of identity are not commandeered by the forces of hate.

Moreover, it makes no sense to lay claim to particular resources because of one's status as a social group member unless the meaning of such membership, and the value associations that come with it, are relatively knowable and fixed. The claim that we must be able to speak effectively in the broad languages of identity is prior to the claim for the particular resources needed to pursue valuable projects in light of that identity, for the latter presupposes a settled sense of that identity. Insisting on resources that connect with identities (such as support for the use of a language, protection of a burial ground, recognition of a national holiday, and so on) simply as a stand-alone demand based on the sacredness of identities assumes a fixed determination of the nature of that identity, not as an outcome of an ongoing social discussion but as a social, biological, or metaphysical 'fact'.[7]

Liberal approaches to culture and identity

Various thinkers working in (or at the edges) of liberal political philosophy have attempted to show how accommodation of the special status of identity and identity-based interests is consistent with the traditional liberal commitments to liberty and (generic) equality. Will Kymlicka, for example, famously describes what he calls a 'societal culture' that is meant to exemplify the connection between group practices and individuals' self-concept. A 'societal culture', says Kymlicka, is 'synonymous with "a nation" or "a people" – that is, as an intergenerational community, more or less institutionally complete, occupying a given territory or homeland, sharing a distinct language and history'. Such cultures, Kymlicka argues, give meaning to the choices and goods that people pursue autonomously, thereby giving value to the autonomy (freedom) expressed in that pursuit.[8]

6 C Taylor, *Multiculturalism and the 'Politics of Recognition'* (Princeton University Press 1992) 25.

7 See S Benhabib, *The Claims of Culture: Equality and Diversity in the Global Era* (Princeton University Press 2002) 50. Another example of this might be the language of 'queering' in regard to gay and lesbian life. As is well known in academic settings, it is perfectly acceptable to refer to gay and lesbian experiences as 'queer life' (after all, Queer Studies is the name of programmes of study in many universities in the United States). But calling gay people or lesbians 'queer' was for some time understood to be insulting and denigrating, and part of a pattern of marginalization that had profound effects on the ability of homosexuals to pursue valued lives in settings of respect and recognition. But the fact that the use of such language now (often) lacks those connotations has to do not with the reference or (literal) meaning of such terms, but the fact that the designation can now be seen as emanating from the community itself. To refer to oneself and one's identity group with a particular terminology that is under one's discursive control, as it were, is fundamentally different from cases where that same language is imposed by others. The dynamics of social self-determination, specifically, determination relative to public discourse and the representation of identity, is what is at stake in such cases.

8 W Kymlicka, *Multicultural Citizenship: A Liberal Theory of Minority Rights* (Clarendon Press 1995) 18. See also A Margalit and J Raz, 'National Self-Determination' (1990) 87 *Journal of Philosophy* 439.

Note that on this approach, freedom is a value, not as an empty set of opportunities but as a necessary means to achieve the substantive goods that give meaning to one's life. Insofar as one's societal culture forms a community that defines and gives meaning to such goods, then protecting the social forms that constitute the value of those pursuits is therefore intertwined with valuing freedom or, for our purposes, autonomy. Now some have pointed out a tension in these claims, for if freedom is valued because of its connection to the ability to pursue the good, it is unclear how the connection to any *particular* culture (or set of social goods) can be defended. Autonomy, on this view, merely requires that I have a choice among goods and that different cultures (whether mine or another's) be available to me to provide a variety of those goods. That is, insofar as freedom (autonomy) means being able to step back from any particular commitment and revise it in the face of social possibilities, and there are several cultural avenues and traditions I could choose in my society other than the one I grew up with (let us imagine), then there is no autonomy-based argument for the survival of *my* culture in particular.[9]

Others in the liberal tradition have taken a different tack, namely attempting to acknowledge the often self-defining nature of social group membership but stressing how very complex and, in some cases, malleable the meaning of such membership can be. Indeed, it is claimed that for any particular cultural form, strong protections for the continued practice of specific traditions, languages, rituals, and other marks of societal cultures belies the complex *heterogeneity* of cultures and other identity groups.[10] This is echoed in the scepticism many have about the idea that identities are concretely fixed, unified, and self-transparent. We are all heterogeneous beings, it is argued, with connections to cultural histories that are themselves more like threaded rivers than straight lines. And particular associations with social groupings, such as seeing oneself as most saliently a *woman* or a *gay man* or a *Catholic*, and so forth, all vary in intensity depending on variable settings that may call them to mind.[11]

For example, Kwame Anthony Appiah explains how very transitory and manipulable some identities can be, and various formal and informal studies over the years confirm this. Appiah cites the Oklahoma Robbers Cave study where children were given artificial labels and almost immediately began fiercely attributing positive and negative characteristics to members of the groups and forming strong bonds and oppositions in association with them.[12] He also quotes Ian Hacking's claim that identities come into being often only after labels are invented for them and are given public purchase, implying the social constructedness of such labels even if they carry with them psychological depth.[13]

The point here is that social practices and treatment produce identities that afterward will feel psychologically fixed, as if they hang on biological or physiological structures. It further might imply that the particular dimensions along which we embrace these identities are in some ways up to us, since both the treatment producing the sense of identity and

9 See Taylor (n 6); KA Appiah, *The Ethics of Identity* (Princeton University Press 2005) 123.

10 See, for example, Benhabib (n 7); A Gutmann, *Identity in Democracy* (Princeton University Press 2003); Appiah (n 9); A Sen, *Identity and Violence: The Illusion of Destiny* (Norton 2006).

11 See, for example, JS Phinney, 'When We Talk About American Ethnic Groups, What Do We Mean?' (1996) 51(9) *American Psychologist* 918.

12 Appiah (n 9). There are several other examples of this, such as Jane Elliott's 'blue-eyed/brown-eyed' experiment (see http://janeelliott.com/).

13 I Hacking, *Rewriting the Soul: Multiple Personality and the Structure of Memory* (Princeton University Press 1998).

the internalization of it might appear to be reversible by human action. This emphasis on choice is similarly stressed by Sen, who lays out in illuminating detail how various global cultural identities are each plural rather than singular in their histories and inner dynamics. A Muslim, for example, may identify prominently with her religion but can also look to her gender, nationality, profession, and so on for the locus of her conception of herself, and this locus may well shift in different situations and/or over time. He writes, 'Given our inescapably plural identities, we have to decide on the relative importance of our different associations and affiliations in any particular context.'[14]

It surely is the case that our self-conceptions contain any number of cultural and historical dimensions, and it may be of value (to some) to become educated about not only how many of these there are but how malleable each one is. However, a given person may not realize this or may not experience it this way, in which case it is not clear how it is a matter of *choice* for that person to take up or reject any particular strain in the complex array of that identity.

What this shows really is not that Sen or Appiah is wrong in his central inferences, but rather that their projects are straightforwardly *normative*. They cannot be saying that their descriptions of the multiform and ephemeral nature of our identities are simply facts to be discovered like historical facts. Rather, they are using historical and psychological observations to mount a case that we all *should think of ourselves and our identities differently*. We should stop thinking that our race or ethnicity is either pure or homogeneous or that they demand from us a particular behavioural profile. We should stop treating others along these lines as well.

Of course one element of their analysis cannot easily be gainsaid, namely that insofar as one's self-conception rests on an overly unified understanding of that identity, and the history and breadth of that social group belies such unity, then one's self-conception rests, as it were, on a mistake. And such a mistake perhaps should be corrected. But even for someone who has multiple dimensions to her cultural identity, the range of these dimensions is still fixed – one cannot simply decide to become another race or ethnicity individually – and the particular aspect of that identity that is dominant in any one social space may be imposed by the power dynamics of that space, and not by one's specific choice. Appiah and Sen are welcome to recommend that people think of their identities differently in order to achieve inner peace, self-knowledge, or historical awareness; but merely pointing out that we have such complex identities does not by itself show that one must see (aspects of) them as simply up to us to choose or shape.

A recurring theme in the liberal approach to cultural identities is the need for the protection of a right to *exit* – the right to extract oneself from associations and commitments – and that this right must take precedence over any call for the protection of cultural forms.[15] Although some pluralists insist that even protecting the right to exit is itself culturally parochial,[16] this right is generally seen as a universal limitation on whatever claims might be made for the recognition or protection of identity groups in a just society. That is, group interests can be identified and given special weight, but only if membership in such groups is in some way voluntary, if the right to disavow such connections is protected by the group itself.

14 Sen (n 10) xiii.

15 See, for example, M Halbertal and A Margalit, 'Liberalism and the Right to Culture' (2004) 71(3) *Social Research* 529; Barry (n 3).

16 B Parekh, 'Superior People: The Narrowness of Liberalism From Mill to Rawls' (1994) 4743 *Times Literary Supplement* 11.

However, it is not clear that this interest in being able to exit the social categories that form identities is uniform either in its weight or its meaning. For some social identities, the idea that one can (and should be given the right to) separate from them is crucial, but for others it is not only unimportant but virtually incoherent: the idea that we should be able to 'exit' a social grouping that defines us, such as being a minority group member or a man or woman (that is, regarding most ascriptive identities) can appear absurd to many.[17] In addition, the particular factor among the multiple aspects of our identity that becomes prominent in our self-conceptions may often be pressed upon us by external treatment or social location. Indeed, a person may develop a sense of pride in her heritage in response to insulting references to it by those around her. But emphasizing the right to *exit* a social group and the identity that goes with it is of questionable importance to many, and in some cases can be seen as destabilizing to the cohesiveness and psychological power of that very identity. Moreover, political structures which *encourage* questioning all commitments and developing an openness to revising them (as well as the geographical and symbolic mobility that this involves) will skew the priorities of political institutions from the point of view of those who have no need to make such changes and moreover are harmed, in a unique way, when openness to change is a social priority.

In some cases, those who adopt a seemingly stultifying traditional lifestyle and who take no steps to adopt a stance of critical scepticism about that lifestyle appear to observers to be lacking agency, as weak and victimized, when in fact their sense of that identity is powerful and fulfilling. For example, Saba Mahmood has argued that women who embrace traditional Islam and who adopt what observers might see as self-stultifying and self-abnegating value formations occupy a precarious status in the standard accounting of who counts as an agent. However, when what it means to have a practical identity *at all* is understood as having one's own, independent, and equally powerful place in a social world, such women will not be seen as agents, period. The 'agency' that embraces traditional roles would not count as having a practical identity at all, and hence would lie outside even the realm of possibility of autonomous agency. This, she argues, is problematic if not dangerous in the current global political landscape, where respect for plural identities and fragile social subject positions cannot be taken for granted.[18]

Consider also the account Jonathan Lear has given of the experience and value orientation of the Crow Indians in the United States, as exemplified by the oral history given by their onetime leader, Plenty Coups. Lear recounts how after 1887 the Crow lost their traditional homeland and were living on a reservation under the control of the U.S. government. The telling passage from that history that spurs Lear's inquiry is historian Frank Linderman's account of a conversation with Plenty Coups:

> Plenty Coups refused to speak of his life after the passing of the buffalo, so that his story seems to have been broken off, leaving many years unaccounted for. [Plenty Coups said] 'I can think back and tell you much more of war and horse-stealing. But when the buffalo went away the hearts of my people fell to the ground, and they could not lift them up again. After this nothing happened.'[19]

17 Though of course not to all: some may well feel disorientation from their ascribed identity – gender, for example – and face a series of choices about what to do about this disorientation.

18 See S Mahmood, *The Politics of Piety* (Princeton University Press 2005).

19 F Linderman, quoted in J Lear, *Radical Hope: Ethics in the Face of Cultural Devastation* (Harvard University Press 2006) 2. I also consider this case in 'Autonomy and Social Disorientation' in G Levey, *Authenticity, Autonomy and Multiculturalism* (Routledge 2015).

What is interesting about such a claim is that many things *did* happen to the Crow after this point (around 1887), as Plenty Coups and his people took up a farming life, he negotiated with the U.S. government for a settlement with his people, and so on. However, Plenty Coups's statement, according to Lear, was more than merely an expression of malaise, more than saying that 'nothing *much* happened'. The claim expressed a view of both history and the collective experience of the Crow that moves Lear to develop a view of agency and value that emphasizes the deep social embeddedness of identity. For Lear, Plenty Coups's claim makes sense in that for events to have meaning, for things 'to happen', there must be a functioning social nexus that allows practices that are definitive of the basic value categories of the persons involved to operate. The social practices of the Crow, which were structured around an elaborate warrior culture, including the hunting of buffalo and the protection of territory by their own efforts, were no longer allowed to function and so were socially unavailable. The narrative that made the life of the Crow intelligible came to an end when the buffalo were decimated and traditional tribal life was ended.

Lear unpacks this story in light of a theory of action according to which actions take place always under a description that makes them meaningful as intelligible sequences of events. The practices of the Crow, for example the Sun Dance, the counting of 'coups' as marks of bravery, hunting, and military endeavours, and the roles of men and women organized around such practices, were all necessary to make meaningful the complex intentions of the individual members of the Crow nation. The virtues of the Crow, which guided moral reflection and structured intentional action, revolved around participation in such practices.

This is clearly a story of oppressive eradication of a culture by a dominant regime (the United States). My point in bringing it up here, however, relates to Lear's account of action and value as lived out in the years prior to that eradication. The webs in which the identities of the Crow are enmeshed were so pervasive that options to engage in alternative pursuits, even ones that were variations of traditional rituals and activities, would not only be valueless for the Crow, but would have been literally meaningless. Activities get their meaning, on this view, because of the way they are understood through the lens of a practical social identity, one that is not served well or expanded by new, irrelevant options. In this way we can see how, for some, identities can be concretized and stable without the need for reflective detachment and critical re-evaluation.

At least this is true, I submit, when these identities are stable and life affirming for the person. As I will explain further, the fact that we can and should call such persons autonomous implies that our concept of autonomy (and, related to it, freedom) should be able to absorb cases where reflective attachment and considerations of alternative life paths are not required for agency.

This, I think, is the crucial departure between liberal accounts of the dynamics of identity and those that posit the recognition of identity-based interests as a reason for rejecting liberalism. That is, insofar as liberal principles require that people question and critically reappraise their identities to avoid oppression, then for those who think it is precisely such questioning that undercuts the force and satisfaction that comes from that identity will reject those liberal principles. The question will be, then, whether the emphasis on autonomy that underlies such principles requires this position, namely the view that identity formations and social group membership are always oppressive when they discourage the questioning and separation that is entailed in valuing the autonomy of such persons.

But before facing this question directly, we should be careful about what is meant by choice here. For example, Appiah points out how two different kinds of choice are involved in the determination of our identities: the choice of *which* identity should predominate and *how important* it should be for one's pursuits, values, and social connections.[20] I have already cast doubt on the ways that the ability to make such choices can be assumed in the general case, but it might also be useful to keep this distinction in mind in thinking about the possibility of self-alteration by way of reflective decisions and choices. Appiah advances a key insight here, namely, that it is one thing to say we have a choice among the social identifiers that define ourselves (and this is the dimension of choice I have resisted as a safe assumption about all agents); it is another, however, to say we can choose what it *means* to be this or that sort of person, what the implications are and should be, in our judgement, for being a member of a social group. It may be that I cannot choose whether or not to be a male,[21] but what being a male means to me, what I might ask my fellow citizens to do because of that identity, how important I would like those requests to be, and, in turn, what others might do in response to all those judgements on my part, may well be seen as up to me, as a choice.

What I have suggested in this section is that these liberal responses to the challenge of multiculturalism have not adequately dealt with the role that choice plays, and does not play, in claims for special recognition of identity-based needs. What is needed, however, is a more nuanced understanding of the nature of autonomous agency itself, both in the general sense relevant to politics and law as well as applied to cases of what appears to some observers to be constrained identity formations and social practices. Moreover, such an account of autonomy (and hence identity) must further support the special status of identity-based interests described earlier.[22] I turn now to a sketch of such an account.

Respecting autonomy and entrenched social identities

As I have argued elsewhere, the conception of autonomy at issue here and the political principles it supports should be *anti-perfectionist* in the sense that the justification of values and principles should not rest on controversial conceptions of moral value, philosophical or religious outlook, or ideals of the good life.[23] For this reason, 'autonomy' does not refer necessarily to an ideal of (say) an independent and self-generated life, though it may be defined that way in other contexts. In such contexts autonomy serves as a character ideal that features independence, self-creation, and willingness to experiment in lifestyle and value.[24]

Seen in this way, the concept of autonomy functions as a status marker and a central social value around which legal structures and policy are constructed. It is a status marker in that it refers to the aspect of citizens that grounds relations of respect from others and expressed in law. For example, as autonomous persons, citizens should be immune from certain forms of

20 Appiah (n 9) 32.

21 However, as I said earlier, for some this may be a choice in some sense. As I discuss elsewhere (J Christman, *The Politics of Persons* (Cambridge University Press 2009) 123), even sex/gender need not be seen as outside the purview of reflective judgement in all cases, though it is understood that way for most people most of the time.

22 This is, in effect, to adopt a version of the third strategy that G Levey lists to respond to the alleged clash between respecting autonomy and cultural diversity, namely the option of 'reformulating the concept' of autonomy. G Levey, Chapter 2 this volume. Below I respond to what he thinks is a shortcoming of that strategy.

23 See Christman (n 1) ch 10.

24 This is the traditional liberal understanding of autonomy stated as a perfectionist ideal. See, for example, JS Mill, *On Liberty* (Hackett 1859/1978) ch 3 for elaboration.

paternalism; they should be given equal status as participants in collective decision-making; and they should be afforded certain basic rights and protections. Those who lack autonomy may be treated differently from this (though it is a delicate and complex question how they ought to be treated, and nothing said here implies that they be ignored, abused, or excluded from social and political processes).

As a guiding value, autonomy refers to the way practices of education and social promotion of collective goods are organized. Children are educated to gain skills required by autonomy, and family law attempts to protect children from abuses that prevent that development. In the famous U.S. case *Wisconsin v Yoder*, for example, a key question before the Supreme Court was whether special exemptions granted to members of the Old Order Amish religion regarding childhood education would harm children in this way.[25]

On the view I favour, autonomy attaches to individuals (only), but such individuals are what they are because of past and present social relations of a complex sort. This is to leave room for the ways in which the components of a person's value systems, self-concept, orienting commitment, and so on, have meaning because of their place in an ongoing social narrative. This narrative has, in turn, essentially historical as well as social elements, even if it is attached to an individual as such.

However, it is crucial to avoid over-extending this point. To say that our self-concepts are socially constituted is not to say – and indeed we should not say – that these self-understandings are necessarily composed of *particular and fixed* relations with other people or social roles. This would mean that people (all of us) who go through radical change in their lives change who they are, literally. We might say in a moment of exaggeration that we cannot *imagine* living without X (a loved one), or not being a mother or brother; but loved ones die and that surviving version of ourselves is still us.

Even at the general level, however, including social elements in the make-up of the self will have important implications for what we say about autonomy and social identities, for the question of whether a person is or can remain autonomous will depend crucially on the social setting he or she exists in. Alienation from some element of one's character may well ensue if the social constituents of one's self-concept are unsupported, made inoperative or unavailable, or publicly denigrated (as might happen regarding one's ability to practise one's religion with others in public).

With this in mind, let us construct the outlines of a conception of autonomy that can function in these contexts. To do so, it must capture the capacity of persons to judge the values and commitments that define their lives and motivate their choices. Therefore, a major requirement for autonomy will be basic *competence* in the capacity to deliberate, judge, and choose.

Many theorists have claimed that competency is all that is required for autonomy, as long as such competences are spelled out in rich enough detail.[26] I would insist, however, that more than that is required, in that being competent does not capture the ways in which the values and motives that move us to action may well be things we cannot see as our own or embrace. For that reason, we should add that a person should be able to reflectively embrace the value system that structures her choices as well as being able to competently act upon it.

The crux of such a view can be expressed in the following way: a person is autonomous relative to the basic action-motivating elements of her character if, were she to critically

25 *Wisconsin v Yoder* (1972) 406 US 205.

26 See, for example, DT Meyers, *Self, Society, and Personal Choice* (Columbia University Press 1989); B Berofsky, *Liberation From Self: A Theory of Personal Autonomy* (Cambridge University Press 1995).

reflect on such elements in light of the processes by which they were developed, she would not be alienated from them as part of her ongoing autobiographical narrative. Such reflection, to adequately express agential authority, must not be constrained by distorting factors, must be invariant over a variety of conditions, and must express basic competence to critically self-reflect and effectively form intentions to act on the basis of such elements.[27] The reference to self-narrative here merely points to the requirement that one sees one's life as an intelligible sequence of acts and experiences of which oneself is the subject.

In order to see the contours of autonomous agency at work here it is necessary to take a closer look at the ways that practical identities figure in the reflective self-acceptance that autonomy involves. The view I just sketched, like others in this literature, combines competence conditions – the capacity to effectively reflect and form desires and intentions to act without distorting and pathological interferences – and 'authenticity' conditions which concern whether the motives and personal characteristics that move one to act are truly one's own in a special sense (and not, for example, merely surreptitiously inculcated into the person's motivational nexus externally). Although conceptualized as a characteristic of individual persons, autonomy in this sense is meant to attach to selves who can be understood to be themselves social products and socially configured. We are self-governing individually, but the practical identities in virtue of which we govern ourselves may well be seen as socially and historically structured.

Political and social institutions, then, if they are committed to respect for autonomy, should be designed to prevent or eradicate this sort of alienation. Indeed, I would argue that seeing autonomy as relative to one's history makes the claim for recognizing identity-based claims even more powerful, at least when they are well grounded in sociological fact. This is because attention to the historical conditions under which one's identity has been socially treated and defined, where that involves patterns of oppression and degradation, would cause alienation among current members of certain marginalized groups if recognition of special needs (associated with that history) were not acknowledged.

The type of alienation I describe as inimical to autonomy can be seen quite clearly in the case discussed earlier of the Crow and Plenty Coups, their leader. At the time of their cultural disbanding (around 1887), they could not conceive of how to go on in any way that made cultural sense. For a time, life on reservations and in the forced confinement of the (oppressive) U.S. policies that applied to them, actions took on the form of mere survival as individuals, though not as cultural members. This is expressed starkly by Plenty Coups's report that after this date 'nothing happened'. Lear brings out starkly the way in which the Crow were alienated from their opportunities and surroundings until they found a way to refashion life in the new environment, recapturing a transformed version of traditional activities but shaped by these new circumstances. In this way, some measure of autonomy, in my sense, could be redeveloped since this deep alienation was eventually overcome.[28]

27 The full version of this model is in Christman (n 1) ch 7. To be more precise, the view is that relative to some characteristic C, where C refers to basic organizing values and commitments, autonomy obtains if:

1 The person is competent to effectively form intentions to act on the basis of C;
2 The person has the general capacity to critically reflect on C and other basic motivating elements of her psychic and bodily make-up;
3 Were the person to engage in sustained critical reflection on C over a variety of conditions in light of the historical processes (adequately described) that gave rise to C;
4 She would not be alienated from C in the sense of feeling and judging that C cannot be sustained as part of an acceptable autobiographical narrative organized by her diachronic practical identity; and
5 The reflection being imagined is not constrained by reflection-distorting factors.

28 Lear (n 19) 135.

In addition, seeing autonomy in the way I describe deflates one particular line of criticism by defenders of identity claims against autonomy-based conceptions of justice, namely that seeing autonomy as the central object of respect in principles of justice privileges choice, mobility, change, and separation over solidarity and social group cohesion. As I have argued, autonomy requires only hypothetical reflection in the weaker sense I sketched, so that if a person is not alienated from her connections with social groups (or traditions or cultural practices) that constitute her fundamental values, then valuing autonomy does not imply devoting social resources to encouraging separation and disconnection from such groups.

In this way, the contrast between the use of this conception of autonomy as a basis for claims to respect identity-based interests and the standard liberal response is notable, specifically in two important ways. The first is that the connection with cultural practices and group-related interests here is tied directly to autonomy itself, not to the goods that autonomous selves pursue, as others have suggested.[29] Second, as I will explain, the claims that this connection to autonomy underscores are not best articulated in the language of (constitutional) rights – to the survival of one's culture, for example – but rather as constraints on deliberation in the determination of social policy.

Most importantly, however, the view of autonomy sketched here does not presuppose that self-governing persons have current powers to step back from their social roles, values, and identities in order to critically evaluate those structures from that disembodied perspective. Nor does it assume that, for the non-alienated individual, autonomy means being able to fundamentally *alter* one's practical identity or religious profile. What matters is that a person can competently and reflectively *accept* (without alienation) those aspects of herself that function in this way. She does this not by asking herself whether being such a person is best, all things considered, but rather *how being such a person* enables her to pursue an intelligible self-narrative in light of her past, her future, and her surrounding social conditions. When she *cannot* see that socially embedded path as intelligible, when it is so rife with contradictions, internal conflicts, fear, and disorientation, she counts as alienated in my sense and hence may lack autonomy. But unless such alienation is in evidence, there is no autonomy-based assumption that she either chose the way she is or can easily choose to change.[30]

For this reason, the worry raised by Geoffrey Levey about redefining autonomy to better accord with the value of cultures can be obviated. Levey argues that fine-grained accounts similar to this one are too demanding to guide actual legal practices in liberal regimes. Critical reflection on one's lower-order motivations would require liberal states to routinely monitor their citizens' decision-making or compel them to make critically reflective choices.[31] But first, there are many quite acceptable social policies that check on people's reflective consideration of their choices, such as requiring proof of informed consent (which Levey mentions). Moreover, however, the model I proposed allows people to maintain autonomy while acting *un*-reflectively (as Levey says, acting 'on impulse, [or] like sheep'), as long as they would not be alienated from those motives *were they to reflect.*

Further, Levey is surely right that actual legal practice merely functions as a distant approximation of the requirements of philosophical views of autonomy. But using proxies

29 See, for example, Kymlicka (n 8); Margalit and Raz (n 8).

30 Consider, for example, a devoted father or mother: would autonomy require that he or she be able to ask herself if she really *should* love her children? Such a question makes no sense for a happy and devoted parent in most cases, so the requirements of autonomy should not demand it.

31 Levey (n 22).

to approximate the demands of our social ideals, even if imprecise and distant from the fine-grained demands of those ideals, is nevertheless to be guided by those values in the formulation and reconsideration of legal instruments and social policy. Such fine-grained philosophical deconstruction of the requirements of social values is the stuff of the most important court cases in liberal jurisdictions.

Now it is important in this context to acknowledge that the autonomy-based principles of justice and law being projected here are meant to apply to societies with notable and notorious records of past and ongoing violence and power differences among groups (as virtually all societies have). In particular, one must acknowledge the way that certain groups have been marked as objects of degradation, violence, and oppression for generations and continuing in the current age. This is relevant to the specific determination of the autonomy-based interests that social policy and law should be designed to protect, for insofar as one has been victimized in these ways as a member of an identity-based social group, and one's autonomy is tied to one's membership in that group, attempting to repair or protect autonomy-based interests will necessitate attention to this group-oriented victimization.

This connects directly to the way that claims are made for special recognition of the interests tied to identity-group membership that are at issue here. The disrespect of non-recognition involves the failure to acknowledge and show respect for the way that such an identity label has marked the person (or persons like her) in a way that has involved injustice in the past, in particular that has taken away from her the power to help determine the public and social meanings of such membership. Discrimination, marginalization, oppression, and overt violence (motivated by such discrimination) are instances of social patterns of degradation of the type of person an individual is, which is to say, denigration of the meanings of that group membership.

The demand for social recognition based on the value of autonomy, then, can be seen as shorthand for the following, long-winded claim: the ability to define and express interests based on membership in an identity-based social group is fundamental to autonomy, as a derivative of the capacity for self-acceptance in light of one's history and social embeddedness. Recognition of identity, then, involves respect for the capacity to express interests associated with that identity in the public deliberation of policies that affect one's well-being. This implies that in debates over social policy and the common good, special weight should be given to claims made on the basis of autonomy as manifested in citizens' relations either to cultural practices or the treatment of particular (historically marginalized) groups with which they identify.

Now it should be noted that claiming special weight for group-related interests need not usher in calls for basic constitutional rights protecting those interests. What is being defended here is that group-related interests should get *special weight* in democratic decisions when the conditions of citizen autonomy are at stake. This implies that special provisions should be made at the legislative level to allow claims made on behalf of identity-based interests to be given procedural priority in a way that gives them special weight in deliberation about policy. This is because the claims being made, we are assuming, are ones that are linked to the possibility of enjoying autonomy as we have defined it, to avoid the alienation that results when social conditions render the person's identity with certain social groups (or with the interests associated with being a member such groups) of lower social value and therefore the object of disrespect.

As many have said, such interests and such groupings are not fixed and unproblematic. This is the main reason that these interests are expressed in the design of democratic procedures rather than constitutional rights. So what must be claimed is that representatives of the interests in question have a defensible claim to speak for the identity groups in question, but that those who are so represented are always able to reject that interpretation of their interests. Procedurally, representative associations that speak for identity groups will be answerable to their members, and the legitimacy of these representatives will be a function of the general support they receive from those members.[32]

In this way, it is important to maintain sensitivity to the way that *internal* dynamics of social groups may well undercut the assumption of a unified understanding of that social identity by all members. A similar point is examined by Avigail Eisenberg when she points to the tension between taking what she calls a 'sociologically realistic' sense of group homogeneity, which would carry with it an admission that identities are more negotiable and fluid than is often claimed, and an essentialist understanding of membership that occludes internal variability and contestation within groups.[33] Others have worried that seeing identities as fixed and based on a static understanding of group traditions and self-understandings affords cultural elites undue power and may exonerate them from violations of basic human (liberal) rights, in particular violations of the autonomy of individual members to engage in resistance and renegotiation of group identity.

On the view sketched here, representatives of the identity-based interests of groups are answerable both externally and internally for the claims in question as part of a deliberative dynamic in which those claims are made in connection with various other competing interests in the general population (and within the group).

This is akin to Habermas's view that the establishment and valuation of both private and public autonomy must be co-original, in that individual self-government is incomplete without collective self-government and vice versa. The requirements of democracy (and more generally, for him, communication and discourse) both presuppose and support the enjoyment of individual autonomy. Only if I can claim participation or representation in effective public fora, where my unique perspective and voice functions on an equal footing with competing voices of my co-citizens, can sense be made of my own ability to govern myself in a social setting that partially constitutes my identity. Insofar as that identity has group-oriented dimensions such as ethnicity, race, gender, or sexuality, only when the interests associated with that group membership get particular play in those public discussions, can I be said to be afforded respect as an autonomous individual.[34]

This position contrasts in subtle but crucial ways with the standard liberal positions outlined earlier (defended by Kymlicka, Sen, Appiah, and others). For on their view of the value of autonomy (and freedom), it is the *actual* access to alternative social options and/ or to rival understandings of people's entrenched identities that is required. On my view, however, only if people suffer the types of *alienation* from those identities (or from the representatives expressing interests based on them) are exit options required. In practice, this may mean that access to social programs and resources that allow individuals to leave a group, tribe, or religious organization are available. But it precisely does not require that exploration of those options must be promoted as a shared social value.

32 For discussion of the role of identity groups in democracies, see A Gutmann, *Identity in Democracy* (Princeton University Press 2003).

33 Eisenberg, Chapter 4 this volume.

34 See J Habermas, *Between Facts and Norms* (MIT Press 1996) ch 8; J Habermas, 'Struggles for Recognition in the Democratic Constitutional State' in A Gutmann (ed), *Multiculturalism* (Princeton University Press 1999) 107.

Eisenberg points out, rightly, that 'in practice these practices may or may not in fact be inalienable and nonnegotiable.'[35] This is correct for many, and indeed the suspicion that certain identity claims are actually more like preferences or interests than is often admitted is part of many liberals' analyses of these conflicts. But I have argued here that one *need not* be skeptical that values based on practical identities be unsheddable or non-negotiable to respect the autonomy of those who hold such values.

The argument I have constructed here has the following general form: autonomy involves non-alienation from factors that function in our basic value orientations; such factors have social constituents, such that their meaning and value are part of social practices and relations of a particular sort; when those practices and relations are denigrated or destroyed, alienation is likely to occur, hence restricting citizens' autonomy; so protecting autonomy will mean giving special weight to the interests connected to those social groups. Correspondingly, public claims on policy based on identity interests must follow the contours of the requirements of autonomy set out: one must claim that failure to alter this or that social policy would prevent the person from pursuing a social self-narrative shaped by her practical identity without abiding alienation.

It follows from all this, then, that due attention to social identities and the recognition of them does not entail the rejection of autonomy-based conceptions of justice, once the notion of autonomy has been formulated in acceptable ways. Attacks on traditional (liberal) conceptions of justice can be seen as overdrawn if they presume that the culprit is insisting that autonomy is fundamental for justice. I think also, however, that such a conception of the autonomous person is strong enough to ground claims of injustice for those social group members who find themselves deeply alienated from the social conditions in which they are asked to pursue their values and find meaning in their identities.

35 Eisenberg (n 33).

4 Three approaches to the protection of religious freedom

Choice, interest, identity

Avigail Eisenberg

More than other rights, the right to religious freedom has been the subject of intense public debate over the last few decades. Whereas freedom of religion has historically been understood as a right that offers the individual protection to choose her religious commitments free of coercion, it is now increasingly viewed as a right aimed at protecting an identity, similar to a cultural or ethnic identity, in order to treat people fairly. There are several possible ways to interpret the nature of a religious commitment; *religion as choice* and *religion as identity* are not the only alternatives,[1] nor are they mutually exclusive approaches. But lately, what has been referred to by legal scholars as the *choice* and the *identity approaches*,[2] which have shaped legal cases, reveal different political aims, impose different obligations and pressures on political institutions, and motivate distinctive ideas about the nature of citizenship and the public sphere.

Here, I examine the identity approach to religious freedom in relation to two other approaches in order to assess some of its political and legal implications. The cases considered here are drawn from Canada, the United States, and Europe. They indicate that when religion is understood as an identity, courts are willing to consider evidence and values related to historical injustice and group inequality that are less likely to be considered when religion is interpreted as an individual choice. At the same time, in adopting the identity approach, judges are also more likely to overlook the pluralism within religious groups and may sometimes buy into stereotypes about a group's character and practices. The evidence shows that, increasingly, a perspective that considers religion to be an identity guides judges to recognize a distinct set of values and concerns at stake in conflicts about the rights of

1 'Religious institutionalism' is a third perspective that is gaining recognition in the courts. See, for example, discussions by J Cohen, 'Freedom of Religion Inc.: Whose Sovereignty?' (2015) 44 *Netherlands Journal of Legal Philosophy* 169; MW McConnell, 'Accommodation of Religion' (1985) 1985 *The Supreme Court Review* 1; R Schragger and M Schwartzmann, 'Against Religious Institutionalism' (2013) 99 *Virginia Law Review* 917.

2 R Moon, 'Religious Commitment and Identity: Syndicat Northcrest v Amselem' (2005) 29 *Supreme Court Law Review (2d)* 201; R Moon, 'Government Support for Religious Practice' in R Moon (ed), *Law and Religious Pluralism in Canada* (University of British Columbia Press 2008) 217. Noah Feldman makes a similar distinction between 'liberty' and 'equality' approaches to religious freedom (N Feldman, 'From Liberty to Equality: The Transformation of the Establishment Clause' (2002) 90 *Cal L R* 673). Ayelet Shachar notes a similar distinction between 'fair inclusion' and 'privatized diversity' (A Shachar, 'When Law Meets Diversity: Implications for Women's Equality' in S Vertovec (ed), *International Handbook of Diversity Studies* (Routledge 2015) 234). Also, for a philosophical defence of a choice-centred approach to cultural and religious practice, see B Barry, *Culture and Equality: An Egalitarian Critique of Multiculturalism* (Harvard University Press 2001).

DOI: 10.4324/9781315413617-6

religious minorities, while at the same time raising challenges and dilemmas with respect to the fair treatment of individuals and minorities within religious minorities.

The first part of this chapter examines the advantages of an identity approach to religious freedom by distinguishing it from two other approaches, one that views religion as a choice and the other that views religion as an interest. The second part examines some of the key implications of assessing conflicts in terms of identity, including some of the trade-offs that occur when this approach is adopted by judges and other public decision-makers.

The proposal here is not to explain how people come to have their religious commitments because, as we know, people may choose their religious beliefs, view religion as part of their identity, or consider their religion instrumentally, for instance, as providing them with community or access to activities and services. Nor is my aim to explore the ontological status or the sociological function of religion. Rather, the aim is to assess the different approaches taken to religious freedom in public decision-making, especially by courts. How does religion as choice, interest, or identity structure political and legal decision-making? What kind of pressure does each approach exert on public institutions to address specific kinds of questions? Does each approach lead decision-makers to consider different kinds of evidence? To address these questions requires understanding each approach as distinct from other possible approaches.

Religion as choice

Freedom of religion in Canada and the United States has been understood primarily as a right intended to protect an individual's freedom to choose religious beliefs as long as these choices do not harm others. This understanding follows what Richard Moon calls, in the context of Canadian jurisprudence, the 'choice approach'.[3] According to one understanding of the choice approach, individuals are rational choosers, and the ideal liberal state is one that protects the individual's rights in order to protect his or her capacity to choose important affiliations and commitments without coercion from outsiders. Following from this, the sovereign value of religious freedom is the freedom to follow the dictates of one's deepest and most personal religious commitments and thereby to decide for oneself what beliefs ought to guide one's conscience.

Although the choice approach seems to reflect a classic liberal view of individual freedom,[4] it offers, at best, superficial consideration of several ideal conditions of individual autonomy such as those discussed by Deveaux and Levey in this volume, including the presence of critical capacities, fair procedures for deliberating about choices, the absence of false consciousness, and the opportunity to exit our religious communities. As Deveaux recognizes, courts are usually looking for evidence that individuals are neither directly nor explicitly forced by external agents into adopting particular practices and beliefs.[5] This kind of evidence is usually satisfied by a sincerity test, which is a low-threshold legal test used to assess whether individuals are credible and consistent in their adherence to their religious beliefs

3 Moon, 'Religious Commitment and Identity' (n 2), 201.

4 The choice approach can be derived from doctrines other than the classic liberal view. With respect to religion, the requirement that individuals be free to follow their conscience was also meant to avoid the potentially intolerable possibility that the state could place people's souls in eternal jeopardy by forcing them to follow a mistaken religious doctrine (see McConnell, 'Accommodation of Religion' (n 1), 15–16).

5 M Deveaux, Chapter 5 in this volume.

and practices.[6] In practical contexts such as court settings, to press individual believers with questions meant to detect false consciousness or assess their critical capacities to choose religious beliefs, as the ideal might require, can easily become too intrusive and may permit judges too much latitude to second-guess believers and deny their choices. This illustrates one of the paradoxes of autonomy, noted throughout this volume, namely that, as Levey describes it, when liberal states establish demanding conditions as evidence of individual autonomy, they quickly cease to be liberal states.[7]

In diverse societies, the chief asset of the choice approach is its flexibility and thereby its capacity to treat people from diverse religious and cultural communities fairly. The approach provides legal protection across different religious and spiritual belief systems by asking judges to focus narrowly and recognize only the individual's authority to make religious choices. In this way, the approach requires very little from the state and certainly does not require the state to protect any particular religious belief or practice. The protection of individual religious choice requires neither that the state eliminate every cost associated with the practice of religion nor that all religions be treated equally by the state. Instead, religious choice can be respected as long as no law or publicly endorsed practice prevents individuals from following their religious faith. As we know, individual choices often involve absorbing costs and, unless these costs function as covert obstacles to practising a religious faith, they are not the concern of the state. As Moon puts it, citizens should not expect the public purse to subsidize their religious choices.

Moon illustrates the distinction between choice and identity in a series of Canadian cases about Sunday closing laws. In 1985, the Supreme Court of Canada heard a case involving the Lord's Day Act,[8] a national law that required businesses to close on Sundays. The law was challenged on the grounds that it discriminated against non-Christians by imposing costs on Jews, Muslims, and other religious minorities, whose Sabbath falls on Saturday or Friday, and who were thereby required to close their businesses two days a week (on their own Sabbath and on Sunday). According to Moon, had the Court applied the choice approach, as it had in the past, it would have found that the Lord's Day Act does not violate religious freedom because it does not prohibit those who hold Saturday or Friday as the Sabbath from closing their businesses on these other days as well. As long as the law does not coerce or prohibit anyone from following their religious practices, but instead only requires them to close on Sundays in addition to any other day they choose to close, it does not violate religious freedom. As some judges observed regarding Ontario's Retail Business Holidays Act, which also mandated businesses to close on Sundays, the state cannot be expected to bear the costs of the choices its citizens make:

> The economic harm suffered by a Saturday observer who closes shop on Saturdays is not caused by the . . . *Act* . . . . It results from the deliberate choice of a tradesman who gives priority to the tenets of his religion over his financial benefit.[9]

6 J Woehrling, 'L'obligation d'accommodement raisonnable et l'adaption de la société à la diversité religieuse' (1998) 43 *McGill Law Journal* 325. I discuss the application of the sincerity test in recent Canadian cases in A Eisenberg, 'What Is Wrong With the Liberal Assessment of Religious Authenticity?' in GB Levey (ed), *Autonomy, Authenticity and Multiculturalism* (Routledge 2015) 145, 149–152.

7 GB Levey, Chapter 2 in this volume.

8 The Lord's Day Act was struck down in *R v Big M Drug Mart Ltd* [1985] 1 SCR 295.

9 *R v Edwards Books and Art Ltd* [1986] 2 SCR 713, para 168.

In sum, the choice approach to freedom of religion does not require that lawmakers eliminate every state-imposed cost associated with the practice of religion or that all religious faiths be treated the same by the state. Nor does the approach prohibit public practices or laws that favour one religious group over another as long as these practices and laws do not prevent anyone from following their religious faith.[10] In a religiously diverse society, freedom to choose one's faith often involves costs and, unless these costs are covert obstacles that prohibit people from practising their religions, citizens should not expect the public purse to subsidize the choices they make with respect to the religious beliefs and practices they follow.

Religion as interest

Whereas the concept of 'rights' is invoked within legal and political contexts to indicate that a claim refers to fundamental values which, *ceteris paribus*, ought not to be compromised or negotiated away, the concept of 'interest' is invoked within legal and political contexts to indicate that a claim may be balanced against other interest claims, or that it is open to revision so that compromises can be reached in cases where different interests conflict. The concept of 'interest' is thereby intended to signal that a claim is negotiable; this is considered especially important in contexts of democratic decision-making. For instance, an interest-based approach to democracy is one in which individuals hold their interests voluntarily and can revise or compromise their interests. An interest might be chosen, but what makes it an interest does not depend on whether it is chosen or not, but rather on whether it can be compromised. In contrast to choice (or identity as discussed later), an interest is the kind of claim that is not usually considered integral to the individual's conception of herself (as would be the case with an identity claim). As Daniel Weinstock explains it, interests are about what people want rather than who they essentially are.[11]

In diverse societies, the capacity of individuals and groups to compromise their interests engenders peaceful coexistence among groups with real differences. For instance, Robert Dahl[12] (following James Madison) distinguished between a 'faction' and an 'interest group' on the basis of the capacity of a group to compromise with other groups, and argued that democracy works where individuals in interest groups engage in ongoing processes of negotiation and compromise with each other. In contrast, 'factions' resist compromise and fail to build coalitions across their rigid boundaries which, in Dahl's view, makes them destructive to democracy. Following this view, diversity is compatible with democracy where individuals and groups consider their distinctive claims to be interests that they are willing to compromise, and democracy is jeopardized by factionalized groups that are rigidly defined by matters they consider inalienable and non-negotiable.

As these concepts are conventionally used, choices and interests can have much in common, and a religious claim may be formulated as a choice or as an interest without losing any meaning. But here, choice and interest are proposed as concepts that elicit different political and legal approaches to religious freedom, each with a distinctive set of values

10 This aspect of the choice approach would, however, be prohibited in the United States given the 'anti-establishment' clause of the U.S. Constitution.

11 D Weinstock, 'Is "Identity" a Danger to Democracy?' in I Primoratz and A Pavković (eds), *Identity, Self-Determination and Secession* (Ashgate 2006) 15, 21.

12 R Dahl, *Preface to the Democratic Theory* (University of Chicago Press 1956).

that guides decision-making. Where choice is the guiding value, the aim will be to resolve conflicts about religious freedom by ensuring that laws do not prohibit people from freely choosing their religious commitments. Where interest is the guiding value, religious commitments may be treated as matters that can be compromised and limited in relation to other similarly important interests, and religious freedom may be best protected by balancing religious interests against other non-religious interests that are at stake in a conflict. Whereas the choice approach maintains that individuals should be free to choose their religious commitments without having to compromise (but with no expectation that the state will compensate them for their choices), the interest approach emphasizes the importance of compromise.

Religion as identity

A third kind of claim is an 'identity claim', which is a claim for the recognition or protection of a belief or practice considered to be integral to the self-understanding of an individual or group. Identity claims are usually considered non-negotiable because they are attached to matters of deep importance to an individual's sense of self and thereby matters whose prohibition or restriction could be experienced as disrespectful and could lead to the marginalization of a minority.

When understood in these terms, identity claims can be distinguished from choices or interests on the basis of whether they are flexible or voluntary claims. Claims that are presented as 'identity claims' in the public sphere are intended to be non-negotiable features of individual and group-based identities rather than 'choices' some individuals have made (and can 'unmake') or 'interests' that can be revised and compromised. This is not to deny that people sometimes 'choose' their identities or assert that they cannot compromise some aspects of their identities.[13] Rather, the point is that, in political and legal contexts, a religious claim is presented as an 'identity claim' chiefly in order to signal its connection to matters so deeply important to the claimant's sense of self that they ought not to be compromised or abandoned. Whereas these deeply important matters may or may not *in fact* be inalienable and non-negotiable, the claims are formulated as matters of identity strategically to invoke a framework that asks others to treat them as though they were inalienable and non-negotiable. What follows is that political and legal actors use an identity approach when they treat a claim made for the protection or accommodation of a religious or cultural practice as though it were a non-negotiable feature of a person that the state must respect in order to treat people as equals.[14] For instance, claimants sometimes invoke identity by arguing that the state is forcing them into a dilemma between choosing their religion or their citizenship, their state or their community and family, in order to highlight the inflexibility of their claim and its relation to their sense of self.

For example, according to an identity approach, a law that requires businesses to close on Sundays may be interpreted as violating religious freedom if it appears to expose minorities

13 For instance, J Christman (Chapter 3 in this volume) develops a philosophical account of social identity that avoids exaggerating both the group essentialism found in many political accounts and the capacities or opportunities people have to choose their identities.

14 Two discussions of identity politics that focus on the non-negotiable character of identity claims are J Waldron, 'Cultural Identity and Civic Responsibility' in W Kymlicka and W Norman (eds), *Citizenship in Diverse Societies* (Oxford University Press 2000), 155, and D Weinstock (n 11).

to disrespect or disadvantage, or if it is viewed as denying them dignity as members of a particular group. According to Moon, if religious belief is viewed as part of the individual's identity, 'then its unequal treatment may be experienced by the individual as an interference with his or her dignity and as a failure to treat him and his [*sic*] group with equal respect'.[15] What follows, using the identity approach, is that laws that convincingly have the effect of alienating or marginalizing some citizens on the basis of their religious commitments are also ones that deny religious freedom.

Moon argues that, in Canada, a shift in the judicial interpretation of religious freedom from choice to identity can be traced back to the first cases decided by the courts using the Canadian Charter of Rights and Freedoms,[16] which was entrenched in the Constitution in 1982. In the 1985 *R v Big M Drug Mart Ltd*,[17] the majority of the Court adopted an identity approach by recognizing that laws which favour mainstream religious groups can have the effect of displaying disrespect for individuals outside the mainstream. Chief Justice Dickson, writing the decision for the majority, articulated the shift from a choice to an identity approach:

> In proclaiming the standards of the Christian faith, the [*Lord's Day*] *Act* creates a climate hostile to, and gives the appearance of discrimination against, non-Christian Canadians . . . . The theological content of the legislation remains a subtle and constant reminder to religious minorities within the country of their differences with, and alienation from, dominant religious cultures.[18]

Whereas before 1985 the Canadian court adopted an approach to religious freedom that assessed law and policy in terms of their impacts on individual choice, after 1985 the court begins to consider arguments about minority inclusion, to use a discourse about equal respect for religious minorities, and to display sensitivity to religious freedom not only for individuals, but also for collectivities.[19]

From a political vantage, a shift from choice to identity is not surprising and can be viewed as the product of a broad set of political struggles that have occurred over the last 50 years in Western states in which group-based identities have been invoked to advance claims for equality and justice. Since at least the 1970s, many different kinds of groups, including religious ones, have made claims before domestic and international courts and legislatures for the recognition and protection of some aspect of their identity in order to contest the ways in which they have been treated by the state.[20] Numerous states have responded to these claims by entrenching legal protections for minorities, by developing multicultural policies, and by interpreting long-standing policies in more culturally sensitive ways. Canada has

15 Moon 2008 (n 2) 232.
16 *Canadian Charter of Rights and Freedoms.*
17 See (n 8) and related discussion.
18 Ibid. paras 97–8; also see para 134.
19 Several scholars disagree with Moon on this point and argue that the Canadian approach remains choice-based and individualistic. See B Berger, 'Law's Religion: Rendering Culture' in R Moon (ed), *Law and Religious Pluralism in Canada* (University of British Columbia Press 2008) 264 and J Borrows, 'Living Law on a Living Earth: Aboriginal Religion' in R Moon (n 2) 161.
20 See A Eisenberg and W Kymlicka, 'Bringing Institutions Back In: How Public Institutions Assess Identity' in A Eisenberg and W Kymlicka (eds), *Identity Politics in the Public Realm* (University of British Columbia Press 2011) 1.

been at the forefront of these developments in part because it was the first state to adopt multiculturalism as an official national policy and because, at the height of what has come to be known as the 'age of identity politics', Canada passed major revisions to its constitution, adding a number of group-based rights and official recognition of multiculturalism.[21] But Canada is not the only country to embrace such reforms. Since 1970, more than 40 national constitutions have been amended to offer protection for some kind of identity-based rights,[22] and numerous transnational and international covenants and conventions have been created in which the protection of some feature of identity figures prominently. Regimes that have undergone such major rights-based reforms in the last 30 years provide especially clear evidence of an emerging recognition that the protection of individual freedom and equality sometimes depends on the protection of group-based identities.

In decisions of the European Court of Human Rights (ECtHR), for instance, it is not uncommon to find legal argumentation about religious freedom that adopts an identity approach. For instance, in *Lautsi and Others v Italy* (2011),[23] a case about whether a crucifix should be removed from a schoolroom wall, the choice approach is articulated in the concurring opinion of Judge Bonello, who argued that 'with or without the crucifix on a school room wall', the Lautsis enjoyed freedom of religion because freedom of religion is premised on the presence or absence of individual choice; it 'consists in the rights to profess freely any religion of the individual's choice, the right to freely change one's religion, the right not to embrace religion at all'.[24] In contrast, the dissenting judges argued that religious freedom 'confer[s] on States a positive obligation to create a climate of tolerance and mutual respect among their population', which cannot be fulfilled 'where they mainly have regard to the beliefs held by the majority'.[25] The role of the court is not to question whether individuals are free to choose, but rather to accept individuals' religious commitments (or non-commitments) as given and then to ask whether the state treats individuals with these commitments with equal respect. The decision carries the language of identity by implying that religious freedom is experienced not merely through individual choice, but through respect, esteem, and inclusion as well.

Similarly, in *Leyla Sahin v Turkey* (2004),[26] the majority decided that officials of the University of Istanbul, who prohibited Sahin from wearing her headscarf, did not violate her freedom of religion because such a prohibition may be required in order to protect public order and pluralism in a majority Muslim society. In the majority's view, the claimant's insistence on wearing a veil is her choice, which has consequences with respect to her access to university education in Turkey; therefore the claimant, not the state, is liable. In contrast, in

21 Multiculturalism is recognized in section 27 of the Canadian Charter of Rights and Freedoms, which directs the court to interpret the Charter 'in a manner consistent with the preservation and enhancement of the multicultural heritage of Canadians'.

22 Explicit mention of 'identity', or articles that directly address cultural rights or 'indigenous identity', can be found in the constitutions of Argentina, Belize, Bolivia, Brazil, Bulgaria, Croatia, Ecuador, Guatemala, Kosovo, Mexico, Nicaragua, Panama, Paraguay, Peru, Poland, Romania, Slovakia, Slovenia, and Venezuela, as well as statutes passed by regions in Italy, Spain (Cataluña), and Germany. In most cases, these provisions have been entrenched in the last 30 years. See I Ruggiu, *Il giudice antropologo. Constituzione e tecniche di composizione dei conflitti multiculturali* (Franco Angeli 2012) 219, 224–233.

23 *Lautsi and Others v Italy* [2011] 3 Reports of Judgments and Decisions 61.

24 Ibid. Bonello J concurring 103.

25 Ibid. Malinverni J and Kalydjieva J dissenting 112.

26 *Leyla Sahin v Turkey* [2005] 9 Reports of Judgments and Decisions 173.

the dissenting opinion, Justice Tulkens argued that Sahin's headscarf did not threaten public order or exhibit inappropriate proselytizing. Instead, the university effectively excluded Sahin from access to public education in Turkey, forcing her to complete her studies in Vienna, and forcing her and other devout Muslims into 'silent exclusion [and] a return to religious schools'.[27] According to Tulkens, the conflict is not primarily one about choice (which is not mentioned in the judgment), but rather about the exclusion of citizens from access to education and should be considered in light of the Report of European Commission Against Racism and Intolerance, which points to 'the climate of hostility existing against persons who are or are believed to be Muslims'.[28]

The case of *SAS v France*[29] provides a more complex example in which all three approaches are evident and clearly in tension with each other. The majority on the ECtHR decided to uphold a French law prohibiting the full-face veil on the basis that the law is, in its opinion, a fair response to the legitimate government objective of preserving the conditions of 'living together'. The majority failed to identify which specific conditions are required for living together and, partly for this reason, the two dissenting judges characterized the majority's reasoning as 'far-fetched and vague',[30] and then employed the discourse of identity to assess the case. They did so by first pointing to the connection between respecting the dress-code law and respecting women's identities or 'personalities' in relation to their approach to religion and, in this connection, noting the gravity of what is at stake for women so restricted.[31] They argue that laws which prohibit full-face veils 'further exclude [devout Muslim women] from society and aggravate their situation'.[32] 'Living together', they argued, requires including people who follow diverse traditions and dress codes, whereas the ban ironically excludes women who wear a full-face veil from access to the core activity of citizenship – namely, 'living together'.

The majority on the court surveyed several arguments presented by the state for the face-veil ban before it arrived at the decisive value of 'living together'. It cited two counterarguments it considered important albeit not decisive to its view of the case. The first was that the legislative restriction may contribute to the discrimination already suffered by Muslims,[33] and the second was that the law posed a dilemma for veiled women, forcing them to choose either forgoing their religious identity or being isolated from the public sphere, including being denied access to hospitals and government offices.[34] In the words of the majority, women who use the full-face veil

> are thus confronted with a complex dilemma, and the ban may have the effect of isolating them and restricting their autonomy, as well as impairing the exercise of their freedom to manifest their beliefs and their right to respect for their private life. It is also understandable that the women concerned may perceive the ban as a threat to their identity.[35]

27 Ibid. Tulkens J dissenting, para 19.
28 Ibid. Tulkens J dissenting, paras 19 and 20.
29 *SAS v France* [2014] 43835/11 ECtHR (Selected for Case Reports).
30 Ibid. para 2.
31 See, for example, ibid. paras 2, 7, 17, 21.
32 Ibid. para 21.
33 Ibid. Majority judgment para 149.
34 Ibid. paras 17, 18, 25.
35 Ibid. para 146.

Yet, despite the majority's recognition that the burden on some women is great, and that the antiveiling law may be part of a broader problem of group-based discrimination, it upheld the legal restriction, averring that the ban is a legitimate 'choice for society'. Thus, the majority ended its decision by employing the language of choice in relation to the state, not the individual claimant, whose religious commitments are instead characterized on several occasions as part of her identity. In this way, *SAS* illustrates a mix of the choice, interest, and identity considerations. Insofar as the religious practice is viewed as a matter of identity, then it may be a non-negotiable feature of a Muslim woman's self. Upholding the law may thereby exclude those who veil from access to public benefits because, as the court recognized, they will not or cannot compromise their religious commitments.

Conversely, if the practice is treated as a matter of choice, then the question is whether the burden of the criminal law imposed on a woman is too great in the sense that it de facto removes her freedom to choose her religious commitments. In this respect, the majority in the *SAS* case recognized that the legal prohibition places a great burden on women who use the full-face veil. It isolates them, threatens their identities, and impairs their exercise of religious freedom, but it does so to very few women, and those whom it affects can always *choose* to risk being penalized. The majority thereby acknowledged that the law restricts women's freedom to manifest their beliefs, but considered this a problem primarily because it will lead to their social exclusion and isolation, and not because it will effectively prohibit them, as individuals, from choosing their religious commitments. In this sense, the practice was treated as an interest of some women rather than an individual right. As an interest, veiling is a practice that may be compromised in light of other important values – such as living together – that the majority recognized to be at stake in this case.

From a perspective informed by the three approaches discussed earlier – choice, interest, and identity – *SAS* displays a mix of considerations in tension with each other. In keeping with the choice approach, the court recognized two leading choice-based concerns, the first being that women may be coerced into veiling by outsiders, which it decided is not a convincing reason to uphold the law. Second, the decision also seems to acknowledge that the legal prohibition restricts individual choice about what is for some people a deeply important religious commitment. Yet, at the same time, the court noted that the restriction will only affect a few women. In this way, the court ignored the sanctity of individual religious choice, which is otherwise at the heart of the choice approach to religious freedom.

In keeping with the identity approach, the court recognized the connection between a religious practice and social exclusion. Veiling, it acknowledged, can be a non-negotiable part of a person's identity whose prohibition can lead to social exclusion and, in reference to government services such as hospitals, to being denied access to the benefits of citizenship. Further to this, by recognizing that the law generates a dilemma for women who veil, the court seemed to acknowledge that the practice is non-negotiable or nearly so for some women. Yet, rather than this leading the majority to decide against the state-imposed prohibition, as one might expect, the recognition of veiling as part of identity led the court instead to note that only a few women will be affected to this extent because only a few are, like the claimant, unwilling to go out in public without being veiled. So the court abandoned the identity approach and settled for an interest-based approach, which allows France to retain the law based, in part, on the rationale that 'living together' is a societal interest that sometimes requires people to compromise their religious commitments, including, in this case, their interest in wearing a veil outside their home.

Today, evidence that courts are sometimes sensitive to the identity-related nature of minority claims can be found in many leading decisions about religious freedom in Canada, the

United States, and Europe, even though the identity approach is not usually the approach informing the majority's decision. Nonetheless, some recognition of identity may indicate an increasing awareness, throughout Western states, that state policies ought to accommodate the practices and beliefs of some cultural and religious minorities. Notwithstanding the official backlash against multiculturalism in Europe, most people recognize that to build an inclusive citizenry requires public recognition of diversity and that, minimally, courts should be prepared to assess whether accommodating some minority practices is necessary in order to treat people as equals.

Implications

The first implication and central benefit of an identity approach is that it is instrumentally useful and more effective than the choice or interest approaches at tracking social exclusion and historical injustice towards groups. In part, this is because the approach treats certain features of a group's religion or culture, such as a particular practice, as a non-negotiable part of the individual's or group's identity and, therefore, as significant to what is required to treat an individual respectfully or to include group members as equal citizens. By focusing on a religious practice or commitment such as veiling, laws or policies that have restricted the group by restricting its practices can be identified and examined to determine if these restrictions constitute a pattern of discrimination, disrespect, and disadvantage. Consequently, if judges were to interpret religion as identity, they might be more willing to consider the connection between the prohibition of a religious or cultural practice and state-driven discrimination against the group. Similarly, if minorities wish to contest legal restrictions on their practices, they can draw the connection between the restriction on their practices and the exclusion and disrespect they have suffered on the basis of their identity.

A good illustration of this instrumental use of identity as a 'tracking device' is reflected in the 1990 US case of *Employment Division v Smith*,[36] in which a law that criminalized peyote was challenged on the grounds that it denied religious freedom to members of the Native American Church, who use peyote in their religious ceremonies. The Church submitted evidence and arguments to the US Supreme Court showing that the practice of 'peyotism' has a rich history in the spiritual practices of indigenous people in North and Central America dating back to 1560.[37] The Church further argued that part of its mission was to reconnect members to their historical rituals, which include ingesting peyote in order to help members see themselves 'not as people whose place and way in the world is gone but as people whose way can be strong enough to change and meet new challenges'.[38] According to this part of their submission, the problem with prohibiting the drug was less a matter of impeding individual choice than of further marginalizing a group that had already suffered marginalization at the hands of a colonizing state. Whereas the criminal prohibition on peyote impedes individuals in the community from choosing to follow one of their religious commitments, the injustice the community claims to experience is not simply a matter of having the choices of their members restricted. Rather, the prohibition on peyote today fits into a history of group-based exclusion and a narrative of persecution that is far more profound to the group's sense of dignity than what a snapshot assessment of individual choice reveals.

36 *Employment Division v Smith* [1990] 494 US 872.

37 *Employment Division, Human Resources of Oregon v Smith* [1988], 485 US 660, 668–669.

38 *Employment Division, Human Resources of Oregon v Smith* [1990], 494 US 872, 915.

Cases that involve historical injustice are often ones in which the restrictions on religious or cultural practices can be framed as matters of disrespect to group identity and, for this reason, the identity approach is helpful in these cases. But it is also helpful in cases that have little to do with historical injustice. In *SAS*, for instance, the Grand Chamber stated that it was 'very concerned' about the manner in which the legal prohibition on the full-face veil contributes to Islamophobia and exposes Muslims in France to ongoing disrespect. The court emphasized that 'a State which enters into a legislative process of this kind takes the risk of contributing to the consolidation of the stereotypes which affect certain categories of the population and of encouraging the expression of intolerance.'[39] A similar connection between a religious practice and societal discrimination against a group characterizes one of the leading cases about religious freedom in Canada, *Multani v Commission scolaire Marguerite-Bourgeoys*,[40] which explicitly protects religious freedom in terms of democratic inclusion in a diverse society. In *Multani*, a Quebec school board prohibited a Sikh boy from wearing his *kirpan* (a ceremonial knife of symbolic significance that is to be worn at all times by Sikhs) to school. According to the school's no-weapons policy, the *kirpan* is considered a weapon, whereas according to the Sikh boy and his family, it is a central article of faith. The Supreme Court ruled that the school's policy unfairly denied Multani's religious freedom, arguing that the regulation may expose religious minorities to disrespect:

> If some students consider it unfair that G may wear his kirpan to school while they are not allowed to have knives in their possession, it is incumbent on the schools to instil in their students this value that is at the very foundation of our democracy . . . . Accommodating G and allowing him to wear his kirpan under certain conditions demonstrates the importance that our society attaches to protecting freedom of religion and to showing respect for its minorities.[41]

The court decided that to respect the Sikh practice meant recognizing the *kirpan*'s distinctiveness as a religious article of faith and therefore not treating it as a knife. It also decided to protect religious freedom not merely as a matter of choice, but also as a matter of identity. If the decision in *Multani* had been framed only in terms of individual choice, the Court's leading question would be whether the school's no-weapons policy placed a significant burden on Multani's right to practise his religion. Argumentation along these 'choice' lines would have to address whether the school's no-weapons policy denies the right of Sikhs to choose their religious commitments and whether the costs borne by orthodox Sikhs who choose to send their children to private schools, where *kirpans* are allowed, rather than public schools, where *kirpans* are prohibited, were too high. Whether or not consideration of these questions would have led to a decision in favour of Multani is uncertain, but clearly it would not have led the Court to consider how restricting *kirpans* in public schools might expose Sikhs to disrespect in Canadian society.

SAS and *Multani* both illustrate that some conflicts can be framed both in terms of denying individual choice and in terms of denying individuals equal citizenship and democratic inclusion.

39 *SAS v France*, para 149.
40 *Multani v Commission Scolaire Marguerite-Bourgeoys* [2006] 1 SCR 256.
41 Ibid., introductory remarks; see also para 79.

The identity approach is the only approach that directs us to consider these questions. Under the framework of identity, the assessment of religious freedom can involve tracking social exclusion and historical injustice towards religious groups. Sometimes this entails assessing whether the law has prevented access of a religious minority to the benefits of citizenship by placing them in a position of having to make an unacceptable choice between religious commitments related to their sense of themselves – that is their identity – and features of citizenship such as being law-abiding.

A second implication of the identity approach is that it is more group-focused than the choice approach. It connects individuals to groups through collective practices and, through these collective practices, to a set of policies and sometimes a history that has targeted these practices in order to target and exclude the group. The approach sheds light on how a policy or rule can be considered unjust not only because it impairs an individual's freedom to choose to follow a religious practice, but also because the restriction targets a religious group to which the individual belongs and marginalizes her as a member of that group. Evidence relating to the meaning and importance of the practice to the group helps to illuminate this collective dimension, which can be overlooked by assessments that narrowly focus on whether an individual believer is (sufficiently) free to choose.

This second implication can be both a benefit and a liability for claimants. One of the leading concerns of recognizing that a religious practice is part of a group identity is that it provides an incentive for group leaders or 'experts' to downplay pluralism within the group by exaggerating the importance and unqualified uniformity of the group's devotion to a contested practice. The hope is that doing so will enhance their chances of winning legal recognition and protection. If a practice can be credibly represented as a 'group practice' rather than an individual choice or interest, then claimants can more easily argue that legally restricting the practice excludes the group.

In this respect, it is worth recognizing how unhelpful the individualist choice-based standard is to arguments that try to show the exclusion, marginalization, and disrespect groups have suffered in the past. Where claimants rely on providing convincing evidence of structural discrimination and historical injustice, the individualistic and sometimes idiosyncratic ways in which people keep their faith may be an impediment to establishing the claim. Judges can better track the connection between a legal restriction on a religious practice and discrimination against a group if there exists a static understanding of which practices are integral to the group's beliefs and commitments and who counts as a member of the group. If religious practices are idiosyncratic and membership is fluid, then it becomes more difficult for courts to establish that a legal restriction on a religious practice is actually a covert means to exclude group members from the public sphere or otherwise deny them the equal benefits of citizenship. This is well illustrated in *SAS*, where internal group pluralism with respect to veiling is uncontested and obvious to the court. The fact that veiling is not a pervasive or essential practice for devout Muslims makes it more difficult for the claimant to argue that a connection exists between the legal prohibition and discrimination against Muslims as a group. A far stronger argument for striking down the law could be developed if all Muslim women wore the full-face veil.

In short, where religion is treated as a matter of identity, groups are caught in a dilemma: they must choose whether to provide public decision-makers with a sociologically realistic and often pluralistic depiction of the group or an essentialist one. The former may show a group's membership to be fluid and its practices to be internally contested, but it thereby provides a weak basis from which to prove social exclusion and unjust group-based treatment. The latter, however, runs the risk of admitting definitions of group identity that are static and stereotypical and that thereby exclude and disadvantage some members. Whereas courts might find it helpful to use a particular religious commitment or practice to trace social exclusion, the real-world political dynamic created by the strategic deployment of an identity claim invites courts effectively to strengthen a narrow and non-voluntary understanding of group identity.

One might conclude from this that the identity approach ought to be avoided because its success sometimes depends on judges ignoring internal group pluralism and accepting group stereotypes. While this risk is real, it is not a sufficient reason to abandon arguments based on identity because the alternatives to the identity approach can have worse outcomes. After all, one leading alternative to which many courts and governments remain strongly attracted is the choice approach, which is insensitive to claims about group-based marginalization and exclusion in the first place.

A third implication of the identity approach is that it can place a significant burden on public institutions – courts in particular – to provide a stable and publicly acceptable method of assessing whether the law unfairly restricts a religious practice and, if so, whether the practice ought to be accommodated. In one sense, this burden is no different from what courts deal with whenever they address structural inequality related to gender or race (although these cases can be difficult as well). All such cases require a legal assessment of whether rules, effectively rather than merely intentionally, exclude an identifiable group from access to the public sphere in the absence of a compelling state interest.

Yet, unlike cases that involve structural social inequality related to race and gender, in religious cases the disputed practices which minority claimants relate to their religious commitments – veiling, *kirpans*, Sabbath observance, peyotism, and so on – are sometimes poorly understood and elusive from a legal standpoint. For one thing, Western courts usually recognize that religious commitments vary from one believer to the next, which means that legislation can run afoul of the practices of some adherents and not others, as was true in *SAS*, or it can prohibit practices that are optional for group members, such as peyotism among members of the Native American Church.[42] And even if a court is willing to accept a practice as a non-negotiable feature of the claimant's identity, it must still assess the meaning and significance of the practice in order to determine whether the legislative restriction impairs an important part of the religious or cultural element of the practice and thereby denies the claimant some important freedom or matter of equality. For instance, is the applicant's inconsistent use of a full-face veil in *SAS* a credible reflection of a sincere religious belief, or does it display a wildly idiosyncratic interpretation of the practice? In addressing this kind of question, courts decide which elements of disputed practices are religiously significant, thereby distinguishing elements that may be legally restricted from those that ought to be protected for the purpose of protecting freedom and equality.

Without a doubt, making these kinds of assessments is difficult and, as many studies report, courts have made mistakes. Judges sometimes employ crude stereotypes about minorities that entrench conservative values or trigger cultural defensiveness within minority groups. Such instances have proven especially problematic for women.[43] Yet only by understanding what is at stake in identity claims can public decision-makers come to

42 On the problem of individual variation in religious practice and its legal protection, see WF Sullivan, *The Impossibility of Freedom of Religion* (Princeton University Press 2007).

43 SM Okin, 'Feminism and Multiculturalism: Some Tensions' (1998) 108 *Ethics* 661; A Shachar, *Multicultural Jurisdictions* (Oxford University Press 2001).

understand the normative weight that minorities attach to specific practices. Without such understandings, judges are left to 'reason by analogy', that is, to use majority practices as their standard for what 'equality looks like' and thereby forgo the opportunity to reflect on the possibility of 'false equality' or equalities that do not matter.

It is important to recognize that the risks associated with misinterpreting identity are less symptomatic of cases where the choice or interest approaches are adopted; for this reason, these other approaches remain attractive today. In contrast to the identity approach, the choice approach merely asks whether claimants are free to choose their religious and cultural commitments, allowing that they must absorb some costs for the choices they make. By taking this approach, judges can often avoid inquiring into the exact nature and significance of the religious practice to the believer because, as far as the court is concerned, what matters about the disputed commitment is only that it is sincerely held. Once sincerity has been established, the focus of the choice approach turns to assessing whether the costs that religious believers absorb for their choices effectively prohibit them from acting in accordance with the choices they have made. Just as some judges argued in Canada that Sunday closing laws do not prohibit Jews from observing the Sabbath, but rather that their observance imposes on them the cost of having to close shop on Saturday as well as Sunday, judges on the ECtHR might have argued that the French law prohibiting full-face veils does not prohibit the claimant in *SAS* from wearing the veil, but instead, by veiling, she chooses to absorb a cost which includes working at home, relying on others to buy her groceries or to pick up her children from school, and so forth. According to the choice approach, the only relevant question for the court is whether this cost is so high that it effectively amounts to a legal prohibition on a deeply held religious belief. In contrast, the identity approach can require that judges interpret the significance of religious commitments and practices, and pass judgment on these practices, while having little understanding of them.

Conclusion

Choice, interest, and identity represent distinct ways to understand religious commitments that are tied to different frameworks for public decision-making regarding the protection of religious minorities. These frameworks in turn illuminate different kinds of injustices that are associated with limiting minority religious practices. Each framework operates according to a partial and limited perspective on religious and cultural commitments and, as such, they are all liable to distort religious claims. Clearly distinguishing among these frameworks helps to illuminate some challenges that courts confront in deciding cases having to do with the protection of religious minorities.

The first challenge to confront is that the choice approach is limited in ways that are increasingly impossible to ignore. For example, state policies that ban veils among public employees, or favour religious symbols on school walls, attract criticism today, in large part because they are viewed as buying into the myth that individuals come to their religious commitments in a fully voluntary way and should be liable for the consequences of their choices. Even though the identity approach does not inform the decisions of judicial majorities in most legal cases, it may increasingly inform the way in which publics respond critically to these decisions.

Second, while the strategic and often deeply political ways in which the need for religious accommodation is defended in the public sphere can obscure internal group pluralism, a sociologically realistic approach to religious practices may be unsuited to advancing a convincing legal case for rectifying injustice towards a group, and this fact is the source of a dilemma for many groups that have just grievances against state policies. As the identity approach shows, the most convincing case for tracking injustice sometimes creates an incentive for groups to generalize and even exaggerate the importance and role of their practices.

Finally, courts and other public institutions are expected to have the capacity to understand and reflect fairly and critically on the practices and distinctive standpoints of different groups and be sensitive to the struggles that have informed them. This means that sometimes courts must assess evidence about the role and significance of a religious practice, even if doing so places onerous demands on them, because the alternative to recognizing different conceptions of the world presents even greater challenges.

5 Appeals to choice and sexual equality

Debates over religious attire

Monique Deveaux

Introduction

Calls to restrict or regulate certain gendered customs[1] associated with cultural and religious minority communities in liberal democracies – notably Muslim women's veiling – often appeal to the norm of sexual equality. While the precise content of this norm is rarely spelled out, those in favour of restricting such practices typically point to the rights of girls and women to live self-directed lives free of strong social constraints and to be regarded as having value and dignity equal to that of boys and men. In this familiar narrative, proponents of restrictions on the *hijab* (headscarf) and/or the *niqab* (face veil) see sexual equality as closely intertwined with the norm of personal autonomy. Yet, paradoxically, those who object to such restrictions, including women from the affected groups, also reach for ideals of choice and freedom to oppose state interference. In this chapter, I suggest that this dual appropriation is made possible by the contrasting conceptions of autonomy that undergird these opposing positions.

Proposals to restrict gendered practices of religious and cultural minorities rely upon an ideal of substantive autonomy that requires not only that one live a self-directed life relatively free of excessive family and social pressure, but that the content of one's choices be compatible with the liberal value of personal autonomy. Conversely, those who defend such customs – and/or women's right to practice them – ground their position in a thinner, more procedural account of autonomy. According to this conception, one acts autonomously insofar as one makes important decisions according to certain criteria, such as reflexivity or authenticity. These different accounts of what autonomy requires in turn inform contrasting understandings of what sexual equality entails. I argue that while proponents and critics of restrictions on veiling share a common commitment to women's legal and political equality, they disagree on whether such equality is compatible with extensive sex-role differentiation. Not surprisingly, then, rhetorical appeals to ideals of choice and women's equality do little to reduce normative conflict over Muslim veiling practices. Respectful and productive political dialogue about putatively competing commitments to

Author's note: This chapter draws some material from my chapter 'Regimes of Accommodation, Hierarchies of Rights' in C Maillé, G Nielsen, and D Salée (eds), *Revealing Democracy: Secularism and Religion in Liberal Democratic States* (Peter Lang 2013) 77.

1 In using the term *gendered* to refer to customs such as veiling that have come under the scrutiny of governments in liberal democracies, I do not mean to suggest that only minority groups (not the majority society) reinforce sex-differentiated norms – this would of course be false.

DOI: 10.4324/9781315413617-7

sexual equality and cultural/religious accommodation has, therefore, been rendered difficult or, at worst, impossible.[2]

In what follows, I argue that moving past this impasse would require, as a first step, that these divergent conceptions of personal autonomy and sexual equality be made more explicit in public debates about controversial customs. In particular, stakeholders in disputes over the status of sex-differentiated practices ought to say (and defend) what they think autonomy requires and what role it plays in sexual equality. A deliberative democratic approach to resolving disagreements over whether to legislate against controversial customs could help to throw into relief underlying disagreements about the value and demands of both autonomy and sexual equality. It would also reveal inconsistencies in key normative claims surrounding these principles.

I urge that these principles be made the subject of democratic deliberation whenever public proposals are made to regulate or restrict gendered practices. Nevertheless, I will argue that the conception of autonomy most suited to a highly diverse liberal society is a minimalist version of procedural autonomy supplemented by the insights of relational-autonomy feminist thinkers. By engaging in public deliberation about the contested meanings of key norms of sexual equality and autonomy, we may come to better understand competing appeals to choice, freedom, and women's equality in the controversies over Muslim veiling in liberal democracies.

Appeals to sexual equality

When France banned 'conspicuous signs' of religion from state schools in 2004 (in a move widely understood to target the Muslim headscarf), lawmakers invoked the ideals of sexual equality and *laïcité* (secularism). Feminist activists and public intellectuals joined with politicians in citing the need to protect girls from family pressures to wear the *hijab*, which they saw as symbolically separating girls from fellow students and preventing them from taking up a range of activities and career paths. In the years that followed, legislation was also passed in Belgium, as well as in a number of European municipalities (including Barcelona and several Swiss cantons) and regions (such as Russia's Stavropol region). These laws banned women from wearing the face-veiling *niqab* and *burqa* (a full-body outer garment incorporating a face veil) on public transport and in public places such as hospitals, schools, and government offices.

Asked by the French National Assembly to determine the constitutionality of a law banning face coverings, the Constitutional Council replied in the affirmative, stating that the face veil was at odds with French republican norms of civic life and that women who wore it 'find themselves placed in a situation of exclusion and inferiority clearly incompatible with the constitutional principles of freedom and equality'.[3] The council argued, in other words, that 'religious freedom considerations were outweighed by the arguments concerning sociability and gender equality.'[4] This assertion of the primacy of sexual equality over other values (such

2 In most liberal constitutional democracies, *sexual equality* and *gender equality* are used interchangeably in the legal instruments that refer to the state's commitment to the equality of women and men. As a consequence, I use both terms here without distinguishing them in the way that scholars of sex and gender frequently do.

3 JR Bowen, 'How the French State Justifies Controlling Muslim Bodies: From Harm-Based to Values-Based Reasoning' (2011) 78(2) *Social Research* 325, 328.

4 Ibid. 328.

as religious freedom) arguably signalled a hierarchy of rights that required greater normative defence. But such a defence was not deemed necessary, in the French context, because sexual equality was seen both as a core aspect of citizenship and as constitutively secular.

Citizenship, religion, and sexual equality

Liberal democracies conceive of citizenship in terms of universal values, including secularism. As sexual equality came to be seen as part of this universal civic identity, it too became linked with the ideal of religious neutrality, especially in states with a strong republican tradition such as France, where headscarf politics first emerged. In France, as Joan Scott explains, '*laïcité* means the separation of church and state through the state's protection of individuals from the claims of religion. (In the United States, in contrast, secularism connotes the protection of religions from interference by the state.)'[5] From this point of view, sexual equality, as one dimension of a secular, civic identity, therefore requires detachment from explicit signs of religious affiliation. If the norms of the religion in question draw attention to sexual differences in a particular way, then the removal of symbols of that religion from the public sphere becomes a matter of urgency. The close relationship between *laïcité* and gender equality thus has to do with the (symbolic) assurance of the universality of women's citizenship:

> Within the prevailing narrative of French republicanism, women are recognized as free and equal citizens because their citizenship or public identity is abstracted both from their gender identity, but also from any religious identity that might be assigned to them through a politics of recognition.[6]

Public discourse linking sexual equality to ideals of both religious and gender neutrality is not limited to the French republican context. In Québec, Canada, legislation that would have banned the *niqab* from public places was introduced in 2010 and again in 2013. While neither piece of legislation passed, both treated the principles of sexual equality and secularism as fundamentally intertwined. The first of these, Bill 94, stated that religious 'accommodations' (in public domains) must be consistent with the right of gender equality and the principle of religious neutrality.[7] A key aim of the later proposed legislation (Bill 60, known as the Charter of Values[8]) was to amend Québec's 1976 Charter of Human Rights and Freedoms so as to make clear that the principles of secularism and gender equality limit the right of religious freedom and therefore the kinds of 'accommodations' that can be made to individuals in respect of their faith.[9]

5 J Scott, *The Politics of the Veil* (Princeton University Press 2007) 15.

6 E Daly, 'Laïcité, Gender Equality and the Politics of Non-Domination' (2012) 11 *European Journal of Political Theory* 292, 293.

7 National Assembly Bill 94: An Act to Establish Guidelines Governing Accommodation Requests Within the Administration and Certain Institutions 2010, ch 2(4).

8 Bill 60: Charter Affirming the Values of State Secularism and Religious Neutrality and of Equality Between Women and Men, and Providing a Framework for Accommodation Requests National Assembly Bill (2012–2014) (Québec Charter of Values).

9 Feminists from the majority Québec society in general applauded this clarification: the Conseil du statut de la femme du Québec (CSF) had previously urged the government to add a second sexual equality clause to the existing Charter so as to ensure that sexual equality would be understood to *trump* religious freedom. See the CSF's Gazette des femmes (September/October 2007) 23.

The singling out of Muslims as a racialized community in need of a lesson and directive in Québec's liberal values was a common theme in the media coverage and the public opinion revolving around the two bills. Not surprisingly, women's centres in the province reported a dramatic rise in the public harassment of women wearing the *hijab* and the *niqab* following the introduction of the proposed charter in the legislature.[10]

Sexual equality and difference

It is worth taking a closer look at the connection that proponents of veiling regulations in Québec, France, and other liberal democracies draw between the Muslim headscarf and women's inequality in Islam. The core belief expressed in the rhetoric surrounding the introduction of such proposed legislation was that head and face veiling effects women's physical separation from men (for religious or other purposes), and that this in turn reflects their sexual subordination.[11] Separateness, in this view, denotes difference, and difference inescapably denotes inferior status. The lack of both sexual and cultural integration signalled by the *niqab* in particular (but even, for some critics, the *hijab*) is seen as an impediment to the realization of the universal rights guaranteed by citizenship (in France or Québec, for example). In the French context, sameness was not only about gender integration and women's parity with men, but also about access to French civic identity:

> Ascriptions of difference, conceived as irreducible differences, whether based on culture or sex or sexuality, are taken to preclude any aspiration to sameness. If one has already been labelled different on any of these grounds, it is difficult to find a way of arguing that one is or can become the same.[12]

Yet the belief that sexual equality (like civic equality generally) requires gender integration in the sense of sameness, is, to say the least, controversial. More importantly, it is also illusory, or only rather selectively applied, given that in liberal democracies women's bodies are (typically) highly differentiated from men's. As feminist sociologists, anthropologists, and cultural studies theorists (among others) have amply demonstrated, a wide range of feminine bodily practices in the West, sustained by the fashion and beauty industries, cosmetic surgery, and advertising generally, serve to uphold bodies that are marked as female. Yet these are not seen, in the main, as incompatible with the principle of gender equality. The sexual sameness demanded by proposed bans on headscarves and *niqabs*, thus, is perhaps better understood in terms of a gendered ideal of autonomy for women, rather than genuine sex blindness. As Wendy Brown explains,

> The equation of secularism with women's freedom and equality often traffics in the tacit assumption that bared skin and flaunted sexuality is a token if not a measure of women's freedom and equality. Sexual difference is already written into this assumption

10 'Violence Against Muslim Women on the Rise, Group Says' (CBC News 2 October 2013) <www.cbc.ca/news/canada/montreal/violence-against-muslim-women-on-the-rise-group-says-1.1876564> accessed 3 May 2017.

11 S Bilge, 'La patrouille des frontières au nom de l'égalité en genre dans une "nation" en quête de souveraineté' (2010) 42 *Sociologie et Société* 197, 220.

12 Scott (n 5) 13.

> . . . since the equation of freedom with near nakedness in public is itself a gendered rather than generic sign of freedom: rarely is it suggested that men in loincloths are free whereas those in three-piece suits lack autonomy and equality.[13]

Brown's insight – that there is a covert expectation of sexual differentiation built into the Western conception of gender equality invoked by antiveiling laws – highlights the lack of even-handedness in many political appeals to sexual equality. Whether viewed as an expression of female modesty or as a different manner of sexualizing women ('sexualization that is robed, secreted from public view'[14]), the *hijab* is taken to be incompatible with a normative commitment to gender equality in ways that Western women's sexualized self-presentations are not. The neutrality and universality of this conception of sexual equality, at least as it is invoked in political discourses about minority women, is thus doubtful. This recognition is in part what gives rise to the suggestion that discussions of the gendered practices of minority religions or cultures should also ask about comparable mainstream social practices.[15]

Formal, substantive, or symbolic equality?

The inconsistency of the gender-sameness ideal also reveals that appeals to sexual equality are very often calls for formal rather than substantive equality. That is, the kind of equality demanded by antiveiling laws is same (or similar) treatment for men and women vis-à-vis the law, but not substantive, equal freedom in economic, social, and political life. The frequent references to the *hijab* (and its variants) as a so-called symbol of women's subordination and oppression evince this preoccupation with merely formal and symbolic dimensions of equality. In the Canadian context, the sexual-equality defence of legislation to ban religious garb from public places is arguably on a collision course with the substantive sexual equality guarantees stipulated by the Canadian Charter of Rights and Freedoms.[16] This is because legislation that prohibits women from wearing the veil in public places may be interpreted as jeopardizing their (substantively) equal access to critical public services (such as health care and child care) as well as to education and employment: government jobs (including the provincially run childcare system, hospitals, civil service) would be off limits to *niqabis* and *hijabis*, as would teaching jobs in public schools and possibly universities. Legal challenges to the proposed *niqab* ban on the grounds of its discriminatory impact on women are therefore likely.[17] For example, the 2011 Ministry of Immigration policy

13 W Brown, 'Civilizational Delusions: Secularism, Tolerance, Equality' in C Maillé, G Nielsen, and D Salée (eds), *Revealing Democracy: Secularism and Religion in Liberal Democratic States* (Peter Lang 2013) 52.

14 Ibid. 52.

15 A Eisenberg, *Reasons of Identity* (Oxford University Press 2009) 49; A Galeotti, 'Relativism, Universalism, and Applied Ethics: The Case of Female Circumcision' (2007) 14(1) *Constellations* 91; GB Levey, 'Liberal Autonomy as a Pluralist Value' (2012) 95(1) *The Monist* 103; A Phillips, *Gender and Culture* (Polity Press 2010) 25.

16 Canadian Charter of Rights and Freedoms (Constitution Act 1982, pt 1; Canada Act 1982 (UK), ch 11, sch B).

17 B Baines, 'Bill 94: Quebec's Niqab Ban and Sex Equality' (Women's Court of Canada 12 May 2010); no archived version available. However, freedom of religion rather than sex equality has subsequently been invoked more often in the Canadian context to defend the *niqab*. In February 2015, the Federal Court ruled in favour of Zunera Ishaq's challenge to a rule restricting her right to wear a *niqab* while taking the Oath of Citizenship; religious freedom grounds were central to her case. See note 18 below.

prohibiting women from wearing the *niqab* in Canadian citizenship ceremonies has recently been challenged.[18] Some evidence suggests that countries with strong anti-sex-discrimination laws are reluctant to introduce veiling restrictions precisely because of the prospect of legal challenges on grounds of sexual discrimination.[19]

The emphasis on formal rather than substantive equality implied by the proposed antiveiling legislation did not sit well with many Muslim women in Québec during this period.[20] Rather than target ostensibly symbolic markers of their subordination, many asked why the government did not redress the tangible inequalities they face in economic and social life. For example, immigrants (both men and women) from North and West Africa have much higher rates of unemployment than the general population, despite their higher levels of educational attainment on average. Moroccan and Algerian immigrants experience 17.5 per cent and 27.2 per cent unemployment respectively, as opposed to 8.2 per cent for the general population; for those who immigrated to Québec less than five years ago, these figures jump to 33.6 per cent and 35.4 per cent.[21] Structural barriers to Muslim women's access to education, employment, social programs, legal services, and housing were, however, not part of the public conversation about the *niqab* as discussed by media and politicians.

Québec's political leaders have arguably sought to mark the province's transition to a modern, secular society by appealing to an ideal of citizenship that uses recent immigrants – especially Muslims – as a cultural and racial foil. Similarly, in France, Scott writes:

> The headscarf controversies were largely an affair of those who defined themselves as representatives of a true France, with North Africans, Muslims, and 'immigrants' consigned to the periphery . . . . The veil became a screen onto which were projected images of strangeness and fantasies of danger – danger to the fabric of French society and to the future of the republican nation.[22]

Pointing to gender equality as a reason to oppose the *hijab* and/or *niqab* in liberal states also fits within a broader trend – namely, using women's equality to justify the 'current retreat from multiculturalism'.[23] By contrast, the justification offered for similar bans adopted in the past by Syria, Egypt, and Turkey highlight political and security concerns related to Islamic fundamentalism. In portraying Muslim women as thoroughly saturated by religion,[24] the rhetorical appeal to gender equality also depends upon an essentialist and static view of culture, at least in connection with the roles of women.[25] That the definition of gender roles and status play a pivotal role in national identity-building exercises should not surprise us, of course; many a commentator has noted the way that women have

18 *Ishaq v Canada* (Citizenship and Immigration) [2015] FC 156 <http://decisions.fct-cf.gc.ca/fc-cf/decisions/en/item/108049/index.do> accessed 3 May 2017.

19 B Sauer, 'Headscarf Regimes in Europe: Diversity Policies at the Intersection of Gender, Culture and Religion' (2009) 7 *Comparative European Politics* 75.

20 Québec Charter of Values.

21 A Lenoir-Achdjian et al., *Les difficultés d'insertion en emploi des immigrants du Maghreb au Québec: Une question de perspective* (2009) 15(3) *Report by the Institute for Research on Public Policy.*

22 Scott (n 5) 10.

23 A Phillips and S Saharso, 'The Rights of Women and the Crisis of Multiculturalism' (2008) 8(3) *Ethnicities* 292.

24 Brown (n 13) 50–52.

25 A Phillips, *Multiculturalism Without Culture* (Princeton University Press 2007) 8.

historically been seen to 'embody the nation' as well as to represent particular aspects of cultural otherness: 'Women . . . become the signifiers of national differences in the construction, reproduction and transformation of national categories. . . . It is women who come to "embody" the nation as such.'[26] Women's equal status – understood as women's legal and political equality, combined with parity of gender roles – therefore becomes a focal point in the process of national identity formation, especially when that identity is under threat.

Yet if legal challenges to veiling regulations can be made using sex discrimination laws, then clearly even legal sexual equality is not reducible to a single meaning (even within a single society). The demand that gender equality be given automatic legal precedence over other important principles, such as religious freedom, is thus problematic not least because of the contested and multivalent character of this norm. Feminist organizations have sometimes seen it as politically advantageous to insist that there is indeed a hierarchy of rights, with sexual equality at the top. For instance, Eisenberg discusses the strategic decision, by the feminist campaign opposed to sharia religious arbitration in Ontario, to steer clear of issues of religious freedom and pluralism and focus exclusively on women's equality.[27] According credence to religious freedom and pluralism was thought to weaken or even jeopardize the gender justice message.

While feminists may understandably be reluctant to open up a conversation about the meaning and application of sex equality in diverse societies, this is arguably a conversation we can no longer ignore. What do legal and political commitments to sexual equality consist of? How are these commitments to be balanced with other values, such as cultural and religious freedom? What policies best further goals? These large questions need to be revisited in light of the demands of diversity. Yet increasingly, questions about the meaning and demands of sexual equality in plural societies are only raised in connection with the practices of minority women, with the effect that 'a "crisis" frame of gender equality dominates the debate, characterized by a strict divide between a majority- and a minority-based gender equality agenda.'[28] This crisis framing encourages problematic ad hoc decision-making because it 'explicitly restricts gender equality issues to minority groups, and sets aside policies initiated to approach these "minority-specific" problems from the broader equality agenda'.[29]

The role of autonomy in assessing gendered customs

As noted in the introduction, an overly narrow notion of sexual equality as sameness (selectively understood) is undergirded by a substantive conception of autonomy. According to this conception, individuals are autonomous if their lives proceed on the basis of projects and commitments that they and they alone actively choose. The ideal of a self-directed life expressed by a substantive notion of autonomy might be thought to lead to an affirmation of difference, not sameness. After all, following John Stuart Mill's argument, different individuals surely want different things, resulting in diversity of beliefs and lifestyles, do they not?

26 N Meer, C Dwyer, and T Modood, 'Embodying Nationhood: Conceptions of British National Identity, Citizenship, and Gender in the "Veil Affair" ' (2010) 59 *The Sociological Review* 84, 85.

27 Eisenberg (n 15) 49.

28 M Teigen and T Langvasbraten, 'The "Crisis" of Gender Equality: The Norwegian Newspaper Debate on Female Genital Cutting' (2009) 17 *Nordic Journal of Feminist and Gender Research* 257.

29 Ibid. 257.

Yet group-based diversity is not especially encouraged by a normative ideal of substantive or strong autonomy, for the concept valorizes expressions of independence from one's social and cultural milieu and views with scepticism choices that appear to align with those of one's families and peers. The selective gender integration valued by the French and Québec governments in their appeals to sexual equality find their analogue in substantive autonomy's affirmation of an idealized agent who is independent and self-choosing, with a coherent and distinct life plan. This conception of the autonomous person as self-determining and sovereign has of course been widely challenged by a wide range of thinkers of many theoretical stripes, from communitarian to poststructuralist, postmodern to psychoanalytic. Even some Kantians object to a caricatured ideal of autonomy as precluding particularistic attachments or relationships of mutual dependence. Onora O'Neill has argued that in invoking an idealized account that reduces autonomy to independence and 'mere sheer independent choice',[30] we overlook 'the deeper reasons for valuing autonomy',[31] which have to do with living one's life in accordance with one's deepest moral beliefs and therefore go beyond mere 'preferences'.

Autonomy and independence

Theorists of multiculturalism have been particularly concerned to challenge an idealized conception of autonomy as independence, on the grounds that such a conception is incompatible with a commitment to cultural group rights. Insofar as multiculturalism affirms the importance of group-based identities and arrangements to the well-being of many citizens in liberal societies, it cannot readily endorse the belief that people are free if they have managed to resist strong socialization. In earlier work,[32] I argue that neither the strong conception of autonomy as requiring evidence of reflectively chosen, independent options,[33] nor the more moderate 'self-definition' account that is ostensibly content-neutral and emphasizes individuals' capacities for leading authentic lives,[34] is an appropriate ideal for adjudicating disputes about religious or cultural practices in a multicultural society. Both conceptions overemphasize personal or individual authenticity and view strong forms of socialization as incompatible with individual agency. This is particularly problematic when considering women's lives, for it leads to the conclusion that women who practice sex-differentiated customs have little or no agency. Uma Narayan notes that strong accounts of autonomy as independence and personal authenticity lead us to imagine only two possibilities: 'In the prisoner of patriarchy model, the veil is entirely imposed on the woman – she veils because she must. In the dupe of patriarchy model, she veils because she completely endorses all aspects of the practice.'[35] The political limitations inherent in the idealized account of autonomy that figures in the dupe and prisoner of patriarchy models are particularly evident in debates over veiling legislation. Notably, such explanations cannot readily account for

30 O O'Neill, *Bounds of Justice* (Cambridge University Press 2000) 39.
31 Ibid. 49.
32 M Deveaux, *Gender and Justice in Multicultural Liberal States* (Oxford University Press 2006).
33 Such as Robert Young's conception: see R Young, 'Autonomy and Socialization' (1980) 89 *Mind* 565; R Young, *Personal Autonomy: Beyond Negative and Positive Liberty* (St. Martin's Press 1986).
34 Such as D Meyers, *Self, Society and Personal Choice* (Columbia University Press 1989).
35 U Narayan, 'Minds of Their Own: Choices, Autonomy, Cultural Practices, and Other Women' in L Antony and C Witt (eds), *A Mind of One's Own: Feminist Essays on Reason and Objectivity* (Westview Press 2002) 419.

examples of legal and political activism by women defending their access to the *hijab* and the *niqab*.[36] Many of those on both sides of the conflict insist that autonomy is the trumping value: sceptics of veiling insist that the lack of autonomy expressed by this custom justifies its prohibition (at least in public places), while religious/cultural group members insist that their decision to veil validates it. In insisting that headscarves, *niqabs*, and/or *burqas* necessarily symbolize women's lack of autonomy and their subordination to men, veiling legislation in Québec and elsewhere succumbs to a substantive ideal of autonomy as requiring a fully self-directed life free of overt socialization.

Minority religious or cultural group members also often emphasize the language of choice in opposing state restrictions on practices that have come under scrutiny, though it is not clear that this serves them especially well. In so doing, they may lock themselves into a position that denies problematic aspects of customs as well as the possibility of internal transformation. At the level of political rhetoric, it also raises problems: in the case of veiling, calling the *hijab* or *niqab* a woman's choice stands in some tension with the claim that covering one's head is required by Islam (and therefore, insofar as she is devout, not a choice). While the normative currency of autonomy within liberal democracies seems to demand this framing, it arguably fails to capture the more complex realities of human agency as well as of the way that social practices evolve and are sustained.

Among feminist thinkers in particular, there is a long-standing and widely shared worry that substantive and thick procedural accounts of autonomy do not capture the complexities of women's agency within 'oppressive social environments'.[37] For instance, the language of free choice tends to individualize the story of how customs evolve – some women choose to wear the *hijab*, and others choose not to wear it. Similarly, we may find ourselves automatically suspicious of 'given' relationships and attachments (especially those with dimensions of dependence) as possible sources of pressure and socialization. Thus, one consequence of employing strong autonomy in debates over contested social practices is that it may lead us to assume that agency is nearly impossible in some coercive social contexts; it is 'as if the measure of how much agency we have is how little coercion has been exercised'.[38]

Disempowering circumstances such as economic dependency, denigration, and intimidation in one's intimate relationships, and ongoing abuse and violence can of course immobilize individuals and make it hard for them to exit. The claim that disempowering circumstances are tantamount to coercion, and so block all agency, may be a strategically useful stance when advancing certain political struggles. Feminist advocacy around domestic violence and sexual assault has frequently taken this approach. But the dichotomy between agency and coercion is otherwise unhelpful for understanding the dynamics of gendered religious and cultural practices in diverse liberal societies. There is a real 'risk of effectively

36 There have been several court challenges in Canada involving the *niqab*. The most high profile concerned an Ontario woman, Zunera Ishaq, who challenged a Ministry of Immigration rule that would prohibit her from wearing a *niqab* during the oath of citizenship ceremony (see n 18, above). Ishaq won her case at the Federal Court of Canada; a subsequent challenge by the federal government to stay the ruling pending a Supreme Court appeal was unsuccessful, and Ishaq took her citizenship oath in October 2015.

37 C Mackenzie and N Stoljar, 'Introduction: Autonomy Refigured' in C Mackenzie and N Stoljar (eds), *Relational Autonomy: Feminist Perspectives on Autonomy, Agency, and the Social Self* (Oxford University Press 2000) 22.

38 S Madhok, A Phillips, and K Wilson, 'Introduction' in S Madhok et al. (eds), *Gender, Agency, and Coercion* (Palgrave Macmillan 2013) 5.

locating coercion as unique to specific "non-Western" contexts',[39] as argued by postcolonial feminists like Narayan. Moreover, the ideal of substantive autonomy may encourage the blanket assumption that girls growing up in families that are religious and even patriarchal in structure are completely incapable of shaping any significant aspects of their lives, such as decisions about schooling, work, and relationships. But this seems patently false. Equally unsatisfying is the belief, implied by some strong accounts of procedural autonomy, that girls or women who undergo traditional gender role socialization can only ever exercise 'episodic' or 'programmic' autonomy at best.[40]

Kimberly Hutchings has argued that when feminists employ an agency/coercion binary, it has the effect of casting women as either 'choosers' or 'losers'; either free or utterly determined.[41] Proponents of legislation prohibiting women from wearing religious headscarves and face veils in public settings have portrayed the *hijab* as a custom that is imposed on women and functions as an enduring symbol of their subordinate status. The insistence by *hijabis* in liberal democracies that they 'choose' the veil is readily dismissed as reflective of their false consciousness. One problem with this view, however, is that it implicitly equates personal autonomy with the rejection of religious or cultural practices. Saba Mahmood has suggested that by locating women's agency in visible portrayals of resistance to social and religious strictures, we overlook the possibility of embedded agency, which can be exercised in a wider range of contexts.[42] Women can and do reflect upon their lives and make choices even within quite constraining circumstances: they redefine and renegotiate the strictures they face, as feminist anthropologists and sociologists like to say.

This is not to say that these circumstances are unproblematic or do not need changing, however. To assume that evidence of embedded agency or explicit choice signals the absence of unequal or coercive relationships and structures that need to be challenged would be foolish. Accordingly, the idea of 'agency as inequality's opposite'[43] must be resisted. Accounting for the exercise of autonomy – or, if we prefer, 'agency' – amidst conditions of gender subordination and oppression is a difficult but nonetheless important undertaking. In my view, autonomy still has a role to play in conversations about contested social practices, as do the concepts of choice and consent. I do not go so far as those who advocate a Foucauldian 'post-agency' position, according to which 'the liberal grammar of consent and self-determination' is swept aside, and 'the vocabulary of consent and choice becomes irrelevant.'[44] Nevertheless, an idealized account of autonomy is surely counterproductive in debates about the religious and cultural practices of minorities, most especially those associated with recent immigrants and members of religious minorities.

39 K Wilson, 'Agency as "Smart Economics": Neoliberalism, Gender, and Development' in S Madhok et al. (eds), *Gender, Agency, and Coercion* (Palgrave Macmillan 2013) 97.

40 As suggested, for example, by Meyers (n 34).

41 K Hutchings, 'Choosers or Losers? Feminist Ethical and Political Agency in a Plural and Unequal World' in S Madhok et al. (eds), *Gender, Agency, and Coercion* (Palgrave Macmillan 2013) 23.

42 S Mahmood, *The Politics of Piety: The Islamic Revival and the Feminist Subject* (Princeton University Press 2005) 167.

43 C Hemmings and AT Kabesh, 'The Feminist Subject of Agency: Recognition and Affect in Encounters With "the Other" ' in S Madhok et al. (eds), *Gender, Agency, and Coercion* (Palgrave Macmillan 2013) 31.

44 E Lépinard, 'Autonomy and the Crisis of the Feminist Subject: Revisiting Okin's Dilemma' (2011) 18 *Constellations* 205, 214.

One can, of course, reject an idealized view of autonomy as, essentially, independence marked by complete freedom of will, without abandoning the concept altogether:

> That one is autonomous does not mean that one's choices are uninfluenced or uncaused, for it is doubtful that such a notion is even coherent. Autonomous agency does not imply that one mysteriously escapes altogether from social influence but rather that one is able to fashion a certain response to it.[45]

Of the alternative conceptions of autonomy developed in response to criticisms of more idealized conceptions, two are especially useful for discussions about contested religious and cultural practices: procedural approaches to autonomy, which deny that autonomous lives must have any particular content and instead emphasize the importance of capacities for reflection and choice; and the idea of 'relational autonomy',[46] which insists that 'persons are socially embedded and [that] agents' identities are formed within the context of social relationships and shaped by a complex of intersecting social determinants, such as race, class, gender, and ethnicity'.[47] In my view, procedural and relational accounts of autonomy are not mutually exclusive. Both offer resources for rethinking autonomy in ways that do not depend upon binaries (such as coercion and agency, or coercion and equality), or privilege idealized versions of independence and choice. Whereas substantive autonomy subjects the content of individuals' life choices to scrutiny, procedural accounts, broadly speaking, place the spotlight on individuals' capacities and opportunities to live a life in keeping with their own reflective values and attachments.

Neither procedural nor relational accounts of autonomy require that one's choices depart dramatically from those endorsed by one's family or community, because they do not conflate autonomy and ideals of self-determination or individual sovereignty.[48] Instead, both begin from a broader account of agency allowing us to see that reflecting on one's values and attachments may come in a variety of forms, and may consist not only in rejecting, but also affirming, those values. Nor need the exercise of autonomy require overt actions: one's agency in the context of social and cultural practices may relate to internal, psychological processes, as well as to one's capacities for reflection, criticism, and reimagining.[49] Theorists of relational autonomy are particularly attentive to the internal dimensions of autonomy, and can enrich and complicate our understanding of key aspects of procedural autonomy: 'recognizing that agents are both psychically internally differentiated and socially differentiated from others calls for a reconceptualization of certain notions . . . such as integration, identification, critical reflection, and self-realization.'[50]

Seeking a way to capture the complexities of, and limits to, women's agential possibilities in so-called traditional religious and cultural settings in the West, Marilyn Friedman has advanced a content-neutral approach that stresses women's capacities and competencies for

45 L Barclay, 'Autonomy and the Social Self' in C Mackenzie and N Stoljar (eds), *Relational Autonomy: Feminist Perspectives on Autonomy, Agency, and the Social Self* (Oxford University Press 2000) 54.

46 C Mackenzie and N Stoljar (eds), *Relational Autonomy: Feminist Perspectives on Autonomy, Agency, and the Social Self* (Oxford University Press 2000); J Nedelsky, *Law's Relations: A Relational Theory of Self, Autonomy, and the Law* (Oxford University Press 2011); J Nedelsky, 'Reconceiving Rights as Relationship' (1989) 1 *Review of Constitutional Studies* 1.

47 Mackenzie and Stoljar (n 37) 4.

48 Deveaux (n 32) 160.

49 Ibid. 177; see also S Madhok, 'Action, Agency, Coercion: Reformatting Agency for Oppressive Contexts' in S Madhok et al. (eds), *Gender, Agency, and Coercion* (Palgrave Macmillan 2013) 108.

50 Mackenzie and Stoljar (n 37) 21.

acting in ways that reflect their 'wants, desires, cares, concerns, values, and commitments'.[51] Friedman is attentive to the relational dimensions of autonomy: she recognizes that our very capacities for autonomy are constituted through our social relationships, some of which have constraining and even oppressive dimensions. With this social backdrop in mind, she argues that 'autonomy competency is the effective capacity, or set of capacities, to act under some significant range of circumstances in ways that reflect and issue from deeper concerns that one has considered and reaffirmed.'[52] Following Friedman, I argue that paying attention to women's capacities for autonomy, even amidst strong sociocultural constraints, serves as an important corrective to stereotypes that reinforce the image of women of certain minority religions and cultures as largely lacking in agency.

Concern about these stereotypes is partly what has led to the emergence of a 'post-agency' perspective,[53] whose adherents worry that critical or revised conceptions of autonomy that reveal the agency of disempowered subjects fail to challenge familiar oppositions at a deep level. They propose that we focus instead on how structures of power give rise to particular expressions of subjectivity – a notion that encompasses what we may recognize as agency – but drop the normative baggage associated with autonomy.

Although it is tempting to heed the call to abandon discussions of the agential capacities of individuals, fraught as these are, I think it would be a mistake. We need, in my view, to ask about the degree to which, in any given circumstance or context, women are able to reflect upon, and possibly renegotiate and redefine – or indeed refuse – particular expectations, roles, and activities.

As relational autonomy feminists remind us, the internal and external processes that mark our relationships with particular norms and arrangements are always mediated through a set of social relationships. Our capacity for critical reflection on these norms is also limited or constrained by a range of relationships and social structures, such as those with particular gender scripts. Although it is not a simple matter, it is nonetheless possible for individuals to identify possibilities for responding to and renegotiating different aspects of their lives in a variety of contexts. Some of the most insightful descriptions of women's capacities for agency in constrained, even oppressive, circumstances emerge in discussions of economic empowerment initiatives in the global South. For example, reflecting on empowerment-building work with women in Afghanistan and Bangladesh, Naila Kabeer writes:

> However socially embedded women – and men – may be in the ascribed relationships of family, kin and community, it is in principle possible for them to attain a reflexive distance from these relationships, to become simultaneously observers of, and participants in, their own society. If it is through the 'given' relationships of family and kinship that women gain their sense of identity and personhood, then it is through participation in other 'chosen' forms of associational life that they may be able to acquire a reflexive vantage point from which to observe and evaluate these relationships.[54]

The post-agency view rejects this emphasis on capacities for procedural autonomy on the grounds that it still relies upon a flawed view of the relationship between human agency and structures of power. In my view, however, a thin procedural approach to autonomy

51 M Friedman, *Autonomy, Gender, and Politics* (Oxford University Press 2003) 6.

52 Ibid. 13.

53 E Lépinard (n 44) 214.

54 N Kabeer, 'Empowerment, Citizenship and Gender Justice: A Contribution to Locally Grounded Theories of Change in Women's Lives' (2012) 6 *Ethics and Social Welfare* 216, 223.

that asks about agents' capacity for reflection and action can provide valuable tools for asking about agency in unequal and even coercive contexts. The availability of tangible alternative options is also important when assessing individuals' procedural autonomy: 'for choice to be meaningful there have to be alternatives, the possibility of having chosen otherwise'.[55] Such options ought to be assessed in terms of the sociocultural norms and strictures of one's own identity or community – such as asking what an ultra-orthodox Jewish woman living in a particular setting may be 'permitted' to do. Of course, they also need to be assessed in relation to the broader social, economic, and political structures that condition our abilities and opportunities to act. As noted, North African Muslim women in Québec face a high rate of unemployment, structural racism, and discrimination in other areas of social life, factors which arguably limit the options open to them, such as whether to leave an abusive relationship, to have or not have additional children, or to undertake higher education. Particularly in the case of economically disadvantaged women, we need, as O'Neill says, to take 'seriously the ways in which their effective capacities and their opportunities for action (in Sen's terms, their capabilities and entitlements) constrain their possibilities for refusal and renegotiation'.[56]

Adaptive preferences theory

The ways in which economic deprivation and constrained social circumstances may limit and shape women's choices takes us into the difficult territory of adaptive preferences theory. Adaptive preferences are thought to be formed under conditions of unfreedom – whether economic, social, political, or a combination of these – and are therefore not thought to be authentic choices. How free are girls to choose to wear the *hijab* in Western countries? Some critics of veiling suggest that Muslim women in the West, at least in some settings, are not genuinely at liberty to form authentic preferences and so to make free choices.

It is tempting to simply dismiss the charge of adaptive preferences as invalid by virtue of the obvious fact that non-Muslim women's preferences, tastes, and choices are also shaped by their peer groups, families, and society at large. But suppose a more neutral case were to be made in support of critically scrutinizing all gendered practices that seem to be reflective of highly adaptive preferences. My response to this is threefold. First, it is surely the case that the place to contest gendered cultural practices that do not violate core rights is in the social sphere/civil society, not the courts. Second, if we think of adaptive preferences as problematic insofar as they are incompatible with a person's basic flourishing – as, say, Martha Nussbaum and Serene Khader have argued – then it is odd that Muslim women's veiling should trigger the adaptive preferences designation: surely it is not the case that wearing a *hijab* prevents a woman from developing capabilities, or flourishing, in key areas of her life. And finally, the charge that the *hijab* and/or *niqab* reflects the adaptive preferences of women who claim to choose it entails the suggestion that they lack autonomy in important areas of their lives. But this is not something that can be assumed in advance of extensive consultation and deliberation. More generally, while adaptive preferences surely do pose important problems from the vantage point of social justice, it is not clear that we should see them as 'autonomy deficits' at all, as Khader argues: 'If the problem with adaptive preferences is that they are unchosen, we should think that all unchosen preferences are

55 Ibid. 218.
56 O O'Neill (n 30) 167.

worthy of public interrogation . . . [but] we do not.'[57] Indeed, the suggestion that Muslim women who wear the *hijab* or *niqab* in a Western society suffer from adaptive preferences should lead us to question customs common to Western women that are arguably harmful, such as extensive body modification surgeries, say; but these do not attract the scrutiny of lawmakers.

The adaptive preferences framework also pivots on a notion of authentic preferences that in itself is difficult to defend. A similar problem besets some procedural approaches to autonomy, especially when applied to the problem of women's agency in oppressive contexts. For example, the background conditions for determining the validity of women's choices stipulated by Friedman strike me as too demanding in some circumstances. In addition to the presence of explicit consent, she cites two conditions for women's procedural autonomy:

> First, women's choices would have to be made under conditions that promoted the general reliability of their choices. This would require that women be able to choose among a significant and morally acceptable array of alternatives and that they be able to make their choices relatively free of coercion, manipulation, and deception. Second, women must have been able to develop, earlier in life, the capacities needed to reflect on their situations and make decisions about them.[58]

Despite Friedman's willingness to acknowledge that women in traditional gender roles might nonetheless be procedurally autonomous, given adequate competencies for self-reflection, I suspect that many religious and cultural arrangements would fall afoul of her conditions – including some that arguably ought not to be restricted, such as arranged marriage or religious education. It is useful to recall here Mahmood's warning of the danger of conflating autonomy and resistance, and in so doing, neglecting more embedded forms of agency. In making a similar criticism of Friedman (as well as Nussbaum), Andrea Baumeister writes:

> Because it may be difficult to establish whether women who continue to endorse traditional practices and life-styles genuinely had the opportunity to develop a more autonomous life, there is a danger that only the rejection of such a life-style will be taken as conclusive proof that the women indeed had, in Nussbaum's language, the opportunity to develop the relevant capabilities or in Friedman's terms enjoyed the conditions for the exercise of procedural autonomy.[59]

Friedman rightly takes a dim view of practices that prevent women from developing the capacity for reflection and action. However, it is less obvious that she is in fact urging a heavy-handed response to all such situations, in statements such as: 'If positive evidence reveals cultural conditions that impede the development of autonomy competencies in women or that prevent its exercise, then the consent of women living under those conditions does not justify the rights-violation practices.'[60] The operative term in this sentence, in

57 S Khader, *Adaptive Preferences and Women's Empowerment* (Oxford University Press 2011) 75.
58 M Friedman (n 51) 188.
59 A Baumeister, 'Empowering Minority Women: Autonomy Versus Participation' (2012) 11 *Contemporary Political Theory* 285, 289.
60 M Friedman (n 51) 192.

my view, is 'rights-violation': provided that we are talking about violations of existing rights, and not simply customs that appear sexist, then it seems to me that Friedman is correct. But were we to extend this requirement more broadly, to any practices or arrangements that appear to subordinate women, even if no actual rights violations have occurred, this would arguably require equal scrutiny of a wide range of customs of both mainstream and minority cultures. But it is not obvious that this would advance the causes of women's equality and agency.

The procedural approach to autonomy

I have argued that a more pared-down version of a procedural account of autonomy, one informed by the insights of relational theories of autonomy, provides the best array of tools for thinking about women's agency in constraining circumstances. But might such an account lack the critical capacity to help in adjudicating disputes over controversial – and possibly harmful – practices? I have argued elsewhere that this conception directs us to ask about the concrete supports for women's agency in diverse contexts, and to develop policies accordingly:

> Formal respect for the procedural autonomy of women in traditional communities would mandate certain protections against such harm, and support services funded by the liberal state whose aim would be to empower vulnerable women. If they are to resist, revise, and reform aspects of their cultural traditions, women's procedural autonomy therefore must be respected and protected.[61]

Again, however, the background conditions that shape women's capacity to negotiate aspects of the expectations and demands they face are not limited to structures within minority communities. Rather, they extend far beyond, to the local, regional, national, and even, arguably, global social and economic structures that impact their lives. This is why even suitably revised principles of autonomy and sexual autonomy by legislators or citizens seeking to regulate contested practices ought to give serious consideration to the broader structures that condition minority women's capacities and opportunities for agency. To fully consider these structures in the course of policy debates about contested practices, however, requires the meaningful inclusion of affected women in processes of fair political deliberation.

Conclusion: contesting norms in democratic deliberation

In earlier work, I have defended a deliberative democratic approach to contested religious and cultural practices in liberal states. This approach (which I do not flesh out fully here) stresses the importance of creating a variety of deliberative processes and spaces in which affected stakeholders can discuss and make decisions about social practices that are in tension with existing laws or core liberal values. I argue that these procedures of political deliberation, which are not required to yield deep moral consensus, ought to be bound by principles of non-domination, political inclusion, and revisability.[62] Political deliberation

61 M Deveaux (n 32) 174.
62 Ibid.

about contested practices may take the form of extensive, democratically structured government consultation with different community groups that have valuable perspectives on a particular custom, including hands-on knowledge of its benefits or harms. But in many instances, it will also need to include deliberative decision-making forums organized by communities themselves, which in turn feed into broader legislative processes. Strategic compromises are encouraged in this model of democratic deliberation.

A deliberative approach to resolving conflicts of culture poses certain risks, especially as there are no guarantees of liberal outcomes. But for now I would like to note the benefits. As an overriding concern, we need to make it possible to tell more complicated stories about these practices: Why do some community members participate in them and why do others not? What different meanings and purposes are attributed to them? What benefits are claimed on their behalf? Are these practices different in some contexts? Do the people who participate in them wholly endorse them, and what concerns or qualms do they have about them? The efficacy of case law is not at all clear in answering such questions. Instead, we need to move to political deliberation – the legislative realm – as a means of evaluating controversial practices.

To propose that we approach disputes about contested practices through public deliberation is also to invite debate about contrasting understandings of what sexual equality and autonomy entail, rather than using these principles as mere trump cards in wedge politics. As I have argued, these norms, so important to debates about women's status, are multifaceted and frequently contested: Do we endorse formal/legal or substantive sexual equality? If the latter, what precisely must it consist in? What aspects and expressions of personal autonomy are critical, and how are they best supported and protected? None of these questions can be answered *a priori*, in my view, without wide consultation with the affected communities. If cultural, religious, and racial/racialized minorities are excluded from processes of multicultural policy formation, subsequent legislation fails the normative test of democratic legitimacy and is arguably unlikely to be effective in practice.

It may be difficult, of course, to protect democratic deliberation about contested social practices from power asymmetries and entrenched stereotypes about cultural and religious groups. Moreover, whether we are talking about informal community consultation over proposed government legislation, open public hearings, or specially designed community political dialogues, valid concerns arise in connection with different agents' capacity and opportunities for political participation and influence. Depending on how inclusive the process is and how it is structured, some voices may be weighted too heavily and some may be muffled.

There are challenges to fair political participation, whether we are talking about government consultations with religious and cultural communities or closed forums that are open to group members alone.[63] Still, it is important to remember that in many cases of legislative initiatives to regulate cultural practices (from veiling restrictions to laws preventing forced

63 I agree with Baumeister that much more work needs to be done to 'define the background conditions that need to be met for women to make effective use of the opportunities for participation and voice that [deliberative] models aim to facilitate' (Baumeister [n 59] 286). I also note Eisenberg's reminder that where cultural conflicts specifically concern the unequal political status of some members, such as membership disputes within indigenous groups, the insistence on fair and equal terms of deliberation may seem no different than the requirement that cultural groups adhere to the norm of sexual equality (Eisenberg [n 15] 78).

marriage), affected women who have sought to be heard have been blocked by legislators and bureaucrats – those who are in positions of power outside of their 'own' communities. Those of us who urge that minority communities themselves must play a central role in assessing whether contested practices ought to be reformed or prohibited clearly need to keep thinking about how to avoid 'simply re-inscribing existing power relations'.[64] Critics may still object to public deliberation about contested practices on the grounds that it singles out minority arrangements for special scrutiny and reinforces the impression that integration is wholly the responsibility of these communities.[65] But a limited procedural account of autonomy, informed by a relational understanding of how our capacities for agency come to be shaped, can provide a helpful orientation to these challenges, including focusing our thinking about what political agency minimally requires.

Legislative attempts to prohibit or regulate controversial practices, which are frequently antidemocratic and frankly racist in tone, often have to do more with wedge politics and national identity building than with genuine concerns about minority women. But when particular practices or arrangements do come to the attention of legislators and become the subject of legislation, some response on the part of the broader society (and minority communities in the spotlight) is surely required. Ideally, that response will include a demand for deliberative forums in which members of the affected communities – most especially women, in the case of the *hijab* and the *niqab* – play a leading role.

Extensive inclusion of diverse stakeholders in political deliberation about contested practices complicates the story in important ways and paves the way for political compromises in three ways. In the first place, invited consultations as well as forums for public deliberation help to bring to light the issues and problems that different sectors of the affected communities perceive as important. The picture that emerges may and often does contrast sharply with the one that politicians imagine, as the example of antiveiling legislation in Québec has shown. Second, democratic consultation and deliberation can go a long way towards restoring broken trust and exposing false stereotypes and assumptions. The inclusion of affected communities signals respect for minority citizens' values and perspectives, and, arguably, is thus vital to the legitimacy of any subsequent proposed legislation. Finally, on pragmatic grounds, an inclusive, deliberative democratic approach to dealing with conflicts of culture can help policymakers draw on the expertise and experience of minority community organizations that have often grappled with the problems at hand for much longer.

My argument that we ought to move to a democratic and deliberative framework for dealing with the status of gendered customs like the *niqab* is not meant to lend credibility to opportunistic controversies generated in the course of wedge politics. We absolutely need to acknowledge the danger of according legitimacy to structures that are permeated by stereotypes about minority communities, unexamined attitudes of entitlement, and institutionalized power asymmetries. Having said this, there have been some surprising outcomes where broadly democratic deliberation has been used as a means to shape policy responses to a disputed custom.[66] Nor is it the case – to anticipate another objection – that formal deliberation and government consultations would necessarily replace the grassroots

64 A Baumeister (n 59) 293.

65 This assumption is made in media commentaries about contested practices, as Meer, Dwyer, and Modood suggest (n 26) 100.

66 For examples, see Deveaux (n 32).

political activism that has been so instrumental in bringing forward gender issues in immigrant and minority communities. While the *hijab* is, notably, not one of the issues that Muslim women's groups in liberal democracies have pressed, women's groups have nonetheless mobilized in impressive ways against proposed veiling regimes, in many cases forging cross-cultural links and solidarities.[67] What is crucial is that deliberative conversations about contested customs not be reduced to overly simplistic appeals to the multivalent norms of sexual equality and autonomy. Instead, public deliberation about disputed customs and corresponding policy proposals can offer ways to explore and debate the different meaning of these contested yet nonetheless valuable liberal principles.

67 In Belgium, according to one report, 'the hijab affair has to some extent . . . provoked the "interculturalization" of white feminist organizations that had not previously addressed the issue of cultural and religious diversity among women in Belgium. Some organizations inspired by the philosophy of active pluralism, are gradually engaging in intercultural dialogue and incorporating principles such as inclusive neutrality into their visions and activities.' G Coene and C Longman, 'Gendering the Diversification of Diversity: The Belgian Hijab (in) Question' (2008) 8 *Ethnicities* 302, 316.

6 Why the individual must be defended – seemingly against all anthropological odds

Olaf Zenker

Introduction

Generally speaking, personal autonomy refers to the capacity to govern oneself and 'to live one's life according to reasons and motives that are taken as one's own and not the product of manipulative or distorting external forces'.[1] Prominently related to the philosophy of, among others, Immanuel Kant, personal autonomy emerged as a key value of the Enlightenment and Western liberal modernity in general. The autonomous person is typically identified with the modern idea of the individual (if not the 'cult of the individual', to use Emile Durkheim's memorable phrase – see below). As a specific historical and sociocultural configuration, this celebration of 'individualism' has been based – as Steven Lukes points out[2] – on the two core values of 'equality' and 'liberty', which have been intimately linked to four basic ideas: the ultimate value and dignity of each human being, his or her capacity for self-direction and autonomy (as just mentioned), the right to privacy, and the potential for unique self-development and self-cultivation.

Such individualism has come in different varieties that are sometimes presented as intrinsically belonging together, although this is arguably not necessarily the case. These basic versions include, among others, the idea that every existence is either an individual or a collection of individuals (ontological individualism); that all knowledge emerges within the individual and derives from her sensations (epistemological individualism); that all explanations of social phenomena must ultimately be rooted in the meaningful actions of individuals (methodological individualism); that the individual is either the object or the source of morality (ethical individualism); that the individual has the prime responsibility for her spiritual destiny (religious individualism); that government is (or should be) based on the consent, representation, and protection of equal individuals and their rights (political individualism); that individuals are (or should be) free to engage in contractual relations within a market (economic individualism); and that the individual can be conceived as a pre-social entity with given interests, wants, purposes, and needs (that is, as an abstract individual), with which actually existing socio-cultural arrangements resonate more or less adequately.[3]

1 J Christman, 'Autonomy in Moral and Political Philosophy' in EN Zalta (ed), *Stanford Encyclopedia of Philosophy* (Spring 2015 edn); see <http://plato.stanford.edu/archives/spr2015/entries/autonomy-moral/> accessed 23 September 2016.

2 S Lukes, *Individualism* (*Key Concepts in the Social Sciences)* (Blackwell 1973).

3 Lukes (n 2); P Birnbaum and J Leca (eds), *Individualism: Theories and Methods* (Clarendon Press 1990); C Bird, *The Myth of Liberal Individualism* (Cambridge University Press 1999).

DOI: 10.4324/9781315413617-8

As one of the four basic ideas of the 'celebration' of the individual, personal autonomy crosscuts and permeates these different varieties of individualism. In underscoring the power of agents to have authority over their own actions, the idea of individual autonomy thereby objects by definition to paternalistic interventions from outside, as the latter undermine the ability of agents to govern themselves, that is, their autonomy. Thus conceptually opposed to paternalism, personal autonomy becomes haunted by a profound paradox that arises when paternalism is applied precisely *in order to* protect and secure personal autonomy – in other words, when a person's actions are interfered with against that person's will for the purpose of advancing that person's 'real' good.[4] This paradox of personal autonomy becomes particularly – though not exclusively – apparent in contexts of cultural diversity, where individual choices might appear not to conform to expectations – often originating in the West – of 'truly' autonomous behaviour. Such situations might then be interpreted as inviting paternalistic interventions in order to uphold that individual's 'true' autonomy against her own non-autonomous 'will', thereby instantiating problems associated with the 'guardian function' of external agents such as the state, as highlighted in the introduction to this volume.

While constituting an important quandary in Western philosophy and an intricate practical problem in the workings of modern law as exported globally from the West, individualism with its attendant paradox of personal autonomy has been categorically challenged by prominent and time-honoured anthropological arguments. Within the history of anthropology as a modern discipline, a dominant strand of thought has followed Durkheim in debunking the individual with its proclaimed personal autonomy, exposing it as a Western particularity rather than an idea of universal applicability. In other words, seen from such a perspective, the paradox of personal autonomy reveals itself to be a pseudo-problem, as the individual with her personal autonomy turns out to be a misplaced concept to begin with – a concept, in other words, in need of abandonment. The main thesis of this chapter is that this widespread anthropological conclusion is mistaken. I will argue instead that for a number of reasons the universality of the individual must be defended, a move that would appear to go against all anthropological odds but that is, in fact, not only consistent with anthropological thinking, but even a logical and necessary outcome of it. Ultimately, my argument thus amounts to little more than a reaffirmation that the paradox of personal autonomy inscribed into the figure of the universal individual is a real one and continues to constitute a thorny theoretical, politico-legal, and moral problem to be reckoned with.

In the first part of this chapter I trace the prevailing line of anthropological reasoning that is critical of the individual, starting with Durkheim's argument about 'the cult of the individual', moving onto Marcel Mauss's discussion of historically variable notions of the 'person' and 'self' and Louis Dumont's case for individualism as a Western exception, and ending with recent anthropological arguments about 'dividuals' and 'porous subjects'. Subsequently, I show how these ideas have been imported into cultural psychology, where they have been further developed into influential arguments about a profound ideal-typical contrast between the 'independent self' of the West and the 'interdependent self' of, basically, the rest. Such arguments, it seems, ensure that mainstream anthropology has tended to favour 'methodological holism/collectivism' and dismiss, as ethnocentric, 'methodological individualism'. In the second part of this text, I critically engage, in turn, with this

4 Christman (n 1).

widespread anthropological critique of the individual. After briefly summarizing arguments from psychological and cognitive anthropologists against the strong relativism of cultural psychology and mainstream anthropology, I focus on four main reasons why the individual must be defended, which are situated within the fields of logic, social theory, epistemology, and morality. Thus attempting to rehabilitate the individual from within anthropology, my chapter reaffirms the continuing relevance of the predicaments surrounding the paradoxes of personal autonomy for both social theory and legal practice that the contributions in this volume attend to in various ways.

The anthropological case against the universal individual

In 1861, Sir Henry Sumner Maine published *Ancient Law*, a study on ancient law's 'connections with the early history of society and its relation to modern ideas', as the book's subtitle reads.[5] In one of the foundational texts of anthropology as a modern discipline and highly influential for subsequent legal theory and practice, Maine forcefully argues for a comparative and historical jurisprudence, strongly criticizing ahistorical approaches such as the state-of-nature and social contract theories of, for instance, Thomas Hobbes, John Locke, Jean-Jacques Rousseau, and Immanuel Kant. Most legal systems, Maine claims, do not recognize the rights-bearing individual so central to the modern West, privileging instead group rights. Such systems, according to Maine, do not change much over time. However, those rare systems that actually are progressive follow a trajectory famously summarized as 'a movement *from Status to Contract*':[6]

> The movement of the progressive societies . . . has been distinguished by the gradual dissolution of family dependency, and the growth of individual obligation in its place. The Individual is steadily substituted for the Family, as the unit of which civil laws take account . . . . Starting . . . from a condition of society in which all the relations of Persons are summed up in the relations of Family [i.e., through status], we seem to have steadily moved towards a phase of social order in which all these relations arise from the free agreement of Individuals [i.e., through contract]. In Western Europe the progress achieved in this direction has been considerable.[7]

It is somewhat ironic that despite Maine's insistence on a historical approach, his scheme nevertheless lent itself to universalist-evolutionary interpretations, in the course of which the individual was seen as increasingly 'freed' from its former embeddedness in a constraining culture of group-specific rights.

It was such a reading of a quasi-natural individualism freed and distinguished from the social facts of the *conscience collective* characterizing traditional societies that Emile Durkheim strongly argued against.[8] By nature, humans are not free and equal, as the French *Declaration of the Rights of Men and of the Citizen* proclaimed in 1789; instead, it was the social facts of modern society characterized by a high degree of division of labour, combined

5 HS Maine, *Ancient Law: Its Connections With the Early History of Society and Its Relation to Modern Ideas* (Cambridge University Press [1861]2012).
6 Ibid. 170, emphasis in the original.
7 Ibid. 168, 169–170.
8 See, e.g., E Durkheim, *The Division of Labor in Society* (Free Press [1893]1984) 162.

with its deep Christian roots, that led to collective representations of all humans as free and equal by nature. 'The cult of the individual' is as much a social and cultural fact, Durkheim insists, as any other religious celebration of society (such as, for instance, Australian totemism); it merely differs with regard to the underlying social structures determining the particularities of this civil religion that have come to prevail in the modern West.[9]

Durkheim's argument proved highly influential, laying the foundations for subsequent anthropological studies claiming to unmask allegedly universal individualism as a mere Western particularity. Marcel Mauss made an important contribution in this direction when, in a lecture given in 1938, he sketched a history of the ways in which different societal structures produced divergent senses of the 'person' and 'self'.[10] According to Mauss, during the first tribal stage of *personnage*, people are conceived merely in their outward appearance as role-takers or characters, exhibiting a limited stock of structural features of their clan from which they cannot be separated (such as the names or reincarnated souls of mythical figures). In the next classical stage of *persona*, humans end up being regarded as 'complete entities, independent of all others save God'.[11] Yet their politico-legal existence as free and responsible citizens still lacks inner life and conscience. This situation changes in the third stage, Christianity, when human beings start to be imagined as moral persons (*personne*). All political, legal, and economic life is seen as rooted in individuals, who are – literally – 'indivisible', rational and equipped with a sacred soul and proper conscience. With the emergence of modern psychology in the Western stage of *moi*, this individual finally turns into a 'self' that is increasingly knowledgeable of it-*self*, *self*-conscious and *self*-interested. Hence, the modern individual, far from being a pre-social entity that has been merely freed from 'Civilization and its Discontents' (to use the Freudian phrase),[12] is analysed by Mauss as the historical product of a peculiar social formation.

This approach of situating individualism as a modern ideology in a broad anthropological perspective was taken up with particular verve by Louis Dumont.[13] Combining what he describes as 'the intellectual history of our modern civilization' with comparative studies in social anthropology, he sets himself the task of demonstrating that the supreme moral value attached to the autonomous individual is actually a peculiar exception to the rule prevailing among civilizations, past and present, which normally valorize society as a whole. In his attempt to explain this historical peculiarity, Dumont turns to religion and contrasts the historical sociology of Western Christianity with that of traditional Hinduism: both, Dumont insists, knew the figure of 'outworldly individuals' who had to renounce the world and leave society behind in order to develop their own independent spiritual destiny. However, while the Hindu world-renouncer continues to exist only outside ordinary social life, the specific Western history of Christianity (especially through the roles played by the Catholic Church and the Protestant Reformation) allowed the outworldly Christian gospel to infuse the structures of society itself. In this way, a truly individualistic society emerged

9 E Durkheim, 'Individualism and the Intellectuals' in E Durkheim (ed), *On Morality and Society: Selected Writings* (University of Chicago Press [1898]1973) 43.

10 M Mauss, 'A Category of the Human Mind: The Notion of Person; the Notion of Self' in M Carrithers, S Collins, and S Lukes (eds), *The Category of the Person: Anthropology, Philosophy, History* (Cambridge University Press [1938]1985) 1.

11 Ibid. 14.

12 S Freud, *Civilization and Its Discontents* (J. Cape & H. Smith 1930).

13 L Dumont, *Essays on Individualism: Modern Ideology in Anthropological Perspective* (University of Chicago Press 1986).

in which modern Christians can simultaneously be individuals and 'inworldly'. Although this peculiar model of moral individualism, originating in the West, has meanwhile been exported around the globe, Dumont claims that its future is uncertain because moral holism still ultimately constitutes the most common model through which non-Western societies make sense of themselves.

This line of anthropological reasoning, which undermines the universal applicability of individualism by exposing its historical and cultural particularity and insists instead that holism prevails in many societies, has recently been joined by debates about 'individuals' and 'dividuals'. While also rejecting individualism as a central motivating force in Hinduism, McKim Marriott and Ronald Inden suggest doing so for a different reason: these authors claim that Hindu thinking is actually particulate rather than holistic, meaning that the person is here conceptualized rather as a 'dividual'.[14] Prominently taken up by Marilyn Strathern when differentiating Melanesian concepts of selfhood from the Western individual, this 'dividual' has emerged within contemporary anthropological debates to stand for sociocentric notions of personhood, whereby the person is considered to be divisible, composite, and fractal, comprising interrelated but essentially independent components;[15] such sociocentric persons reveal themselves as heteronomous actors who essentially follow sociocultural scripts.[16] Anthropological arguments in this mould, exemplified by Strathern's insistence on relationality and 'partial connections',[17] continue to proclaim that 'the porous dividual more closely approaches an accurate ontology than the atomistic Western individual'.[18]

The widespread anthropological insistence that the Western conception of what is variably described as 'the individual', 'the person', or 'the self' is of little value when dealing with non-Western societies has been taken up and further elaborated within cultural psychology. In recent decades, cultural psychology has developed into a strongly relativist subdiscipline within (if not against) general psychology, which typically operates with precisely those universalist assumptions about the unitary, self-conscious, and egocentric individual that Mauss identified as the rather late and peculiar form of the *moi* (see above). In contrast, cultural psychologists have propagated 'the study of the way cultural traditions and social practices regulate, express, and transform the human psyche, resulting less in psychic unity for humankind than in ethnic divergences in mind, self, and emotion'.[19] Against this backdrop, the Durkheimian tradition within anthropology of the individual as a Western particularity has been favourably received by cultural psychologists, who have often subscribed to the following often-quoted and influential dictum by Clifford Geertz:

> The Western conception of the person as a bounded, unique, more or less integrated motivational and cognitive universe, a dynamic center of awareness, emotion, judgment,

14 M Marriott and RB Inden, 'Towards an Ethnosociology of South Asia Caste Systems' in KH David (ed), *The New Wind: Changing Identities in South Asia* (Mouton 1977) 227.

15 M Strathern, *The Gender of the Gift: Problems With Women and Problems With Society in Melanesia* (University of California Press 1988).

16 K Smith, 'From Dividual and Individual Selves to Porous Subjects' (2012) 23 *The Australian Journal of Anthropology* 50.

17 M Strathern, *Partial Connections* (Updated Edition, AltaMira Press 2004).

18 Smith (n 16) 60.

19 RA Shweder, 'Cultural Psychology – What Is It?' in JW Stigler, RA Shweder, and GH Herdt (eds), *Cultural Psychology: Essays on Comparative Human Development* (Cambridge University Press 1990) 1.

> and action organized into a distinctive whole and set contrastively both against other such wholes and against a social and natural background is, however incorrigible it may seem to us, a rather peculiar idea within the context of the world's cultures.[20]

In an influential text, Richard Shweder and Edmund Bourne follow up on the question of whether the concept of the person actually does vary cross-culturally.[21] For this, they employ an experimental task approach, comparing how Indian (Oryas) and Western (American) subjects describe their close acquaintances. Noting that Oryas do so in more concrete and context-dependent ways while Americans use more abstract and context-independent formulations, the authors conclude that the two sets of actors maintain opposing conceptions of the person: Oryas tend to conceive of the person in a sociocentric way that subordinates individual interests to the good of the collectivity and does not distinguish between individual and social roles. Americans, in contrast, have a predominantly egocentric conception of 'an autonomous, abstract individual existing free of society yet living in society'.[22]

Building on arguments from social and cultural psychology (like Shweder's and Bourne's) as well as anthropology, Hazel Rose Markus and Shinobu Kitayama (1991) offer a synthesizing model of alternative 'construals of the self': for the 'independent self' prevalent in Western societies, others are important for comparison and reflected appraisal, but the self is seen as complete, whole, and autonomous without them; attributes, abilities, and motives are seen as internal and their expression (through which one stands out) is valued.[23] By contrast, the 'interdependent self', which prevails in Asian, African, Latin American, and southern European cultures, includes others '*within* the boundaries of the self because relations with others in specific contexts are the defining features of the self' (emphasis in the original);[24] important attributes of the self, and its value, follow from external, public relationships and one's capacity to fulfil role expectations and maintain harmony (rather than from standing out). Based on a number of empirical psychological studies (especially on Japan), the authors claim that these differences in self-construal have much more profound consequences for people's cognitions, emotions, and motivations than previously imagined.

While influential within cultural psychology, such arguments about dichotomized conceptions of independent, individualistic, egocentric, separate, autonomous, idiocentric, or self-contained selves, on the one hand, and interdependent, collective, sociocentric, holistic, organic, allocentric, ensembled, contextualized, or relational selves, on the other, arguably still constitute a minority position within psychology in general. In anthropology, however, according to Nigel Rapport and Joanna Overing, the situation has been somewhat different:

> In much mainstream [anthropological] debate, sensitivity to the individualistic is still denigrated as 'methodological individualism': as erroneously couching explanation in terms of characteristics of individuals, their behaviours and interests, and so procuring insufficient purchase on the broader and deeper conditions of socio-cultural 'realities'.

20 C Geertz, 'On the Nature of Anthropological Understanding' (1975) 63 *American Scientist* 47.

21 RA Shweder and EJ Bourne, 'Does the Concept of the Person Vary Cross-Culturally?' in RA Shweder and RA LeVine (eds), *Culture Theory: Essays on Mind, Self and Emotion* (Cambridge University Press 1984) 158.

22 Ibid. 190.

23 HR Markus and S Kitayama, 'Culture and Self: Implications for Cognition, Emotion, and Motivation' (1991) 98 *Psychological Review* 224.

24 Ibid. 245–246.

> The centre-ground of anthropology, in other words, continues to be a preserve of 'methodological collectivism' – positing social phenomena as determined by factors which bypass individual rationality, and hence envisaging cultural development quite independently of individual consciousness. Here is a continuing insistence that the distinction between the individual and the societal is specific to the West and must be collapsed in favour of the latter – or at least of 'social relations' . . . for anthropology persuasively to encounter cultural others.[25]

Of course, there have been some anthropological studies that put special emphasis on the cross-cultural importance of the self and individual in understanding culture and society. Thus Anthony Cohen advances an alternative anthropology of identity that puts 'self-consciousness' centre stage, insisting that any understanding of collective phenomena has to be approached from the self upwards.[26] Continuing this conversation, Nigel Rapport has argued in a number of interrelated works[27] that 'individualism' as a particular historical-cultural conceptualization of person or self must be distinguished from 'individuality', referring to 'the universal nature of human existence whereby it is the individual who possess agency', and that 'this individuality of consciousness and agency is extant whatever the currency of individualism as a cultural norm.'[28] Yet such anthropological studies have clearly constituted a minority position. Jan Patrick Heiss and Albert Piette make this point as well when rhetorically asking in the introduction to their recent special issue, *Towards an Anthropology of the Individual* (*Zeitschrift für Ethnologie*), 'does the anthropology of the individual not exist?'[29] It is to a critical engagement with this neglect and denigration of the individual and the concomitant celebration of methodological holism that I turn now.

An anthropological case to be made in support of the universal individual

Within anthropological debates, numerous empirical examples of non-Western societies have been presented in which the category of the individual apparently does not matter. As such, these ethnographic case studies have seemingly lent substance to the theoretical conclusion that the idea of the autonomous individual cannot claim universal applicability. Yet, to begin with, it is far from clear that these ethnographic and historical arguments depicting the individual as a modern Western particularity are actually empirically accurate. For instance, Alan Macfarlane argues that English individualism demonstrably reaches back at least to the thirteenth century, thus hardly constituting a modern phenomenon as is commonly believed.[30] Conversely, ethnographic studies highlight the presence of individualistic and egocentric behaviour in seemingly sociocentric contexts outside 'the West'.

25 N Rapport and J Overing, 'Individualism – Individuality' in N Rapport and J Overing (eds), *Social and Cultural Anthropology: The Key Concepts* (Routledge 2000) 178.

26 AP Cohen, *Self Consciousness: An Alternative Anthropology of Identity* (Routledge 1994).

27 See, e.g., N Rapport, *Transcendent Individual: Towards a Literary and Liberal Anthropology* (Routledge 1997); N Rapport, *I Am Dynamite: An Alternative Anthropology of Power* (Routledge 2003); N Rapport, *Human Nature as Capacity: Transcending Discourse and Classification* (Berghahn Books 2010); N Rapport, *Anyone: The Cosmopolitan Subject of Anthropology* (Berghahn Books 2012).

28 N Rapport, 'Individualism' in A Barnard and J Spencer (eds), *The Routledge Encyclopedia of Social and Cultural Anthropology* (Routledge 2010) 378.

29 JP Heiss and A Piette, 'Individuals in Anthropology' (2015) 140 *Zeitschrift für Ethnologie* 6.

30 A Macfarlane, *The Origins of English Individualism: The Family, Property and Social Transition* (Blackwell 1978).

According to Uni Wikan,[31] people in Bali demonstrate poise, grace, and etiquette *not* because of an aesthetic self-styling as *dramatis personae* without any individuality (*pace* Geertz 1975),[32] but rather because negative passions are seen as offensive and harmful to others and may provoke sorcery in retaliation; public performances of refined aestheticism thus ultimately function as defence mechanisms by and for individuals in the true sense of the word. Similarly, studies from South Asia show that sociocentric conceptions of selfhood do not necessarily preclude forms of 'intrapsychic' autonomy[33] or practical engagement by selves of a more egocentric variety (*pace* Shweder and Bourne).[34] In this vein, Martin Sökefeld offers the example of a northern Pakistani whose skilful management of multiple and conflicting identities, the author claims, requires a universal self endowed with reflexivity and agency.[35] Furthermore, Eiko Tada argues that in Japan intrapersonal conflicts can be observed between sociocentric role expectations and egocentric interests and desires – *pace* Markus and Kitayama's one-sided emphasis on the cultural norm of interdependent selves in East Asia.[36]

For Papua New Guinea, often celebrated as a radical other to 'the West', Kenelm Burridge equally insists that locals actually figure both as 'persons' prescribed by culture and social order (what he calls 'someone') and as 'individuals' transcending conventions in their search for self-realization (temporarily adopting the stance of 'no one');[37] such an oscillation between personhood and individuality, Burridge proclaims, is constitutive of human beings everywhere. In a similar vein, commenting on the dividual-individual debate, Harri Englund and James Leach note that according to 'the current anthropological wisdom, *all* persons are both dividuals and individuals'.[38]

In addition to empirical reasons for casting doubt on the claim regarding the peculiarity of the Western self, psychological and cognitive anthropologists have also questioned this thesis on methodological and conceptual grounds. Melford Spiro argues that reported differences between the Western and non-Western self may actually be the product of differences in the techniques and samples of investigation, as well as of insufficient data to fully support the often far-reaching claims.[39] Furthermore, both Spiro and Naomi Quinn point out the lack of terminological and conceptual clarity with regard to key terms such as 'person', 'self', and 'individual'.[40] Importantly, they also stress that the self as mere self-representation cannot be automatically equated with the self as it is lived – that is, the extensive self as 'the totality of what an organism is physically, biologically, psychologically, socially, and culturally'.[41] In his attempt to integrate and reconcile both social science and cognitive science notions of the self, Maurice Bloch correspondingly proposes a multi-layered model

31 U Wikan, 'Public Grace and Private Fears: Gaiety, Offense, and Sorcery in Northern Bali' (1987) 15 *Ethos* 337.

32 C Geertz, 'On the Nature of Anthropological Understanding' (1975) 63 *American Scientist* 47.

33 KP Ewing, 'The Illusion of Wholeness: Culture, Self, and the Experience of Inconsistency' (1990) 18 *Ethos* 251.

34 Shweder and Bourne (n 21).

35 M Sökefeld, 'Debating Self, Identity, and Culture in Anthropology' (1999) 40 *Current Anthropology* 417.

36 E Tada, *Maintaining a Balance: Between Hito ('Person') and Kojin ('Individual') in a Japanese Farming Community* (PhD dissertation, University of California at San Diego 1991).

37 K Burridge, *Someone, No One: An Essay on Individuality* (Princeton University Press 1979).

38 H Englund and J Leach, 'Ethnography and the Meta-Narratives of Modernity' (2000) 41 *Current Anthropology* 225, 229.

39 ME Spiro, 'Is the Western Conception of the Self "Peculiar" Within the Context of the World Cultures?' (1993) 21 *Ethos* 107, 114.

40 Spiro (n 39) 107–153; N Quinn, 'The Self' (2006) 6 *Anthropological Theory* 362.

41 Quinn (n 40) 362.

of the self that includes 'meta-representation' (explicit re-representations of one's self to oneself and others) as only one level, and only as a potential one, in addition to other interrelated levels.[42]

This brief overview of empirical, methodological, and conceptual arguments may suffice to highlight that the claim of an alleged absence of the individual in non-Western societies, as propagated in much of the anthropological and cultural-psychological literature, is far from being uncontested. However, in the remainder of this chapter, I will refrain from further engaging with these arguments. Instead, I will offer four different arguments – pertaining to logic, social theory, epistemology, and morality, respectively – to explain why, to my mind, the individual actually is an appropriate analytical and moral figure.

First, looking at the issue in logical terms, it turns out that the *historical* argument about the presence of the individual in the West and its alleged absence in the rest is actually immaterial for the *systematic* question of whether 'the individual' is a useful idea of universal applicability.[43] Thus, even if it was historically true that the individual did not figure in many societies (which, as I have pointed out, is contested), this historical truth – logically speaking – would be irrelevant for the independent systematic question of whether 'the individual' is actually a helpful universal idea. Put differently, the systematic appropriateness of a universal concept for the analysis of a social setting is logically independent of the historical question of the extent to which the people within any such setting endorse and use this concept themselves.

Unfortunately, this logical truth is not always acknowledged in anthropological arguments. Instead, according to James Laidlaw, it is a widespread weakness among anthropologists

> to invoke the authority of a single (inevitably a currently fashionable and usually continental) philosopher, first as a supplier of ideas that refute some 'dominant Western assumption' [such as 'the individual'] (as if a French, German, or Slovenian philosopher were not also Western), and then to discover that philosopher's doctrines lived out by a people in some non-Western setting – New Guinea highlanders who speak fluent Heidegger, Spinoza, Deleuze, or Levinas – as if this demonstrated simultaneously the truth of the One and the virtue of the Other.[44]

However, such argumentation, as widespread as it may be, is logically unwarranted: using historical arguments about the alleged absence of 'the individual' in order to substantiate a systematic argument against its appropriateness as a universal analytical category commits the fallacy of a *non sequitur*. In other words, we cannot acquit ourselves of the duty to establish, with good reasons, our own etic concepts of analysis simply by transferring that duty to our interlocutors – as if the reconstruction of emic concepts simultaneously solved the problem of which etic terms the observing anthropologist, in turn, should use to describe and analyse these emic ideas and related practices.

Such an approach is not only problematic in logical terms, but also unacceptably paternalistic in that observers do not dare to differ from their informants – as if driven by the

42 M Bloch, *Anthropology and the Cognitive Challenge* (Cambridge University Press 2012) 117–142.

43 H Seiffert, 'Historisch/Systematisch' in H Seiffert and G Radnitzky (eds), *Handlexikon zur Wissenschaftstheorie* (dtv 1989) 139.

44 J Laidlaw, *The Subject of Virtue: An Anthropology of Ethics and Freedom* (Cambridge University Press 2014) 40–41.

fear that these exotic others could not cope with disagreeing anthropologists. By contrast, I believe that if we dignify our colleagues as equals by allowing ourselves to disagree with them, surely we should bestow the same honour upon our informants. This is neither to claim that the actually existing world of knowledge production is not characterized by massive power asymmetries nor that, following from this, researchers in relatively privileged positions have no duty to actively level the playing field for all interested parties to participate on as equal a footing as possible in scientific arguments. However, such a politics of levelling differential access should not be confused with the paternalism of an epistemological obligation to succumb to the view of the other merely because of her (formerly) subaltern position.

Whether or not 'the individual' is a useful universal idea, therefore, is a systematic question that requires systematic arguments supporting or undermining the concept, since the mere historical fact of whether others do or do not cherish this idea proves inconsequential from a systematic perspective. In the following I will concentrate on such systematic arguments that, to my mind, justify defending 'the individual' – with all the problems of personal autonomy that its practical implementation in and beyond the law entails.

I thus turn to the second argument in favour of the individual, which is related to social theory, where debates supporting or rejecting 'methodological holism' or 'methodological individualism' have an honourable and well-documented history.[45] Introduced as a doctrine by Max Weber, methodological individualism initially referred to the need to explain social phenomena in terms of 'the particular acts of individual persons, since these alone can be treated as agents in a course of subjectively understandable action'.[46] Around the mid-twentieth century, Friedrich von Hayek and Karl Popper propagated methodological individualism primarily as a political means to defend liberalism against a 'historicism' that was seen as conducive to totalitarianism.[47] In the 1980s, within an upsurge of interest in rational choice theory drawing attention to collective action problems such as free-rider incentives,[48] demands for providing micro-foundations for social macro-phenomena resurfaced within a broader interest in 'the micro-macro link'.[49]

For my purposes here it is not necessary to summarize these controversies, but rather to pinpoint my main argument in favour of the universal individual. One bone of contention within these debates has been the question of 'voluntarism': methodological holists have been accused of reducing actors to cultural dopes who, in their mere enactment of sociocultural structures, lack agency;[50] such holists, in return, have retorted that methodological individualists easily fall prey to reductionist ideas of 'rational choice', radical egotism, and

45 L Udehn, *Methodological Individualism: Background, History and Meaning* (Routledge 2001); J Heath, 'Methodological Individualism' in *The Stanford Encyclopedia of Philosophy* (Spring 2015 edn) <http://plato.stanford.edu/archives/spr2015/entries/methodological-individualism/> accessed 23 September 2016.

46 M Weber, *Economy and Society: An Outline of Interpretive Sociology* (University of California Press [1921]1978) 13.

47 FA von Hayek, *The Counter-Revolution of Science: Studies on the Abuse of Reason* (Free Press 1952); KR Popper, *The Open Society and Its Enemies* (Routledge & Sons 1945).

48 J Elster, 'The Case for Methodological Individualism' (1982) 11 *Theory and Society* 453.

49 JC Alexander, B Giesen, R Münch, and NJ Smelser (eds), *The Micro-Macro Link* (University of California Press 1987).

50 See, e.g., L Holy and M Stuchlik, *Actions, Norms and Representations: Foundations of Anthropological Inquiry* (Cambridge University Press 1983).

creativity in a world incorrectly presumed to be void of structural constraints.[51] Following the celebrated intuition of Karl Marx that people make their own history but not under structural conditions of their own choosing,[52] several attempts have been made at synthesizing 'structure and agency'.[53] However, as Rapport and Overing rightly point out,[54] each proclaimed synthesis ultimately ends up putting stronger causal emphasis on one or the other, that is, either on structure or on agency.[55]

This state of affairs possibly becomes easier to handle if the problem is framed in terms of 'structural determinism' rather than of 'voluntarism': a compromise between a deterministic and non-deterministic theory of social practice seems impossible, whereas voluntary action under conditions of structural constraint can be easily imagined. As a matter of fact, Marx's mentioned intuition is not at all in need of any synthesis, siding unambiguously with non-determinism, while Marxian statements of faith have often favoured the opposite of structural determinism. In other words, supporting a non-deterministic social theory evidently does not imply that there are no powerful structural constraints or that voluntarism or rational choice prevails at all times. To the contrary, such a commitment merely insists that for people to have at least in principle the potential (even if rarely instantiated) to also act on motives that are their own, 'someone' – or rather 'anyone' in Rapport's terminology – endowed with genuine agency must be assumed.[56] Why not call her 'the individual' with at least the potential for personal autonomy? In sum, if one wants to allow for the possibility of social practice to be oriented not only through people's affects and ingrained habituation, but also through their instrumentally or value-rational reflections – as suggested by Max Weber[57] – it seems difficult not to assume that people at least sometimes do behave like autonomous individuals.

The third reason that, to my mind, makes it rather difficult not to decide in favour of the individual is related to epistemology: does the very question of whether to decide in favour of or against the individual not already presuppose – at least for the analyst – the universal existence of the very subject position of an individual with relative personal autonomy (i.e., the ability to decide for oneself) that is at issue in the first place? Is there a way in which a decision against the universal individual can be taken without simultaneously making use of the very capacity to act for oneself that one thereby denies everyone else, namely personal autonomy?

51 See, e.g., B Kapferer (ed), *The Retreat of the Social: The Rise and Rise of Reductionism* (Berghahn Books 2005).

52 K Marx, 'The Eighteenth Brumaire of Louis Bonaparte' (Excerpts) in LH Simon (ed), *Karl Marx: Selected Writings* (Hackett [1852]1994) 187, 188.

53 See, e.g., PL Berger and T Luckmann, *The Social Construction of Reality: A Treatise in the Sociology of Knowledge* (Penguin Books 1967); T Parsons, *Social Systems and the Evolution of Action Theory* (Free Press 1977); P Bourdieu, *Outline of a Theory of Practice* (Cambridge University Press 1977); A Giddens, *The Constitution of Society: Outline of the Theory of Structuration* (University of California Press 1984); MS Archer, *Culture and Agency: The Place of Culture in Social Theory* (Cambridge University Press 1988); NP Mouzelis, *Back to Sociological Theory: The Construction of Social Orders* (St. Martin's Press 1991).

54 N Rapport and J Overing, 'Agent and Agency' in N Rapport and J Overing (eds), *Social and Cultural Anthropology: The Key Concepts* (Routledge 2000) 1, 2.

55 See also R Jenkins, *Pierre Bourdieu* (revised edn, Routledge 2002).

56 N Rapport, 'Apprehending Anyone: The Non-Indexical, Post-Cultural, and Cosmopolitan Human Actor' (2010) 16 *Journal of the Royal Anthropological Institute* 84; Rapport (n 27).

57 Weber (n 46) 24–26.

This raises tricky questions of reflexivity – taking a step back, observing oneself, and thereby turning the preconditions of observation and representation into the explicit object of reflection. However, rather than merely turning in on oneself in an unspecified reflexive move of self-reference, the observations of others and the observations of oneself observing others should be actively aligned in such a way that the formal and substantive presumptions underlying the observational process are repeated in a self-similar way. Through this process, what underlies the act of observing is consciously made to simultaneously determine what is observed; the observed is thus defined recursively – that is, in terms of the preconditions of its own act of being observed. Recursivity is thus introduced as an epistemological principle, allowing an evaluation of the extent to which what is said is consistent with both that and how it is said. A recursive epistemology, in this sense, is hence applicable to itself. In other words, the more recursive a theory, the more it treats the capacities of the observer and the observed as alike in principle.

As I explore in greater detail elsewhere,[58] under conditions of epistemological indeterminacy and normative pluralism, which arguably characterize anthropology's workspace, such an epistemological recursivity constitutes a superior epistemological criterion for theoretically positioning oneself, because there is no reason to assume that the observing anthropologist has in principle any better capacity to apprehend the 'true' nature of the social world than any other actor; hence their symmetrical epistemological treatment. Against this backdrop, when applying a recursive epistemology to the problem of the universal individual, such an approach arguably ends up supporting the subject position of the autonomous individual by necessity precisely because the very act of deciding for or against this universal notion already presupposes it to have universal applicability.

This leads me to my fourth and last reason in support of the autonomous individual, which transposes this epistemological argument into the field of morality: precisely because we cannot be sure, ultimately, whether or not the individual is a useful universal category, we end up being morally obliged in principle to allow others to opt out of this model of personal autonomy. This dilemma seems to be at the heart of the paradox of paternalism for the sake of personal autonomy sketched at the beginning of this chapter. If there were no profoundly nagging doubts about the appropriateness and hence legitimacy of overriding other people's seemingly non-autonomous actions for the sake of their 'true' autonomy, this paradox would lose its sting. But what if the other is right? What if those acts that I believe to be expressions of true universal autonomy – and thus the benchmark legitimating the paternalistic overruling of others' preferences – are, in fact, merely specific to my own culture? How can I ever be sure that those seemingly repulsive decisions by others are not, in fact, expressions of their 'true' personal autonomy, which only seem strange to me due to my own parochial culture?

Evidently, none of us can ever be sure. Hence, the moral obligation to allow others (and, of course, oneself) under certain conditions to opt out of mainstream definitions of personal autonomy, and hence also the continual and contested process of defining those conditions under which opting out may be legitimate. Paradoxically, however, constructing such an exit option out of 'the individual' requires us to adopt, yet again, the individual as the

58 O Zenker, 'Anthropology on Trial: Exploring the Laws of Anthropological Expertise' (2016) 12 *International Journal of Law in Context* 293; O Zenker and K Kumoll, 'Prologue: Opening Doors Beyond *Writing Culture*' in O Zenker and K Kumoll (eds), *Beyond Writing Culture: Current Intersections of Epistemologies and Representational Practices* (Berghahn Books 2010) 1.

underlying role model that makes possible, in the first place, the use of personal autonomy to decide against making 'the individual' and 'personal autonomy' part of one's own cherished moral and legal points of reference.

In short, the autonomous individual reveals itself as operating in what Douglas Hofstadter calls a 'strange loop' – that is, 'a paradoxical level-crossing feedback loop' in which 'despite one's sense of departing ever further from one's origin, one winds up, to one's shock, exactly where one had started out', namely with the individual and its personal autonomy.[59] Many of the drawings of the Dutch artist M.C. Escher, especially his famous 'Drawing Hands' (1948), visually exemplify this loop – moving up or down one hierarchical level strangely and inconclusively leads one back eventually to where one started. In this way, the strange loop of the universal individual seems impossible to escape: even in deciding against being an 'individual', one simultaneously takes up anew the position of the deciding individual. This paradox is illustrated in a very immediate and funny way in the scene from the movie *Life of Brian* by the British comedy group Monty Python (also referred to in Ian Kalman's chapter in this volume): when Brian addresses a crowd and tells them, 'You're all individuals,' all but one from the audience respond in unison, 'Yes, we are all individuals.' This one dissenter, in proclaiming 'I am not [an individual],' gets caught in the strange loop of simultaneously opting out of and instantiating the role model of the universal individual. Of course, this quandary of the individual is mirrored in the complementary predicament of paternalism, in having to decide when the individual under one's guardianship truly is 'the individual'. This is where the practical problems of personal autonomy really start.

Conclusion

In the first part of this chapter, I gave a brief overview of a prominent line of anthropological reasoning descending from Emile Durkheim, which has claimed to undermine the universal applicability of the notion of the autonomous individual through revealing the historical and sociocultural particularity of this concept, namely its alleged confinement to Western modernity. Apart from discussing anthropological work directly concerned with the individual, I also engaged with developments in cultural psychology, where these arguments had meanwhile migrated. Limitations of space prevented me from further engaging with a related mode of thought in poststructuralism and postmodernism regarding the death of the subject. However, as I argued at the beginning of the second part, such historical truths about seemingly non-individualistic understandings of personhood in non-Western societies – even if they were historically true, which is contested – are logically immaterial when we concern ourselves with the systematic truth of whether or not the individual is a useful and appropriate figure of universal applicability. As Stephen Reyna succinctly points out with regard to comparable *non sequitur* arguments about Foucauldian 'regimes of truth' widely popular in anthropology, 'regime-of-truth arguments, while they may tell you something about what people believe to be true, beg the point of providing warrant for whether or not what people believe to be true, is true.'[60]

59 DR Hofstadter, *I Am a Strange Loop* (Basic Books 2007) 102.

60 SP Reyna, 'Hard Truths: Addressing a Crisis in Anthropology' in O Zenker and K Kumoll (eds), *Beyond Writing Culture: Current Intersections of Epistemologies and Representational Practices* (Berghahn Books 2010) 163, 165.

Against the backdrop of this logical argument, I have offered three more systematic arguments from the fields of social theory, epistemology, and morality in support of the universal individual. As I have tried to show, a non-deterministic social theory cannot do without affording actors under observation at least the potential to behave like 'autonomous individuals', even if such moments might empirically be rare. A recursive epistemology equally leads to the principal assumption of a potentially universal individual equipped with personal autonomy, since the very act of deciding about the universality of the individual already requires what it purports to decide about: universal individuality. Finally, the moral desire to, in principle, allow others (and oneself) to opt out of a potential tyranny of the individual leads back, in a strange loop, to the very model of this individual autonomy.

This argument does not solve any of the concrete problems and predicaments surrounding the paradoxes of personal autonomy in social theory and legal practice. As such, it does not, of course, deny the crucial importance of legally instituting safeguards for anyone to opt in or out of 'individual' as well as 'not-so-individual' rights, of providing that the marginalized are adequately empowered in the ongoing negotiations regarding the actual contents of such rights, or of ensuring that abstract rights sufficiently turn into actual capabilities on the ground. These are all very important questions that follow from taking the problem of personal autonomy seriously. My goal in this chapter has been much more circumscribed, attempting to provide reasons in the first place as to why the universal individual must be defended – only seemingly against all anthropological odds. As I have argued, the autonomous individual is not just a pseudo-problem to be easily abandoned – the paradoxes of personal autonomy constitute real problems that are going to stay. Precisely because they stay and, as paradoxes, are unlikely to be solved, they can and must be processed. For anthropology, there remains much to be done, descriptively and normatively.

Part II

Autonomy in context: empirical illustrations

A: The majoritarian assessment of personal autonomy

7 Cultural diversity in the workplace

Personal autonomy as a pillar for the accommodation of employees' religious practices?

Katayoun Alidadi

This chapter addresses the issue of cultural and, in particular, religious diversity in the workplace, inquiring whether the concept and discourse of personal autonomy provide support for or, rather, fuel opposition to certain religious practices in the secular European workplace. I start by discussing the concept and the paradox of personal autonomy as I understand them in a culturally diverse context. My aim is to assess what personal autonomy signifies in the discussion concerning claims for accommodation of employees' religious or philosophical beliefs and practices. In order to illustrate the very divergent viewpoints that, in my opinion, can be justified with reference to personal autonomy in the area of EU anti-discrimination law, I draw on two recent opinions delivered by Advocate General Kokott and Advocate General Sharpston in the Court of Justice of the European Union (CJEU) regarding, respectively, the Belgian *Achbita v G4S* case and the French *Bougnaoui v Micropole SA* case. These two independent but topically related cases involve the wearing of a headscarf in the workplace, and the CJEU's rulings will impact workplace accommodation of employees' religious attire in Europe for some time to come.[1] I argue that the valuation of the personal autonomy of people from minority backgrounds can operate as an argumentative pillar for allowing accommodation of certain religious practices. At the same time, however, the concept is susceptible to (mis)representation and can be mobilized to argue positions that delegitimize even modest accommodations. Autonomy not only serves as 'a coordinating mechanism between different normative systems' or as 'justification for individuals' preferences',[2] but also at times provides justification for the exclusion of religious minorities who seek the security, safety, and comfort of mainstream employment. In this sense, the debate surrounding accommodation of religious practices aptly illustrates the paradoxes of personal autonomy encountered by projects of culturally sensitive law.

'Accommodative law' and the paradox of personal autonomy

The concept of human autonomy or self-governance may seem straightforward at first glance,[3] and one may think its realization or facilitation through legal means would be

1 See Case C-157/15, *Achbita v G4S Secure Solutions NV*; Case C-188/15, *Bougnaoui v Micropole SA*, both issued 14 March 2017.

2 Concept note for this collective volume, *(Not) Outside My Culture: The Paradoxes of Personal Autonomy in a Plural Society*; see <http://intra1:8080/mpi-eth/idatDownload.eth?subDir=3605&FileName=2014_CfP_Personal_Autonomy_140117.pdf&saveMode=true> accessed 25 April 2017.

3 See, e.g., J Christman, 'Autonomy and Social Disorientation' in G Levey (ed), *Authenticity, Autonomy and Multiculturalism* (Routledge 2015) 28: 'An autonomous agent is one who is able to act for reasons (or more generally, to act on value considerations) that are *one's own*, and to do so competently' (emphasis in original).

DOI: 10.4324/9781315413617-10

unequivocal as well. However, beyond a cursory examination, human autonomy as a concept – with many competing interpretations[4] – exhibits an inherent elusiveness that is a product of the complexity of human psychology.[5] People are motivated in their seemingly autonomous actions by beliefs, intentions, desires, pressures, and so on, which have been shaped through various processes, including a lifetime of socialization.[6] If people are led to choose certain courses of action over others because of internal pressures shaped by inescapable outside influences (or an interplay of various influences), are they then really being autonomous agents when they make legally significant choices? These philosophical considerations play a key role in Western liberal legal debates:[7] how is the law to facilitate 'free actions and preferences' when even under the best conditions people are bound by various commitments, affiliations, and loyalties which promote, privilege, or even demand certain actions or abstentions?

Cultural diversity and its recognition or accommodation by the law is a case in point, illustrating this very 'paradox of personal autonomy', which lies in the fact that, while the law seeks to open up autonomous fields of action for the individual, it can at best only facilitate choosing among respective sources of influences, pressures, and demands, at times privileging some over others. Law or policies may divert or alleviate some societal pressures, but the vacuum that the lifting of these pressures creates is rapidly filled as other influences or forces are allowed free range. What is more, some consider religion antithetical to human agency and even as a key *obstacle* to free agency.[8] Should the law then facilitate, even privilege, religion's hold over individuals? Is 'accommodative law' – by which I refer to laws, rules, or practices that favour the opening of personal choices and value pluralism within the majoritarian legal system, in particular for minorities that are not historically anchored – in the end conducive to the personal autonomy of individuals from minority backgrounds?[9]

4 For a discussion of procedural approaches versus substantive approaches to autonomy, see AE Galeotti, 'Autonomy and Multiculturalism' in Levey (n 2) 47ff.

5 See, generally, M Cottam et al., *Introduction to Political Psychology* (Erlbaum 2004) 1–2: instead of acting in rational pursuit of self-interests, psychologists have demonstrated a more complex picture of human behaviour, recognizing that '[p]eople are imperfect information processors, struggling mightily to understand the complex world in which they live. People employ logical, but often faulty, perceptions of others when deciding how to act, and they are often unaware of the causes of their own behavior. People often do things that are seemingly contrary to their own interests, values, and beliefs.'

6 M Bratman, 'Planning Agency, Autonomous Agency' in J Taylor (ed), *Personal Autonomy: New Essays on Personal Autonomy and Its Role in Contemporary Moral Philosophy* (Cambridge University Press 2005) 33–34. Peter Jones notes that 'For the majority of the world's believing population, their religious beliefs are a consequence of their socialization, either by their family or by the larger community or society in which they live.' See P Jones, 'Belief, Autonomy and Responsibility: The Case of Indirect Religious Discrimination' in Levey (n 2) 71.

7 Michael Bratman (n 5, 34) refers to the difficulties of 'reconciling our self-understanding as autonomous with our self-understanding as embedded in a natural order'.

8 See, e.g., Charlemagne, 'Antwerp's Muslim Headscarf Row, the Story on the Ground' *The Economist* (17 September 2009). The column presents interviews with three main protagonists in the headscarf debate, one of whom was then mayor of Antwerp Patrick Janssens, who says, 'I cannot imagine that young Muslims, when they study science, when they go to university in more numbers, will not liberate themselves from their religion. I do not mean they will become atheist. But they will realise that religion does not become dominant over all other values.'

9 Since 'accommodative laws' open up space towards other normative systems, they thus imply a degree of *legal pluralism* within (spatio-temporal) boundaries.

When it comes to the workplace setting, legal techniques that allow employees to escape external pressures in the form of direct or indirect commands from employers can certainly be seen to increase employee autonomy. But if this freed-up space is swiftly taken up by religious needs and claims, the paradox resurfaces and the question remains: does the application of legal instruments, most prominently human rights and anti-discrimination law as applied to secular employment situations, not simply lead to a redirection of control over employees, namely from the (external) demands of the dominant culture to (internalized) cultural and religious forces?[10]

It can be argued that the circumstances of cultural and religious diversity arguably do matter in this consideration. Cultural or religious practices may be so internalized in relatively culturally homogeneous settings that members consider them part and parcel of their identities, and the possibility to question, criticize, or revise practices may be severely limited.[11] In contrast, routine confrontation with otherness and alternative world views and ways of life in contemporary contexts of diversity can enable human agency to play a more substantial role regarding religion and culture, even if these remain embedded in the history and traditions of a group as a whole. At times, religionists living in conditions of diversity will feel a need for justification of much of what has been taken for granted. People may find their traditional beliefs and practices challenged and will want to grasp, perhaps for themselves foremost, why adherence to such beliefs and practices makes sense in today's world. Then, in the face of otherness and potential adversity, culture itself and the adherence to certain cultural and religious practices can transform into something of a more solid and active *choice*,[12] namely a personal preference (often backed by a community) that seeks to confirm, reproduce, and possibly alter given beliefs and practices. Of course, such choices – even if not backed by intense social pressures – give voice to a form of individual autonomy that remains closely connected to one's background and convictions, but the 'autonomy scale' seems more prominent. Individual autonomy, then, is the vehicle for respecting and accommodating cultural and religious commitments of individual members of (minority) religions.[13]

10 I refer to culture in the traditional Boasian sense of 'a system of shared beliefs, values, customs, behaviours, and artifacts that the members of society use to cope with their world and with one another, and that are transmitted from generation to generation through learning', rather than a broader understanding of culture as frames (Erving Goffman), as is often posited in sociological circles. See F Stuart, 'Becoming "Copwise": Policing, Culture, and the Collateral Consequences of Street-Level Criminalization' (2016) 5 *Law and Society Review* 278. However, understanding culture in the latter way amplifies some of the arguments presented here.

11 See W Wagner et al., 'The Veil and Muslim Women's Identity: Cultural Pressures and Resistance to Stereotyping' (2012) 18 *Culture and Psychology* 521–541. Wagner reveals significant differences in Muslim women's reasons for wearing a veil in a Muslim majority society (Indonesia) compared to a country where Muslims form a minority (India). In the latter case, cultural identity and religiously inspired arguments were much more prevalent.

12 This is in contrast to many 'default rules'. On the concept of choice and the importance of good default rules that make active but cumulatively overwhelming choice-making redundant, see CR Sunstein, *Choosing Not to Choose: Understanding the Value of Choice* (Oxford University Press 2015).

13 This approach is an example of what Levey, in this volume, calls 'more sophisticated accounts of liberal autonomy . . . which recognize individuals as social and cultural beings'. On this discussion in the family law context, see M Deveaux, 'Personal Autonomy and Cultural Tradition: The Arranged Marriage Debate in Britain' in B Arneil et al. (eds), *Sexual Justice/Cultural Justice: Critical Perspectives in Political Theory and Practice* (Routledge 2007) 157.

Thus, within an understanding of human autonomy as procedural and non-comprehensive, legal instruments of human rights and non-discrimination arguably do increase the personal agency of minority employees in the sense that individuals then also maintain the option of adhering to culturally embedded practices while retaining the benefits of participation in a mainstream workplace.

Equality, religious freedom, and reasonable accommodation in the European workplace: revealing the two faces of autonomy

Considering that the human rights to freedom of thought, conscience, and religion and to non-discriminatory treatment irrespective of religion or belief form the most solid legal anchors in the European legal framework for the freedom to express one's religion and conscience, the focus of this chapter will be on accommodation of religious practices in employment under these two legal frameworks.[14]

The role of autonomy is key in the formulation of Article 9 ECHR and its application by the European Court of Human Rights (ECtHR).[15] However, the choice factor – the fact that a religionist could change his or her practices – has at times been the justification for an attenuated level of protection of the exercise or manifestation of religious freedom.[16]

Personal autonomy, along with human dignity, is seen as the core value underpinning the notion of equality, which has the status of a fundamental principle of EU law and is applied specifically in various settings including, according to Directive 2000/78, in the workplace setting.[17] The exercise of personal autonomy requires that 'individuals should be able to design and conduct the course of their lives through a succession of choices among different valuable options.'[18] Depriving people of this autonomy by referring to religion or beliefs or other 'suspect classifications' is particularly egregious, as such discrimination is seen as a violation of human autonomy. In the words of Advocate General Poiares Maduro:

> Access to employment and professional development are of fundamental significance for every individual, not merely as a means of earning one's living but also as an important way of self-fulfilment and realisation of one's potential. The discriminator who discriminates against an individual belonging to a suspect classification unjustly deprives her of valuable options. As a consequence, that person's ability to lead an autonomous life is seriously compromised since an important aspect of her life is shaped not by her own choices but by the prejudice of someone else. By treating people belonging to these groups less well because of their characteristic, the discriminator prevents them from exercising their

14 While accommodation of religious beliefs raises similarly significant issues of personal autonomy, many recurrent accommodation requests by religious minorities (and, as the Eweida case shows, also for practising Christians in Europe) involve externalized practices such as dress code, the observance of religious holidays, or prayer practices. It is of no small significance that the two first cases regarding religion or belief discrimination to come before the CJEU involve the issue of the Islamic headscarf in two highly secular countries.

15 It includes, among other rights, the 'freedom to change [one's] religion or belief and freedom, either alone or in community with others'.

16 See, e.g., the freedom to resign doctrine in the jurisprudence of the Strasbourg institutions (reversed since *Eweida v the UK,* 15 January 2013).

17 See, e.g., CJEU, C-303/06, Coleman, Opinion of Advocate General Poiares Maduro, para 73.

18 Ibid. para 9.

> autonomy. At this point, it is fair and reasonable for anti-discrimination law to intervene. In essence, by valuing equality and committing ourselves to realising equality through the law, we aim at sustaining for every person the conditions for an autonomous life.[19]

However, under EU anti-discrimination law, religion or belief is one of several 'discrimination strands', which enters into competition (even if not necessarily conflict) with various other 'strands', including gender, ethnic origin, sexual orientation, age, disability, and so on. Interestingly, choice (and thus autonomy), if it comes into play at all, has a much more subdued role in considerations regarding the protection against discrimination on the basis of these other grounds. For instance, in the case of the protection of people with disabilities, remedies or accommodations are almost never bolstered by a perceived 'choice' of the individual role with regard to his or her disability.[20] The fact that the requester *did not choose* to live with a disability leads to much less ambiguous, more emphatic social and legal responses. From here it is but a small step to contrast this situation with that of religious employees who seek to manifest their religion in the workplace: unlike the disabled employee, the religious employee could often *choose* to take off his or her religious dress or symbols or refrain from overtly engaging in certain religious practices when in a professional setting.

The availability of 'choice' undercutting the autonomy of religious minorities: the AG opinion in the *Achbita* case

EU Directive 2000/78 makes no distinction regarding the 'choice factor' involved in the different discrimination strands; in principle, the protection against different forms of discrimination applies to the ground of religion or belief just as it does to sexual orientation, disability, and age. There are some differences when it comes to the justification tests,[21] and an employer's duty to reasonably accommodate is limited to persons with disabilities.[22] The choice factor nevertheless has a tendency to sneak into legal argumentation. There are many examples, but the one to which I will refer here is the opinion of Advocate General Kokott in the *Achbita* case,[23] which provides a useful vehicle for exploring the role of autonomy

19 Ibid. para 11, cited by AG Sharpston in her opinion of 13 July 2016 in the case C-188/15, *Asma Bougnaoui and Association de défense des droits de l'homme (ADDH) v Micropole SA*.

20 See T Mitchell and M Kovera, 'The Effects of Attribution of Responsibility and Work History on Perceptions of Reasonable Accommodations' (2006) 30 *Law and Human Behavior* 733.

21 On the strand hierarchy discussion in equality law, see M Pearson, 'Religious Discrimination and the "Hierarchy of Rights": Non-Existent, Appropriate or Problematic?' (2016) 16 *International Journal of Discrimination and the Law* 37–50.

22 Art. 5 EU Directive 2000/78.

23 CJEU, Case C-157/15, *Samira Achbita and Centrum voor gelijkheid van kansen en voor racismebestrijding v G4S Secure Solutions NV*, Opinion of Advocate General Kokott, delivered on 31 May 2016. On 14 March 2017, after this chapter was finalized, the CJEU issued the two highly anticipated judgments in the *Achbita* and *Micropole* cases. In its *Achbita* judgment, it partially follows AG Kokott's advice. The Court rejects the argument that private company neutrality policies constitute direct discrimination or even indirect discrimination under certain stated conditions (e.g., consistent and systematic application of the policy, limited to employees who come into contact with customers). These being the first CJEU judgments on religious discrimination under EU law, many questions do remain (e.g., the interaction with the *Eweida* case and other ECtHR cases) and will have to be worked out in the years to come. The focus of this chapter is, however, on the approaches and more elaborate reasoning advanced in the respective AG opinions.

in anti-discrimination law. This AG opinion and the opinion by AG Sharpston in a similar French headscarf case precede the CJEU's highly anticipated (first) landmark decisions involving religious discrimination in the workplace, and they represent starkly divergent approaches to the protection against religious discrimination in the EU.

While Advocate General Kokott acknowledges that the term 'religion or belief' under the EU Directive 2000/78 is to be interpreted broadly, meaning including both the *forum internum* and *forum externum*,[24] she nonetheless proceeds to argue that an employee should not be protected from dismissal for following certain religious practices (here: wearing a headscarf) in the same way that he or she is protected from dismissal on the basis of *religious status* because the employee can choose to abandon religious practices or follow other ones.[25] This is in stark contrast to the opinion delivered by Advocate General Eleanor Sharpston on 13 July 2016 in the French case of *Asma Bougnaoui v Micropole SA*. In her opinion in the Bougnaoui case, AG Sharpston argues that the dismissal of a Muslim design engineer for wearing a headscarf while dealing with customers (which the employer argued had 'embarrassed a number of its employees') constitutes *direct* discrimination based on religion.[26]

In her opinion in the *Achbita* case, AG Kokott comes to a different conclusion. In order to reject the stance that employment exclusion based on religious dress (the headscarf) could amount to direct discrimination, AG Kokott reasons as follows:

> [I]n its previous case-law concerning various EU-law prohibitions on discrimination, the Court has generally adopted a broad understanding of the concept of direct discrimination, and has, it is true, always assumed such discrimination to be present where a measure was inseparably linked to the relevant reason for the difference of treatment.
>
> However, all of those cases were without exception concerned with individuals' immutable physical features or personal characteristics – such as gender, age or sexual orientation – rather than with modes of conduct based on a subjective decision or conviction, such as the wearing or not of a head covering at issue here.[27]

24 See para 35: 'The term "religion" used in Article 1 of Directive 2000/78 must be understood in a broad sense. It includes not only the faith of an individual as such (*forum internum*) but also the practice and manifestation of that religion, including in public spaces (*forum externum*). . . . The overarching objective of that directive is to create a working environment that is free from discrimination. . . . If this objective is to be achieved to best effect, the scope of that directive cannot be defined restrictively.' AG Sharpston similarly addresses this same question in the *Bougnaoui* case (n 25, para 85–86): 'Does the prohibition laid down by Directive 2000/78 extend not only to the religion or belief of an employee but also to manifestations of that religion or belief? (86) In my view, it does.' In its *Achbita* judgment, the CJEU adopts this expansive definition of religion: 'the concept of "religion" in Article 1 of that directive should be interpreted as covering both the *forum internum*, that is the fact of having a belief, and the *forum externum*, that is the manifestation of religious faith in public' (para 28).

25 One could argue that people can also change their religion, and that this ground does not merit protection under anti-discrimination law. AG Kokott certainly does not go this far, but the argument does demonstrate the slippery slope of attaching protection to presumably unchangeable or immutable characteristics only.

26 CJEU, Case C-188/15, *Asma Bougnaoui and Association de défense des droits de l'homme (ADDH) v Micropole SA*, AG Opinion Sharpston (13 July 2016), para 88. In para 63, AG Sharpston reasons that the protection against direct discrimination given by EU law (where the direct-indirect discrimination dichotomy is key) is stronger than under the ECHR, which contains less specific discrimination provisions.

27 See (n 22) para 44–45 (references omitted).

This then leads to the conclusion that the neutrality policy adopted by the employer, the security services company G4S, *subsequent*[28] to the employee headscarf dispute 'cannot properly be classified as constituting direct discrimination': 'The deciding factor for the purposes of assuming the presence of direct religious discrimination as defined in Article 2(2) (a) of Directive 2000/78 is that, on account of religion, one person "is treated less favourably than another is, has been or would be treated" . . . There is nothing in the present case to indicate that an individual was "treated less favourably".'[29] This statement represents a reversal of AG Kokott's considerations on religious discrimination discussed earlier, as the employee, Samira Achbita, was dismissed plainly for seeking to adhere to a religious practice that falls under the *forum externum*, which AG Kokott had earlier in the same opinion recognized as covered under 'religion or belief'. What is more, AG Kokott takes the argument a step further when she insists that such a ban constitutes 'a genuine and determining occupational requirement'.[30] The partial characterization of religion as a choice thus in effect implies a significant hollowing out of anti-discrimination protection for employees with religious or philosophical commitments.[31] Under such a restrictive interpretation, EU law does not protect against religion or belief discrimination, but merely against *religious status* discrimination. Since the expectation is a religion-free workplace, the pressure on religious employees not to cross lines can hardly be considered in keeping with a 'working environment that is free from discrimination', the stated overarching goal of the EU Directive. The demands to 'pass' and 'cover' that this approach justifies and bolsters – as Yoshino has convincingly argued in the case of sexual minorities[32] – are not benign, but in fact tantamount to conversion demands in a context where socially and legally sanctioned 'covering' (e.g., in the form of laws and practices requiring the *unveiling* of Muslim women) is becoming the contemporary form of discrimination, whether religious or otherwise.[33] More importantly, the characterization of belief or religion as a choice is open to challenge on various grounds. As Peter Jones observes,

> We cannot simply choose or decide what to believe in the way that we might choose to take a holiday in Spain . . . . We can believe only what seems to us to be the case. If I have good reason to believe that Barcelona is in Spain, . . . I cannot choose to believe

28 The employer argued that prior to this explicit policy, there was an 'unwritten rule' banning religious symbols in the workplace. AG Kokott (too readily) accepts this argument.

29 Para 47–48.

30 Para 84. See also para 94: 'In such a case, a policy of neutrality is absolutely crucial, not only because of the variety of customers served by G4S, but also because of the special nature of the work which G4S employees do in providing those services, which is characterised by constant face-to-face contact with external individuals and has a defining impact not only on the image of G4S itself but also and primarily on the public image of its customers.' However, AG Kokott also does not support 'back-routing' employees (i.e., giving religiously visible employees alternative jobs that entail little or no customer contact). Her opinion, then, encourages conditions that lead to very widespread employment exclusion of Muslim women wearing headscarves and other visibly religious employees. On this issue generally, see K Alidadi, 'From Front-Office to Back-Office: Religious Dress Crossing the Public – Private Divide in the Workplace' in S Ferrari et al. (eds), *Religion and the Public – Private Divide* (Ashgate 2012).

31 Unsurprisingly, then, AG Kokott argues against the extension of a de facto duty to reasonably accommodate on the basis of religion or belief. See para 110.

32 K Yoshino, 'Covering' (2001) 111 *Yale Law Journal* 769.

33 The term 'status performativity' is used to argue that protecting certain identities may require protecting some practices or characteristics that are constitutive of those identities.

otherwise. Beliefs therefore would seem to be (in a suitable sense) imposed upon us by the world.[34]

However, if we value the notion of personal autonomy, there is a case to be made for considering the choice factor a bolstering argument – that is, a *pillar* – for promoting reasonable accommodation on the ground of religion or belief. Notably, human autonomy constitutes such a pillar for the accommodation of the mutable characteristic of religion or belief more than it does for accommodation on grounds involving immutable characteristics such as disability and, to a large degree, gender, age, and sexual orientation.[35] Certainly, autonomy arguments are often presented by accommodation protagonists, for instance, by those arguing in favour of allowing female Muslim employees to wear headscarves or other religious dress in the workplace. One may argue in favour of accommodating the religious dress worn by various minorities because it allows these individuals the freedom to choose how they wish to live out their faith and shape their identities in a visible way. Allowing Muslim women to wear headscarves, full-face veils, or other religious dress is to be preferred over a paternalistic approach, as it allows these women the freedom to choose for themselves – in other words, to act as autonomous agents. But in discussions on the limits of accommodation, the paradoxes of personal autonomy become amplified as the value of freedom or agency (for example, to change one's religious practices in certain contexts) is utilized not only by protagonists but also by antagonists of particular accommodation practices. Two strands of positioning can be distinguished here. First, some commentators, such as AG Kokott, may argue against strengthening the legal right of religious accommodation because of the presence of a choice element in the case of employees seeking accommodation for religious practices. One could see this as a 'nudge'[36] towards toning down one's religion in public space, something Stanley Fish has called the demand to 'wear one's religion lightly' under an increasingly more muscular liberalism.[37] Certainly, choices are motivated by intentions and have consequences, but why should adhering to one's (minority) religion systematically carry negative consequences if society values (religious) freedom and pluralism?

A second position goes much further. Some observers view the *banning* (that is, the removal of choice) of religious practices or dress in the workplace as 'liberating' for presumably oppressed girls and women of religious minorities.[38] Essentially, choice is denied to

34 P Jones (n 5), 70. However, he recognizes that there are differences, as belief is 'non-fully evidentiary' and 'affords people a domain of epistemological discretion that they do not have in relation to simple factual matters' (ibid. 71).

35 On mutable versus immutable characteristics, see D Schiek, 'A New Framework on Equal Treatment of Persons in EC Law?' (2002) 8 *European Law Journal* 290, 309–312; see also A Lester and P Uccellari, 'Extending the Equality Duty to Religion, Conscience, and Belief: Proceed With Caution' (2008) 5 *European Human Rights Law Review* 567–573: '[u]nlike the other characteristics which are protected under . . . anti-discrimination legislation, religion is not an essential, immutable element of the individual's birthright and identity.'

36 R Thaler and C Sunstein, *Nudge: Improving Decisions About Health, Wealth, and Happiness* (Yale University Press 2008). In this pioneering book, Thaler and Sunstein favour a thoughtful 'choice architecture' to nudge us in beneficial directions in various areas of life, arguing that this does not limit freedom of choice.

37 Stanley Fish, 'Our Faith in Letting It All Hang Out' *New York Times* (12 February 2006).

38 This has been a recurrent argument in favour of banning religious minority dress in the educational context: it was the argument behind the French law of 2004 banning the wearing of conspicuous religious

a vulnerable minority group so that (majority-dominated) institutions of schools and the workplace can be religion-free zones. Antagonists may seek to enable these women to exercise another, allegedly more genuine, form of personal agency in modern societies, which is to choose their own future without the pressures and dogma of a woman-unfriendly religion such as Islam.[39] However paradoxical it may seem to be, a *prohibition* is considered capable of effectively opening up a whole world of possibilities for vulnerable people.[40] But their efforts to free people from one source of pressure can quickly turn into something else entirely, creating space for new demands, laws, regulations, and social pressures. As Galeotti writes, such toleration-limiting autonomy argumentation (which she calls 'lack-of-autonomy judgments') 'entails a conflict with liberal public morality and often nurtures double standards'.[41] The vulnerable individual that is targeted, it seems, is caught between competing demands and pressures instead of being freed and given a true choice that would allow him or her to realize personal autonomy and self-governance.

It is important to notice how opposing arguments can both draw on the same discourse of personal autonomy, with one potentially giving unwarranted weight to culturally internal pressures and the other approaching a paternalistic standard that replaces (in the best case) internal pressures with external ones derived from the majority culture.[42] The notions of autonomy and choice seem to allow for this apparent contradiction. To be sure, one can wonder if Muslim women, or any other religionist for that matter, can truly exercise free will if their ultimate aim in life is to follow the 'right way', the will of God, which is given from above. In such situations, 'choice' never transcends hierarchy;[43] rather, one (grand) hierarchy merely transcends and obliterates another (more mundane) subordination. In this sense, the debate surrounding accommodation of religious practices aptly reflects the paradoxes of personal autonomy encountered by projects of culturally sensitive law.[44]

---

symbols in French public schools (loi no 2004–228 du 15 mars 2004 encadrant, en application du principe de laïcité, le port de signes ou de tenues manifestant une appartenance religieuse dans les écoles, collèges et lycées publics) and was also used in the Belgian *burqa* affair and the Antwerp public school headscarf row before it.

39 See AE Galeotti, 'Autonomy and Multiculturalism' in Levey (n 2), 45: 'The claim is that people observing those practices or engaging in such behavior exhibit some defect in their personal autonomy regarding their values, attitudes and choices.' Galeotti is primarily referring to female genital mutilation (FGM), but also mentions Islamic veiling practices.

40 One can observe that this is by no means guaranteed, as external restrictions such as bans on women's religious attire may trigger even more culturally internal restrictions, for example, where parents or husbands restrict the freedom of Muslim girls or women more than when the latter can don headscarves and other conservative dress in public.

41 See (n 38). Accordingly, Galeotti favours a purely political conception of autonomy rather than a comprehensive notion of autonomy.

42 Jennifer Denbow has observed a similar development when it comes to women's health and reproductive decisions in the United States, with certain actions such as sterilization and restriction of abortion being defended by some experts in terms of promoting women's autonomy. See J Denbow, *Governed Through Choice: Autonomy, Technology, and the Politics of Reproduction* (New York University Press 2015).

43 The controversial statements by Laurence Rossignol, the French minister for women's rights who compared women who wear the *burqa* to 'negroes' who supported slavery, can be seen in this light: despite having a 'choice', the women cannot be free. See K Willsher, 'French Women's Rights Minister Accused of Racism Over Term "Negro" ' *The Guardian* (30 March 2006).

44 See K Alidadi, 'Reasonable Accommodations for Religion and Belief: Adding Value to Article 9 ECHR and the European Union's Anti-Discrimination Approach to Employment?' (2012) 37 *European Law Review* 693; E Bribosia, J Ringelheim, and I Rorive, 'Reasonable Accommodation for Religious

Reasonable accommodation and personal autonomy

While EU non-discrimination law and Article 9 of the European Convention on Human Rights (ECHR) are now applied to private-sector employment,[45] a duty of reasonable accommodation on grounds of religion or belief retains a more controversial status under current EU law. The face-off between two advocates general in (the first) two Muslim headscarf cases in which the CJEU has been asked to give a preliminary ruling makes this abundantly clear.[46] This legal concept, which was first introduced in the United States in the context of religious employment discrimination, was explicitly foreseen as a right only for persons with disabilities under EU law. The question of whether to extend a similar right for reasons of religion or belief in Europe has generated ample debate and controversy. For instance, scholars who support protection against religious or belief discrimination have argued against adopting an explicit duty of accommodation, questioning the appropriateness and feasibility of strengthening religious rights in the European context, where existing tensions between religious freedom and other values and rights (including non-discrimination of other vulnerable persons) are hard to deny and some forms of religious expression in the public sphere generate anxiety and restrictive legislation.[47]

In this debate, the right to reasonable accommodation is sometimes misinterpreted as an unrestricted right to workplace adaptations and a complete exemption from carrying any personal burden for one's religious commitments.[48] But reasonable accommodation is in the first place (if not solely) a procedural right, enabling an employee to raise an issue and negotiate space for the respect of religious beliefs or the practice of aspects of religion. Herein also lie its limitations. When anchored in law, employee requests derive a *prima facie* legitimacy, as they must be given due regard by the employer or management. This does not mean that accommodations must or will be extended in any and all workplace situations or settings, but it does imply that avenues of accommodation should be explored and if possible pursued by those in an employment relationship.[49] Once the request is made, the onus is on the party receiving the request to justify a certain course of action, which should take into account the interests of the requesting party. The concept resonates strongly with the idea that individuals, 'as rational agents, are best left to make their own decisions and to chart their own course in life'.[50] Reasonable accommodation is thus supported by choice- or autonomy-based arguments for cultural recognition.

Minorities: A Promising Concept for European Antidiscrimination Law?' (2010) 17 *Maastricht Journal of European and Comparative Law* 137.

45 See *Eweida and others v the UK* App no 48420/10, 59842/10, 51671/10 and 36516/10 (ECHR, 15 January 2013); Council Directive 2000/78/EC of 27 November 2000 Establishing a General Framework for Equal Treatment in Employment and Occupation, *OJ 303 L* 02/12/2000, 16–22.

46 See infra. Compare Opinion AG Kokott, 31 May 2016 with Opinion AG Sharpston of 13 July 2016.

47 See, e.g., L Waddington, 'Reasonable Accommodation: Time to Extend the Duty to Accommodate Beyond Disability?' (2011) 36 *NTM/NJCM-Bulletin* 186. For a discussion of the different positions in this debate, see K Alidadi, *Religion, Equality and Employment in Europe: Towards a Duty of Reasonable Accommodation for Religion or Belief?* (Hart Publishing 2017, forthcoming).

48 H Bielefeldt, 'Misperceptions of Freedom of Religion or Belief' (2013) 35 *Human Rights Quarterly* 33.

49 See AG Sharpston in *Bougnaoui* (n 25), at para 128: 'Whilst the employee does not, in my view, have an absolute right to insist that he be allowed to do a particular job within the organisation on his own terms, nor should he readily be told that he should look for alternative employment.'

50 See Levey (n 2).

It must be stated that while individuals are to be held responsible for the costs associated with their choices, including potential 'costs' attached to religious practices,[51] such costs or burdens are not an invariable given, but rather a variable that law and society can mediate (particularly if those costs are created or perpetuated though legal support for majoritarian standards). The 'unburdening' that takes place by means of reasonably accommodating (or by mandating employers to provide accommodations which do not amount to undue hardships) is not a 'subsidy' of these choices, but a removal of undue obstacles to the free exercise of religion by (in most cases) minorities in diversified Western societies.[52]

To be sure, there are other illustrations of 'accommodative laws' confronting the paradoxes of human autonomy in a complex world. In the area of gender equality, the reasonable accommodation of mothers who wish to continue breastfeeding their infants after returning to work is another illustration of an accommodation where choice is the triggering element for claiming and exercising a right. It is up to the woman to take the initiative to claim an accommodation (often legally recognized) by (in most cases) engaging in negotiations with her employer for time and space to pump and safely store milk while at work. However, the promotion of 'natural (and intense) motherhood' also anchors 'progressive' modern pressures on women to engage in demanding and, to some, unnecessary activities of intense mothering, which often include exclusive, long-term, or on-demand breastfeeding, lest they be labelled bad mothers. French feminist Elisabeth Badinter has criticized the modern 'natural motherhood' movement for promoting demanding parenting models – exemplified by the conservative *La Leche League* – that jeopardize and set back women's equality and liberation and hinder women's diverse aspirations (not to mention delaying child independence and impeding the development of the father-child relationship by overemphasizing the mother's role).[53] In this sense, culture and autonomy face off in the arena of contemporary gender equality debates as well.

Conclusion

In questions of religious diversity, the role of personal autonomy as a directing principle for European law remains pervasive.[54] Normative stances, including what we understand under

51 P Jones (n 5) 66.

52 For an opposing opinion, see, e.g., A Eisenberg, 'Choice or Identity? Dilemmas of Protecting Religious Freedom in Canada' *RECODE Working Paper No. 24* (2014): 'In a religiously diverse society, freedom to choose one's faith often involves costs and, unless these costs are covert obstacles to prohibit people from practicing their religions, citizens should not expect the public purse to subsidize our choices.' See also P Jones (n 5) 69: 'I cannot reasonably expect to choose a belief, the demands of which make me less eligible for employment, and yet be able to offload the costs of my choice onto an employer.'

53 E Badinter, *The Conflict: How Modern Motherhood Undermines the Status of Women* (Metropolitan Books 2011). Badinter is a fierce and prominent voice in France in favour of religious headscarf bans in the workplace, in particular in the much-debated *Baby-Loup* case, and consequently does not seem to take the side of personal autonomy when it comes to all women and their rights and values. Badinter has even called for women to boycott Western companies that produce Islamic clothing. See A Focraud, 'Contre les vêtements islamiques, Elisabeth Badinter appelle au "boycott" ' *Le Journal du Dimanche* (2 April 2016).

54 As not all cultures put the same value on personal autonomy, this remains a presentation from the Western liberal perspective that highly values individual choice and self-direction; see D Copp, 'Rationality, Autonomy and Basic Needs' in N Roughley (ed), *Being Humans: Anthropological Universality and Particularity in Transdisciplinary Perspectives* (Walter de Gruyter 2000) 348. See also CE Rasmussen, *The Autonomous Animal: Self-Governance and the Modern Subject* (University of Minnesota Press 2011).

human autonomy and which role we seek to assign to it, no doubt colour our legal reasoning and are instrumental in assigning appropriate meaning to key discrimination terms such as '(in)direct discrimination', 'genuine and determining occupational requirement', and 'objectively and reasonably justified'. One can see that the freedom of religion or belief, and the reasonable accommodation that can be considered an implied part of some understandings of this 'first human right', increase the options available for minorities in a pluralist society. The choice factor, however, can also operate to weaken and muffle protection under legal instruments such as EU anti-discrimination law, as its relevance is considered a distinguishing factor between the discrimination strands. In the words of AG Kokott:

> [U]nlike sex, skin colour, ethnic origin, sexual orientation, age or a person's disability, the practice of religion is not so much an unalterable fact as an aspect of an individual's private life, and one, moreover, over which the employees concerned can choose to exert an influence. While an employee cannot 'leave' his sex, skin colour, ethnicity, sexual orientation, age or disability 'at the door' upon entering his employer's premises, he may be expected to moderate the exercise of his religion in the workplace, be this in relation to religious practices, religiously motivated behaviour or (as in the present case) his clothing.[55]

In this sense, autonomy does not serve as 'a coordinating mechanism between different normative systems' or as 'justification for individuals' preferences', but rather as a justification for exclusion of religious minorities who seek the security, safety, and comfort of mainstream employment. The margin of appreciation left to individuals in such cases forces them into an Antigone's dilemma that 'accommodative law' should seek to avoid within contemporary Western societies. What seems most needed in this context is an understanding of personal autonomy that leads to substantive equality and opens up space for different conceptions of the good life, one that challenges the exclusionary effects that are linked to the element of 'choice' and prizes value pluralism and intercultural interaction in diverse societies.

55 AG Kokott, *Achbita* case (n 22), para 116.

8 Adopting a face veil, concluding an Islamic marriage

Autonomy, agency, and liberal-secular rule

Annelies Moors

Introduction

In the Netherlands a wide range of Islam-related practices have been at the centre of heated public debate in the course of the last decade. In this contribution, I focus on two of these practices – face veiling and what is commonly referred to as 'Islamic marriages'[1] – which have not only drawn the attention of the media, but also of politicians, policymakers, and parliamentarians.[2] Various attempts have been made to ban these practices. In the case of face veiling, this concerns either proposals to prohibit wearing face coverings in all public spaces or more limited locational and functional prohibitions. With respect to Islamic marriages, nearly forgotten legislation has been revived, while the association of Islamic marriages with forced and cousin marriages has triggered new legislation. However, this chapter only marginally engages with the question of whether governmental actors have succeeded in producing and implementing specific laws or regulations. Rather, it broadens the scope and investigates the wider range of effects that the problematization of these practices produces.

My point of departure is that face veiling and Islamic marriages did not simply appear as problems in need of regulation, but that particular actors turned these practices into issues that require state intervention. In order to better understand how debates about face veiling and Islamic marriages emerged and the work they do, I use Foucault's notion of problematization, which draws attention to how producing and presenting particular issues

1 The term 'Islamic marriages' refers here to those marriages that the couple involved believe to be valid under Islamic law and that are concluded without the prior conclusion of a civil marriage. According to Dutch law, these Islamic marriages do not have legal effects. Moreover, it is prohibited to conclude a religious marriage prior to a civil marriage (Art. 1:68 Civil Code), but only the religious functionary concluding the marriage is punishable by law (Art. 449 Penal Code). According to Islamic law, the presence of a religious functionary is not required for a marriage to be valid.

2 In this contribution I use the results of two research projects in which I am engaged, one focusing on face veiling (see A Moors, 'The Dutch and the Face Veil: The Politics of Discomfort' (2009) 17(4) *Social Anthropology* 392; A Moors, 'The Affective Power of the Face Veil: Between Disgust and Fascination' in B Meyer and D Houtman (eds), *Things: Material Religion and the Topography of Divine Spaces* (Fordham University Press 2012); A Moors, 'Face Veiling in the Netherlands: Public Debates and Women's Narratives' in E Brems (ed), *The Experiences of Face Veil Wearers in Europe and the Law* (Cambridge University Press 2014)), the other on Islamic marriages (see A Moors, 'Unregistered Islamic Marriages: Anxieties About Sexuality and Islam' in M Berger (ed), *The Application of Sharia in the West* (Leiden University Press 2013)). This contribution builds on these earlier publications. Since 2013, my research on Islamic marriages has been funded by the European Research Council (ERC) advanced grant 'Problematizing "Muslim Marriages": Ambiguities and Contestations' (ERC Project 2013-AdG-324180).

DOI: 10.4324/9781315413617-11

as a problem is part and parcel of the process of governing.[3] When practices are turned into problems, the language used does not simply describe reality, it also (co)produces it. In other words, discursive practices have material effects. In our case, this raises a number of questions: How, by whom, and under what conditions have face veiling and Islamic marriages become defined as 'problems'? What kinds of questions does this raise? What answers do these questions evoke? And what wider societal effects does this all engender? At the same time, we need to recognize that there is potentially always a gap between hegemonic discourses and how subjects respond to them.[4] This is evident when we turn to the narratives of the women concerned and analyse how they engage with the ways in which these practices have become problematized.

Although wearing a face veil and concluding an Islamic marriage are different kinds of practices, in both cases participants in public debate directly or indirectly draw on personal autonomy and related notions such as free choice or free consent. In doing so, tensions between 'women's rights', 'cultural rights', 'gender equality', 'the freedom of religion', and/or 'the freedom of expression' become apparent. Hegemonic discourse treats both face veiling and Islamic marriages as contributing to gender discrimination against Muslim women and to their oppression by their families and 'the community'. The women engaging in these very practices commonly state, however, that they themselves opt to cover their faces or to conclude Islamic marriages, and that they frequently do so against the wishes of their parents. Criticizing attempts to ban face veiling and Islamic marriages, they appeal to civil rights, in particular the freedom of religion and the principle of non-discrimination, and point to the double standards employed by those arguing for such bans. Hence, these issues seem to be classic cases of minoritized women defending their right to choose to engage in practices that the majority society considers discriminatory and detrimental to them. Before analysing the kinds of work the concept of 'personal autonomy' does in these debates, I first briefly turn to how debates about personal autonomy and cultural rights are gendered.

With respect to liberal democracies, Susan Okin's influential essay 'Is Multiculturalism Bad for Women?' functions as a paradigmatic text.[5] Okin argues that even if 'Western liberal cultures' also still practise many forms of sex discrimination, they have 'departed far further' from their 'distinctly patriarchal pasts' than others, as women in these Western cultures are 'legally guaranteed many of the same freedoms and opportunities as men'.[6] In her view, recognizing cultural rights is highly problematic in the case of cultural minorities that are characterized by strong patriarchal control of men over women, especially in the domestic sphere and with respect to sexuality and reproduction. Okin has been widely criticized for using a strongly reified and static notion of culture and for limiting minority women's agency to active resistance against their own 'cultural tradition'.[7] Juxtaposing second-hand

3 N Rose and P Miller, 'Political Power Beyond the State: Problematics of Government' (1992) *British Journal of Sociology* 173; C Bacchi, 'The Turn to Problematization: Political Implications of Contrasting Interpretive and Poststructural Adaptations' (2015) 5(1) *Open Journal of Political Science* 1.

4 J Butler, *Excitable Speech: A Politics of the Performative* (Routledge 1997).

5 SM Okin, 'Is Multiculturalism Bad for Women?' in J Cohen, M Howard, and M Nussbaum (eds), *Is Multiculturalism Bad for Women? Susan Moller Okin With Respondents* (Princeton University Press 1999).

6 Ibid. 16.

7 See, for instance, the responses to her essay in J Cohen, M Howard, and M Nussbaum (eds), *Is Multiculturalism Bad for Women? Susan Moller Okin With Respondents* (Princeton University Press 1999); L Abu-Lughod, 'The Debate About Gender, Religion, and Rights: Thoughts of a Middle East Anthropologist' (2006) 121(5) *PMLA* 1621.

cases of male domination in the private spheres of minority cultures with the formal gender equality in Western liberal society's public sphere, she provides little or no insight into the wide range of positions the women concerned take up with respect to such practices.

This variety of positions is central to Deveaux, who discusses how personal autonomy and cultural traditions are at stake in debates about arranged marriages in the United Kingdom. She proposes moving from questioning whether 'contested cultural practices undermine or support personal autonomy' to investigating 'the range of actual and possible individual and social responses to specific customs and arrangements'.[8] Employing a broad understanding of agency, she argues for a 'thinner, less idealized view of autonomy' that takes into account the various ways in which 'women in traditional cultures challenge, revise, and reaffirm aspects of cultural practices and arrangements.'[9] In other words, her concern is about agents' abilities to reflect upon and respond to social practices, which includes how 'vulnerable group members may revise and reinvent certain traditions to empower themselves.'[10] Deveaux's approach is critical of labelling people's relationships to cultural practices as a matter of either autonomous choice or oppressive constraints and points out how employing liberal norms of consent and choice frame contested cultural practices as overly static.[11] Arguing against simple binaries of force versus choice, she highlights the need to empirically investigate the motivations of women who engage in practices that to the majority public may seem contrary to their interests.[12]

In the following, I start with tracing how and under what conditions wearing a face veil and concluding an Islamic marriage have become problematized in the Netherlands. In the next section, I then present the range of motivations, desires, and intentions the women who engage in such practices present. In doing so, I focus on how notions such as autonomy or agency are employed both in hegemonic discourse and in the narratives of the women themselves. I conclude with a note on how liberal-secular rule produces more and less acceptable forms of religion and sexuality, and hence considers some expressions of autonomy desirable and other expressions undesirable and even transgressing what may be tolerated.

Problematizing face veiling and Islamic marriages: a lack of personal autonomy

In the course of the first decade of this century, both wearing a face veil and concluding an Islamic marriage have been turned from non-issues into hotly debated topics. In the case of face veiling, the issue concerns an exceedingly small number of women who have become hypervisible in public space. Islamic marriages, in contrast, are more widespread, yet remain largely invisible to the general public. Still, there are notable similarities in how

8 M Deveaux, *Gender and Justice in Multicultural Liberal States* (Oxford University Press 2006) 173.

9 Ibid.

10 Ibid. 179.

11 Ibid. 184.

12 S Bracke and N Fadil have elaborated on the ways in which this problematic opposition works in the case of headscarf debates (S Bracke and N Fadil, 'Is the Headscarf Oppressive or Emancipatory? Field Notes From the Multicultural Debate' (2012) 2(1) *Religion and Gender* 36), drawing on the work of S Mahmood, *Politics of Piety: The Islamic Revival and the Feminist Subject* (Princeton University Press 2005). While not referring to Mahmood's work, Deveaux also criticizes approaches that assume that the only way to express agentic power is through resistance to authority.

both issues have become problematized, with much debate centring on women's personal autonomy or, rather, the lack thereof.

The emergence of the 'burqa *debates'*

Although not a completely new phenomenon, it was only in early 2003 that face veiling became a major issue of public debate in the Netherlands.[13] This happened when three Moroccan-Dutch students who had started to wear face veils were refused entry to a school for vocational training and adult education and raised a complaint with the Equal Treatment Commission.[14] In the end, the various parties opposing face veiling at educational institutions were all satisfied with the outcome of the case. Individual schools could prohibit face coverings as long as they did not refer to religion and if they provided valid justification such as, in this case, impeding communication and hindering identification, thereby posing a security risk.[15]

At the time, there were no voices expressing the desire to prescribe a prohibition at the national level, let alone to implement a general ban, but two years later the situation changed dramatically. In December 2005, a parliamentary majority voted in favour of Geert Wilders's resolution 'to prohibit the public use of the *burqa* in the Netherlands', and the Netherlands became the first country in Europe to attempt to introduce such a general ban.[16] The arguments used were also very different. Wilders's resolution explicitly referred to a specific Islamic garment, 'the *burqa*' (or 'the *niqab*'), and stated that the *burqa* is a symbol of women's oppression and is, therefore, inhumane, that it is unacceptable that people appear in public who cannot be identified, and that it widens the gap between the native Dutch and others.[17]

Wilders was not alone in drawing heavily on the common trope of Muslim women's subordination, amplifying and sedimenting this discourse through the performative power of words. When the media reported on the 2003 case, a variety of terms such as face veil, *niqab* (the term the women themselves use), *chador*, and *burqa* were used interchangeably to refer to face coverings, with the term *niqab* mentioned far more often than the term *burqa*. Within a few years, however, this had changed, and by 2006 the variety of terms had narrowed down to one preferred term, *burqa*.[18] This is remarkable, as face-veiling

13 For an overview of debates about and attempts to ban face veiling in Europe, see R Grillo and P Shah, 'Reasons to Ban? The Anti-*Burqa* Movement in Western Europe' (2012) 12(5) *Working Paper Max Planck Institute for the Study of Religious and Ethnic Diversity*; E Brems (ed), *The Experiences of Face Veil Wearers in Europe and the Law* (Cambridge University Press 2014). For an analysis of how the media hype around face veiling was generated at particular moments, see A Moors, 'The Dutch and the Face Veil: The Politics of Discomfort' (2009) 17(4) *Social Anthropology* 392, 396ff.

14 Moors (n 13) 396.

15 See CGB case no. 2003–40 <www.mensenrechten.nl/publicaties/oordelen/2003-40> accessed 29 July 2016. In a rather similar case in 2000 (see <www.mensenrechten.nl/publicaties/oordelen/2000-63> accessed 29 July 2016), the CGB stated that there was no objective justification for a prohibition against face veiling. At the time, neither the media nor politicians paid any attention to this case.

16 Parliamentary document 29754, no. 41. France implemented a ban on wearing face coverings in public space on 11 April 2011, and Belgium did so on 23 July 2011.

17 Parliamentary document TK 29754, no. 41.

18 A Moors, 'The Affective Power of the Face Veil: Between Disgust and Fascination' in B Meyer and D Houtman (eds), *Things: Material Religion and the Topography of Divine Spaces* (Fordham University Press 2012).

women in the Netherlands do not wear the Afghan-style *burqa* (a one-piece garment with a mesh in front of the eyes), but rather cover the face with a thin piece of cloth, often leaving the eyes visible, a style more commonly worn in parts of the Middle East. The point, however, is not that a technically incorrect term is used to describe face veils, but rather that '*burqa*' is an overdetermined term that evokes Muslim women's gender subjugation. In 2001 and 2002 this term had already regularly been used in the media (and hence was known to the public) as evidence of the particularly gender-repressive nature of the Taliban regime in Afghanistan. In the years to come, not only was this link between face veiling and the Taliban regime reiterated in the media, but the term *burqa*, with its associations of women's oppression, was also employed in similar ways in parliamentary debates and in popular culture.[19]

These attempts to ban the face veil need to be seen within the context of an ongoing process of the culturalization of politics and citizenship.[20] From the early 1990s on, those who had previously been labelled guestworkers and ethnic minorities were increasingly categorized first and foremost as Muslims (with some also defining themselves as such). Simultaneously, Islam came to be seen as the root cause of a wide range of societal problems and, more generally, as incompatible with European values.[21] By the end of the twentieth century, a populist anti-Islam movement had started to gain ground, arguing that the way of life of the majority population was under threat of Islamization. Proposing a more muscular neo-nationalism, its proponents distanced themselves both from the ancient regime of a pillarized society they (or their parents) had freed themselves from in the 1960s and from the 'multicultural tolerance' of the 1980s.[22] An early exponent of this trend was Pim Fortuyn, whose popularity skyrocketed after the 9/11 terror attacks that marked the beginning of the global 'war on terror'.[23] His murder in May 2002 by an animal rights activist a few days before the national elections and the enormous election victory of the List Pim Fortuyn led to a political landslide. In the years to come, and especially after the murder of Theo van Gogh in November 2004 by a young Moroccan-Dutch man who claimed to have committed the murder on religious grounds, mainstream political parties also increasingly adopted an anti-Islam stance.

19 Ibid.

20 M Mamdani, *Good Muslim, Bad Muslim: America, the Cold War, and the Roots of Terror* (Three Leaves Press 2004); A Moors, 'The Dutch and the Face Veil: The Politics of Discomfort' (2009) 17(4) *Social Anthropology* 392; P Geschiere, *The Perils of Belonging: Autochthony, Citizenship, and Exclusion in Africa and Europe* (University of Chicago Press 2009).

21 A major turning point was Frits Bolkestein's speech at the Liberal International in Lucerne in 1991, in which he asserted the incompatibility of Islam and Western, liberal values (*NRC Handelsblad* 21 September 1991); another was Paul Scheffer's article 'The multicultural drama', in which the author, a prominent Labour Party ideologue, considers Islam the main reason for the failure of the integration of minorities (*NRC Handelsblad* 29 January 2000).

22 See P van der Veer, 'Pim Fortuyn, Theo van Gogh, and the Politics of Tolerance in the Netherlands' (2006) 18(1) *Public Culture* 111–124. 'Pillarization' refers to the segregation of society along confessional and ideological lines ('pillars'), with the elites of these pillars cooperating in state administration; see A Lijphart, *The Politics of Accommodation: Pluralism and Democracy in the Netherlands* (University of California Press 1968).

23 Pim Fortuyn had already published his *Tegen de Islamisering van onze samenleving* ('Against the Islamization of Our Society') in 1997. Half a decade after his murder, two new anti-Islam political movements had emerged: Geert Wilders established his Party for Freedom in February 2006, and Rita Verdonk launched her movement Proud of the Netherlands in October 2007.

The turn to 'Islamic marriages'

In the same year that Wilders was preparing his resolution for a general ban on face veils, Islamic marriages also emerged as a topic of debate and policymaking. Whereas prior to 2005 almost no attention had been paid to Islamic marriages, in the years since there have been two distinct peaks in media attention, the first occurring in 2005 in relation to the Hofstad network and the second in 2008 centred on 'Salafi imams'.[24]

The sudden hype over Islamic marriages in 2005 emerged in the context of the trial of the members of the Hofstad network, when journalists started to report on the Islamic marriages that were concluded in the circles related to this network. These marriages were not only unregistered, but were also concluded in a highly informal manner, without the knowledge, let alone the involvement, of the parents of the young women. Many newspaper articles referred to information provided by the two Dutch civil security services, the AIVD and the NCTb (now NCTV), with the NCTb even publishing a report in February 2006 asserting that Islamic marriages represented a threat to national security.[25] The main arguments were that these marriages could function as a means to recruit women for the violent jihad, that they might indicate that a man is entering the last phase prior to becoming a martyr in a terrorist attack, and that they could in time become a threat to the democratic rule of law, as ultra-orthodox Muslims refuse to register civil marriages on ideological grounds.[26]

In 2008, Islamic marriages again became a topic of extensive public and parliamentary debate. This time the targets were imams attached to Salafi mosques, who were accused of concluding Islamic marriages between partners who had not yet performed civil marriages. The regulation prohibiting religious functionaries from concluding such religious marriages, part of the early nineteenth-century institutionalization of civil marriage as the only form of marriage with legal effects, had largely remained dormant until it was revitalized in the course of these 2008 debates on 'Salafi imams'.[27] In this case, members of Parliament, including the social democrats (PvdA), the Christian democrats (CDA), the right-wing liberals (VVD), and Geert Wilders's anti-Islam Party for Freedom (PVV), played a pivotal role in turning Islamic marriages into a matter of public concern. The press extensively reported on the parliamentary questions they posed and the investigation of Salafi imams and mosques that the parliamentarians requested. These Islamic marriages were considered evidence of and an instrument for the development of a strictly orthodox Islamic 'parallel society' that deliberately distanced itself from Dutch society. As had been the case with the newspaper articles in 2005, the arguments presented by members of parliament resonated strongly with the reports produced by the Dutch security services (especially AIVD 2007).[28]

Although two different categories of Muslims were the targets of these two media hypes – first violent jihadist and later Salafi imams – the women entering into these marriages were

24 For an analysis of the media hype surrounding Islamic marriages, see A Moors, 'Unregistered Islamic Marriages: Anxieties About Sexuality and Islam' in M Berger (ed), *The Application of Sharia in the West* (Leiden University Press 2013) 149ff.

25 NCTb, *Informele islamitische huwelijken. Het verschijnsel en de (veiligheids)risico's* (NCTb 2006).

26 Ibid. 26–27.

27 In their report *Informele huwelijken in Nederland: een exploratieve studie* (Universiteit Leiden 2009) 8ff., J van der Leun and A Leupen describe debates in the field of law about the relationship between civil and religious marriages.

28 AIVD, *De radicale da'wa. De opkomst van het neo-radicalisme in Nederland* (AIVD 2007).

framed in similar terms: they were by and large defined as victims. During the first hype it was argued that they were recruited by unscrupulous male extremists who employed 'loverboy-like' practices in order to mobilize the women for the jihad.[29] In the case of Salafi imams, the women were viewed as the victims of those who wanted to institutionalize sharia and its assumed gender inequality.[30] In the years since these two media moments, debates about these 'Islamic marriages' have engendered attempts to establish laws regulating other kinds of marriage that had become associated with Islam, that is, forced marriages and cousin marriages.[31]

Face veiling: oscillating between a limited and a general ban

In the meantime, face veiling remained an issue of debate and policymaking. Depending on the composition of the coalition government, parliamentarians and policymakers either attempted to impose a general ban or worked towards a number of functional bans (in education, health, and public transport, for civil servants, and in government buildings), with the most recent coalition agreement including a more extensive version of such functional bans.[32] The fact that the social democrats also now insisted on imposing a locational or functional ban rather than leaving it up to individual institutions needs to be seen in the broader context of shifts in Dutch identity politics, with policymakers on the right and on the left increasingly agreeing that (post-)migrants will only integrate if the Dutch national identity is more firmly established. The net result is that public discourse and national policymaking have become more explicitly assimilationist, placing increasingly high demands on Muslims in particular to prove their belonging to the nation and their loyalty to the state. The cabinet's 2011 Memorandum of Integration officially declared the end of Dutch multicultural society.[33]

Both those arguing for a limited ban and those proposing a general ban link face veiling to women's subjugation. When the cabinet argued for locational or functional bans on face veiling in 2008, specific reference was made to Islamic face veils.[34] Analysing the problems that face veils can cause in society, the cabinet argued that they 'hinder open communication, . . . are considered oppressive to women, and, to many, are a symbol of a fundamentalist Islam that does not suit Dutch society'. The cabinet further explained that it 'considers open communication between citizens, participation, and equal chances for men and women essential values of Dutch society and our democratic rule of law'.[35] In a similar vein, when in 2012 the cabinet explained its reasons for banning face coverings in all public places, it argued that what matters is 'not the quantity of the phenomenon, but

29 NCTb (n 25) 22.

30 AIVD (n 28) 68.

31 M De Koning, O Storms, and E Bartels, 'Legal "Ban" on Transnational Cousin-Marriages: Citizen Debate in the Netherlands' (2014) 4(2–3) *Transnational Social Review* 226.

32 See coalition agreement, 29 October 2012, <www.rijksoverheid.nl/documenten-en-publicaties/rapporten/2012/10/29/regeerakkoord.html> accessed 5 August 2016.

33 See<www.rijksoverheid.nl/documenten/kamerstukken/2011/06/16/aanbiedingsbrief-integratienota-integratie-binding-burgerschap> accessed 29 March 2017.

34 See the letter to Parliament of 8 February 2008, which argued for specific, functional bans on face coverings: Parliamentary document TK 2007/08 31 200 VII, Nr. 48, 8 February 2008.

35 Ibid. 3.

its fundamental incompatibility with the social order in our country'.[36] Such a ban is considered legitimate because it protects an important element of public order: the equal treatment of men and women. The fact that women (and not men) need to conceal themselves is seen as an expression of an unequal position in public life, as 'in our society covering the face is a symbol of women's subordination to men.' Moreover, according to the Cabinet, covering the face hinders women's participation in society and is an obstacle to women's efforts to exert their social and economic human rights on an equal footing with men. In addition, the Cabinet stated that a prohibition would protect those women who might cover their faces because of physical or social pressure from their environment. In this way, a stance against face veiling has become a matter of principle.[37]

The women involved: an excess of agency?

If both in the case of face veiling and with respect to Islamic marriages the hegemonic discourse frames women as victims, how then do the women engaged in these practices position themselves? In their narratives they refer to two different discourses – one the discourse of religion, of submission to God; the other the liberal discourse of civil rights, in particular freedom of religion, freedom of expression, and non-discrimination.[38] Women who wear a face veil refer to religious commitment as their motivating force, whereas among women who have concluded Islamic marriages, some highlight religious considerations while others foreground practical or instrumental reasons.

Wearing a face veil: religion and civil rights

The common denominator in the narratives of women who have adopted face veiling with some level of consistency is their strong commitment to Islam and their desire to become more pious Muslims. For them, wearing clothing that covers more of the body, including a face veil, is first and foremost a recommended or obligatory religious practice. Doing so is, above all, an act of worship and a means to express their love for God. In addition, face veiling functions as a technique of the self, a self-disciplinary practice that produces certain feelings and sensations and helps to shape their actions.

Narrating their move towards adopting a face veil, the women concerned adamantly distance themselves from any suggestion of force or social pressure. Instead, they frame their motivations in terms of affective experiences as well as of acquiring Islamic knowledge. Some women had started to wear the face veil because of an intensely felt urge to do so. For others, it was through learning about Islam that they understood the need to change their appearance. For many it was a combination of both. Whereas some appreciated a literal interpretation of the central texts and followed the opinions of Salafi-oriented religious

36 See the Explanatory Memorandum to the 2012 Draft Law banning face coverings in all public places: Parliamentary document TK 33165 nr. 3, 6 February 2012.

37 Ibid. 2.

38 Starting ethnographic fieldwork with face-veiling women in 2007 and with women concluding Islamic marriages in 2009, I have conducted topical life-story interviews with more than 20 women who either wore a face veil, had done so previously, or were seriously considering doing so. I have collected in-depth information about how women have concluded Islamic marriages and their motivations for doing so in more than 20 cases. In addition, I have had numerous informal conversations with women engaged in these practices.

scholars, they all agreed that, because there is a difference of opinion among Islamic scholars over whether wearing a face veil is obligatory or not, they had to use their own judgement and evaluate the evidence themselves. They also pointed out that if wearing the face veil is to serve as a genuine act of worship, one needs to do it with a pure intention in order to please God. Such an emphasis on the importance of intentionality resonates with the liberal discourse of personal autonomy and choice and stands in strong opposition to the portrayal of these women as pressured by their environment to adopt face veiling. On the contrary, their narratives time and again highlight how their families as well as their husbands have tried to convince them not to cover their faces, sometimes because they fear for their safety.

In discussing attempts to ban face veiling, the women concerned employed a liberal civil rights discourse and pointed to the inconsistencies and double standards that, in their eyes, characterize arguments to implement such a ban. They considered the bans to be not only an infringement of their freedom of religion, but also of their right to be able to choose how to appear in public and what to wear like other women in the Netherlands can do.[39] To them the ban was a form of discrimination because it excluded face-veiling women from access to education, health care, public transport, or, in the case of a general ban, all public space. More generally, they also pointed out that there are other categories of women, such as orthodox Christian women, who prefer not to work outside the house when they have small children and for whom immaterial, religious values are more important than paid employment, yet these women are not similarly targeted. While they recognize that their style of dress in public may create a sense of discomfort, they also pointed out that there is a much wider range of sartorial practices, forms of body language, and behaviour that may also cause a feeling of unease among the general public. Only in the case of face veiling, however, do such feelings become grounds for legislation.

Concluding Islamic marriages: religious and practical motivations

Islamic marriages are not a new phenomenon in the Netherlands. Among (post-) migrant Muslims, Islamic marriages were sometimes concluded prior to civil marriages because people adhered to the sequence of rituals common in their country of origin, where there could be a considerable lapse of time between concluding the marriage contract and celebrating the wedding, which signalled the moment of cohabitation. If they followed the same sequence in the Netherlands, then the civil marriage was usually concluded close to the wedding. In more conservative circles, the period 'in-between' concluding the marriage contract and celebrating the wedding was sometimes used as a 'dating period'.

There were, however, also more specific reasons for the parties concerned to first (or only) conclude an Islamic marriage. Some couples simply were not able to enter into a civil marriage because, for instance, they did not have legal residency status or did not have the required documents. Others did not fulfil the conditions for a civil marriage because they were too young or were already married. Some also preferred not to conclude a civil marriage because they considered it financially too disadvantageous. In all these cases couples

39 See also the petition and the letters posted on the Facebook page *Blijf van mijn niqab af* ('Hands off my *niqab*'), an initiative of face-veiling women in response to the latest threat to implement locational and functional face-veil bans in the Netherlands; see <www.facebook.com/blijfvanmijnniqaabaf/> accessed 1 July 2016.

might conclude an Islamic marriage if they felt the need to conform to the expectations of their own social circles or because they themselves were strongly convinced of the necessity to make their relationship *halal* (permissible under Islamic law). In other words, for some the main reason to conclude an Islamic marriage was more instrumental, accommodating the desires of their families, while for others religious conviction was the driving force.

Some young couples opted for an Islamic marriage in order to appease their parents. In more conservative Muslim circles in the Netherlands, parents may find it hard to accept that their sons, and even more so, their daughters, are involved in 'a dating relationship'. The couple may then feel strong social pressure to enter into a marriage for which they themselves do not yet feel ready. In such cases, concluding an Islamic marriage may be a convenient solution. To their parents and the community at large, dating is more acceptable once the Islamic marriage contract has been concluded. Such an Islamic marriage may, occasionally, also function as a means for women to convince their families to agree to a marriage with the man of their choice. Although family pressure in circles of Muslim migrants, especially those who have been present in the Netherlands for a longer time, has gradually diminished, parents may still refuse to accept the partner a daughter has chosen. Some may, for instance, be hesitant about a partner from another ethnic background, or one who is not a born Muslim but has converted to Islam. Once the Islamic marriage has been concluded, parents may well resign themselves to the situation, realizing that there is not much they can do.

There are also couples for whom religious considerations are the main motivating force behind concluding an Islamic marriage. For them, an Islamic marriage is their first priority because it makes their relationship *halal*. They often strongly support the normative notion of gender segregation and reject the idea of free dating. Before the marriage contract is concluded, the couple only meet a limited number of times, always in the company of others or in a public setting. They use these meetings to exchange ideas about their concerns and ambitions, what they expect from each other, and how they would like to organize their marital life. Such Islamic marriages are not only very different from the Dutch mainstream notion of dating and marriage, but also from those arranged marriages among (post-)migrants, when parents focus more on family relations and material matters than on character and religiosity. Still, their commitment to an Islamic marriage does not imply that they reject a civil marriage. Rather, they deal with the civil marriage in a pragmatic manner. At some point in time, they may well conclude a civil marriage because it is the most convenient way to organize the relationship with their spouses and children (including paternity) and to guarantee certain material rights, such as entitlements to a spouse's pension and rights to a share in any inheritance that may be forthcoming. In doing so, they act much the same way that non-Muslim Dutch do when dealing with the question of whether to officially marry or not.[40]

Women's autonomy, agentic power, and liberal-secular rule

Face veiling and concluding Islamic marriages are strong examples of minority women engaging in practices the majority considers detrimental to them. In order to better understand

40 In the course of the last 30 years, the Netherlands has witnessed a trend towards increasingly informal marriages. A growing number of couples simply cohabit without entering into a civil marriage or concluding another form of contract; see J Latten, 'Trends in samenwonen en trouwen. De schone schijn van burgerlijke staat' (2004) 52(4) *CBS Bevolkingstrends* 46.

the divergent positions governmental actors and the women concerned take up, it is not very helpful to frame these contestations in terms of the presence or absence of personal autonomy. Instead, we need to engage with the different notions of agentic power and liberal-secular rule that the various parties concerned employ.

As is evident from the above, in these debates one particular trope was persistently present, that is, Muslim women's lack of autonomy. In the hegemonic discourse the women concerned were framed as victims of the men of 'their own community' and as suffering from a particularly strong form of gender oppression. State actors have often taken for granted that Islamic practices such as covering the face and concluding an Islamic marriage are signs or instruments of women's subjugation. This is not surprising when we consider the long history, dating back to colonial times, that links such practices to Muslim women's gender subordination.[41] Moreover, to a liberal secular public, engaging publicly in religious practices in itself stands in a tense relationship to the notion of personal autonomy. In the Netherlands this is further compounded, as such practices may well evoke memories of the old system of pillarization that many consider a relic of the past. It is not so much these acts in themselves – covering the face with a thin piece of cloth or conducting a private ritual and calling it a marriage – that are deemed problematic. Rather, what turns these acts (*Islamic* face veils and *Islamic* marriages) into particularly pressing problems in need of regulation is the fact that those engaging in them are Muslim women inspired by Islamic motivations.

Yet the women themselves often deny being pressured into wearing a face veil or entering into an Islamic marriage; they insist that they themselves have opted to do so, more often than not against the wishes of the people closest to them in their immediate surroundings. Those driven primarily by religious motivations – virtually all women who wear a face veil more or less consistently and many of those who conclude an Islamic marriage – stress that they opted to engage in these practices as a form of worship and submission to God, as part of their project to live a pious life. The notion of individual agency this entails does not start from an inert desire to be free of restraints; rather, these ethical practices may more productively be seen as a form of wilful submission.[42]

At the same time, while these women's acts are not motivated by resistance to authority, their desire to follow religious prescriptions pushes them to oppose both mainstream and minority cultural practices. Moreover, those who conclude Islamic marriages mainly for instrumental reasons often accommodate some cultural-religious practices (no free dating) and reject other cultural practices (forced marriage). In other words, when they opt to wear a face veil or to conclude an Islamic marriage, the women concerned cannot simply be defined as lacking autonomy or agentic power. Rather, what is at stake is that state actors and the wider public deem the forms of agentic power they exert to be undesirable.

41 L Ahmed, *Women and Gender in Islam: Historical Roots of a Modern Debate* (Yale University Press 1992); M Yeğenoğlu, *Colonial Fantasies: Towards a Feminist Reading of Orientalism* (Cambridge University Press 1998).

42 This builds on Mahmood's argument about the ethical practices of women involved in the mosque movement in Egypt. She warns against equating agentic power solely with resistance to authority or domination. Instead, she proposes a broader understanding of agentic power as 'a capacity for action that specific relations of subordination create and enable' (ibid. 17; 28), which can include wilful submission; see S Mahmood, *Politics of Piety: The Islamic Revival and the Feminist Subject* (Princeton University Press 2005).

This is also evident when we shift the focus from engaging in religious practices to attempts to prohibit them. When they reject attempts to ban such practices, many of the women concerned employ a liberal-secular discourse and claim their rights as citizens. In doing so, they engage in the cultural politics of national belonging. Whereas politicians have increasingly emphasized the need for a stronger and more homogeneous notion of Dutchness, these women draw on alternative notions of Dutchness, be it the pillarized system of governance or 'multicultural tolerance', to argue respectively for the right to practise their religion in orthodox ways and for the right to opt for an alternative lifestyle.

While it has not been possible to implement a general prohibition against wearing face coverings or to prevent Islamic marriages, problematizing these practices has nonetheless had material effects. Not only has it engendered lower-order regulations (for instance at educational institutions) and triggered indirect legal consequences (such as legislation restricting cousin marriages),[43] it has also produced particular categories of people. Problematizing certain practices (and not others) marks some people as belonging to a stigmatized minority driven by particularistic interests and simultaneously enables the majority to position itself as the unmarked category representing the public and the common good.[44] As majority and minority positions are always inherently unstable, debates about face veiling and Islamic marriages are performative in the sense that they contribute to the (re-)constitution of particular majority and minority positions. Whereas donning a face veil and engaging in an Islamic marriage are seen as imposed on women, majority practices in the fields of dress and marriage are self-evidently considered expressions of individual autonomy.[45] This force-versus-choice binary overlooks how the ability of all individuals to exert agentic power is always constituted through processes of subjectivation, that is, subject formation through submission to normative structures.[46]

To better understand the positions various actors take up in contestations about face veiling and Islamic marriages, we need also to briefly turn to the notion of liberal-secular governance. To many of the women concerned, adopting a face veil and concluding an Islamic marriage are religious practices. Liberal-secular forms of governance claim to be grounded in the separation of church/religion and state, as well as in the divide between the public and the private, with the former the domain where public opinion is shaped through rational deliberation and the latter the sphere of intimacy, passions, and emotions. In practice, however, the secular state does not simply relegate religion, sexuality, and family relations to the private sphere; it also defines and regulates these fields and in doing so categorizes some forms as more acceptable and other forms as less acceptable and even beyond the pale of what may be tolerated.[47] Face veiling and Islamic marriages are deemed problematic

43 De Koning et al. (n 31).

44 Mah, Harold, 'Phantasies of the Public Sphere: Rethinking the Habermas of Historians' (2000) 72 *The Journal of Modern History* 153, 167ff.

45 W Brown, *Regulating Aversion: Tolerance in the Age of Empire and Identity* (Princeton University Press 2006).

46 For a discussion of how this works in the case of dress, see A Moors and E Tarlo, 'Introduction: Islamic Fashion and Anti-fashion: New Perspectives From Europe and North America' in E Tarlo and A Moors (eds), *Islamic Fashion and Anti-Fashion: New Perspectives From Europe and North America* (Bloomsbury 2013).

47 T Asad, 'Trying to Understand French Secularism' in H de Vries (ed), *Political Theologies* (Fordham University Press 2006); S Mahmood, 'Religious Reason and Secular Affect: An Incommensurable Divide?' (2009) 35(4) *Critical Inquiry* 836. Both Asad and Mahmood, who have theorized how secular power

because they are linked to highly undesirable forms of religion and sexuality. In contemporary liberal societies such as the Netherlands, where women's emancipation has increasingly come to be defined in terms of sexual freedom and the public display of women's bodies, the full covering of face-veiling women and the rejection of non-marital sexual relations are viewed as signs of women's oppression. With citizenship increasingly defined in terms of shared values rather than with respect to legal rights and obligations, it has become evident that particular categories of the population are, far more than others, distrusted and required to provide evidence of their internalized commitment to the substantive (majoritarian) values in which regulations and laws are grounded. When the women concerned state that it was their own choice to engage in such practices, state actors in general have great difficulty recognizing such actions as an expression of personal autonomy. In response to the women claiming sameness with other Dutch citizens (in their position vis-à-vis the state), state actors tend to highlight their difference from other Dutch citizens based on the private values they presumably adhere to. One could then argue that the women concerned show a stronger commitment to the proclaimed principles of secular rule – the separation of state and religion, of the public and the private – than those attempting to ban these practices.

has constituted religion as a category in specific ways, have developed this argument with a focus on religion. For insightful discussions about how sexuality and secular rule are intertwined, see especially J Scott, *Sexularism* (Robert Schuman Centre for Advanced Studies Distinguished Lecture, European University Institute 2009; see <http://cadmus.eui.eu/bitstream/handle/1814/11553/RSCAS_DL_2009_01.pdf?sequence=1> accessed 9 February 2017); J Surkis, 'Hymenal Politics: Marriage, Secularism, and French Sovereignty' (2010) 22(3) *Public Culture* 531; M Fernando, 'Intimacy Surveilled: Religion, Sex, and Secular Cunning' (2014) 39(3) *Signs* 685, with the latter highlighting how secular rule simultaneously constructs and trespasses the public-private divide (ibid. 687).

9 Unregistered Muslim marriages in the UK

Examining normative influences shaping choice of legal protection

Rajnaara C. Akhtar

Introduction

Unregistered marriages are reportedly on the rise within Muslim communities in Europe.[1] Such unions are the outcome of couples concluding a religious ceremony of marriage which does not adhere to the requisite legislative instruments that confer state recognition on an official marriage, with all the subsequent rights and responsibilities attached to and protected by the law. The focus of this chapter is on the seemingly autonomous decision made by a couple choosing to enter into an unregistered marriage; how such a family arrangement is constructed vis-à-vis the practices in wider society, namely cohabitation; and the implications of legal intervention for personal autonomy.

Marriage and the family remain very central to Muslim communities, reflective of their historic positioning as 'central to the development of law in Islamic lands'.[2] Normative religious influences ensure that Muslim couples entering into marriages abide by religious formalities, and many weddings are celebrated with the pomp, ceremony, and grandeur associated with any publicly celebrated nuptials – regardless of whether the marriage is legally registered or not. The decision to remain unregistered, however, places couples beyond the reach of the state and its family law infrastructure, and the exercise of autonomy is demonstrated in the way they negotiate within themselves the often conflicting demands of religion, law, and culture in coming to this family arrangement. The outcome is a precarious relationship which is presumably regulated by Islamic legal traditions, yet such regulations are largely unenforceable in the jurisdiction of the state of residence and thus are voluntary and reliant on goodwill and social pressure for implementation.[3] In England and Wales, the relationship resulting from an unregistered marriage is comparable in many ways to that of cohabiting couples, who have few guaranteed legal rights arising from the relationship regardless of its duration.[4] As outlined by Probert et al., 'Cohabitants have no

1 R Grillo, *Muslim Families, Politics and the Law: A Legal Industry in Multicultural Britain* (Routledge 2015); A Moors, 'Unregistered Islamic Marriages: Anxieties About Sexuality and Islam in the Netherlands' in MS Berger (ed), *Applying Shariah in the West: Facts, Fears and the Future of Islamic Rules on Family Relations in the West* (Leiden University Press 2013) 141; R Akhtar, 'Unregistered Muslim Marriages: An Emerging Culture of Celebrating Rites and Conceding Rights' in J Miles, P Mody, and R Probert (eds), *Marriage Rites and Rights* (Hart Publishing 2015) 167.

2 M Khaddury, 'Marriage in Islamic Law: The Modernists Viewpoints' (1977–1978) 26 *The American Journal of Comparative Law* 213.

3 R Sandberg et al., 'Britain's Religious Tribunals: "Joint Governance" in Practice' (2013) 33 *Oxford Journal of Legal Studies* 263, 269.

4 A Barlow et al., *Cohabitation, Marriage and the Law, Social Change and Legal Reform in the 21st Century* (Hart Publishing 2005) 1–3.

DOI: 10.4324/9781315413617-12

obligation to support each other financially, either during their relationship or upon its end, and the courts have no power to transfer assets between them.'[5] There are obvious correlations between these two relationship types, and both are presumably the outcome of the autonomous decision-making of the parties who enter into them, no doubt prompted by a range of personal beliefs, cultural factors, and other influences. However, unregistered Muslim marriages are treated as conceptually problematic for a number of reasons, resulting in calls for legal interventions to challenge their position and restrict couples from entering into them. One such call comes from the Register Our Marriage (ROM) project, which is campaigning for mandatory registration of all religious marriages, although the project focuses on Muslim marriages.[6] ROM goes so far as to question whether criminal sanctions should be imposed upon ministers who perform unregistered religious marriages.[7] The intervention is said to be required for the purposes of protecting vulnerable parties in the event the relationship breaks down. Notably, it does not call for the law to accommodate such relationships (neither unregistered marriages nor cohabitation) by expanding the legal rights from which these couples can benefit. Calls for modernization in the law have also been made by the Law Commission of England and Wales, which conducted a comprehensive review of family law in 2015 and concluded that one of the three main grounds supporting the need for law reform is the increase in 'religious-only' marriages.[8] However, the Law Commission recognized the lack of empirical evidence in the area, and has not yet defined its proposed parameters for intervention.

Historically, cohabiting couples have remained beyond family law's legal provisions, and the rapid growth in cohabitation arrangements arguably provides one of the normative bases underpinning unregistered marriages, as it provides for a legitimate relationship without an officially recognized marriage ceremony.[9] Both types of relationship are a manifestation of negotiations taking place at a personal and social level, and while some decisions may be more informed than others, it is worthwhile to investigate the underlying motivations which lead to calls for legal interventions aimed at preventing one type of relationship (unregistered marriages), while the other (cohabitation) benefits from a proposed parliamentary bill – the Cohabitation Rights Bill – which seeks to reinforce the right to such a family arrangement by extending the legal safeguards in place for unmarried couples as a solution to the legal quagmire they often find themselves in.[10]

This chapter compares the legal effects of unregistered marriages and cohabitation in order to deduce the extent of parallels and divergence between the two. The focus shall be on the question of autonomy, exploring whether and to what extent these family arrangements foster and/or inhibit an individual's personal autonomy. The analysis will converge on the question of unregistered Muslim marriages in England and Wales as contrasted with the legal position of cohabiting couples, and identify any associated disparities between these two arrangements. Questions arise as to whether parallels can be drawn between the normative

5 J Herring, R Probert, and S Gilmore, *Great Debates in Family Law* (2nd edn, Palgrave 2015) 176.

6 A Khan, 'Register Our Marriage (ROM) Campaign on Unregistered Religious Marriages' (briefing by Aina Khan, 11 February 2016).

7 As is the case in the Netherlands.

8 The Law Commission, *Getting Married, A Scoping Paper* (17 December 2015) 17.

9 'Cohabiting couple families were the fastest growing family type between 1996 and 2016, more than doubling from 1.5 million families to 3.3 million families.' *Families and Households in the UK: 2016*, Office of National Statistics (see <www.ons.gov.uk/peoplepopulationandcommunity/birthsdeathsandmarriages/families/bulletins/familiesandhouseholds/2016> accessed 12 April 2016).

10 Cohabitation Rights Bill 2017–2019.

religious influences that prompt unregistered marriages and other influences precipitating cohabitation, as well as the rights and avenues available for dispute resolution in both cases. These two seemingly congruent practices have received widely differing social and political responses, with legal interventions being proposed for the former, while individual autonomy remains safeguarded for the latter. Arguments advocating legal intervention aimed at limiting the phenomenon of unregistered marriages will be critically assessed and explored in light of the lack of rights vested in cohabiting couples by the law and the impact this has on vulnerable parties. This gives rise to a number of pertinent questions, namely, how do the outcomes of these two family arrangements differ from one another, and do these disparities warrant different legal responses? Alternatively, should all family arrangements be equally protected and safeguarded by the state in the best interests of the parties in light of new cultural norms derived from the autonomous decision-making of individual citizens?

The question of autonomy and its practice in the context of contemporary plural societies is at the core of this volume. For the purposes of this chapter, autonomy refers to the individual right – in law and policy – to self-govern where personal family arrangements are concerned. At present in England and Wales, a couple can autonomously decide to marry, cohabit, enter into any other form of religious or non-religious marriage, or choose not to live together. Parties who conclude a state-recognized ceremony of marriage are protected by law from factors such as duress and lack of consent in entering the marriage. For those in other relationship types, there is a distinct lack of safeguards against such coercion. However, the decision on the part of couples to exclude the state from their relationship can be defined as a form of self-governance in family arrangement, and is accepted in both law and mainstream culture in the United Kingdom today. Finally, consideration of these pertinent issues will revolve around the idea of newly developing cultural norms among British Muslims concerning marriage, the increase in cohabitation, and the impact of these factors on the decision of whether to register – thereby choosing state legal protection through the medium of family law – or not.

Marriage and cohabitation

Marriage, as defined by the state, has a long history. It has been almost 150 years since Lord Penzance's famed definition of marriage was first espoused, in which he pronounced that marriage in the Christian tradition (and therefore in the state context) is defined by certain parameters:

> I conceive that marriage, as understood in Christendom, may for this purpose be defined as the voluntary union for life of one man and one woman, to the exclusion of all others.[11]

In considering Lord Penzance's definition of marriage, all that appears to remain integral today is that it is a 'voluntary union'. In England and Wales, marriage is no longer presumed to be exclusively between a man and a woman,[12] and while optimists consider it to

11 *Hyde v Hyde and Woodmansee* (1866) LR 1 P&D 130.

12 The Marriage (Same Sex Couples) Act 2013 states that 'Marriage of same sex couples is lawful.' This was preceded by the Civil Partnership Act 2004, which granted same-sex civil partnerships rights which were similar to those within a civil marriage.

be for life, statistics reflect that in 42 per cent of the cases, it is for a limited time span.[13] Clearly Lord Penzance was advocating a Christian-centric narrative in which little was left amorphous. He portrayed the institution of marriage as one which could only be entered into by defined individuals – a man and a woman – elevated and protected 'to the exclusion of all others'.[14] While the accuracy and relevance of this definition has been critiqued by numerous academics,[15] and most recently elements of it have been challenged in the United Kingdom by legislation which permits same-gender civil unions,[16] it still remains a commonly recognized description.[17]

Registration of a marriage under English law can take one of two possible forms. Anglican religious ceremonies are a distinct category and do not require a separate registration. For any non-Anglican religious ceremony to be recognized by the state, a separate civil ceremony must be performed unless the ceremony is conducted in a place solemnized for the performance of wedding ceremonies.[18] This requirement extends far beyond Muslim marriages to include Roman Catholic, Baptist, Methodist, Hindu, and Sikh marriages. Where buildings are not solemnized for the performance of a registered marriage, any ceremony of marriage remains unregistered and therefore unrecognized by the state. The resulting relationship is not one over which the state can exercise jurisdiction in the same manner that it can with a recognized marriage that conforms to the requisite state legislation.

Where family arrangements are concerned, there is a tangible departure from the state's Christian-centric narrative of marriage. In the post-modern world, increasing cultural diversity, individualization of lifestyles, and a decline in religious adherence have presented many challenges for the state. Statistics from the recent census reveal the growing move away from the traditional family arrangement of marriage and towards a less formal and less secure structure. Cohabitation is the fastest growing type of family arrangement in England and Wales,[19] a trend that is mirrored in many other so-called secular democracies in the world.[20] As with unregistered marriages, cohabitation can have a number of underlying motivations, including serving as a 'prelude to marriage',[21] as a 'do it yourself' marriage,[22] or as an alternative to marriage.[23] It is estimated that by 2033, the number of cohabiting couples in England and Wales will reach 3.8 million – thus accounting for a quarter of all couples.[24] As pointed out by Wood et al., even though legally recognized marriages are still

13 Office for National Statistics, 9 February 2013 (see <www.ons.gov.uk/ons/rel/vsob1/divorces-in-england-and-wales/2011/sty-what-percentage-of-marriages-end-in-divorce.html> accessed 4 April 2017).

14 Lord Penzance described marriage as a 'union for life', which did not reflect the reality even in 1866. This element of his definition will not be considered in any detail here as it remains defective.

15 For example, R Probert, 'Hyde v Hyde: Defining or Defending Marriage?' (2007) 19 *Child and Family Law Quarterly* 322; S Poulter, '*Hyde v Hyde* – A Reappraisal' (1976) 25 *International and Comparative Law Quarterly* 475.

16 The Marriage (Same Sex Couples) Act 2013.

17 S Gilmore and L Glennon, *Hayes and Williams' Family Law* (Oxford University Press 2014) 13–16.

18 The Places of Worship Registration Act 1855 and the Marriages Act 1949.

19 Office of National Statistics (n 9).

20 B Perelli-Harris and L Bernardi, 'Exploring Social Norms Around Cohabitation: The Life Course, Individualization, and Culture' (2015) 33 *Demographic Research* (article 25), 701.

21 Barlow et al. (n 4) 65.

22 Ibid. 68.

23 Ibid. 72.

24 H Wood et al., *Cohabitation: Law, Practice and Precedents* (6th edn, Jordan Publishing 2015) lxiii.

the most common form of relationship, the sheer numbers of cohabiting couples mean that this issue is significant and must be acknowledged by the law.[25]

Yet despite the increasing frequency of and attention to cohabitation, the concept itself remains underdetermined. Probert defines cohabitation as a 'non-marital co-residential relationship'[26] and outlines the difficulties that arise from the wide range of relationships that fall under the rubric of cohabitation. For example, bigamists or people who otherwise enter into a marriage that falls short of the state's legal requirements will be deemed cohabitees as a default position resulting from the lack of recognition of their 'marriage'.[27] However, Probert rightly views such relationships as distinct from other cohabitants, as their decision to undertake a ceremony of marriage, illegal or invalid though it may be, sets them apart from those who 'set up home without such preliminaries'.[28] The distinction is drawn on the grounds that cohabitation may not be deemed an acceptable family arrangement from a normative religious perspective for some, who then opt to go through a marriage ceremony (whether valid or invalid). There is, therefore, a binary division between marriage and cohabitation for these couples, and one could speak of a conscious decision to enter into both types of family arrangements, each within its own distinct conceptual framework – a marriage as far as the religious community is concerned, and cohabitation as far as the law is concerned. This autonomous negotiation between two distinct cultures results in an arrangement which satisfies the constituent elements of both. It can thus be argued that Muslim couples are formulating a new cultural practice that reflects their embeddedness in the British communities of which they are a part while at the same time remaining true to the norms of their religious community.

Unregistered Muslim marriages and personal autonomy

While the registration of marriages in England dates back at least to Lord Harwick's Marriage Act of 1753, in most Muslim-majority jurisdictions around the world it is a relatively recent phenomenon. Unregistered marriages were the norm prior to the emergence of the modern nation states, and to a large extent they continue to be widespread.[29] From Indonesia to Pakistan and from Jordan to Morocco, the move towards formal registration of marriages occurred during periods of transition. In many of these countries, unofficial, unrecognized, and unregistered marriages, much like the unregistered Muslim marriages in the United Kingdom today, continue to take place, presenting similar problems.

In England and Wales, the importance of registration is closely linked to the legal protections the law offers to a married couple, who form the 'ideal' family unit.[30] From guaranteed rights to inheritance,[31] shared matrimonial property,[32] and financial protections, a registered

25 Ibid.

26 R Probert, *The Changing Legal Regulation of Cohabitation: From Fornicators to Family, 1600–2010* (Cambridge University Press 2012) 5.

27 Ibid. 4.

28 Ibid.

29 Moors (n 1) 142.

30 *Supporting Families: A Consultation Document* (Home Office 1998); see <http://webarchive.nationalarchives.gov.uk/+/http:/www.nationalarchives.gov.uk/ERORecords/HO/421/2/P2/ACU/SUPPFAM.HTM> accessed 12 April 2017.

31 Administration of Estates Act 1925, S.46 (Intestacy).

32 Matrimonial Causes Act 1973, S.24.

marriage provides numerous safeguards to the family unit. Those entering into an unregistered marriage may well believe that these rights are likewise protected in their cases, as do many cohabiting couples who labour under the false impression that the 'common-law' spouse is in fact recognized by the law.[33] However, the reality is that the end of an unregistered marriage can leave the vulnerable party without recourse to any financial remedies, regardless of how long the marriage lasted, except in certain circumstances.

The lack of registration is an issue mirrored in numerous jurisdictions, including the Netherlands[34] and Egypt. Moors[35] uses the term *urfi* or 'tradition' to describe the temporary unregistered religious marriages frequently observed in Egypt, which provide young people with a means by which they can enter into a sexual relationship with each other without long-term marital commitments. Anecdotal evidence from young Muslims in Britain appear to suggest that unregistered marriages are similarly entered into during periods of 'engagement', when the families may not be ready to support a *nikkah* – the Islamic marriage ceremony deemed necessary for a couple in order to live together and embark on a sexual relationship – but the couple are less inclined to wait for their wedding night before commencing a sexual relationship. In both the latter and the former scenario, the *nikkah* is indeed conducted, but in the former case it is a temporary relationship from the outset, and in the latter case usually conducted in secret, to be repeated later with family and friends present. Normative religious influences are powerful in both scenarios, as the individual faithful Muslims do not wish to transgress 'God's laws' by entering into such relationships outside of the marriage bond, yet they may also not want to adhere to the marriage for life either, as in the Egyptian example. It should be noted that such temporary unions are not considered valid, but rather voidable or void, depending on the Islamic scholarly opinion being adhered to. For those who do not wish to be bound by a marriage for life, interesting parallels can be drawn to the trends that surrounded the increase in cohabitation in Britain in the 1970s. Probert identifies one group within society – students – who took advantage of the freedoms offered by moving out of their homes at a relatively early age and cohabiting without parental knowledge.[36] Similarly, young Muslims may be entering unregistered marriages without parental knowledge in order to bridge the gap between conservative religious ideals of a sexual relationship only occurring exclusively within marriage and wider cultural norms that accept cohabitation, sexual liberalism, and the possibility of engaging in a sexual relationship without it constituting a lifelong commitment. In all cases, autonomous navigation between competing interests is apparent.

In 2015 I conducted an empirical study involving a modest sample of 20 participants who were engaged in unregistered marriages.[37] Within the sample, the duration of the marriages varied from one year to, in one case, 15 years. There was no discernable pattern; duration appeared to reflect individual autonomy in decisions regarding the marriage. The wedding celebrations ranged in cost from a few hundred pounds to £35,000. Hundreds of people celebrated as guests at the weddings, and the ceremonial aspects reflected a mixture of normative religious influences and popular cultural trends such as music and dancing. The

33 Probert (n 26) 198–217.

34 See for example: J van der Leun and A Leupen, *Informele Huwelijken in Nederland: een Explorative Studie* (Universiteit Leiden 2009).

35 Moors (n 1) 143.

36 Probert (n 26) 189.

37 See Akhtar (n 1).

religious ceremony (*nikkah*) was identified as one of the most important aspects of the day, the other being the opportunity to celebrate the nuptials with friends and family. Pomp and ceremony were also important facets of the big day, despite that fact that no subsequent legal rights between the couple come about as a result of the ceremony. Most of the participants simply stated that a civil ceremony had not been a priority while the grand celebration of wedding rites was being planned. A significantly reduced focus on the civil ceremony seemed to be linked to the idea that the validity of the marriage according to Islamic rites would not be impacted at all in the absence of a civil ceremony.[38]

The study indicated that low priority and lack of time are the main reasons marriages remain unregistered in the United Kingdom. Nevertheless, it is clear that the decision not to register a marriage may have an array of other, less obvious motivations. Moors presents the case study of Egyptian couples entering into unregistered (and, for some, temporary) marriages,[39] where the women are older, more mobile, and better educated than the younger Egyptian men they marry.[40] In these examples, the women are often nationals of 'Western' states and they do not 'aspire to a "real" marriage',[41] thus the decision has more to do with satisfying various personal interests such as the desire to have a sexual relationship, even if only for the duration of a holiday, without transgressing Islamic traditions. Thus, a holiday romance may well entail an unregistered marriage for a Muslim couple,[42] without any subsequent rights attached to it.

Another possible reason for unregistered marriages is the high cost associated with getting married, which can make it unattainable for many young people. In such cases, an unregistered (and perhaps secret) marriage enables a sexual relationship to begin, which may be formalized later when the couple are in a financial position to marry officially. This conflict between religious ideals and community norms means that the option of unregistered marriages for young people provides an indispensible avenue for fulfilling basic physical and emotional needs while adhering to their faith. This narrative challenges what can be termed the 'paradigm case' for unregistered marriages – the disadvantaged female spouse and empowered male bread-winning spouse which results in the 'wife' being left homeless and penniless upon the breakdown of the relationship. While the paradigm case is the most frequently invoked in media discourse, these various scenarios present a complex picture of the nuanced material circumstances and other considerations that can induce unregistered marriages.

Cohabitants and the law

In England and Wales, the legal position of unregistered and cohabiting couples is quite similar. The legal consequences vary with the circumstances in each individual case. There is a spectrum of rights associated with cohabitants, the most common of which is

38 The participants' understanding of their legal positions was not explored in the study, as the sample was relatively modest and, as an initial foray into the field, it was deemed inappropriate to tackle this potentially problematic factor without adequate opportunity to explain the legal ramifications and deal with any resulting concerns which could arise for the participants.

39 Moors (n 1) 146–147.

40 O Magued and S Laila, 'Age Discrepant Marriages in Egypt' in N Hopkins (ed), *The New Arab Family* (The American University in Cairo Press 2003).

41 Moors (n 1) 146.

42 A discussion of the debate over the legitimacy of temporary or *urfi* marriages within Islamic jurisprudence is beyond the scope of this chapter.

the absence of any rights at all.[43] Generally speaking, there are in fact no ***guaranteed*** rights; rather, the granting of rights appears to be very much at the court's discretion. Despite this fact, myths about the rights associated with cohabitation abound, including the oft-cited 'common-law spouse'. The idea of the common-law spouse emerged when legislative changes were discussed in the 1970s.[44] It has since lived on as a powerful myth, bolstered by anecdotal evidence such as the category 'common-law spouse' appearing as an option under 'relationship status' on insurance application forms. In actual fact, there are no rights attributable to a 'common-law' spouse, as there is no legal recognition of this term. Barlow and James summarize the position as follows:

> On relationship breakdown, there is certainly no 'divorce-law equivalent' for cohabiting couples. There is no duty to pay maintenance to a former cohabitant, nor to redistribute property between the partners according to family law principles when cohabiting partners separate. Instead, strict property law normally applies. This is the case even where one partner was totally financially dependent on the other during a long-term relationship and/or the other partner has gained advantage from the domestic and/or child care services provided.[45]

The issue of property where cohabitees are concerned is complex and depends on a number of factors. Unlike with a married couple, no automatic property right is inferred, and property interests would have to be registered by way of a trust. The only exceptions are where both parties made a financial contribution to the purchase of the property, or there was an express agreement (whether formal or informal) that the other party would have a property right, and that party relied upon this to such an extent that it would be deemed 'inequitable' not to give effect to it.[46] This is deemed a 'constructive trust'. Only in limited circumstances would a property interest arise in the absence of such a contribution, such as in the case *Cooke v Head*,[47] which related to a dispute over a bungalow built by a couple on land they had acquired. In this case, the woman had contributed to the mortgage payments although not to the initial downpayment, but she also put a great deal of her own physical labour into the project, helping to demolish parts of the previous building, working with cement, painting, and so forth. It was clear that the Lords in this case felt it would be inequitable to deprive her of a financial interest in the property despite the absence of any express agreement of property rights. In the absence of rights for cohabitees, Lord Denning creatively took a wide view of the factors of significance. These included any statements made to third parties which reflected the principals' intentions; the way in which they saved for the property; how mortgage instalments were paid; the amount of direct cash contributions made by each of them; the actual amount of the work each had undertaken on the property and the nature of this work; and the part that each party played in planning and designing the house.[48] In this case, Ms Cooke was awarded one-third of the property. The

43 Wood (n 24).
44 Probert (n 26) 185.
45 A Barlow and G James, 'Regulating Marriage and Cohabitation in 21st Century Britain' (2004) 67 *The Modern Law Review* 148.
46 *Gissing v Gissing* [1971] AC 886.
47 [1972] 1 WLR 518.
48 Ibid.

case shows the court's willingness to treat the parties equitably and more in line with married couples. However, it should be noted that her contribution to the physical construction work was deemed 'quite unusual . . . for a woman', and thus added to the burden of contribution expected. This case is an early illustration of the judiciary's recognition of the inequities that can arise from the lack of formal legal protection afforded to cohabiting couples. In reality, however, the burden of proof is set so high that it is unattainable for many. Further, it should be noted that the costs, time, and knowledge required to bring such proceedings places any such endeavour beyond the reach of many cohabitees.

The decision in *Cooke v Head* can be contrasted with the case of *Burns v Burns*,[49] in which the court concluded that, following a 19-year relationship and despite substantial contributions to raising children, paying bills, and so forth, the female cohabitee failed to establish a 'common intention' between her and her partner which would give rise to a trust in the property in her favour. Thus, she walked away destitute – something that would be inconceivable for a married couple.

Case law surrounding cohabitation is complex and uncertain. The judiciary approaches each case based on its merits and, as a result, the area of cohabitee rights is a quagmire. Lawyers advising cohabitants operate in a field that is multifaceted and dependent largely on the cohabitants' pre-existing knowledge of law and practice, ensuring that they construct their relationship and property interests in a manner that protects legal and beneficial interests. Indeed, one of the most comprehensive volumes on cohabitation rights runs to some 756 pages,[50] reflecting how complex the lack of clear legislation makes this field. This uncertain legal position is identical for unregistered marriages, as these couples are also cohabitees in the eyes of the law.

The lack of legal redress for the inequitable treatment of cohabitees (when compared to married couples) is very much policy driven. Since the 1990s, governments have continued to espouse the virtues of marriage, as recognized by the law, as the ideal model for raising children.[51] While cohabitation has been largely ignored by the legislature to date, it has been up to the judiciary to develop creative solutions to tackle unfairness; however, in most cases inequity reigned supreme. The Law Commission has advocated legal reform and recommended a statutory scheme designed specifically for cohabitants; however, thus far no such legislation has been approved.[52] The solution has been increasingly located within private orderings, such as cohabitation agreements. This is something that remains open to all who choose not to register their relationships as marriages – both cohabiting and unregistered couples – but once again it requires knowledge, time, and financial means to obtain legal advice and pay for the drafting of the agreement. Furthermore, the likelihood of such contracts being upheld is yet to be tested,[53] and as cohabitees are considered the least likely to enter formal legal arrangements,[54] it may prove to be a solution not fit for purpose. However, such an arrangement does provide a solution to the oft-cited problem of vulnerable women exploited within unregistered marriages.

49 *Burns v Burns* [1984] CH 317.
50 Wood et al. (n 24).
51 *Supporting Families* (n 30).
52 *Cohabitation: The Financial Consequences of Relationship Breakdown* (2007) The Law Commission No 307.
53 Probert (n 26) 259.
54 Ibid.

Protecting vulnerable spouses in unregistered marriages?

As is the case with cohabitation, women are often perceived to be the vulnerable spouse in unregistered marriages, as the notion of the paradigm case outlined above illustrates. This gendered assumption is substantiated by evidence that supports the contention that in most families with children, women are the partners who sacrifice their careers in order to care for the children.[55] A woman's ability to recover her economic position following this break in her career is severely limited,[56] leaving many women in a vulnerable financial position outside of the family unit, where the partnership with the breadwinning spouse is her only remaining option to ensure that her sacrifices are compensated.[57]

Where unregistered marriages in England and Wales are concerned, this potential vulnerability of the spouse has been the focal point of contention. As long as both parties in the relationship understand their limited legal rights by remaining unregistered and agree to stay in the relationship without any form of coercion or duress, one could conclude that they are exercising autonomy in decision-making, and therefore, in my view, any forced intervention becomes highly questionable. After all, the couple are adults who, much like cohabiting couples, are exercising their free will. This raises a question: at what point are state authorities justified in overriding this autonomy? The assumed vulnerability of the female spouse, which may appear to be supported by real as well as sensationalized evidence,[58] can nurture gendered stereotypes about Muslim women and their subservience to men. This paradigm case for unregistered marriages can, however, be challenged. For example, Moors observes that Muslim women may be the instigators of such marriages, and the arrangements may in fact suit them very well.[59] The empirical evidence gathered by Moors also suggests that some women perceive the informal *nikkah* as the only necessary element to the formation of the religiously sanctioned marital relationship.[60] A government-initiated Muslim Marriage Working Group (MMWG), reporting in 2012, also identified a list of potential factors precipitating the decision not to register.[61] While they identified lack of knowledge about the benefits of registration as one such factor, the more prominent reasons were related to cost, convenience, and priorities, all of which reflect autonomous decision-making. While the wisdom of some

55 *Keeping Mum* (Fawcett Society 2010).

56 S Dex, K Ward, and H Joshi, *Changes in Women's Occupations and Occupational Mobility Over 25 Years* (Centre for Longitudinal Studies 2006).

57 In the English case of *Miller v Miller; McFarlane v McFarlane* [2010] UKHL 24, heard before the House of Lords, the judiciary in fact ruled that Mrs Miller, who had sacrificed a high-paying career in the city to care for the children, was entitled to compensation payments from the husband (which was eventually settled at one-third of his annual income of over £1 million, until he reached retirement). This was in recognition of a joint decision they made that she would stop working during the course of their marriage, for which she should not have to pay a financial penalty following divorce. However, this 'compensation' element for distribution of assets upon the breakdown of a marriage has been severely restricted to specific circumstances.

58 Numerous newspaper reports that came out in December 2015 suggested that Britain risks having an 'alternative legal system that discriminates against women'. These reports referred to Machteld Zee's book *Choosing Sharia? Multiculturalism, Islamic Fundamentalism and British Sharia Councils* (Eleven International Publishing 2016), which is itself based on a total of 15 hours spent by Zee at two sharia councils in the UK. The stories wholly failed to take into account other studies which contested these claims.

59 Moors (n 1) 146.

60 Akhtar (n 1) 173–176.

61 MMWG Report 2012.

decisions may be questioned, the suitability of legal interventions aimed at enforcing registration needs to be considered in light of various factors at play, including competing rights and interests and other benefits that partners may gain (or hope to gain) from not registering.

Exploring the Dutch jurisdiction regarding unregistered marriages, Rutten suggests that the decision may be precipitated by a desire to remain outside formally recognized arrangements.[62] This can be due to an array of economic reasons, such as surviving spouse pension claims that would come to an end upon remarriage. While non-religious couples in such instances would simply cohabit, religiously observant Muslim couples would feel compelled to sanctify their relationship in the eyes of God and may therefore decide to enter into an unregistered marriage, the effect of which is, legally speaking, cohabitation. Other economic factors may include the desire by one party to avoid financial obligations upon the breakdown of the marriage, or to avoid paying taxes in some way.[63] Less financially motivated factors may be linked to the formalities of marriage, such as the requirement that specific forms of identification be presented. For people who do not have such documents (e.g., certain migrants), registering their marriage may simply not be possible.

The emergence of a new 'culture' among young Muslims in the United Kingdom is also reflected in the changing circumstances of Muslim marriages. For example, transnational relationships are in decline, as is evidenced by the increase in the numbers of young Muslims marrying partners from within the United Kingdom. Another possible factor is that compelling immigration-related objectives for registering marriages are becoming less prevalent. The MMWG interestingly note:

> Young Muslims appear to be more likely to not register their marriages. This would seem to be less the result of parental pressure and owe more to the strengths of Muslim culture, cultural change and peer group norms. In some cases, the first religious marriage may be an experimental union of partners not ready for commitment, with the parties to the marriage still living at home. In some cases the women may see religious marriages as testing out the relationship.[64]

This portrayal of autonomy and liberated decision-making should be tempered with the recognition of vulnerabilities, especially where the social consequences may have a greater impact on women or where the parties are in a position of unequal bargaining power. For example, within Iranian society, *urfi* marriages have been criticized by women's organizations for being a threat to the family and to women.[65] In societies which remain highly traditional, the impact of a breakup is going to be harsher for women who enter into unregistered marriages than it is for men.[66] Where such arrangements turn out to be temporary, the woman, who is publicly no longer a virgin, will be at a disadvantage when it comes to entering into a socially accepted permanent marriage. In the UK context, this may still remain an issue within traditional Muslim communities. A spouse who is unwilling to register the marriage because he or she benefits financially from *not* registering can also put his

62 S Rutten, 'Protection of Spouses in Informal Marriages by Human Rights' (2010) 6 *Utrecht Law Review* 77.

63 Ibid. 79.

64 Muslim Marriage Working Group, *Report of Working Group* (2012) 4.

65 Moors (n 1) 147.

66 Ibid.

or her partner in a vulnerable position. If the relationship breaks up, the more vulnerable partner's situation can change suddenly and dramatically from being in a secure family unit with a home and high standard of living to being homeless with no protections.[67] However, as outlined earlier, cohabiting couple also face this same vulnerability. Furthermore, the decision to enter into an unregistered marriage may be influenced by purely external factors, such as the 'reputation' of the individuals and families involved, leading to parental pressure to go through an unregistered *nikkah* while the couple is still exploring the chances of success of their relationship. Doing so ensures that community and religious norms are adhered to, but the pressures can compel the couple to formally marry when they 'do not feel ready', thereby infringing on the autonomy of the couple.[68]

While the prevalence of unregistered marriages remains unquantified due to a lack of empirical studies, scholars working in the area agree that it is on the rise.[69] The ROM campaign estimates that 80 per cent of Muslim marriages are unregistered. This figure, however, is based on anecdotal evidence grounded on a divorce practitioner's experience,[70] and is highly unlikely. A more realistic projection appears to be between 27 and 52 per cent.[71] Cohabiting couples face the same legal uncertainties that unregistered marriage gives rise to, resulting in gendered inequality in the distribution of property and the protection of partners. As detailed earlier, in cohabiting couples, it is often the female partner who is left without rights and receives no recompense for her time, labour, and financial contribution to the household. This raises the question of why unregistered Muslim marriages should be singled out for special treatment. It seems that the fairest and most palpable solution lies in legislation which protects cohabitees in all their guises, as has often been suggested in recent decades. The idea of 'couple regulation', as espoused by Barlow and James, advocates the protection of the 'function' rather than the 'form' of a relationship,[72] and seems a fairer approach to the regulation of this fast-growing family arrangement. This would ensure that couples are able to utilise the formal legal system when disputes arise, relying on a coherent set of legal rights. At present, unregistered marriage disputes are often addressed in parallel dispute resolution forums.[73]

Unregistered marriages, cohabitation, and dispute resolution

For unregistered marriages, dispute resolution often takes place in unfair and unrepresentative 'sharia councils',[74] which are accused of implementing rules that discriminate against

67 Examples such as this have been used in documentaries purportedly focusing on Muslim women in Britain and the dangers posed by sharia councils; see, e.g., *Panorama: Secrets of Britain's Shariah Councils* (April 2013).

68 Moors (n 1) 155.

69 Grillo (n 1) 41.

70 Ibid. 42.

71 V Vora, 'The Problem of Unregistered Muslim Marriages: Questions and Solutions' (2016) 46 *Family Law* 95.

72 Barlow and James (n 45) 145.

73 SS Ali, 'A Push to Reform Islamic Divorce Could Make Shariah Councils Redundant in Britain' *The Conversation* (9 November 2016) <http://theconversation.com/a-push-to-reform-islamic-divorce-could-make-sharia-councils-redundant-in-britain-68023> accessed 12 April 2017.

74 R Akhtar, *British Muslims and Transformative Processes of the Islamic Legal Traditions: Negotiating Law, Culture and Religion With Specific Reference to Islamic Family Law and Faith Based Alternative Dispute Resolution* (PhD thesis, University of Warwick 2013); S Bano, *Muslim Women and Shari'ah Councils: Transcending the Boundaries of Community and Law* (Palgrave Macmillan 2012).

women.[75] Other criticisms of these councils include the failure to respect the jurisdiction of family courts in, for example, custody matters, and for forcing women to confront their husbands in 'mediation' sessions, despite evidence of domestic violence or other controlling behaviour.[76] The sharia councils also indirectly penalize women because, despite the councils' discriminatory practices, women are the main users of these forums and are required to pay hefty fees running into hundreds of pounds for their cases to be heard. More often than not, the woman's complaint is that the husband will not pronounce the *talaq* divorce. The absence of an authoritative Islamic legal system in the United Kingdom means that there is an unfair balance of power between the spouses. A husband can utter the word '*talaq*' three times and he has pronounced a divorce signifying the end of the marriage.[77] The woman, on the other hand, unless she has reserved the right to a delegated *talaq*,[78] must approach a sharia council or a religious scholar to validate her own instigation of a divorce. In many Muslim majority jurisdictions there is usually a judicial procedure, much like in England and Wales, which provides safeguards against abuse of this process and guarantees greater parity between the husband and wife.[79] In the UK context, the lack of such Islamic religious authority means that women can be severely disadvantaged, especially when their husbands refuse to pronounce the *talaq* themselves.[80] This situation compels Muslim women to conduct proceedings to obtain the religious divorce before a sharia council,[81] an unelected, unaccountable, and unrepresentative body that is, conversely, deemed to have religious authority in granting the divorce.[82]

Such plural dispute resolution bodies have existed since the 1980s, and the intervening decades have seen increasing caseloads. As Sandberg et al. found, of the 27 cases they observed at a sharia council, more than half involved unregistered couples.[83]

Cultural assimilation and personal autonomy: unregistered or cohabiting

The plurality of reasons motivating people not to register marriages can also be seen with cohabitation. The number of people in this type of relationship has steadily increased since the 1970s,[84] and its current positioning in society reflects a new cultural norm. As detailed earlier, one can locate unregistered marriages at the intersection of the culture of cohabitation and normative Islamic religious influences. This is a newly emerging cultural norm among young Muslims.

75 Baroness Cox has repeatedly tabled the Arbitration and Mediation Services (Equality) Bill to counter the operation of sharia councils on the basis of discriminatory practices.

76 Ibid.

77 L Carroll, 'Muslim Women and "Islamic Divorce" in England' (1997) 17 *Journal of Muslim Minority Affairs* 97.

78 Known as the *talaq-I'tafwid*.

79 For example, Indonesia; see S van Huis and T Wirastri, 'Muslim Marriage Registration in Indonesia: Revised Marriage Registration Laws Cannot Overcome Compliance Flaws' (2012) 13 *Australian Journal of Asian Law* 1.

80 This is also the case concerning Jewish women seeking to obtain a *get* (a document of divorce) under Rabbinical law; see Carroll (n 77) 100.

81 Sandberg et al. (n 3) 272.

82 S Ali, 'Authority and Authenticity: Sharia Councils, Muslim Women's Rights and the English Courts' (2013) 25 *Child & Family Law Quarterly* 113.

83 Sandberg et al. (n 3) 272.

84 Barlow et al. (n 4) 1.

What can be said about culture in this context? Britain has long been hailed as a progressive, multicultural society, defined by Modood as a society that recognizes 'group difference within the public sphere of laws, policies, democratic discourse and the terms of a shared citizenship and national identity'.[85] While the term 'culture' itself is difficult to define, its correlation to religion is virtually universal. From the seventeenth century to the first half of the twentieth century, the philosophical countenance of culture was very much in line with T.S. Eliot's portrayal: 'No culture has appeared or developed except together with a religion: according to the point of view of the observer, the culture will appear to be the product of the religion.'[86] However, this symbiosis between religion and culture is now understood in broader terms, and cultural norms are no longer primarily rooted in religious practice. The post-modern reality is that any given culture can be influenced by a multitude of religions, as well as political and social norms distinct from religious conviction. Perhaps Eliot was reflecting the Englishman's worldview at the time, but it is clear that globalized society is very different today and diversity is its key axiom. Nevertheless, manifestations of culture (often encompassing religion) remain a key feature of an individual's identity.

The broad range of academic discourse on culture considers its complex issues from a range of perspectives, including the community/society rubric as well as from the individual's autonomous self-identification perspective. Reservations about the use of the term 'multiculturalism' as an empirical description of societal diversity abound,[87] and yet a discussion about culture in any given European context cannot but be termed under such a rubric. There exist many cultures in which personal autonomy is greatly affected by normative influences that can be traced to religio-cultural origins, as intimated by Eliot. Where the Muslim community in Britain is concerned, the social-cultural perspective influences the issue of integration, while the autonomous individual perspective provides the underlying adaptation process by virtue of which British Muslims are forming a new and unique culture, facilitated by the influence of personal autonomy in the application of religious narratives within their particular social settings. Thus, knowledge of the British legal system and knowledge about Islamic family laws are being fused to give rise to new cultural practices, and unregistered marriages are a manifestation of this process. Scholars such as Menski have observed a hybrid form of religious laws that can be traced to migration patterns.[88] The entrenchment of British Muslims in the United Kingdom, and especially the increase in the numbers born in Britain, demand further investigation into such religio-cultural manifestations. Thus it remains the case that 'multiculturalism refers to a project that attempts to pluralise the terms through which subjects can understand their socio-cultural inter-relatedness against a core set of values about the importance of life.'[89]

Contemporary discourse on British-born Muslims must recognize the emergence of a new hybrid culture wherein British norms are amalgamated with Islamic cultural traditions through the exercise of personal autonomy. Regarding multiculturalism, Tie elucidates an epistemological inference which 'empowers subjects to entertain both their embeddedness within interpretative traditions and their capacity to alter the terms of their embeddedness'.[90]

85 T Modood, *Multiculturalism* (Polity Press 2007) 2.
86 TS Eliot, *Notes Towards the Definition of Culture* (Harcourt, Brace and Co. 1949) 13.
87 R Mehdi et al. (eds), *Law and Religion in Multicultural Societies* (DJØF Publishing 2008) 17.
88 D Pearl and W Menski, *Muslim Family Law* (3rd edn, Sweet and Maxwell 1998) 276.
89 W Tie, *Legal Pluralism, Toward a Multicultural Conception of Law* (Ashgate 1999) 30.
90 Ibid. 27.

In this way, the subjects of multiculturalism 'negotiate alterations in their self-perceptions, both within themselves as individuals and as collectives'.[91] This trans-cultural positioning allows for a multitude of factors which may have an impact on an individual's autonomous cultural self-identification. It allows for plural moral and ethical frameworks to contribute to shaping the cultural identity. Thus, focusing on the issue of marriage and the registration of marriages, it would appear that the cohabiting norm provides the framework for the emergence of the cultural norm of unregistered marriages among British Muslims.

The underlying commonality shared by cohabitation and unregistered Muslim marriages is that, in both instances, autonomous actions prompt the decision. The question then arises of why one form attracts calls for legal intervention while the other does not. The Law Commission review of family law in 2015, which listed 'religious only' marriages as among the trends indicating the need for law reform, concluded that 'the problems with the system are such that reform is not a simple matter of deciding whether any particular group should be able to conduct legally binding marriages. Rather, a thorough review of the law as a whole needs to be carried out in order to provide a system that is both more coherent and fair to all.'[92] Interestingly, of the other two underlying reasons supporting law reform, the first is the 'demand for an alternative option' by those who wish to enter into marriages using ceremonies other than civil or religious ones.[93] This may be due to underlying belief systems or a simple preference for a ceremony that is more individually meaningful. The Law Commission reaches a logical and rational conclusion that does not precipitate legislation, but rather recognizes the complexity and plurality that surrounds unregistered marriages and renders finding an adequate solution equally complex.

Those who consciously and autonomously elect to enter into an unregistered marriage are navigating between the culture of the society in which they are citizens and their own religious norms. While they may have differing motivations, the outcome is the same, namely that they are deemed legitimately married in the eyes of their (religious) communities while opting for a cohabiting family unit as far as the law is concerned. This intersection meets the requirements of their religious beliefs while simultaneously conforming to an acceptable British cultural family norm. It can thus be argued that unregistered marriages are in fact the result of a successful integration process whereby British norms have been fused with particular normative religious influences, allowing citizens to autonomously navigate between religious norms and British cultural norms.

Conclusions

The institution of marriage is culturally universal, but it varies widely according to local and regional norms. One no longer needs to travel across geographic boundaries to find these differences; they can now be observed within one and the same jurisdiction. This mixing and merging of different types of family arrangements has presented European nations with many challenges, especially over the past 50 years. All European jurisdictions have faced the question of multiculturalism and its impact on what can be conceived of as cultural norms

91 Ibid. Tie summarizes the theories of Charles Taylor and Frederick Jameson. C Taylor, 'The Politics of Recognition' in C Taylor and A Gutman (eds), *Multiculturalism and 'The Politics of Recognition'* (Princeton University Press 1992); F Jameson, *Sartre: The Origins of a Style* (Yale University Press 1961).

92 The Law Commission (n 8) 18.

93 Ibid. 11.

for their citizens. The nature of family arrangements is also transforming internally, even without the influence of an external culture. In England and Wales, a formal marriage has historically been the focal point of family law. Thus, legally recognized marriages are given special privileges and benefit from certain regulations. Cohabitees have been deliberately excluded from the framework in the interests of preserving the sanctity of marriage, something which recent successive governments in the United Kingdom have maintained. While married couples benefit from the family courts when a relationship breaks down, cohabitees are left unprotected, regardless of the duration of the union. The impact can be colossal, as there is no duty to provide maintenance to cohabitants, and any interest in property which was jointly resided in or looked after by the partners will only be realized if there is a corresponding legal right written into the property deeds. While exceptions exist, the rule is that cohabitees have to pursue property rights through channels other than the family courts, which is an expensive and painstaking process.

In the United Kingdom today, unregistered but religiously sanctioned marriages appear to be a new cultural trend among young Muslims. Research conducted thus far has identified an array of underlying reasons and motivations behind this trend, ranging from a lack of priority being given to civil registration to the choice on the part of couples to engage in a relationship that they know may be temporary. Muslim couples are autonomously structuring their relationships in such a way that they can adhere to the Islamic mandate not to engage in sexual relationships outside of marriage, but at the same time avoid getting themselves bound up in state-recognized marriages with implications for maintenance and other potentially long-term consequences. Parallels can be drawn between such relationships and the choices of cohabiting couples. In both cases, complications arise when one or both spouses are labouring under the false belief that their marriage is recognized by the state and therefore enjoys the protection of statutory family laws.

The issue of unregistered marriages is not problematic when couched in terms of autonomous decision-making, as it has the same effect as cohabitation. However, in the paradigm case, where the parties do not enjoy equal bargaining powers, or when one or both of the parties are misinformed about the legal consequences to the extent that severe and unexpected financial harm may occur upon the breakdown of the relationship, the question of state intervention becomes conceivable. However, the issue of unregistered marriages still requires in-depth empirical investigation before any legal solutions can be proposed.

10 *Quis custodiet ipsos custodes?* Personal autonomy, forced marriage, and the inherent jurisdiction in English law

Alberto H. Neidhardt

Introduction

Autonomy is a notorious source of discord in moral and political philosophy.[1] The conceptualization and practical implications of autonomy have varied over time and continue to give way to controversy within and between distinct intellectual traditions, cultures, and societies.[2] Inevitably, in an interconnected world marked by a plurality of normative systems, conflicting understandings of autonomy routinely come to the fore. Particularly challenging are judicial cases in which the legal competence of a person with some form of intellectual disability who also belongs to a distinct 'normative community' is contested.[3] One noteworthy example of such conflicts are cases of alleged forced marriage, in which the capacity to consent (and to refuse) of adults from non-European backgrounds is disputed. The Parliament of the United Kingdom introduced the Forced Marriage Act (FMA) in 2007 to safeguard the rights of victims of this practice. However, on numerous occasions the legal framework has proven inadequate to deal with volatile scenarios that fall outside the legislative framework and are further complicated by increasing transnationalism. Some distinguished English judges have thus exhorted their colleagues not to hesitate to use every weapon in the judicial arsenal if faced with what appears to be a case of forced marriage.[4] In an attempt to strengthen the legal position of individuals over the age of 18 whose capacity to consent to the marriage is either absent in the first place or is compromised by reason of external pressure, the High Court of England and Wales has declared them 'vulnerable' to the unlawful actions of their families and subject to the powers of its inherent jurisdiction.[5] The jurisdiction, which the FMA did not revoke, confers on the High Court the right and imposes on it a duty to devise innovative judicial mechanisms if statutory law does not offer adequate remedies. In *Re SA*,[6] Judge James Lawrence Munby, the FMA's main architect and champion, explained that the Court now exercises in substance and reality a jurisdiction in relation to vulnerable adults, including those not

1 For Christman, 'autonomy, like many concepts central to contentious moral or political debate, is itself essentially contested. So a theory of autonomy is simply a construction of a concept'; J Christman, 'Autonomy in Moral and Political Philosophy' (2009) *Stanford Encyclopedia of Philosophy* <https://plato.stanford.edu/entries/autonomy-moral/> accessed 3 May 2017.

2 M Fineman, *The Autonomy Myth: A Theory of Dependency* (The New Press 2005).

3 P Schiff Berman in his *Global Legal Pluralism: A Jurisprudence of Law Beyond Borders* (Cambridge University Press 2012) uses the terms 'normative community' to refer to non-state actors such as non-governmental organizations, religious institutions, and ethnic groups, who all have their means of exerting normative pull on their members.

4 *NS v MI* [2006] EWHC 1646 (Fam) 4.

5 In this chapter the terms 'capacity' and 'competence' are used interchangeably.

6 *Re SA* [2005] EWHC 2942 (Fam).

DOI: 10.4324/9781315413617-13

affected by intellectual disabilities, that is indistinguishable from its well-established wardship jurisdiction in relation to children.[7]

The extension of the jurisdiction to forced marriage cases involving vulnerable adults is justified by the shortcomings of statutory law. However, it is not self-evident why the Court should not be bound in such proceedings by restrictions similar to those that delimit *parens patriae* powers over children. Notably, these restrictions have been introduced to protect the welfare of children whose families may not share the same cultural heritage of the majority, but have an equally worthy understanding of domestic care and human dignity. Similarly, the Mental Capacity Act (MCA), introduced in 2005, places safeguards against unnecessarily intrusive decisions in disputes concerning the welfare of incapacitated adults. In particular, the MCA aims at giving voice to incapacitated adults whose desires and views might otherwise be neglected. Marriage cases dealt with under the inherent jurisdiction, however, do not fall within the scope of the MCA.

Against this background, the question is: Who makes sure that the English courts, 'the guardians', will not abuse their powers? *Quis custodiet ipsos custodies* – who watches the watchmen? English judges have consistently argued that the powers granted by the jurisdiction ought to be used so that vulnerable individuals can regain the very autonomy that dire personal circumstances made them lose.[8] However, the current lack of an effective system of checks and balances entails that the potentially limitless powers granted by the jurisdiction over vulnerable adults, with or without legal capacity, may be used at the paradoxical and worrying cost of reducing their right to self-determination. Regrettably, the dangers that could result from an indiscriminate use of the discretionary and potentially limitless powers in non-medical welfare cases, including forced marriage disputes, have generated little critical response in the literature.[9]

The goal of this chapter is neither to provide the reader with a full account of the legal framework put in place to reduce instances of forced marriage[10] nor to offer an account of English and human rights law concerning individuals with intellectual or physical disabilities.[11] The objective is rather to problematize the use of the inherent jurisdiction – in particular by considering the risks of accepting unquestioningly the role and powers of state agencies for protecting the sanctity of individual autonomy – and, possibly, to stir up a constructive debate about its virtues and dark sides.

Preliminary remarks: from family privacy to state paternalism

In contrast to contemporary attitudes to partnership choices, English law bestowed on parents an official role in the making of their children's marriages as early as the seventeenth

7 On the nominal differences between the wardship jurisdiction and the *parens patriae* jurisdiction, see A Grubb et al., *Principles of Medical Law* (Oxford University Press 2010) 511. In this chapter the two terms are used interchangeably.

8 *DL v A Local Authority* [2012] EWCA Civ 253, para 63.

9 With some exceptions: M Dunn et al., 'To Empower or to Protect? Constructing the "Vulnerable Adult" in English Law and Public Policy' (2008) 28 *Legal Studies* 234. Jonathan Herring, instead, discusses and rightly rejects the criticism of those who accuse the High Court of unwarranted judicial activism, but he fails to notice and to examine the lack of limits on the use of the inherent jurisdiction in the case of capable adults. J. Herring, *Vulnerable Adults and the Law* (Oxford University Press 2016) 71–96.

10 R Gaffney-Rhys, 'The Development of the Law Relating to Forced Marriage: Does the Law Reflect the Interests of the Victim?' (2014) 16 *Crime Prevention and Community Safety* 269.

11 European Union Agency for Fundamental Rights, *Legal Capacity of Persons With Intellectual Disabilities and Persons With Mental Health Problems* (Publications Office of the European Union 2013).

century.[12] The Clandestine Marriages Act 1753 codified the requirement of parental consent to marriages of those under the age of 21, then the age of majority.[13] Until the beginning of the twentieth century the inherent jurisdiction itself was used as an instrument of control of minors who did not respect the authority of those in charge of their upbringing.[14] Fathers who wished to put a check on their children could enforce their authority by making the child a ward of the Court of Chancery. Neither the autonomy nor the desires of capable children were given legal weight by the Court. From the eighteenth century, sons and daughters could be prevented from marrying or from meeting with a specific person in accordance with the wishes of their family, thanks to the powers granted by the inherent jurisdiction. State institutions were prevented from intervening in family life unless asked to do so by parents themselves, and in such situations, the Court of Chancery traditionally supported the desires of fathers.

The first half of the twentieth century marked the beginning of a new approach by the judiciary, which started using the wide powers deriving from its *parens patriae* jurisdiction to achieve the child's welfare independently of the stance of the family.[15] From the early decades of the twentieth century, the notion of 'best interests' allowed the Court of Chancery to extend further its *parens patriae* jurisdiction over children, and to make decisions according to what it considered to be the most effective way of ensuring the welfare of the minor. By way of example, one of the motivations behind the introduction of the 1934 Guardianship of Infants Act (GIA) was to allow state authorities to grant consent if any person whose consent was required refused to agree to a prospective marriage.[16] Where the family did not give its permission, the underage parties could apply to the court instead of eloping to the Scottish border.[17] The GIA signalled that parents' sovereignty over the choice of partners was no longer absolute.

Parental authority came to be increasingly suspected of creating unnecessary tensions within family and society and of hiding instances of abuse and discrimination. Social perceptions of the extent of legitimate exercise of parental authority had become markedly different by the 1960s–1970s, and the state was progressively assuming a more prominent role in protecting children against abuses by the family.[18] Not only did a rapidly evolving social and political scenario see unprecedented demands by younger generations for individual liberties and freer partnership choices; the underlying assumptions of the legal and institutional framework also changed.

If until the twentieth century courts' orders in wardship proceedings almost invariably followed parental desires, after the 1960s a strong belief emerged in the public that children's welfare, and individual autonomy more generally, should be absolute. Family involvement in marriage arrangements, and in all important decisions concerning the upbringing

12 R Probert, 'Parental Responsibilities and Children Partnership Choices' in R Probert et al. (eds), *Responsible Parents and Parental Responsibility* (Hart Publishing 2009) 237–238.
13 S Cretney, *Family Law in the Twentieth Century: A History* (Oxford University Press 2003) 4–8.
14 Ibid. 586.
15 Ibid. 589.
16 S 7(9)(1)(b).
17 The CMA did not apply in Scotland, where boys could get married at the age of 14 and girls at the age of 12 with or without parental consent.
18 A Diduck and F Kaganas, *Family Law, Gender and the State: Text, Cases and Materials* (Hart Publishing 2006) 289–293.

of children, was traditionally seen as an extension of parental authority. As a result of these social and cultural developments, it became regarded as suspicious and unwarranted.

This change in social consciousness reached its apex in the latter decades of the twentieth century and had a great impact on family law as well as on medical law. In accordance with the intellectual shift underway, *Gillick*[19] and other high-profile cases decided in the 1980s and 1990s established that family privacy could be subject to state intervention whenever parental decisions did not consider the best interests of the child first and foremost.[20] However, the result of this cultural shift was not that individual autonomy eventually came to prevail over parental responsibilities *and* state prerogatives. Instead, state powers have, over time, become more extensive even than the custodial powers of parents had been originally.[21] Speaking of the jurisdiction, John Seymour thus argued that the *parens patriae* had over time conferred on courts 'wider powers than those possessed by natural parents and so permitted the judge invoking it to do more than fill the shoes of the parents'.[22]

Preventing state abuses: the Children Act 1989

The flexibility of the jurisdiction and the unprecedented powers deriving from it led to increased numbers of wardship and *parens patriae* applications from the 1960s to the 1990s.[23] The jurisdiction became an increasing concern because of its costs, the extent of the discretionary powers of the Court, and its careless use by local authorities.[24] It became important to specify in what circumstances social services could intervene through the Court's jurisdiction and, when this was the case, what factors it should consider when making a decision on behalf of the child. In 1989, in response to these widely held concerns, the Children Act (CA) placed statutory checks on the potential abuses of the jurisdiction.[25]

Although the CA – which is still in place and is regarded by many as one of the most successful reforms in the field of domestic relations – provides for an 'open-door' principle, allowing anyone the right to seek an order from the court in relation to the child's upbringing, a person who is not related in some way to the child must first obtain the court's leave.[26] Under this simple but effective measure, courts are bound by the CA to follow the 'no-order presumption', according to which an order can be made only in cases where the child would be worse off by not making any order at all.[27] Non-intervention was thus elevated by the CA to the status of a guiding principle, demonstrating that protection of vulnerable individuals and respect for family privacy are not necessarily incompatible.[28]

19 *Gillick v West Norfolk* [1986] AC 112, [1986] 1 FLR 224.
20 A Bainham, 'Is Anything Now Left of Parental Rights?' in R Probert et al. (eds), *Responsible Parents and Parental Responsibility* (Hart Publishing 2009).
21 Grubb et al. (n 7) 511.
22 J Seymour, 'Parens Patriae and Wardship Powers: Their Nature and Origins' (1994) 14 *Oxford Journal of Legal Studies* 159, 159 referring to the words of Lord Donaldson in *Re R* [1991] 14 All ER 177, 186.
23 Cretney (n 13) 588.
24 K Standley, *Family Law* (Palgrave Macmillan 2010) 272.
25 Ibid. 33.
26 Ss 9 and 10.
27 S 1(5).
28 FE Olsen, 'The Myth of State Intervention in the Family' (1984–1985) 18 *University of Michigan Journal of Law Reform* 835.

It is important to note that the CA set in place a system of checks and balances partly because of the fear that state agencies could intervene in family life whenever parental decisions did not conform to the majority-held view. Lord Chancellor Mackay explained the policy to which the CA seeks to give effect:

> Unless there is evidence that a child is being, or is likely to be, positively harmed because of a failure in the family, the State, whether in the guise of a local authority or a court, should not interfere. . . . [T]o provide otherwise would make it lawful for children to be removed from their families simply on the basis that a court considered that the state could do better for the child than his family. *The threat to the poor and minority groups, whose views of what is good for a child may not coincide closely with that of the majority, is all too apparent.*[29]

In a scenario marked by a plurality of normative communities and rising inequalities and suspicion between ethnic groups, the emphasis on protection might inadvertently turn the jurisdiction into a proxy for advancing one specific conception of welfare. Accordingly, the CA established that when a court makes decisions concerning the welfare of the child, judges must follow a checklist of relevant factors, including the wishes and feelings of the child.[30]

The jurisdiction can be a tool for empowerment, but also a tool that is susceptible to abuse, with particular risks for normative minorities if the limits to its application are not strictly defined. As the High Court now exercises in substance and reality a jurisdiction in relation to vulnerable adults that is practically indistinguishable from its well-established wardship jurisdictions in relation to children, the question that arises is why the High Court should not be bound, in the case of adults, by restrictions similar to those which delimit judicial powers over children.[31]

Into the 2000s: extension of the inherent jurisdiction to incapacitated adults

For centuries the evolution of the inherent jurisdiction over adults followed a separate course from that of the *parens patriae* jurisdiction over children. Until the mid-nineteenth century, no body of legislation was developed with respect to the specific category of intellectually disabled adults. The role of legal guardian was still being exercised by the Lord Chancellor and the judges of the Chancery Division when the Mental Health Act 1959 (MHA) came into force. By the time the MHA was introduced, judicial attitudes had come to embody the spirit of previous times, especially legal ideas deriving from social Darwinism.[32] Against a legal background characterized by a lack of specific provisions, English judges had claimed for themselves an ever greater 'guardianship role', often replacing the statutory void with benevolent paternalism.[33]

29 Cretney (n 13) 727 (emphasis added).

30 S 1(3)(a). See also Cretney (n 13) 725.

31 Already in *Re G* [1995] 2 FLR 528, 530, Sir Stephen Brown described the jurisdiction as 'not strictly "parens patriae" but similar in all practical respects to it'.

32 AF Tredgold, 'The Definition and Diagnosis of Moral Imbecility' (1926) 6 *British Journal of Medical Psychology* 1.

33 A Dimopoulos, *Issues in Human Rights Protection of Intellectually Disabled Persons* (Ashgate 2010) 110.

The MHA is generally regarded as introducing a historic and positive change in mental health legislation. In consonance with advances in psychiatry and medical treatment, and with the emergence of a human rights culture, the stated goal of the MHA became to de-institutionalize patients and delegate their treatment to community care. In line with this cultural shift, the MHA also revoked the warrant that previously allowed the Lord Chancellor to exercise *parens patriae* powers with respect to incapacitated adults. Starting in the 1960s, only the Court of Protection could exercise such powers with respect to adults, and only in decisions concerning financial matters.[34]

From the late 1980s, however, judges started lamenting the harmful consequences of the watertight barrier imposed on non-financial matters where the welfare of adults was at stake, but the concerned individuals lacked the capacity to make 'best interests' decisions in relation to their surgical, medical, and nursing treatment.[35] In practical terms, the guardianship regime set up by the MHA did not prove successful. A process of judicial lawmaking followed calls for reform by experts, resulting in courts bringing the jurisdiction over adults back to life. In the words of Judge Munby, this process 'was astonishing in [its] speed' and led to what would become, for all practical purposes, 'a new branch of the law'.[36] First, the jurisdiction was extended to cover situations in which the appropriate medical treatment was in question.[37] Then it was also extended to questions of residence and contact.[38]

It is important to note that this process did not take place in a legal void, but drew from the experience acquired in 'best interests' cases involving children, including those with intellectual disabilities. Andreas Dimopoulos explains that

> the evolution of wardship and family law had already familiarised the courts with a process of answering welfare issues for children. The coast was therefore clear for the courts to apply, by way of analogy, the familiar process of dealing with children welfare to adult cases as well.[39]

Mindful of the risks posed by the unfettered *parens patriae* powers in best interests cases concerning children, however, Parliament introduced in 2005 the Mental Capacity Act (MCA).

The MCA, which is founded on the pillar of functional capacity, placed significant restrictions on judicial interventions in welfare cases involving legally incapable adults. There are five key principles underlying the MCA which guide the Court of Protection:[40] every adult shall be presumed to have decision-making capacity unless proved otherwise; incapacity cannot be established unless all practicable means have been taken to help the person make

34 As to the functions of the judge of the Court of Protection, according to s 102(1), 'The judge may, with respect to the *property and affairs* of a patient, do or secure the doing of all such things as appear necessary or expedient.'

35 Starting with Wood J in *T v T* [1988] Fam 52, [1988] 1 FLR 400. M Welstead, 'Vulnerable Adults: The Inherent Jurisdiction and the Right to Marry' (2007) 19 *Denning Law Journal* 258.

36 JL Munby, 'Protecting the Rights of Vulnerable and Incapacitous Adults – The Role of the Courts: An Example of Judicial Law Making' (2014) 26 *Child and Family Law Quarterly* 64, 66–77.

37 *Re S (Adult Patient: Sterilisation)* [2001] Fam 15.

38 *Re F (Adult: Court's Jurisdiction)* [2001] Fam 38.

39 Dimopoulos (n 33) 112.

40 A Weereratne et al., *Butterworths New Law Guide: Mental Capacity Act 2005* (LexisNexis 2008) 15–24.

his or her own decisions; individuals must be free to make unwise decisions; judges must consider the best interests of the incapacitated person and must opt for the least restrictive form of intervention.[41] The MCA thus aims to empower adults affected by disabilities so that they can make best interests decisions autonomously.

The specialized literature has criticized the MCA for not replacing the vague and paternalistic notion of best interests with a more principled approach based on human rights.[42] However, the familiar problem of paternalism denounced by experts seems to follow from the limits of the human rights regime itself rather than from the specific provisions of the Act. International covenants such as the European Convention on Human Rights are universal instruments and were not designed with persons affected by *intellectual* disabilities foremost in the mind. It is no accident that the European Court of Human Rights heard the first case concerning a person with an intellectual disability only 35 years after the ECHR was signed in 1950.[43] A handful of ECtHR proceedings have touched on the right to private and family life of individuals affected by disabilities, and the ECtHR has generally granted a wide margin of appreciation with regard to questions of welfare.[44] Although the UK has also ratified the Convention on the Rights of People with Disabilities, the international human rights regime has not instituted adequate safeguards in cases concerning *intellectually* disabled individuals.[45] The absence of a comprehensive jurisprudence dealing specifically with intellectually disabled individuals weakens the European human rights regime to the point of making it negligible in the difficult search for an equilibrium between empowerment and control to which the MCA is instead devoted.[46]

The MCA, which came into force in 2007, does not cover non-medical decisions. It thus does not bind judges in, among other types of cases, marriage cases.[47] This explicit limitation gave the High Court the leeway, and imposed on it the duty, to develop the inherent jurisdiction further with respect to non-medical welfare cases

> where an individual does not lack capacity in the terms of the MCA 2005 and therefore falls outside the statutory scheme, but other factors, for example coercion and undue influence, may combine with his borderline capacity to remove his autonomy to make an important decision.[48]

Per contra, the concerns that pushed the legislature to take action and introduce the MCA beg the question: why should a similar set of firmly established and clearly spelled-out limits not be in place in cases where the jurisdiction is used to protect vulnerable but capable individuals?

41 S 1(1–5).

42 Dimopoulos (n 33) 128–132.

43 *X and I v the Netherlands*, 26 March 1985, Ser. A No. 91.

44 Most cases concern the custody of children of disabled individuals. On the right to private and family life, see P Bartlett et al., *Mental Disability and the European Convention of Human Rights* (Martinus Nijhoff 2007) 192–195.

45 The CRPD entered into force in 2008. It is not, however, devoted specifically to the rights and needs of persons with intellectual disabilities in mind. See Dimopoulos (n 11) 79.

46 Dimopoulos (n 33) 101–136.

47 S 27(1)(a).

48 *DL* (n 8) para 65.

From medical to situational vulnerability: forced spouses between coercion and protection

It is evident from the case law that the inherent jurisdiction is exercisable in relation to a wide range of civil matters, marriage included.[49] That the inherent jurisdiction could be of help even in forced marriage cases became crystal clear when the Foreign and Commonwealth Office started court proceedings in *Re SK*.[50] Consular offices in Bangladesh had received information according to which a young British adult of South Asian origin was being held by her family against her will. According to the information in the hands of the British authorities, SK's family was planning to force her into marriage. SK was a capable adult and should not have been subject to *parens patriae* jurisdiction. In spite of that, the Court feared that she was being prevented by her relatives from controlling 'her own life and destiny'.[51] Pointing out that, if a child, SK could be made a ward of the Court, Judge Singer held that the inherent jurisdiction can, in an appropriate case, be relied upon and utilized to provide a remedy also in cases concerning adults who do not suffer from intellectual disabilities and can consent to marriage.[52] In *Re SK* the extension of the jurisdiction was evidently justified by the shortcomings of statutory law which would not allow the authorities to swiftly intervene and prevent a forced marriage from taking place.

Indeed, it is common ground in law that a fully autonomous adult like SK can be rendered temporarily incapable of making decisions which carry legal consequences. In order to qualify as legally competent, besides 'internal conditions', persons must also be free from duress, coercion, and manipulation.[53] Accordingly, with respect to forced marriages, duress occurs where a person is subjected to pressures that destroy 'the reality of consent and overbear the will of the individual'.[54] Together with an assessment of cognitive capacity, it becomes critical to consider what degree of pressure within her family and her social environment would suffice to compromise an otherwise free and genuine consent.

This assessment, it ought to be noted, encompasses life-changing and value-laden choices that may either be or come across as unsound and irrational, especially when made or taken in concert by members of a normative minority. When referring to external conditions there is a grey area that has to do with the acceptability by the cultural majority of what may appear to be irrational, life-changing decisions taken under the influence of strong emotions in combination with 'distorted values'. It is precisely in order to avoid entering into this moral and legal minefield that the High Court also held in *Sheffield* that judges only have jurisdiction to evaluate the person's capacity to consent, and not whether a particular marriage is in the adult's best interests.[55]

49 *XCC v AA and others* [2012] EWHC 2183 (COP).

50 *Re SK* [2004] EWHC 3202 (Fam).

51 Para 3.

52 Para 8.

53 Internal conditions provide that a person must be able to understand and retain the information to which she is exposed; she must be able to assimilate the information, to evaluate options, and to weigh alternatives; finally, she must be able to communicate her decision.

54 *Hirani v Hirani* [1983] 4 FLR 232, 233.

55 *Sheffield City Council v E* [2004] EWHC 2808 (Fam). Confirming the reasoning of *Park v Park* (n 94), Judge Munby held that '[i]n relation to her marriage the only question for the court is whether E has capacity to marry. The court is not concerned – has no jurisdiction – to consider whether it is in E's best interests to marry or to marry S. The court is concerned with her capacity to marry, not with the wisdom of her marriage in general or her marriage to S in particular.' Para 102.

Clearly, the capacity of courts to protect the well-being of vulnerable individuals also depends on this external dimension of autonomy, which may be compromised by the cultural norms and family pressures to which victims of forced marriage are often exposed. It is likewise evident that in social contexts marked by a high degree of normative pluralism, the risk is to mistake domestic tensions over partnership choices, which are often imbued with cultural undertones but are nearly universal, for unlawful family pressures. This delicate aspect was specifically addressed by the High Court in *NS v MI*,[56] where the petitioner, a legally capable British girl whose family originally came from Pakistan, successfully applied for nullification of her marriage on the ground of duress.[57] In the judgment, Judge Munby held:

> [W]here the influence is that of a parent or other close and dominating relative, and where the arguments and persuasion are based upon personal affection or duty, religious beliefs, powerful social or cultural conventions . . . the influence may . . . be subtle, insidious, pervasive and powerful. In such cases, moreover, very little pressure may suffice to bring about the desired result.[58]

This broad definition of external pressure shows sensitivity on the part of the High Court to the subtle ways in which a person can feel forced to marry.[59] However, as pointed out by Rebecca Probert, '[i]f this is the degree of influence deemed inappropriate . . . it would seem that a parent is not entitled to promote particular suitors, even if he or she may warn against those deemed unsuitable.'[60] Any involvement of the family in the marriage arrangements is regarded as suspicious, whether the individual is legally competent or not, especially when the influence of the parents or family members is grounded in religious or cultural terms. Individuals could nevertheless decide to delegate certain decisions to their family members because they feel this is the best way to ensure their own well-being. In many such circumstances, their autonomous choices would be framed in cultural and religious arguments, thus giving rise to suspicion and, possibly, judicial intervention.

Re SK demonstrates that the jurisdiction can be a valuable and empowering resource. The extension of the legal protective net over capable adults who are rendered vulnerable by their environment seems to be fully justified in light of the dangers posed by social evils such as forced marriages. It also appears to be in line with an ongoing redefinition of the notion of disability from a purely medical concept to a 'social' one.[61] However, the inherent jurisdiction is an instrument that is susceptible to abuse, with particular risks for normative minorities if the limits to its application are not strictly defined.

56 *NS v MI* (n 4).

57 Matrimonial Causes Act [1973], s 12(c).

58 Para 34. This definition of coercion confirms the one given in *Re SA* (n 7) and is in line with the test of duress established in *Hirani* (n 54).

59 According to *Szechter v Szechter* [1971] 2 WLR 170, [1970] 3 All ER 905, a marriage was valid unless it could be proved that the will of one of the parties had been overborne by fear caused by the threat of immediate danger to life, limb, or liberty. R Probert, *Cretney's and Probert's Family Law* (Sweet & Maxwell 2006) 49–52.

60 Probert (n 12) 251.

61 See World Health Organization, *World Report on Disability* (2011) 4 for a programmatic statement of this shift.

Vulnerability redefined: *Re SA*

Not long after the decision in *NS v MI*, Parliament passed the Forced Marriage Act of 2007.[62] The FMA did not abolish the inherent jurisdiction.[63] As the Family Division of the High Court soon made clear, precautionary measures should be taken whenever possible to prevent forced marriages in order to avoid physical and psychological consequences for their victims.[64] In the words of Judge Munby, the 'court must not hesitate to use every weapon in its protective arsenal if faced with what is, or appears to be, a case of forced marriage'.[65] This is the scenario faced by the Court in *Re SA*.[66]

Proceedings in *Re SA* were initiated by the local authority, which applied for extending the *parens patriae* jurisdiction over SA, a vulnerable 18-year-old who had been a ward since a younger age. SA, who is described as profoundly deaf, could only communicate by British Sign Language (BSL) and also had learning disabilities. The family was of Pakistani origin and could not communicate with SA using BSL. The local authority argued that SA was in need of protection from unsuitable marriages because it feared that the family was planning to marry her off in Pakistan. However, expert evidence stated clearly that SA had capacity to marry according to the test laid down in *Sheffield*.[67] In addition, SA had made a conscious decision that her parents should arrange a marriage.[68] In spite of that the High Court felt 'the need to put in place protective measures to prevent [this] vulnerable adult being taken abroad to be married'.[69] Specifically, the High Court was concerned that SA would not understand the risks entailed in marrying a person limited by his immigrant status or someone who would not be able to communicate in BSL.[70]

Re SA confirmed the extension of the jurisdiction to capable adults that had already been applied in *Re SK*. The High Court maintained that it now 'exercises what is, in substance and reality, a jurisdiction in relation to . . . adults which is for all practical purposes indistinguishable from its well-established *parens patriae* in relation to children'.[71] Accordingly, Judge Munby decided to grant the injunction in favour of the local authority in order 'to protect SA's private life, in particular to ensure that her private life is not jeopardised by her parents' actions in seeking to arrange a marriage for her'.[72] As a result, SA was prevented from leaving the UK and from entering into marriage without the Court's prior consent.[73]

62 Before the introduction of the FMA, the courts had to work their way through a patchwork of laws that were not specifically designed to tackle the practice of forced marriage. R Gaffney-Rhys, 'The Implementation of the Forced Marriage (Civil Protection) Act 2007' (2009) 31 *Journal of Social Welfare and Family Law* 245.

63 H Patel et al., 'In Practice: Forced Marriage: The Concept and Law' (2009) 39 *Family Law* 726.

64 *NS v MI* (n 4) para 7.

65 Ibid. para 4.

66 *Re SA* (n 6).

67 Para 12. Too high a threshold would allow many marriages to be annulled under the Matrimonial Causes Act, ss 12(c) and 12(d). *Re Estate of Park, Deceased, Park v Park* [1954].

68 Para 13.

69 Para 97.

70 Paras 13 and 14.

71 Para 37.

72 Para 130.

73 *Re SA* is therefore in contradiction to the Court's decision in *Sheffield*, where it held that it can only evaluate the person's capacity to consent and not whether a particular marriage is in the vulnerable adult's best interests.

The High Court also specified that the powers that the jurisdiction grants are not confined to vulnerable adults. A vulnerable adult is simply more likely to fall within the scope of the jurisdiction.[74] For Judge Munby, 'the inherent jurisdiction is no longer correctly to be understood as confined to cases where a vulnerable adult is disabled by mental incapacity . . . but extends to a wider class of . . . adults.'[75] Vulnerability is no longer 'a necessary or a sufficient condition to fall within the jurisdiction'.[76] Despite admitting that it would be unwise to try to define who might fall within its jurisdiction, the Court declared that a person over the age of majority

> who does not suffer from any kind of mental incapacity may nonetheless be entitled to the protection of the inherent jurisdiction if he is, or is reasonably believed to be, incapacitated from making the relevant decision by reason of such things as constraint, coercion, undue influence or other vitiating factors.[77]

Absent a set of firmly established limitations on its use, and on account of the broad definition of coercion advanced in *NS v MI*, the jurisdiction could potentially be applied whenever a person, legally competent or not, saw his or her best interests depend on the advice of a family member or third party whose strong influence and whose opinion the Court does not consider beneficial to his or her welfare. Intervention by state agencies – and social services no longer need to apply for leave of the Court[78] – could happen even against the wishes of a capable person who is willing to consent to a marriage being arranged for her.

The dark side of virtue: ignoring personal autonomy

Although the best interests and personal autonomy of vulnerable adults are said to be of absolute priority, where the jurisdiction has been invoked their wishes and feelings are paradoxically given little or no consideration. It cannot but strike one's attention that in *Re SA* as well as in other non-medical welfare cases, attempts to engage directly with the subjective perspective of being vulnerable to a determined situation are missing. The counter-argument could be made that, in conformity with the classical distinction between 'global' and 'local' autonomy, the High Court decided to ignore SA's personal agency in the short term – and her right to marry and establish a family – in order to enable her to better exercise her right to self-determination in the long term.[79] However, there must be strong and cogent reasons for courts to ignore a person's desires and feelings. As Jonathan Herring emphasized, 'Certainly the idea of a court making an order compelling a person to be treated in a particular way without their consent would be seen as an anathema to most lawyers.'[80] If decisions taken under the jurisdiction serve the purpose of protecting personal

74 Para 80.
75 Para 76.
76 Herring (n 9) 81.
77 Para 79.
78 Proceedings under the FMA can be initiated by the victim and by third parties, such as local authorities, which can also apply for protection orders without leave of the Court (unlike under the CA).
79 See *A Local Authority v A* [2010] EWHC 1549 (Fam) para 79.
80 J Herring, 'Protecting Vulnerable Adults: A Critical Review of Recent Case Law' (2009) 21 *Child and Family Law Quarterly* 498, 502.

autonomy, whether local or global, a high value must necessarily be assigned to the wishes and feelings of the vulnerable person concerned.

Hearing SA's voice was of critical importance for understanding to what extent she could participate in her family culture and to what extent she could comprehend it. As Dunn, Clare, and Holland underline:

> If SA valued her cultural heritage, and wished for her mother and father to have an active role in arranging her marriage, surely more attention should have been focused on attempts to work with them as a family to resolve the issue facing the court? Rather than viewing her parents as hostile, inflexible, and lacking in insight and understanding, intervention would then have prioritised the maintenance of close relationships between family members. If this is not the approach taken, inadvertent negative consequences might arise.[81]

We cannot assess the personal cost to SA of the Court's decision because we do not know to what extent SA subscribed to her removal from the influence of her family, to what degree she could express her cultural values, and whether she saw a particular marriage arrangement as a means of improving the quality of her life.

As the Law Commission reminds us, '[f]or both policy makers and practitioners, there is a difficult balance to be struck between maximising autonomy and ensuring adequate protection for those who need it.'[82] What *Re SA* shows is that without a system of checks and safeguards in place, judges may not be in a position to strike an appropriate balance. Had it not been made in the context of non-medical welfare, the decision to ignore SA's views would have arguably contradicted two of the key principles underpinning the MCA: that individuals shall always be presumed to be able to make decisions autonomously, and that they shall be able to make unwise decisions. If *Re SA* were to be decided in accordance with principles regulating the wardship jurisdiction, judges would be explicitly bound by the provisions of the CA to take notice of the concerned person's own wishes. The High Court enjoys discretionary powers identical to those available under the wardship jurisdiction; however, it appears unwilling to accept restrictions similar to those which have been established for preventing abuses of power and disproportionate interventions.[83]

If the cultural background of all members of liberal democratic states acts as an incentive rather than as a deterrent to voice concerns, vulnerable members of all normative communities will be empowered. If the official legal system supports the realization of their wishes, they can make advantageous choices even in the presence of structural constraints.[84] If, instead, no debate about the issue at hand takes place and the judicial approach stays the same, the welfare of vulnerable adults may be ensured in the short term, but the quality of their lives could deteriorate in the long run because their life-course would not match their expectations and wishes. In light of the scarce attention paid to their desires, the state's duty to protect their autonomy might turn out to disempower vulnerable adults.

81 Dunn et al. (n 9) 252.

82 The Law Commission, *Adult Social Care* (Consultation Paper No. 192, 2010) 136.

83 The CA would require that there must be strong evidence before the Court could even contemplate whether the state should interfere.

84 S Anitha and A Gill, 'Coercion, Consent and the Forced Marriage Debate in the UK' (2009) 17 *Feminist Legal Studies* 165.

Conclusion

The inherent jurisdiction has been turned, through a skilful process of judicial lawmaking, into a powerful tool that could be instrumental in protecting the personal autonomy and the well-being of vulnerable adults. Contrary to the view of some experts, I do not take issue with the fact that its reinvention is due to the judicial activism of socially sensitive judges, as there is no evidence that courts have overstepped their legitimate powers and duties. I explicitly reject the claim that the jurisdiction is illegitimate and that a protective framework can only be created by Parliament.[85] Nevertheless, in this chapter I have tried to shed light on the risks of accepting unquestioningly the role and powers of state agencies for protecting the sanctity of individual autonomy, and to stir up a constructive debate about the virtues and dark sides of the inherent jurisdiction. Although the jurisdiction has progressively secured a larger and potentially beneficial supervisory role for the English judiciary, it does not necessarily follow that English law has managed to find the right balance between empowerment and control, between autonomy and protection. In this chapter, I have suggested that the inherent jurisdiction may become an increasing concern because of its financial and social costs, the extent of the discretionary powers of judges, and the potential for indiscreet and careless use by local authorities without any regard to the capable adult's own wishes.

Of course, it may seem uncontroversial for state agencies to take all necessary precautions to guard the interests of society at large. In the eyes of many, the potential risks can be ignored for the sake of protecting individual freedoms and human rights. However, there exist great theoretical and practical dangers that derive from a righteous and yet not principled transition from an exclusively medical to a situational notion of vulnerability. This chapter has presented some of those dangers. In the European scenario marked by the coexistence of a plurality of normative communities, the emphasis on protection might inadvertently turn the powers deriving from the inherent jurisdiction into a proxy for a paternalistic and value-oriented redefinition of welfare and of autonomy. In particular, I have invoked the familiar concerns over the risks inherent in a legal framework that protects the autonomy of vulnerable individuals at the paradoxical cost of reducing their right to self-determination. Limitless and discretionary powers can lead to unnecessary and disproportionate interventions in family life and, at the same time, can undermine, rather than strengthen, autonomy. For this reason, legislation such as the Children Act and the Mental Capacity Act has placed restrictions on the use of the jurisdiction, limiting interventions to circumstances in which it is compelling and establishing the factors to be taken into account when deciding on behalf of the child or incapacitated person. The High Court of England and Wales enjoys powers under the inherent jurisdiction that are indistinguishable from those conferred by the wardship jurisdiction in the case of minors. However, the crucial difference is that in non-medical welfare cases statutory restrictions do not apply. In the absence of a comprehensive human rights regime and adequate domestic legislation, nobody is ensuring that it is not abused and – to answer the question *Quis custodiet ipsos custodes?* – nobody is watching the watchmen. As a result, there is nothing preventing this instrument of empowerment from becoming an instrument of discriminatory social control.

85 For instance, B Hewson, ' "Neither Midwives nor Rainmakers" – Why DL Is Wrong' (2013) *Public Law* 415; J Miles, 'Family Abuse, Privacy and State Intervention' (2011) 70 *Cambridge Law Journal* 31.

11 Balancing migration policy and personal autonomy in private international law

A shattered illusion?

Jinske Verhellen

Introduction

This chapter discusses the difficult balancing act in private international law (PIL), namely balancing PIL (and one of its techniques, party autonomy, which has been introduced into the field of family law) and migration law (migration policy).

Private international law should, first and foremost, be the branch of law that responds to migration and its influence on family life. However, private international law has been absorbed into and even overruled by the various legal and political frameworks relating to global migration. One of the fundamental principles underpinning PIL is cross-border harmony, but because individual countries pursue their own specific migration policies rather than seeking cross-border solutions, migration procedures often lead to far-reaching regulations of family relations. The differing, even opposing, normative stances of private international law, on the one hand, and migration law on the other hand often turn cross-border family situations into very complex legal affairs. More and more, family law is hampered by 'limping' legal relationships – that is, relationships that are considered lawful and valid in one legal order but not in another. For example, people can be considered legally married in one country, but not in another; they can have a national passport under one name, and another passport under a different name; they may be legally recognized as a mother or father in one country, but not in another. Over and above this complexity in the daily lives of a growing number of people, there is much debate among (legal) scholars over giving the persons and families concerned less or more autonomy to make their own decisions regarding legal matters.

This chapter will take cross-border divorces – specifically, the possibility for parties to select the applicable law for their divorce case within a migration context – as a case study to afford some insight into this difficult balancing act. The principle of party autonomy in the field of cross-border divorce is increasingly inserted into national PIL legislation and has even been jointly agreed to among some Member States of the European Union. The question is whether such a noble principle can be implemented when family situations become very complex.

My analysis is based on my ongoing empirical research in Belgium, comparing the objectives of the Belgian legislature to the actual practice of courts and the decisions of spouses going through divorce proceedings. The first research findings from this empirical comparison (hereinafter: study 2012)[1] stem from three sources:

1 J Verhellen, *Het Belgisch Wetboek IPR in familiezaken. Wetgevende doelstellingen getoetst aan de praktijk* (The Belgian PIL Code in family matters: Field-test research of legislative intentions and the actual practice of courts and administrations) (die Keure 2012). This research was conducted with support from the Research Foundation Flanders (FWO – Vlaanderen).

DOI: 10.4324/9781315413617-14

1 A **court decision database** with 656 published and unpublished court decisions.
2 The **database of one of the Belgian PIL centres** containing more than 3,000 files (covering 2006–2010). At the end of 2005, the Belgian government established two Centres for Private International Law, one Dutch-speaking and the other French-speaking.[2] Both individuals and professionals can turn to these legal clinics with their PIL questions regarding family law matters.
3 **In-depth interviews**: In 2010 I interviewed 16 Belgian judges specializing in cross-border family law. The selection of these judges was based on two main considerations: (1) the 'verifiable' PIL expertise (based on the decisions of the judge in question); and (2) the 'expected' PIL expertise (taking into consideration the multicultural/ international character of the judges' jurisdictions).

Complexity in cross-border divorce cases: a typical case

A Pakistani couple, married in Pakistan, live in Belgium. The husband unilaterally requested the dissolution of the marriage in Pakistan. This *talaq* divorce cannot be recognized in Belgium due to the fact that the man has his habitual residence in Belgium. The Belgian PIL Code provides for a specific (read 'severely restricted') recognition regime for 'foreign divorces based on the will of the husband' (Article 57).[3] The basic principle of Article 57 PIL Code is non-recognition of the repudiation. This position is based on fundamental objections to two defining elements: the unilateral character of the marriage dissolution and the presumption that repudiation is the husband's prerogative.[4] When these two elements are present, recognition is not possible unless a number of restrictive conditions are met cumulatively: (1) the deed has been approved by a judge in the state of origin; (2) at the time of the court approval neither of the spouses had the nationality of a state whose law does not acknowledge this mode of marriage dissolution; (3) at the time of the court approval neither of the spouses had their habitual residence in a state whose law does not acknowledge this mode of marriage dissolution; (4) the wife has accepted the dissolution unambiguously and without coercion; and (5) none of the general grounds of refusal provided for in the PIL Code prohibits the recognition (e.g., general public policy clause, rights of defence).[5]

The effect of the non-recognition of the Pakistani *talaq* is that the man is considered to be still married to his first wife, so his subsequent remarriage (which also took place in

2 The Dutch-speaking centre was placed within the non-profit organization Vlaams Minderhedencentrum (since January 2011 Kruispunt Migratie-Integratie; see <www.kruispuntmi.be>) and the French-speaking centre within the Association du Droit des Etrangers (see <www.adde.be>).

3 For an English translation of the Belgian PIL Code (Law 16 July 2004), see *Yearbook of Private International Law* (2004) vol 4, 319–375.

4 The Dutch recognition rule is different. Article 10:58 of the Dutch Civil Code is formulated in a sex-neutral manner. It reads as follows: 'A dissolution of marriage abroad that has exclusively been brought about by a unilateral declaration "of either spouse" is recognized if . . .' See P Kruiniger, *Islamic Divorces in Europe: Bridging the Gap Between European and Islamic Legal Orders* (Eleven International Publishing 2015) 234–235.

5 Article 25 PIL Code.

Pakistan) is not recognized in Belgium.[6] Therefore, the second wife will be denied a family reunification visa on the grounds of polygamy.

In order to get their legal situation regularized, people are advised to 're-divorce' in Belgium (the man needs to get a divorce in Belgium from his first wife, followed by a divorce in Pakistan from his second wife, after which he can remarry his second wife in Pakistan). In some of these divorce cases Belgian courts then use the non-recognized repudiation as proof of the irremediable breakdown of the marriage.[7] This jurisprudence leads to bizarre situations: initially the Pakistani marriage dissolution is not recognized, but it is then used as grounds for divorce in a Belgian divorce procedure. During the interviews judges expressed their concerns about these developments. This practice really does not sit well with one judge in particular, who feels that in accepting repudiation as grounds for divorce, she is violating Belgian public policy, which is justification for refusing recognition of repudiations in the first place. This judge expressed her confusion as follows:

> I always say to lawyers, 'Please don't tell me there is already a repudiation.' I don't want to know it. What's the matter? We are talking here about public policy. About the Belgian international public policy rejecting the recognition of repudiations. But if I have someone living for ten years in repudiation – a repudiation that I cannot recognize . . . I still have the evidence of an irremediable breakdown of the marriage, and in fact I am doing nothing more than agreeing with something that happened elsewhere and that I cannot recognize under Belgian international public policy. That is just the way I breach the Belgian international public order, isn't it? Tell me, because I haven't found the answer yet . . . . That question about repudiation and the fact that I cannot recognize it but that I ultimately agree, approve – or whatever word you want – means that in any case I confirm the situation. This is deeply worrying. So, let us be clear, and let us curb the hypocrisy by recognizing repudiations. That's everything. We must be sure of what we want. But of course we all know that this is a political question.

In some cases that are even more complicated the trouble does not end here. Parties – divorced abroad, but re-divorcing in Belgium – ask Belgian courts to apply the divorce law of the country of their common nationality, in our case Pakistan. I will return to this complication later.

Personal autonomy within this (legal) complexity

Divorce proceedings in Belgium apply the EU Regulation Rome III on the law applicable to divorce and legal separation. This regulation takes as a starting point the possibility for parties to choose the law applicable to their divorce. The spouses may agree to designate the applicable law provided it is one of the following: (1) the law of the state where the spouses are habitually resident at the time the agreement is concluded; (2) the law of the state where the spouses were last habitually resident, provided that one of them still resides there at the

6 Article 27 PIL Code, referring to the public policy clause in Article 21 PIL Code.

7 For an illustration, see Court of First Instance Liège 26 May 2009 (2010) 38 *Revue de Jurisprudence de Liège, Mons et Bruxelles* 1807.

time the agreement is concluded; (3) the law of the state of nationality of either spouse at the time the agreement is concluded; or (4) the law of the forum.[8]

The Recitals of the Rome III Regulation explain that the European legislature – by enhancing the parties' autonomy – aimed to provide for more flexibility and greater legal certainty: spouses know in advance which law will regulate their divorce. In Belgium, this choice of law has been possible since 2004: spouses are allowed to choose between the law of the state of both spouses' nationality and Belgian law.[9] With this choice of law, the Belgian legislature wanted both to improve international harmony and to show respect for people's cultural ties. Letting spouses choose the law of their country of origin not only allows them to reaffirm their connection to the culture of their country of origin, but also assures parties of smoother recognition of the (foreign) divorce in their country of origin, to which they might want to return some day.[10]

It was not an obvious choice to study party autonomy in Belgian divorce proceedings, given that very little relevant case law is available. In 2004 the Belgian legislature took a very innovative approach by introducing a provision allowing the parties involved in a divorce case to choose the applicable law. The lack of applications in the courts suggests that this new element in the PIL Code has not been used much in practice. In order to support this conclusion, I discussed with several judges the possibility for parties to choose the applicable law in divorce cases. The interviews with the judges have been a valuable addition to the available court decisions. The results of this part of the research are interesting not only with regard to the application of the PIL Code, but also in light of the Rome III Regulation, which uses similar justifications to support party autonomy in the field of divorce.

The analysis of the very limited case law and the interviews led to some sobering research findings: in practice, people are only very rarely taking advantage of this major innovation and exercising their autonomy to choose the applicable law. The very few who do tend to make a very pragmatic choice for Belgian law. People mainly want a quick and inexpensive divorce, and Belgian law provides for this. It looks as if the stated objective of connecting parties to (or not disconnecting them from) their country of origin is not being achieved.

Do these bare facts mean that the noble legislative ambitions of flexibility, legal certainty, and cultural diversity boil down to one shattered illusion? Not necessarily, if we are prepared to consider and to address the contextual factors that prevent parties from exercising this personal autonomy in cross-border divorce cases. This chapter briefly approaches three of these contextual factors: (1) the noble PIL principles versus the problems of everyday life; (2) inadequate access to good-quality information on foreign law; and (3) more generally, the instrumentalization of private international law by migration policies.

Concerns other than the choice of the applicable law

The PIL Centre database shows that people are often preoccupied with matters other than which applicable law to choose. They worry about the impact the divorce will have on their

8 Article 5 Council Regulation (EU) No. 1259/2010 of 20 December 2010 implementing enhanced cooperation in the area of the law applicable to divorce and legal separation, in force since 21 June 2012. See T Kruger, 'Rome III and Parties' Choice' *Social Science Research Network* (2012) <http://ssrn.com/abstract=2173334>.

9 Article 55, para 2 PIL Code. This national provision has in the meantime been superseded by the Rome III Regulation.

10 Explanatory Memorandum, Parliamentary Records of the Belgian Senate, Session Extraordinaire 2003, No. 3-27/1, 86.

residence status (their residence status being based on the marriage) or they are faced with difficult problems regarding the documents they have to present (for instance, a 'legalized' marriage certificate). The following queries recorded in the PIL Centre's database illustrate this:

- My client, a woman of Turkish nationality, married in Turkey. Her husband has both Turkish and Belgian nationality. They live in Belgium and want to start divorce proceedings here. Will my client be able to keep her residence permit after the divorce?
- A couple from Gaza were married in Palestine in a traditional ceremony. In Belgium they are registered as 'unmarried'. They want to divorce. What now?
- At the moment of their asylum application a couple from Afghanistan declared that they were married. Now that they have started divorce proceedings in Belgium, they cannot present a marriage certificate from Afghanistan.

During the interviews one judge explained how she even pronounces divorces in cases where there is no marriage certificate. When the parties have always been considered married by the national and local administrative authorities, she said, 'We cannot simply tell the parties that we consider them married, but that they cannot divorce because they don't have a marriage certificate . . . or even worse, tell them at the same time that they cannot remarry because they cannot prove their unmarried status.'

In Belgium, spouses seldom make use of the possibility to select a specific legal system to be applied by the Belgian courts. They simply choose between a Belgian divorce and a divorce procedure in their country of origin. During the interviews judges said that they have the impression that if parties want their foreign law to be applied, they turn to their country of origin and initiate divorce proceedings there. According to one judge, 'Party autonomy is very theoretical.' She thinks that 'people are pragmatic: if they want to divorce, they won't emphasize the fact that they are, for example, Moroccans.'

This is autonomy in a different guise. Personal autonomy does not seem to be a question of choosing between two legal systems, but the reality of choosing to go through two divorce proceedings, one in each country. The queries to the PIL Centre illustrate that spouses often reason in terms of a 'double divorce'. Choice of law is not used to 'anticipate' possible recognition problems in the country of origin. The recognition of a Belgian divorce in the country of origin is a concern, but this concern has so far not resulted in a choice for the application of foreign law. Spouses are simply getting a divorce in their country of origin, whether they are divorced in Belgium or not.

This issue is also related to the fact that the spouses concerned (and/or their lawyers) are often ill-informed and are convinced that they have to divorce in both country of residence and country of origin. This results not only in many limping divorces, but also in a number of other problems, as I discuss in the next section.

Access to information on foreign (divorce) law

If party autonomy is exercised, one could assume that parties take into consideration the advantages and disadvantages of the substantive rules of the applicable divorce law. This implies a thorough knowledge of this substantive law, and raises the question of whether the option of choosing to have a Belgian court apply the law of the state of both spouses' nationality – in other words, opting for foreign divorce law – is an achievable and realistic *optio juris*.

Recital 17 of the Rome III Regulation states:

> Before designating the applicable law, it is important for spouses to have access to up-to-date information concerning the essential aspects of national and Union law and of the procedures governing divorce and legal separation. To guarantee such access to appropriate, good-quality information, the Commission regularly updates it in the Internet-based public information system set up by Council Decision 2001/470/EC.[11]

Recital 18 continues: 'The informed choice of both spouses is a basic principle of this Regulation. Each spouse should know exactly what are the legal and social implications of the choice of applicable law.'

My empirical research in Belgium shows what has actually been common knowledge for a long time: courts lack structural support to properly carry out this task. Although the informed choice of both spouses is a basic principle of the Rome III Regulation, the well-intended EU solution – that is, the website of the European Judicial Network (EJN)[12] – does not settle this 'foreign law problem': the EJN only covers the divorce law of the EU Member States; information about non-EU divorce laws is not available, and the legal information that is available is often not up to date and is difficult to understand for non-lawyers.[13] During the interviews judges referred to this website, but they remain cautious because they know the information is sometimes outdated.

During the interviews several judges emphasized the need for improved access to foreign law. One judge from a Court of First Instance talked about a utopian dream:

JUDGE: What would we need? Something utopian, something completely utopian. Maybe something Internet-based, as this magical resource already exists. A place where the most recent information from every country on divorce would be centralized. The legislative changes of course, but also – and this is where it becomes utopian – the changes in case law and that kind of stuff. A tool which we could all really use, I'm thinking of the Internet . . .

INTERVIEWER: And you would all have the same tool then?

JUDGE: Ah . . . that is why I say this would be utopian, but let us dream a little bit.[14]

Utopian dream or not, 'in a global village there is a need to know foreign law.'[15] Due to globalization and migration there is a need to access foreign law, and this need is likely to

11 The reference is to the website of the European Judicial Network in civil and commercial matters (see <http://ec.europa.eu/civiljustice/index_en.htm>). The European Judicial Network (EJN) was set up by the Council under Decision 2001/470/EC establishing a European Judicial Network in civil and commercial matters (28 May 2001). It began operating on 1 December 2002. The EJN is composed of contact points designated by the Member States.

12 See <http://ec.europa.eu/civiljustice/index_en.htm> and the accompanying national pages. There is one page for each Member State except Denmark. On these pages one can find specific information about the national legal systems.

13 See also K Boele-Woelki, 'For Better or for Worse: The Europeanization of International Divorce Law' (2010) 12 *Yearbook of Private International Law* 17.

14 Translated from French.

15 Holger Knudsen at the conference 'Access to Foreign Law in Civil and Commercial Matters', A Joint Conference of Experts of the Hague Conference and the European Commission held on 15–17 February 2012; see Meeting Report, 23, available at <www.hcch.net/upload/xs2foreignlaw_rpt.pdf>.

increase in the future. There is nothing new in stressing the need for specialization and improved access to good-quality information on foreign law. Private international law in family matters simply cannot exist without a thorough knowledge of foreign family law

Within the Hague Conference on Private International Law much consideration has been given to the issue of assessing the content of foreign law and the need for the development of a global instrument in this area. A number of meetings of experts have already taken place under the auspices of the Hague Conference.[16] These led to the conclusion that the Hague Conference could become a valuable platform 'for co-operation with legal information institutes and governments, to facilitate access to foreign law and play a co-ordinating role in the various ongoing efforts to establish standards for online legal resources'. A 'Hague portal on accessing foreign law' could lead its users to officially recognized providers of legal information.[17] The activities within the framework of the Hague Conference have not led to tangible results. Unfortunately, in March 2015 the Council decided to remove this topic from the agenda of the Hague Conference 'with the understanding that this issue may be revisited at a later stage'.[18] This is a surprising turn. One can only hope that these global initiatives will inspire the European and national authorities to (at least) centralize the information and documentation on foreign law.

Immigration policy constructions resulting in limping divorces

While very little case law exists in relation to party autonomy in Belgian divorce proceedings, the recognition in Belgium of divorces obtained in the countries of origin has resulted in extensive case law. As in other European countries, the recognition of foreign marriage dissolutions raises a number of important questions that will not be discussed here. However, I would like to comment on one particular aspect, namely the limping marital situations created by the current migration policies of several European countries.

Analysis of the many questions addressed to the help desk of the PIL Centre exposed a certain practice of the Belgian embassies and the Immigration Office and revealed complicated 'immigration (policy) constructions' leading to limping divorces: through the non-recognition of foreign marriage dissolutions the person(s) involved is/are considered to be bigamous. As a result, family reunification visas are denied to new spouses.

16 Prel. Doc. No. 11A of March 2009, 'Assessing the Content of Foreign Law and the Need for the Development of a Global Instrument in this Area – A Possible Way Ahead' <www.hcch.net>. The first meeting of experts (February 2007) came to the conclusion that there was a greater demand to facilitate access to foreign law than to harmonize the different takes on foreign law. Therefore the experts suggested investigating thoroughly whether a new instrument for cross-border cooperation would be realistic. In another meeting (October 2008) experts also pointed out the task of many other legal practitioners, such as notaries. Establishing foreign law was no longer regarded as just a task for judges (Prel. Doc. No. 11B of March 2009, 'Assessing the content of foreign law. Report of the meeting of experts on global co-operation on the provision of online legal information on national laws', 6). Several experts also reported on the promising developments of the 'paperless world' and the worldwide digitizing of legal information.

17 Besides this platform for more cooperation, a new global instrument should provide a system for requests of information in the context of a specific dispute. Whether such a system should operate through the existing system of the administrative Central Authorities, through direct cooperation between legal authorities, or through a combination of both was still left open.

18 Council on General Affairs and Policy of the Conference (24–26 March 2015), Conclusions & Recommendations adopted by the Council, 4.

When Belgian embassies and consulates abroad legalize foreign divorce documents, they tend to classify marriage dissolution documents from Islamic countries rather on a pro forma basis as repudiations, even documents from countries where repudiations do not exist, such as Tunisia. This qualification results in the application of Article 57 PIL Code and the attachment of an 'Article 57 sticker' to the passport.[19] This sticker has a huge impact: it takes the shape of a binding opinion that is followed by the immigration office and the local authorities in Belgium. Based on this qualification the recognition of a marriage dissolution of, for instance, a Pakistani man can easily be refused. If this man gets married again to another Pakistani woman who then requests a family reunification visa, the visa will most likely be denied on the grounds of polygamy. It is debatable whether this is still really about the incompatibility of repudiations and polygamy with public policy, or whether it has become about finding ways to control the flow of immigrants from certain countries (such as Morocco, Tunisia, and Pakistan).[20] This is just one illustration of the instrumentalization of private international law by migration law and policy.

Such migration policy constructions add to the complexity of cross-border family situations and in some cases even lead to paradoxical legal outcomes. I return to the case of the non-recognition of the Pakistani marriage dissolution. What if the parties were to re-divorce in Belgium and choose the application of Pakistani divorce law? I refer here to a decision of the Liège court in which the court was legally required to apply Pakistani law, but invoked an escape clause to avoid doing so. Article 19 PIL Code stipulates that, by way of exception, the law designated by the Code does not apply if, on the basis of combined circumstances, it manifestly appears that the matter has only a very slight connection to the state whose law was designated, but is very closely connected to another state. In such a case, the law of that other state will be applied. This provision was intended to introduce a certain degree of flexibility should the application of the relevant conflict rules lead to an undesirable result.[21] The case discussed here demonstrates this 'undesirable result'. The court applied Belgian law (instead of Pakistani law) because there was a valid marriage dissolution in Pakistan which could not be recognized in Belgium.[22] According to the court, it would be paradoxical to apply Pakistani law in a Belgian divorce procedure and refuse at the same time the solution this same law already gave to the marriage breakdown.[23]

Some concluding thoughts

It goes without saying that limping legal relationships lead to legal uncertainty and unpredictability for the persons and families concerned. Personal autonomy could be a meaningful way to moderate the negative effects of limping relationships. Therefore, it remains a noble principle. The ambition to encourage certain positive principles such as flexibility,

19 C Henricot, 'L'application du Code marocain de la famille, à la croisée des jurisprudences belge et marocaine en matière de dissolution du mariage' (2011) *Journal des Tribunaux* 641, 649.

20 J Verhellen, 'Lost in Nationality. Private International Law and Cultural Diversity' in M-C Foblets and N Yassari (eds), *Approches juridiques de la diversité culturelle – Legal Approaches to Cultural Diversity* (Martinus Nijhoff Publishers 2013) 521, 560.

21 Explanatory Memorandum, Parliamentary Records of the Belgian Senate, Session Extraordinaire 2003, No. 3-27/1, 44.

22 Article 57 PIL Code.

23 Court of First Instance Liège 24 November 2009, (2010) 8 *Tijdschrift@ipr.be* 131.

certainty, cultural diversity, and international harmony should be supported. Even if some illusions are shattered, that does not mean we should discard the principle entirely.

Personal autonomy can serve as 'transmitter of cultural diversity in private international law'.[24] However, if the ambition really is to allow parties to select a legal system that meets their expectations, for instance cross-border respect for their cultural identity, sufficient structural means and support should be offered both to the parties and the judicial and administrative authorities. The parties need to be informed about the choices they have and also about the legal, social, financial, and other implications of their choices. Courts and administrations need more expertise and improved access to foreign law.

At the same time we should bear in mind that it is not only the diversity of (legal) cultures and the potential lack of consensus on fundamental underlying principles that generate limping legal relationships. States often pay more attention to the immigration issue than to the risks and problems of limping legal family relationships. Whether it will be possible to balance PIL and migration policy and to bridge their opposing normative stances remains to be seen. In the years to come, this balancing act will be a real challenge to science in law and anthropology, a challenge that is extremely tangible and topical given the current refugee flows to Europe.

24 M-C Foblets and N Yassari (eds), *Approches juridiques de la diversité culturelle – Legal Approaches to Cultural Diversity* (Martinus Nijhoff Publishers 2013) 1, 45.

12 The antireligious bias in personal autonomy

Towards coherence and a solution

Toon Agten

Introduction

Autonomy is a difficult concept with a variety of different meanings. Although autonomy as a concept was first used in a rather specific context, namely to describe the power of a Greek city-state to make its own laws,[1] it has since taken on a different function in moral and political philosophy, where it relates to the ability or inability of individuals to make choices regarding their own lives and how their choices relate to the power of the state to make generally binding rules that regulate human behaviour and, consequently, human choices. Often, paternalism then becomes the antithesis of autonomy. Many authors have tried to tackle the meaning and value of autonomy in Western societies and many still do.[2] However, there is no consensus on the meaning and value of autonomy. For some, respect for autonomy is part of human dignity or even a consequence of human dignity.[3] Defining autonomy, or determining its scope, appears to be next to impossible.[4] Nevertheless, autonomy remains a fascinating lens through which we can think about the relationship

1 A Greek city-state had *autonomia* when its citizens made their own laws, as opposed to being under the control of some conquering power. See G Dworkin, *The Theory and Practice of Autonomy* (Cambridge University Press 1988) 108.

2 In philosophy two of the most influential accounts are those of Immanuel Kant and John Stuart Mill, but more recent philosophers such as Charles Taylor, Harry Frankfurt, Ronald Dworkin, Gerald Dworkin, Joseph Raz, John Rawls, and so on have also addressed the concept of autonomy.

3 On this distinction, see AB Da Silva, 'Autonomy, Dignity and Integrity in Health Care Ethics – A Moral Philosophical Perspective' in HS Aasen, R Halvorsen, and AB Da Silva (eds), *Human Rights, Dignity and Autonomy in Health Care and Social Services: Nordic Perspectives* (Intersentia 2009) 13–52, where he explains the differences between a *humanistic* perspective on dignity (mostly based on a Kantian perspective) and a *non-humanistic* perspective on dignity. Simply put, in a humanistic perspective, dignity is an inherent trait of human beings, whereas in the non-humanistic perspective dignity is a result of the exercise of personal autonomy.

4 I think Gerald Dworkin said it best:

> [Autonomy] is used sometimes as an equivalent of liberty (positive or negative in Berlin's terminology), sometimes equivalent to self-rule or sovereignty, sometimes as identical with the freedom of the will. It is equated with dignity, integrity, individuality, independence, responsibility, and self-knowledge. It is identified with qualities of self-assertion, with critical reflection, with freedom from obligation, with absence of external causation, with knowledge of one's own interests. It is even equated by some economists with the impossibility of interpersonal comparisons. It is related to actions, to beliefs, to reasons for acting, to rules, to the will of other persons, to thoughts, and to principles. About the only features held constant from one author to another are that autonomy is a feature of persons and that it is a desirable quality to have.
>
> It is very unlikely that there is a core meaning which underlies all these various uses of the term.
>
> G Dworkin, *The Theory and Practice of Autonomy* (Cambridge University Press 1988) 6

DOI: 10.4324/9781315413617-15

between the state and its citizens, and about the way that people try to give meaning to their lives.

In this chapter I consider a constitutional issue within the framework of personal autonomy, namely the question of whether or not it is possible to refuse a (potentially life-saving) vaccination based on your own philosophical or religious beliefs. I do so by discussing an actual case of a 17-year-old Dutch girl who refused a vaccination based on her religious beliefs and who consequently died as a result of the complications of the disease.

In this chapter I first analyse the case mentioned to show how it illustrates problems with the interpretation of autonomy in law. Second, I discuss inoculation in general and connect it to a general rise in anti-vaccination movements, especially in the United States. Third, I will take up the case against the background of the human rights framework laid out in the European Convention on Human Rights (hereinafter ECHR or 'the Convention'), with a focus on the question of how to balance personal autonomy against the freedom to manifest one's religion. Finally, I offer an overview of European Court of Human Rights (ECtHR) jurisprudence on personal autonomy and apply the conclusions drawn from that body of case law to the dispute about the Dutch girl's choice.

Refusing treatment for religious reasons

The case

On Saturday, 26 October 2013, a 17-year-old girl passed away due to measles-related complications in the Netherlands (to be more precise in Tholen), in what is often called the 'Bible Belt' of the Netherlands.[5] Details on the case are sparse in both Dutch and Belgian (Flemish) media. Apparently, the girl had suffered from poor health all her life and therefore was already quite weak. Newspapers reported she was physically handicapped and because of a growth in her back she had trouble breathing. She had been confined to a wheelchair from an early age. Nevertheless, she made a very conscious choice – based on her religious beliefs – not to have an inoculation against measles.[6] Eventually, when she got the measles, the combination of her weak health and complications from the illness resulted in her death at an early age.[7]

Public debate

Her death sparked a debate in both the Netherlands and Belgium that pitted the obligation to inoculate children against certain diseases against the right to opt out of this obligation

5 The 'Bible Belt' goes from the south-western part of the Netherlands (Zeeland) to the western part of Overijssel.

6 M Bolwijn, 'Slachtoffer koos voor God' (*Volkskrant*, 29 October 2013) <www.volkskrant.nl/vk/nl/2672/Wetenschap-Gezondheid/article/detail/3534960/2013/10/29/Slachtoffer-mazelen-17-koos-bewust-voor-God.dhtml> accessed 7 July 2016; 'Nederlands slachtoffer mazelen "koos bewust voor God" ' (*Knack*, 29 October 2013) <www.knack.be/nieuws/wereld/nederlands-slachtoffer-mazelen-koos-bewust-voor-god/article-normal-113612.html> accessed 7 July 2016; M Bolwijn, 'Nederlandse tiener die stierf aan mazelen koos bewust voor God' (*De Morgen*, 29 October 2013). <www.demorgen.be/dm/nl/993/Gezondheid/article/detail/1731412/2013/10/29/Nederlandse-tiener-die-stierf-aan-mazelen-koos-bewust-voor-God.dhtml> accessed 7 July 2016.

7 According to newspaper reports, she most likely died of pneumonia or encephalitis, two common, potentially life-threatening disorders associated with measles.

for religious reasons. Several arguments support the inoculation of children. One argument is that inoculation is a child's right. One commentator points out that it is tragic that people – and in this case a child – still die in 'civilized countries' from diseases we can help prevent and control.[8]

A second argument is that refusing certain treatments amounts to denying children the 'right to care and health'.[9] According to one commentator, 'No religion or philosophy has priority over the right to a healthy life.'[10] The argument warns against the pressure that children might face in having to make certain medical choices, but more specifically against religions or philosophical worldviews that would unduly pressure children to take a specific course of action. This reasoning, however, denies children the possibility to have a say, empowering state authorities to determine for them what is in their own best interests.

A third argument in favour of inoculation is a moral one: the inoculation of children is not a choice, but a moral duty in this day and age. According to this view, parents are not free to withhold preventive or lifesaving medication or treatment from minors.[11] By extension, only adults have the right to refuse vaccinations for themselves or – to give another example – blood transfusions, but minors have no such right. Moreover, the parents of children have a duty to allow any form of medical treatment that would protect, save, or help their children, regardless of their own views on the matter and regardless of the wishes of the child.[12]

A final argument in favour of compulsory inoculation is the public health consideration. By not being inoculated against a certain disease the risk of infecting other people unwittingly, and therefore putting them in danger, increases, especially in an epidemic.[13]

By contrast at least three arguments were put forward to respect the girl's choice in this case. The first agrees that there is a right to health, but insists that it was respected in this case: the girl had this right, but merely made a choice not to invoke it.[14] Whether or not this choice was religiously motivated is not relevant. What is relevant is that she made the choice herself in a conscious manner. In this case, the right to health does not mean there is a duty or an obligation to health. No one can be forced to invoke a right; doing so would go against the very essence of what a right is intended to be. This is a response to the first argument made above against the choice of the girl: if one frames a right in this way, it actually becomes an obligation because it suggests what people ought to do, leaving no margin for meaningful choice.[15]

8 B Eeckhout, 'Inenting is een kinderrecht' (*De Morgen*, 30 October 2013) <www.demorgen.be/dm/nl/2462/Standpunt/article/detail/1731864/2013/10/30/Inenting-is-een-kinderrecht.dhtml> accessed 7 July 2016.

9 Ibid.

10 Ibid.

11 E Vermeersch, 'Inenting is een plicht' (*De Morgen,* 3 November 2013) <www.demorgen.be/dm/nl/2461/Opinie/article/detail/1733929/2013/11/03/Inenting-is-een-plicht.dhtml> accessed 7 July 2016.

12 Ibid: '[S]taat het hen niet vrij een minderjarige, zelfs al is het hun eigen kind, beschermende of levensreddende middelen te ontzeggen.'

13 Ibid.

14 H van Eyghen, 'Recht op en plicht tot gezondheid zijn niet hetzelfde' (*De Morgen*, 31 October 2013) <www.demorgen.be/dm/nl/2461/Opinie/article/detail/1732620/2013/10/31/Recht-op-en-plicht-tot-gezondheid-zijn-niet-hetzelfde.dhtml> accessed 7 July 2016.

15 A distinction already clearly seen by W Hohfeld, 'Some Fundamental Legal Conceptions as Applied in Judicial Reasoning' (1913) *Yale Law Journal* 16.

A second argument was invoked by some priests in the Netherlands: the girl made a conscious choice and this choice should be respected.[16] They pointed to the double standards at play in some of the outrage at the girl's choice. They reminded everyone that reformists in the 'Bible Belt' do not protest when someone decides to have an abortion or commits euthanasia. Here, the girl's conscious choice should also be respected.[17] The principal of her school noted that the girl dealt with her faith in a very serious and adult way precisely because of her physical handicap and general weakness all her life.[18] This reasoning is very much based upon a respect for the personal autonomy of individuals, including minors.

The third argument is religious in nature. There are some people who want to have faith in their god and the plan their god has for them. According to these people, having an inoculation would circumvent this divine plan.[19] In other words, if someone gets sick, then it is God's intention and should be respected. One reformist even testified in the newspaper, 'I will not put a needle in a creature of God.'[20] However, not all reformists in the Dutch 'Bible Belt' have the same view on this matter. Some consider vaccinations to be a gift from God and that it is the responsibility of mankind to promote health.[21]

While the above arguments would appear to be irreconcilable, intuitively it seems rather easy to understand both points of view. This may be a sign that an intuitive analysis of the problem does not suffice to deal with autonomy in a consistent way in cases like this. Before we try to find a consistent way of dealing with autonomy, however, it is important to mention the issues at stake in this particular case.

The issues

The girl was 17 years old, still a minor under Dutch law. As will be discussed later, Dutch law conditionally allows assisted suicide for minors over the age of 16. The presumption in this law seems to be that minors over a certain age are capable of forming their own opinions and making valid, conscious choices. Here is where the religious motivation behind her refusal to be inoculated comes into play. The precise dictates of her religion are of lesser importance here; what is important is that her motivation can be traced back to her faith.

Hence the question becomes: Should the fact that a person's choice is motivated by his or her religious belief matter when assessing whether a given action is a genuine expression

16 M Bolwijn, 'Slachtoffer koos voor God' (*Volkskrant*, 29 October 2013) <www.volkskrant.nl/vk/nl/2672/Wetenschap-Gezondheid/article/detail/3534960/2013/10/29/Slachtoffer-mazelen-17-koos-bewust-voor-God.dhtml> accessed 7 July 2016.

17 M van Beek, 'Mensen geven ons nog een trap na' (*Trouw*, 30 December 2013) <www.trouw.nl/tr/nl/5009/Archief/archief/article/detail/3569437/2013/12/30/Mensen-geven-ons-nog-een-trap-na.dhtml> accessed 7 July 2016. In response to the criticism one reformist pointed out, 'Why do people act like this? I just do not understand it. I think they are more narrow-minded. These are people who support abortions: those are carried out 30,000 times per year. I just do not understand that. And then they all freak out because of one death as a result of the measles?' (translation from the Dutch by the author).

18 Ibid.

19 W van de Poll, 'Ouders die niet inenten willen op God vertrouwen' (*Trouw*, 31 October 2013) <www.trouw.nl/tr/nl/5009/Archief/archief/article/detail/3536346/2013/10/31/Ouders-die-niet-inenten-willen-op-God-vertrouwen.dhtml> accessed 7 July 2016.

20 M van Beek (n 17) 'Ik zet geen spuit in een schepsel van God.'

21 W van de Poll (n 19). Research indicates that the degree of vaccinations in the Dutch 'Bible Belt' is on the rise and that more and more people get inoculations against certain diseases and infections.

of personal autonomy? To put it bluntly, if someone acts in a certain way without taking account of any religious or other moral reason, should that be given more or less weight than when someone makes a choice for religious reasons? For the people on the more liberal side of the philosophical spectrum, invoking personal autonomy seems key in cases of abortion and euthanasia, whereas for some more religiously inclined people personal autonomy should be given less prominence or even disregarded in such instances. In the aforementioned case, however, religious people argue that the Dutch girl's personal choice should be respected, and the liberals are the ones having difficulties accepting her choice. Both sides seem to change the value they subscribe to autonomy depending on the situation at hand.

The arguments mentioned above about the right to health and the right to inoculation implicitly point to the next issue: is this a case about a right to die or not? Opponents of the girl's free decision seem to assume that she chose to die for religious reasons. Yet such reasoning is highly problematic. The girl chose to refuse an inoculation for religious reasons. It is true that her choice led to her unfortunate death, but she did not make a conscious choice to die as such. Because of her general physical weakness she faced a higher *risk* of dying as a result of complications, but it seems more likely that she very consciously chose to *live* in a way that corresponds to her moral precepts, which happened to be based on her faith. In my view, this is why it is a mistake to frame this case as a choice to die for religious reasons. This is very much about making a choice to live your life in a certain way and accepting the consequences of your decisions, even if they turn out to be dramatic or even fatal.

It may be relevant at this stage to refer to the legal framework of the Netherlands when it comes to addressing cases such as these. In the Netherlands the assisted suicide of minors over the age of 16 is conditionally allowed by law, and the law in Belgium was changed so that minors can consent to euthanasia under certain conditions as well.[22] So even if some comments tend to steer this case towards a discussion of whether or not there is a right to die, the legal framework in the Netherlands already gives us a (legal) answer to the question. *Qui peut le plus, peut le moins*:[23] it stands to reason that if the girl in the case discussed is old enough to make a valid choice as to the ending of her life, then she can also make a valid choice as to whether or not she wants to accept a form of medical treatment.

Another point to bear in mind is that in the Netherlands, anyone over the age of 16 can decide for himself or herself whether to have a vaccination or not.[24] Between the ages of 12 and 16 the child has to be consulted, but permission from the parents is still needed.[25] So under Dutch law, the girl had the right to refuse her inoculation. This is why the Dutch prime minister made a point of publicly asking people to have the vaccination during the time of the epidemic in the country – the Dutch legislature did not go so far as to force the

22 For the Netherlands: Wet van 12 april 2001, Article 2.3 'Wet toetsing levensbeëindiging op verzoek en hulp bij zelfdoding' (Nederlands Staatsblad No 194 26 April 2001); for Belgium: loi du 28 février 2014 modifiant la loi du 28 mai 2002 relative à l'euthanasie en vue d'étendre l'euthanasie aux mineurs (Moniteur Belge 12 March 2014).

23 The French translation of an expression found in Aristotle's work, although he had a different meaning in mind. Aristotle meant that if you are able to do a hard or complex task, then you can also do simpler jobs as well.

24 Dutch Civil Code Article 447.1, adjusted by the 'Wet van 17 november 1994 tot wijziging van het Burgerlijk Wetboek en enige andere wetten in verband met de opneming van bepalingen omtrent de overeenkomst tot het verrichten van handelingen op het gebied van de geneeskunst (Wet op de Geneeskundige Behandelingsovereenkomst)' (Nederlands Staatsblad 21 December 1994).

25 Dutch Civil Code Article 450.2.

people of the 'Bible Belt' to have the inoculation. But could the legislature have done so? We will return to this issue later.

The question of whether or not people can be forced to have an inoculation when there is an epidemic in a country brings us to the public health considerations in cases such as these. By refusing inoculation one puts other people at risk, especially those who are also not inoculated.[26] When there is a measles epidemic, this may result in an entire region of people being threatened by a preventable disease. The choice not to be inoculated, therefore, affects more than the individual making the choice and creates very real concerns for public health. I will turn to this question when I discuss the human rights dimension of this case, since both Article 8 and Article 9 ECHR can be limited for reasons of public health.[27]

Mandatory vaccination and the rise of anti-vaccination movements

For some time now there has been a trend in Europe and the United States: diseases such as mumps, measles, and the whooping cough are reappearing.[28] This has been the result of a slow but steady decline in vaccination rates.[29] There are several examples on both sides of the Atlantic. In January 2015, in California's Disneyland there was a measles outbreak that eventually caused the first confirmed measles death in the United States in 12 years.[30] In Europe, again in the Netherlands, there was a case of cross-infection whereby a consciously unvaccinated older child infected three babies with the measles in a day-care centre. One of the babies became seriously ill and nearly died.[31] And during a measles outbreak in France between 2008 and 2011, 10 patients died and almost 5,000 patients were hospitalized.[32]

The introduction of vaccines against infectious diseases has been one of the most important contributions to public health of the last century. The WHO estimates that between two and three million lives are saved each year and calls it 'one of the most cost-effective health investments', lauding vaccination as the public health intervention that has had the greatest impact on the world's health after clean water.[33] The major goal of vaccination programmes is the maintenance of 'herd immunity', a phenomenon whereby a critical proportion of a community (between 92 and 94 per cent) is immunized against a contagious disease so that the virus can no longer circulate freely within the population and gain a

26 And based on the reports in the newspaper, the entire region – the 'Bible Belt' – has a lower inoculation rate than the rest of the Netherlands, making it the part of the Netherlands where illnesses such as the measles strike hardest.

27 United Nations Treaty Collection, vol 213 (1955) 230 '[T]he protection of health' in Article 8.2 and 'the protection of public . . . health' in Article 9.2.

28 SP Calandrillo, 'Vanishing Vaccinations: Why Are So Many Americans Opting out of Vaccinating Their Children?' (2004) 37(2) *University of Michigan Journal of Law Reform* 353; R Pierik, 'The Return of the Measles to the Low Countries: A Legal-Philosophical Exploration' (2014) 2 *Netherlands Journal of Legal Philosophy* 103.

29 R Pierik, 'Mandatory Vaccination: An Unqualified Defense' (2016) *Journal of Applied Philosophy* (available at <http://onlinelibrary.wiley.com/doi/10.1111/japp.12215/full> accessed 28 July 2017).

30 E Izadi, 'The U.S. Just Recorded its First Confirmed Measles Death in 12 Years' *The Washington Post* (2 July 2015) <www.washingtonpost.com/news/to-your-health/wp/2015/07/02/the-u-s-just-recorded-its-first-confirmed-measles-death-in-12-years/> accessed 7 July 2016.

31 R Pierik (n 28) 104.

32 R Pierik (n 29).

33 WHO website <www.who.int/topics/immunization/en/> accessed 7 July 2016.

foothold. It is through herd immunity that mass vaccination is so much more effective than individual vaccination.[34]

Traditionally, most well-known among those who refuse vaccinations are members of religious groups; they argue that vaccination interferes with divine providence. But in recent years there has been a noticeable trend towards questioning vaccines on the grounds that the dangers of vaccination far outweigh the benefits. Epidemiologists explain this surge in the modern anti-vaccination movement in terms of a paradox: vaccination over the past decades has been tremendously successful, and many people living in the Western world today have never witnessed the ravages that infectious diseases can cause.[35] This leads more people to believe that it is no longer necessary to have their children vaccinated. At the same time, there has been more discussion about the (alleged) risks of vaccination. Here, an important cause may be the controversy that was caused by Andrew Wakefield and colleagues' 1998 publication about the MMR vaccine causing autism. His article was published in the *Lancet* but has since been fully debunked, the article has been retracted by the journal, and the author has been stripped of his medical license altogether.[36] But the suggested link between vaccines and autism remains 'the most damaging medical hoax of the last 100 years'.[37]

Nevertheless, the modern anti-vaccination movement disputes the overwhelming medical consensus that vaccines are safe and effective. Some believe that diseases such as the measles can even contribute to the growth, development, and immunity-building of children who are otherwise healthy. In this way, children would gain more resilience against other diseases and even cancers later in life. Other vaccine deniers want to ensure an 'all-natural' life for their children, arguing that vaccines contain toxic preservatives that might damage their children. And yet others argue that current vaccine programmes overwhelm children's immune systems because they have to handle several different vaccinations so early in their lives.[38] However, as noted earlier, the medical evidence contradicts all of these statements. A recent systematic review of vaccine research concluded that 'there is evidence that some vaccines are associated with serious adverse events; however, these events are extremely rare and must be weighed against the protective benefits that vaccines provide.'[39]

Autonomy and the ECHR

From respect for private life to a right to personal autonomy

In its case law the ECtHR has developed the right to respect for one's private life, enshrined in Article 8 ECHR as the right to personal autonomy.[40] However, it may be premature to

34 WA Orenstein, PM Strebel, and AR Hinman, 'Building an Immunity Fence Against Measles' (2007) 196 *The Journal of Infectious Diseases* 1434; R Pierik (n 29).

35 SP Calandrillo (n 28) 362.

36 AJ Wakefield et al., 'Ileal-Lymphoid-Nodular Hyperplasia, Non-Specific Colitis, and Pervasive Developmental Disorder in Children' (1998) 351(9103) *The Lancet* 637; retracted (2010) 375(9713) *The Lancet* 445.

37 D Flaherty, 'The Vaccine-Autism Connection: A Public Health Crisis Caused by Unethical Medical Practices and Fraudulent Science' (2011) 45(10) *The Annals of Pharmacotherapy* 1302.

38 R Pierik (n 29).

39 MA Maglione et al., 'Safety of Vaccines Used for Routine Immunization of US Children: A Systematic Review' (2014) 134(2) *Pediatrics* 325.

40 Nevertheless, the Court itself sometimes refers to it as a right and at other times a principle. It is not clear whether the Court is aware of the distinction or if it is using the terms interchangeably.

discuss a *right* to autonomy; it should perhaps more accurately be considered a *value* underlying the fundamental rights system of the ECHR.[41]

At the very least one can say that personal autonomy is a general principle of law within the ECHR. As early as 1990, Judge S.K. Martens noted in his dissenting opinion in the *Cossey* judgment that '[h]uman dignity and human freedom imply that a man should be free to shape himself and his fate in a way that he deems best fits his personality.'[42] He also made the point that human freedom is related to the various rights enshrined in the Convention and that those rights are there to guarantee respect for human dignity and human freedom.[43] This can be seen as the starting point for the recognition of the value of personal autonomy within the ECtHR, and the Court builds upon this in later case law. One of the most notable and important cases in this respect is the *Pretty* judgment, where the Court held:

> Although no previous case has established as such any right to self-determination as being contained in Article 8 of the Convention, the Court considers that the notion of personal autonomy is an important principle underlying the interpretation of its guarantees.[44]

The wording in this paragraph explicitly refers to Article 8, but in later case law the Court has also used the notion of personal autonomy in relation to other Convention rights.[45] So it can be argued that the notion of personal autonomy underlies the interpretation of all Convention rights, not just Article 8.[46] This is important when we move to the relationship between personal autonomy and the right to freedom of religion in Article 9. In any event, holding personal autonomy to be 'a principle underlying the interpretation of Convention guarantees' in effect means the same as finding that 'the essence of the Convention is respect for human dignity and human freedom.'[47]

A more far-reaching interpretation holds autonomy to be a right in and of itself. In this view autonomy becomes a right, and human dignity is the underlying value that autonomy is supposed to protect.[48] This poses a conceptual problem for the following reason: autonomy is supposed to safeguard choice and freedom. As a concept, autonomy may be far from clear (see above), but at least these elements seem to be consistent. Autonomy, then, becomes about taking command of one's own life, a line of protection against paternalism. But through human dignity, paternalism can again enter into the equation. One of the clearest examples of this would be the *Wackenheim* case, in which a person afflicted with dwarfism

41 N Koffeman, *(The Right to) Personal Autonomy in the Case Law of the European Court of Human Rights* (2010) Leiden University, 4 <https://openaccess.leidenuniv.nl/handle/1887/15890> accessed 7 July 2016.

42 *Cossey v United Kingdom* App No 10843/84 (ECtHR 1990) para 2.7.

43 'The principle which is basic in human rights and which underlies the various specific rights spelled out in the Convention is respect for human dignity and human freedom' (n 42).

44 *Pretty v United Kingdom* App No 2346/02 (ECtHR 2002) para 61.

45 *Sørensen and Rasmussen v Denmark* App Nos 52562/99 and 52620/99 (ECtHR 2006) para 54; *Olafsson v Iceland* App No 20161/06 (ECtHR 2010) para 46. (both on the freedom of association in ECHR Article 11).

46 N Koffeman (n 41) 7.

47 Ibid.

48 Ibid. and the authors cited there. Jill Marshall is also of the view that autonomy is a true right that has human dignity as its basis. J Marshall, *Personal Freedom Through Human Rights Law? – Autonomy, Identity and Integrity Under the European Convention on Human Rights* (Martinus Nijhoff Publishers 2009).

said that a prohibition against dwarf-tossing was an act of discrimination because it limited his employment options and was, therefore, an affront to his human dignity. The Human Rights Committee held otherwise, arguing that dwarf-tossing could be banned for reasons of human dignity.[49] This case illustrates how human dignity can sometimes be used as a barrier to autonomy.

For Marshall, 'the right to respect for one's private life, including freedom from unwanted intrusion and a right to autonomy, now means the right to develop one's personality in connection with others, the freedom to live the life of one's own choosing.'[50] Möller goes even further, arguing that 'there exists a general right to personal autonomy, that is, a right to everything which, judged from the perspective of the agent's self-conception, is in his interest.'[51] He holds that *all* interests, even trivial or immoral ones, should be included in this right to autonomy.[52] Still, as with other rights, the right to autonomy is not absolute and can be limited. But Möller makes a strong case for a *prima facie* inclusion of every autonomy interest an individual may have.[53]

The Court itself has also started speaking about a right to personal autonomy, beginning with the *Evans* case.[54] Later on, in the *Tysiac* case, the Court reiterated this: private life is a broad term, encompassing, among other things, 'the right to personal autonomy'.[55] The Grand Chamber even affirmed this 'right to personal autonomy' in its treatment of the *Evans* case.[56] In its more recent case law, the Court now seems to accept the movement from personal autonomy as a 'notion' or 'principle' to a right.[57] Autonomy now seems to be firmly enshrined as one of the elements that Article 8 of the Convention aims to protect.

But some ambiguity still remains. In *Jehovah's Witnesses and Others v Russia*, the Court holds that '[t]he very essence of the Convention is respect for human dignity and human freedom and the notions of self-determination and personal autonomy are important principles underlying the interpretation of its guarantees.'[58] Yet in the same case the Court also explicitly talks about the right to personal autonomy.[59] It is not clear what the Court means by this difference.

49 *Manuel Wackenheim v France*, Communication No 854/1999, U.N. Doc. CCPR/C/75/D/854/1999 (2002) para 7.4.

50 J Marshall (n 48) 70.

51 K Möller, *The Global Model on Constitutional Rights* (Oxford University Press 2012) 73. To be clear, Möller does not argue based on the ECHR alone, but instead argues for a general constitutional right to autonomy. He sees the ECHR also as a constitutional order and uses it as an example for his argument, which is why his book is about a *global* model. Other constitutional orders he refers to include the German and South African ones.

52 An example could be an interest in feeding pigeons in the park. See BVerfGE 54, 143 (1980); K Möller (n 51) 58–60.

53 K Möller (n 51) '[A]ny attempt to limit the scope of rights to certain especially important autonomy interests will come at the price of incoherence of the underlying conception of autonomy; thus, the only way to avoid this incoherence is to include *all* autonomy interests in the scope of rights.'

54 *Evans v United Kingdom* App No 6339/05 (ECtHR 2006) para 57.

55 *Tysiac v Poland* App No 5410/03 (ECtHR 2007) para 107.

56 (n 54) para 71.

57 *A, B and C v Ireland* App No 25579/05 (ECtHR 2010) paras 212 and 216; *Gross v Switzerland* App No 67810/10 (ECtHR 2013) para 58; *V.C. v Slovakia* App No 18968/07 (ECtHR 2011) para 138; *R.R. v Poland* App No 27617/04 (ECtHR 2011) para 180; *Jehovah's Witnesses of Moscow and Others v Russia* App No 302/02 (ECtHR 2010) paras 117 and 135.

58 *Jehovah's Witnesses of Moscow and Others v Russia* (n 57) para 135.

59 Ibid. para 134.

On the one hand, personal autonomy is an aspect of the private life that Article 8 aims to protect. On the other hand, it becomes a general principle of the Convention *as a whole* and not just of Article 8. This conceptual split seems very difficult to maintain: how can something be a right derived from one of the Convention articles, but at the same time also be an 'important underlying principle underlying the interpretation of [the Convention] guarantees'? A possible but perhaps not all that convincing explanation could be that it is in fact first and foremost a principle, on a par with human dignity, and that it does reflect an essential element of the Convention, but that this principle at the same time finds its clearest expression in Article 8.

The inconsistencies of personal autonomy with regard to religion

When it comes to the relationship between personal autonomy and religious beliefs, the case law of the ECtHR is somewhat inconsistent. As Marshall states, '[t]he importance of beliefs and conscience to one's identity cannot be overstated for these enable a person to live by a set of rules and values of fundamental worth to that person.'[60] Within the framework of the Convention, Article 9 protects religious freedom first and foremost. Article 9 primarily protects the sphere of personal beliefs and religious creeds, that is, the area that is sometimes called the *forum internum*. In addition, it protects acts which are intimately linked to these attitudes, such as acts of worship or devotion that are aspects of the practice of a religion or belief in a generally recognized form.[61]

Marshall believes that Article 9 has been largely unsuccessful in upholding individuals' manifestations of religious beliefs. In her view, it would be better if the Court relied more on its case law on personal autonomy and the importance of identity to individuals.[62] In cases where there is a religious dimension but where individuals still wish to rely on their personal autonomy, the Court mainly focuses on Article 9, which is problematic because the Court analyses personal autonomy under Article 8.[63] In *Leyla Sahin v Turkey*, a case about a ban on the wearing of the Islamic headscarf in Turkish universities, the applicant also wanted to invoke Article 8 as well as Article 9. The Grand Chamber did not address the applicant's claim from the perspective of Article 8, focusing instead only on Article 9 and the right of education in Article 2 of Protocol 1 of the Convention. Judge Tulkens points out in her dissenting opinion that the decision of the majority is inconsistent with the Court's Article 8 jurisprudence.[64]

Granted, this case was about headscarves, but it does show that when there is a religious dimension, the Court prefers to rely on Article 9 and not Article 8. This gives the impression that the exercise of one's religious freedom has nothing to do with the personal autonomy of individuals. This is unfortunate, as an analysis under the Court's jurisprudence on Article 8 might have led to very different results.

A good example of this is the case *Jehovah's Witnesses of Moscow and Others v Russia*, in which the Court does in fact connect religious freedom to personal autonomy.[65] The

60 J Marshall (n 48) 140.
61 Ibid. 141.
62 Ibid. also 160–161.
63 Ibid. 144.
64 *Leyla Sahin v Turkey* App No 44774/98 (ECtHR 2005).
65 (n 58).

facts of the case are complex and there are several legal issues at stake. Most relevant is the question of whether the refusal of blood transfusions by Jehovah's Witnesses amounts to encouragement of suicide or is simply refusal of medical assistance.[66] Barring one crucial difference which I will discuss later, this case is principally quite similar to the inoculation case discussed here.

When it comes to the encouragement of suicide, the Court is brief:

> In so far as the domestic judgments can be understood to consider that the refusal of a blood transfusion is tantamount to suicide, in the Court's view, this analogy does not hold, for the situation of a patient seeking a hastening of death through discontinuation of treatment is different from that of patients who – like Jehovah's Witnesses – just make a choice of medical procedures but still wish to get well and do not exclude treatment altogether.[67]

The Court then moves on to examine the other question, namely whether or not the community encouraged its members to refuse medical treatment in life-threatening situations by refusing blood transfusions. It notes that

> the refusal of potentially life-saving medical treatment on religious grounds is a problem of considerable legal complexity, involving as it does a conflict between the State's interest in protecting the lives and health of its citizens and the individual's right to personal autonomy in the sphere of physical integrity and religious beliefs.[68]

It is interesting to note that the applicants in this case did not claim a violation of their rights under Article 8, but rather under Article 9 only. Yet this does not stop the Court from using its jurisprudence on personal autonomy and Article 8 in its own motion.

The Court declares that personal autonomy is an 'important principle underlying the interpretation of [the Convention's] guarantees', which even include activities that may be physically harmful or dangerous.[69] In the sphere of medical assistance, this also includes a possibly fatal outcome as the result of the refusal of a certain form of treatment. For the Court, this would result in an interference of a patient's rights under Article 8 of the Convention.

According to the Court, 'to accept or to refuse specific medical treatment . . . is vital to the principles of self-determination and personal autonomy.'[70] But the Court goes even further: '[F]or this freedom to be meaningful, patients must have the right to make choices that accord with their own views and values, regardless of how irrational, unwise or imprudent such choices may appear to others.' In the *Jehovah's Witnesses* case, the Court recognizes that the authenticity of the refusal of treatment is a legitimate concern, but just because someone's choice also reflects the tenets of that person's faith and the religious community he or she belongs to does not necessarily mean that his or her will was overborne by others. There has to be concrete evidence to that effect.[71]

66 Ibid. paras 131–2.
67 Ibid. para 132.
68 Ibid. para 134.
69 Ibid. para 135.
70 Ibid. para 136.
71 Ibid. paras 138–9.

What makes the *Jehovah's Witnesses* case even more relevant is that the Court explicitly mentions the issue of mandatory vaccination. In general, the Court states that even though patients can make decisions that may be harmful or even possibly fatal, 'the State must abstain from interfering with the individual freedom of choice in the sphere of health care, for such interference can only lessen and not enhance the value of life.' Yet there can still be an overriding public health concern which the State has to protect, such as 'mandatory vaccination during an epidemic'.[72]

The ECtHR has made a similar argument, albeit very briefly, in *Solomakhin v Ukraine*, a case about a man who was vaccinated against diphtheria during a diphtheria epidemic in the region. Afterwards, he complained that this vaccination had caused him several chronic health issues. In this case the ECtHR explicitly acknowledges that compulsory vaccination – if it is an involuntary medical treatment – amounts to an interference with the right to respect for one's private life, including a person's physical and psychological integrity.[73] But the ECtHR then immediately affirms that 'the interference with the applicant's physical integrity could be said to be justified by the public health considerations and necessity to control the spreading of infectious diseases in the region.'[74] The ECtHR does not elaborate upon this argument, but seems to find it quite evident that public health concerns can justify interference in the applicant's private life, especially as the domestic courts had thoroughly examined the circumstances of the epidemic in the region and determined the medical necessity of vaccinating the applicant.

We can compare this to the approach of the U.S. Supreme Court in its famous case *Jacobson v Commonwealth of Massachusetts*.[75] *Jacobson* was decided in 1905, when infectious diseases were among the leading causes of death.[76] Justice Harlan, who wrote the opinion on behalf of the Supreme Court, held that individual liberty is not 'an absolute right in each person to be, in all times and in all circumstances, wholly free from restraint'. He added,

> There is, of course, a sphere within which the individual may assert the supremacy of his own will and rightfully dispute the authority of any human government, especially of any free government existing under a written constitution, to interfere with the exercise of that will. But it is equally true that, in every well-ordered society charged with the duty of conserving the safety of its members the rights of the individual in respect of his liberty may at times, under the pressure of great dangers, be subjected to such restraint, to be enforced by reasonable regulations, as the safety of the general public may demand.

In this case the U.S. Supreme Court agrees that a state may require adults to submit to an effective vaccination when an existing epidemic (smallpox, in the case of Jacobson) endangers a community's population. This, in broad strokes, seems quite similar to the approach of the ECtHR: in principle everyone is considered a free agent, able to make choices about their own lives, but this freedom is not unrestricted, as concessions to freedom sometimes have to be made for the sake of public health.

72 Ibid. para 136.

73 *Solomakhin v Ukraine* App No 24429/03 (ECtHR 2012) para 33.

74 Ibid. para 36.

75 *Jacobson v Commonwealth of Massachusetts*, 197 US 11 (1905).

76 WK Mariner, GJ Annas, and LH Glantz, 'Jacobson v Massachusetts: It's Not Your Great-Great-Grandfather's Public Health Law' (2005) 95(4) *American Journal of Public Health* 583.

The reasoning of the Court in the *Jehovah's Witnesses* judgment can be applied to the Dutch girl's case. As with the Jehovah's Witnesses, her choice has to be respected ***prima facie*** based on her autonomy in health care decisions. As the Court stressed, even if her reasons for refusal are based on her religious beliefs, this does not in and of itself make her choice unfree or in some other way not her own. The fact that her decision increases her risk of fatal complications considering her weak physical constitution is also not enough to justify forcing her to have the inoculation. This much is clear from the Court's reasoning. The crucial difference with this case and the refusal of blood transfusions by Jehovah's Witnesses is that the choice of the Dutch girl might adversely impact the health of other people and therefore touches upon public health concerns. This is not the same for the refusal of blood transfusion, which only affects the refusing individual. So we should include the Dutch girl's choice within the scope of her right to personal autonomy, but as with all rights they can be balanced against other considerations, in this case the 'protection of health' mentioned in Article 8 paragraph 2 of the Convention. If we do that, then it becomes very likely that the Dutch government could have rightfully forced her to have the inoculation, her religious beliefs notwithstanding.

Summary: personal autonomy as a guiding principle

This section began with a short analysis of how the Court's case law on personal autonomy has evolved. Personal autonomy and personal freedom are part of the foundational principles of the Convention as a whole and have their importance as such. The principle of personal autonomy is most clearly reflected in Article 8, and it is in the jurisprudence on this Article where the Court has derived a right to personal autonomy from the right to respect for one's private life. The principle has become a guiding interpretational tool for the Court, whereas the right becomes a tool for individuals to invoke. This right to personal autonomy may be especially important given its relation to the principle bearing the same name, but it is still subject to the same restrictions as other rights: it can be balanced against other considerations or other rights and as such can be limited. One of these possible considerations is the public health concern, which may limit one's right to personal autonomy.

Applied to the case under scrutiny here, this means that the girl's autonomy interest in leading a life in accordance with her religion is part of her right to personal autonomy. As such, it should be protected, but can still be limited. She refused an inoculation against the measles, an infectious disease, during an epidemic, so clearly there were public health concerns at stake here. Whether or not the situation was grave enough to warrant limiting the girl's exercise of her autonomy is less clear. The available information is limited, and it would require an analysis of the severity of the epidemic and also of the threat level of measles as an infection.[77] Erring on the side of caution would mean limiting the girl's freedom to safeguard the health of others.

Conclusions

In this chapter I have reviewed the case of a 17-year-old Dutch girl who refused an inoculation against the measles for faith-based reasons. Due to her generally weak physical constitution, she died when complications arose after she contracted the measles. This case led

77 One could argue, for example, that polio is worse than the measles.

to a debate in the Low Countries, with opinions coalescing around two main opposing positions. Proponents of one position, citing the concept of (personal) autonomy, defended the girl's freedom of choice. They argued that the girl made a conscious choice based on her religion and as such this choice should be respected. Proponents of the other position argued that the girl did not have any personal autonomy in this case because of the public health concerns at issue here. Implicitly, the argument also seemed to be that her choice could not be truly free precisely because it was based on her religion.

Personal autonomy has also made its way into the case law of the ECtHR. There it functions both as a principle and a right. These two functions of personal autonomy can be complementary, and the conceptual difference between them should not be problematic. Personal autonomy as a principle becomes an interpretational tool and general principle of law for the entire Convention, whereas personal autonomy as a right becomes a concrete instantiation of that principle within the scope of Article 8 ECHR.

When it comes to the relationship between autonomy and religion, there seems to be some inconsistency, as the Court tends to look at these cases exclusively from the perspective of the freedom to manifest one's religion as enshrined in Article 9. Most of the time, Article 8 is left completely out of the equation. This disregards the fact that for many people today, religion is a major part of their identity and an essential part of who they are and how they behave. As such, the case law on personal autonomy of Article 8 is extremely relevant. That is why the Court should be more open to analysing cases that have a religious dimension from the perspective of personal autonomy and Article 8.[78] A good example of this is the *Jehovah's Witnesses* judgment, in which the Court clearly made the connection between autonomous behaviour and religion: many people draw upon the tenets of their faith in the choices that they make. This is an evolution that should be encouraged, as it leads to a fairer and more equal treatment of autonomy interests.

I agree with Möller that all autonomy interests should be *prima facie* included in the right to personal autonomy, even those that many people consider silly, trite, or even immoral.[79] This also means that autonomy interests based on religion should be included. Doing so prevents us from discriminating against certain interests on the basis of, for example, the moral views of the majority within a society. It is only during the balancing stage that we can analyse *in concreto* whether certain autonomy interests can be reasonably and proportionately limited by the state. In the Dutch girl's case, there were clearly public health concerns that could be used to trump the exercise of her personal autonomy. This way we can respect personal autonomy as a right that – like other rights – can be limited.

This approach differs from some of the commentaries on the choice of the Dutch girl. The opponents of her freedom of choice seem to argue that she simply has no freedom to choose in this case: she is a minor, her decision is based on her religion and on the views of the community to which she belongs, and her choice would endanger the health of others. Based on this they deny her autonomy *because* there are overriding (public health) concerns. I do not agree with this approach. My view would be that her choice *prima facie* falls within the scope of her personal autonomy, *but* it can be limited by other considerations such as public health. The end result may be the same in this particular case, but the road to get there is very different. This approach seems more consistent on a principled level and would therefore be preferable.

78 This is based on the work of J Marshall referenced in this article (n 48).
79 (n 51).

13 Shaping notions of personal autonomy in plural societies

Addressing female genital cutting in France and the European regulatory framework's approach to this custom

Lucia Bellucci

Introduction

Female genital cutting (FGC, *excision*) is an ancient tradition that consists of the ablation, to differing degrees, of female genital organs. It is widespread in many places, mainly in Africa. It conflicts with the concept of personal autonomy as developed in so-called Western countries to such a degree that the two are virtually incompatible. For this reason FGC deserves special attention in the study of personal autonomy in plural societies.

In the present chapter, it will not be possible to analyse the rich theoretical framework related to the concept of autonomy (see Part I of this volume for more conceptual treatments). It is possible, however, to underline that this notion is strongly connected to issues related to an individual's ability to make decisions.

The concept of autonomy, as most of us interpret it, and the custom of excision reflect differing and opposing narratives. Such tensions can create normative conflicts. The fact that FGC is generally performed on minors exacerbates these conflicts.

Assessing FGC in France, and in particular the reaction of the French criminal justice system to this custom, is useful for the analysis of the aforementioned conflict because France has the richest jurisprudence on FGC and is, to the best of my knowledge, the only country where excision cases are systematically brought to court. It is also one of the few countries, among the 'Western' countries that punish FGC, that has not adopted an act or an article in its penal code to actually prohibit it. In order to bring an FGC case to the French courts, therefore, other charges must be brought, such as personal injury, manslaughter, or failure to render assistance to a person in danger.

In France, FGC is perpetuated mostly by West African immigrants, particularly from sub-Saharan Africa, belonging to the Mandé and Halpulaar ethnic groups.[1] Between the late 1970s and the late 1980s, excision cases were adjudicated by the Tribunal Correctionnel. In the late 1980s, jurisdiction over these cases was transferred to the Cour d'Assises,[2] a move that prompted heated debate.[3]

1 See *Rapport d'activité du GAMS* (GAMS 2001) 1.

2 The Tribunal Correctionnel is part of the Tribunal de Grande Instance and has jurisdiction over offences that may be sanctioned with less harsh punishments (*délits*). The Cour d'Assises has jurisdiction over offences that may be sanctioned with the harshest punishments (*crimes*). While the Tribunal Correctionnel is strictly composed of professional judges, the Cour d'Assises combines these judges, one of whom is the President of the Court, with a popular jury made up of randomly selected French citizens.

3 In the academic context, the journals *Droit et Culture: Revue semestrielle d'anthropologie et d'histoire*, *Revue du MAUSS*, and *Nouvelle Revue d'Ethnopsychiatrie* helped lead the debate. For further details see L Bellucci, *Consuetudine, diritti e immigrazione: La pratica tradizionale dell'escissione nell'esperienza francese* (Giuffrè 2012) 158 (n 416).

DOI: 10.4324/9781315413617-16

In order to carry out a more profound analysis of the conflict between the custom of excision and the criminal justice system, I conducted an ethnographic enquiry into the French criminal trials related to FGC, which I carried out through in-depth interviews and a qualitative content analysis of documents (newspapers, periodicals, academic journals, and grey literature). I analysed all the cases for which I was able to find enough documentation to reconstruct the proceedings (19 cases in total) and conducted 12 in-depth interviews. The trials cover a period of 24 years (1979–2013). I interviewed some of the main social actors in the excision cases tried in France: judges, lawyers, anthropologists who were heard as experts or who have written about and witnessed excision proceedings, interpreters, doctors from the *Protection Maternelle et Infantile* (PMI) centres, and non-governmental organization (NGO) activists fighting for the elimination of excision practices and/or otherwise engaging in the proceedings as civil parties. The data gathered from the interviews were combined with information culled from informal conversations with other individuals familiar with the topic.

In this chapter I will only present two of the trials I analysed, both of which specifically concern the Coulibaly case of 1991. Even though the Coulibaly case was not the first FGC case ruled on by the Cour d'Assises,[4] it is worth consideration for three main reasons. First, after this case, traditional excision was no longer considered a *délit* but a *crime*. Verdicts in excision cases were rendered by a popular jury after an elaborate procedure and an usually highly publicized trial. Second, this case was tried before the Cour d'Assises of Paris and Bobigny. It therefore allows for a comparison of trials before two different Cours d'Assises and their rulings. Third, the case establishes a link between FGC and the idea of violence. I will in fact demonstrate how the response of the French legal system, as it emerges from the trials analysed, associates the custom of excision with the concept of violence, and how this association is reiterated in the texts, including regulatory texts, of the European institutions on the issue.

The fact that FGC is usually performed on minors exacerbates the conflict between the concept of autonomy and the custom of excision. My analysis of the Coulibaly case is therefore preceded by a section that contextualizes the 'ages' at which excision occurs and focuses on the socio-cultural changes in attitudes towards this topic. Section three provides extensive analysis of the Coulibaly case. Section four develops a comparison between the two trials that shape the Coulibaly case and are tried by different courts, and draws on them to analyse what I call 'the social actors of the trials'. Section five illustrates how the excision-violence binomial stems from recent interventions, including regulatory interventions, of European institutions on the subject matter. Section six shows how this binomial also appears in the 'Council of Europe Convention on preventing and combating violence against women and domestic violence' of 12 April 2011 (hereinafter the Istanbul Convention).[5] Section seven concludes the analysis.

The 'ages' of excision, the role of pain, and the body as a vector for education

Across populations, the age or social stage at which excision is traditionally practised varies. Scholars have detected a considerable diversity in the practice of this custom. They classify excision by the age at which a girl or woman undergoes the procedure: until 40 days after birth; from 1 to 4 years old; from 4 to 8 years old; from 8 to 10 years old; from 10 to

4 The Chambre correctionnelle of the Cour de Cassation ruled in the Coulibaly case only on 9 May 1990. In the meantime the Cour d'Assises had already ruled on other cases.

5 See <https://rm.coe.int/CoERMPublicCommonSearchServices/DisplayDCTMContent?documentId=090000168046031c> accessed 3 May 2017.

15 years old; and from 15 to 20 years old.[6] They also classify it according to physiological and social stages: before the first menstrual period; after the first menstrual period; before marriage; during pregnancy; and after a sterile marriage.[7]

Among the Gourmantché, Michel Cartry has observed both a 'black' excision that marks the end of childhood for young girls and is performed without an initiation ceremony, and a 'white' excision that involves girls who are about to get married and is accompanied by an initiation ritual (marriages are celebrated at the end of the initiation ceremony).[8]

Distinct excision practices exist as well among the Sénoufo and the Minianka (an ethnic group related to the Sénoufo), as Bohumil Théophile Holas[9] and Nicole Sindzingre[10] have observed. Among the Sénoufo Fodonon, excision was traditionally conceived as a precondition for marriage and was performed collectively on small groups of five to six girls. In another Sénoufo group, it was performed on girls between the ages of 10 and 15, and was not a precondition for marriage. Only among one Sénoufo group, the Fodombolé, was excision practised collectively at the beginning of the first pregnancy. Among the Minianka, excision was traditionally a precondition for marriage, but it was performed individually.

Denise Paulme has described the practice of excision in the forest of Kissidougou (Guinea), where it often used to be performed by age group in rural areas. Paulme also observed the close ties that excision fostered among women of the same age group.[11] By contrast, Monique Gessain has observed that excision within the Bassari society of eastern Senegal (Etiolo region) is performed individually, according to individuals' maturity.[12]

In both France and Africa, the general trend is to lower the age of excision. In urban African contexts, this trend is not new. As early as the 1950s Holas had already observed that the Minianka were starting to perform some excisions at a younger age.[13] Nevertheless, some ethnic groups have always performed FGC on the very young. According to Annie Raulin,

> the diversity of practices related to excision is a relatively well-known reality, but it is often explained as if it ensued from a diachronic evolution . . . . This interpretation, while not false, nonetheless deserves some qualifications. The diversity of these practices appears . . . in the synchronic dimension as well, not only from one ethnic group to another, but [also] from one sub-ethnic group to another.[14]

6 See I Gillette-Faye, *La polygamie et l'excision dans l'immigration africaine en France analysées sous l'angle de la souffrance sociale des femmes* (Presses Universitaires du Septentrion 1998) 91–94.

7 For this schematization see ibid. 94–96; M Erlich, *La femme blessée: Essai sur les mutilations sexuelles féminines* (L'Harmattan 1986) 32–35.

8 See M Cartry, 'La calebasse de l'excision en pays gourmantché' (1968) 38(2) *Journal de la Société des Africanistes* 189–190.

9 See BT Holas, *Les Sénoufo, y compris les Minianka* (Presses Universitaires de France 1957).

10 See N Sindzingre, 'Le plus et le moins: à propos de l'excision' (1977) 17(65) *Cahiers d'Études Africaines* 68–69.

11 D Paulme, 'L'initiation des filles en pays Kissi (Haute Guinée)' in *Actas da 2a conferência international dos africanistas ocidentais em Bissau*, vol 5 (Ministerio das Colonias 1952) 301.

12 M Gessain, 'Les classes d'âge chez les Bassari d'Etyolo (Sénégal oriental)' in D Paulme (ed), *Classes et associations d'âge en Afrique de l'Ouest* (Plon 1971) 167.

13 Holas (n 9) 115.

14 A Raulin, *Femme en cause: Mutilations sexuelles des fillettes africaines en France aujourd'hui* (Centre Fédéral (FEN) 1987, 51 (translation from French by the author).

In the cases brought before the courts in France, excision had been performed on children – mostly infants. In both France and Africa, the desire to help their daughters avoid the memory of such a strong and therefore unforgettable pain is the mothers' most frequently invoked justification for performing excision on infant girls.[15]

A ruling was issued by the Court of Appeal of Venice on 23 November 2012[16] on the first and, for the time being, only excision trial in Italy since Italian legislation was adopted on female genital mutilation (FGM) in the form of Law no. 7 of 9 January 2006, which includes 'Provisions on the prevention and prohibition of female genital mutilation'.[17] In the text of the trial, the accused mother stated under examination that 'the operation is [usually] done on very small children to avoid pain,' and the father said that he wanted the 'operation to take place within two months of age so that [the child] would suffer as little as possible'.[18] Furthermore, telephone conversations intercepted between the father and the *exciseuse* (a person who performs excisions) revealed that 'it would be best if the "*operation*" could be done on the same day that the child had her "*ears pierced*" so that the pain would "*only last a day*".'[19] The charges were brought against both the parents and the *exciseuse*, and while the statements of the accused reveal a certain confusion between the memory of pain and the feeling of pain, the explanation of pain avoidance seems to reveal changes in the interpretation of pain, which is seen as an indispensible vector of moral education in many West African societies. One could argue that the desire to help their daughters avoid the memory of the pain masks many women's worries about not being able to perform FGC on their daughters when they get older because of the possibility that girls will reject this custom once they have integrated into French, Italian, or other 'Western' society. In fact, empirical research in France has shown that some parents do indeed fear their daughters' refusal.[20] Nevertheless, the pain-avoidance explanation is not limited to European contexts; it has also been articulated in African countries where excision is part of the tradition of many ethnic groups. In many West African societies moral qualities are traditionally inscribed on the body in a number of ways. The markings are visible proof of the bearer's capacity to bravely endure pain and therefore of his or her self-control. The ability to dominate oneself leads to self-respect, which in turn inspires respect in others.[21]

15 See Gillette-Faye (n 6) 96.

16 Court of Appeal of Venice 23 November 2012 (dep. 21 February 2013), n 1485. Other rulings were issued before the adoption of the law of 2006. According to new sources, more cases are currently pending. See 'Perugia, mutilazioni genitali sulle figlie: ai domiciliari una coppia di nigeriani', Umbria24 <www.umbria24.it/perugia-infibulazione-su-due-bambine-ai-domiciliari-coppia-di-nigeriani/307280.html> accessed 3 May 2017 and 'Infibulazione, si difendono i genitori delle bambine: l'operazione è stata fatta in Nigeria dai nonni, noi non ne sapevamo nulla', La Nazione <www.lanazione.it/umbria/infibulazione-sesso-donne-violenza-perugia-nigeriani-bambine-1.110422> accessed 3 May 2017.

17 In GU 14, 18 January 2006, 4. This law introduced arts 583 *bis* and 583, prohibiting the mutilation (or lesion) of female genitalia, into the Italian Penal Code. On this issue, see F Basile, 'La nuova incriminazione delle pratiche di mutilazione degli organi genitali femminili' (2006) 6 *Diritto penale e processo* 678; C de Maglie, *I reati culturalmente motivati. Ideologie e modelli penali* (ETS 2010) 40–41; L Goisis, 'Multiculturalismo e diritto penale in un'ottica comparatistica: l'esempio del Canada. Prime riflessioni alla luce della convenzione di Istanbul' in MA Foddai (ed), *Il Canada come laboratorio giuridico: Spunti di riflessione per l'Italia* (Jovene 2013) 143–157.

18 Court of Appeal of Venice (n 16) 48–49.

19 Court of Appeal of Venice (n 16) 35; italics appear in the ruling.

20 See Gillette-Faye (n 6) 96.

21 See Raulin (n 14) 42.

In fact, traditionally pain should not be expressed;[22] being able to endure it stoically was a sign of courage,[23] and the endured pain was made visible on the body. The pain caused by the excision (as well as by infibulation) was not a by-product of the ritual practice nor was it the result of the *exciseuse*'s lack of skill or caution or inadequate instruments or a failure of technique, as the colonial literature had argued.[24] Pain was not only an inevitable consequence, but also a necessity because of its formative value and transformative action.[25] This was true also of other operations that mark the bodies, such as scarification and tattooing. An analogous link between pain, courage, self-control, and respect could also be made with regard to childbirth. The fact that both in Africa and Europe mothers usually want excision to be practised on their newborns to avoid the memory of pain shows that they do not consider pain to be a vector of moral education anymore. They no longer interpret the experience of enduring pain as a challenge their daughters need to face in order to become stronger and to prepare themselves to overcome the adversities they may be confronted with in their adult lives. Without actually contesting the practice of excision, women break with a tradition that has always valued the endurance of pain. Through the reinterpretation of the role of pain they therefore create a space of autonomy. This leaves the door open to future reinterpretations of FGC.

Even though changes and adjustments related to custom generally occur collectively, within the group,[26] custom is flexible and adaptable. Despite past hesitations regarding this issue, it is a well-established concept in legal anthropology that custom is only seemingly changeless,[27] and the study of FGC supports this argument.

Women's autonomy and the Coulibaly case before the Cour d'Assises of Paris

With the Coulibaly case the French judicial system started to consider excision a criminal act belonging to the jurisdiction of the Cour d'Assises. The case was tried before the Cours d'Assises of both Paris and Bobigny, with differing outcomes.[28]

22 According to Paulme, among the Kissi a girl endures excision without a cry. See D Paulme, *Les gens du riz: les Kissi de Haute Guinée* (2nd expanded edn, Plon 1970) 155. On the topic of self control and the domination of the tongue in the Bambara tradition see D Zahan, *La dialectique du verbe chez les Bambara* (Mouton & Co 1963) 152; L Calderoli, 'Marquages permanents du corps en Afrique subsaharienne: le processus technique comme signifiant' (1993) 89(2) *L'Ethnographie* 105, 125.

23 On the topic, see also S de Ganay, 'Symbolisme de quelques scarifications au Soudan français en rapport avec l'excision' (1947–1949) 3 *Comptes rendus sommaires des séances de l'Institut français d'anthropologie* 7.

24 See, for example, A de Villeneuve, 'Étude sur une coutume somalie: les femmes cousues' (1937) 7(1) *Société des Africanistes* 15.

25 Calderoli (n 22) 120.

26 See N Rouland, 'La coutume et la pensée juridique sauvage' in J Gilissen (ed), *La coutume-Costume*, Recueils de la Société Jean Bodin pour l'histoire comparative des institutions/Transactions of the Jean Bodin Society for Comparative Institutional Law, vol LI, part I *Antiquité, Afrique noire, Amérique, Australie-Antiquity, Black Africa, America, Australia* (De Boeck Université 1990) 11.

27 See SF Moore, *Law as Process: An Anthropological Approach* (Routledge & Kegan Paul 1978) 13–14.

28 See R Verdier, 'Une exciseuse en Cour d'Assises. Le procès de Soko Aramata Keita' (1991) 21 *Droit et Culture: Revue semestrielle d'anthropologie et d'histoire* 184; R Verdier, 'Le double procès de Mme Kéita (Paris-Bobigny, mars-juin 1991)' in E Rude-Antoine (ed), *L'immigration face aux lois de la République* (Karthala 1992) 149.

In the Coulibaly case, excisions had been performed on all six children of one couple. The accused were the *exciseuse*, Mrs Aramata[29] Souko Keita, and the parents of the young girls, Mrs Semité Diarra and her husband, Mr Sory Coulibaly. They were accused before the Cour d'Assises of Paris of acts of violence causing mutilation, perpetrated on a minor under 15 years of age, and of being accomplices to this offence.[30] Michel Erlich was the appointed expert.[31] The trial lasted three days. The parents were given a five-year suspended sentence and two years' probation,[32] and Mrs Keita, the *exciseuse*, was sentenced to five years' imprisonment.[33]

This trial shows that the notion of autonomy must be considered with regard to FGC not only because of the issue of young girls' freedom to decide what happens to their bodies, but also because of women's relationships to their husbands and the rest of society. As in many other FGC cases, the mother accused in this trial seems to have had very little independence. Instead of leading to improvements and gains in their economic independence, migration often implies a considerable loss of autonomy for West African women: in France they usually become housewives and cannot count anymore on the small personal incomes that they often have in their home countries. They also often live in a chronic state of isolation from European society, while their husbands provide for the maintenance of the family. Even though they have migrated to a country where women are predominantly financially independent from their husbands, West African women lose financial independence instead of gaining it. One can suggest that this paradox has an impact on their interpretation of the notion of autonomy, considering that the lack of financial independence reinforces women's dependence on their husbands, extended families, and, more generally, their ethnic communities. For example, this paradox may also contribute to their desire for endogamous family unions and relationships: most West African immigrants want their daughters to marry somebody from their community, either in France or in their home country.

Moreover, the Coulibaly case implicitly shows that the parents' autonomy has been emphasized in order to avoid describing excision as a binding cultural obligation. In her closing argument the *Parquet* (prosecutor), Mrs Commaret, deemed that cultural pressure was not irresistible. Certain Malian immigrant associations and families had resisted it. She also added that a constraint presupposes not only that it be irresistible but also unforeseen; in other words, to be justified it must impose itself on you unexpectedly, suspending all reflection. Excision is instead an organized act, anticipated and premeditated.

Furthermore, the Coulibaly case depicts FGC as an act of violence. Commaret described excision as 'an illegal and mutilative act of violence'. She continued by arguing that excision

29 In Commaret's summation the *exciseuse* was called 'Ramata'. In some sources, the second name appears as 'Soko'.

30 See G Levasseur, 'Violences volontaires. Excision' (1991) 3 *Revue de science criminelle et de droit pénal comparé* 565; M Peyrot, 'L'excision, crime coutumier' Le Monde (Paris, 8 March 1991) 11.

31 See Peyrot (n 30) 11. For some information from Peyrot's work translated into English, see 'The Prosecution of Aramata Keita, Sory Coulibaly and Sémité Coulibaly, Paris, March 1991' (1992) *Passages* <http://quod.lib.umich.edu/p/passages/4761530.0003.002/—prosecution-of-aramata-keita-sory-coulibaly-and-semite?rgn=main;view=fulltext> accessed 3 May 2017.

32 See Commission nationale consultative des droits de l'homme (CNCDH), *Étude et propositions sur la pratique des mutilations sexuelles féminines en France* 2004, 71 <www.cncdh.fr/ sites/default/files/ cncdh-_etude_msf.pdf> accessed 3 May 2017; E Rude-Antoine, *Des vies et des familles: Les immigrés, la loi et la coutume* (Odile Jacob 1997) 233. Another source states that the sentence was five years' imprisonment, including three years in jail and a two-year suspended sentence. See Levasseur (n 30).

33 See also Rude-Antoine (n 32) 233.

was a 'marking of inferiority, but also a mutilating and dangerous wound . . . . Who would dare deny it? All the doctors who have come before the bar in succession were in agreement on its injuriousness.'[34]

The prosecutor linked FGC with the *exciseuse*'s economic interests and detached it from a cultural background: 'Draped in her dignity, emerging from behind a wall of silence only to utter contradictory statements', Aramata Keita denied 'any active participation in these medical interventions'. And yet, a number of elements were gathered against her. Furthermore, Aramata Keita belonged to the caste of the *forgerons*,[35] whose members benefit from 'power and prestige heightened by the lucrative nature of their activities'. Prosecutor Dominique Commaret argued that excision is

> an attractive financial operation when frequently performed . . . . Therefore, if respect for custom implies a certain financial sacrifice relative to the meagerness of the incomes of the families who have daughters excised, the persistence of these practices is particularly lucrative for those of this profession. It seems that the gulf which in past years separated the abortionists – the *faiseuses d'anges* ('angel makers') – from their clientele appears again between the *exciseuse* and those who solicit her services.[36]

The Coulibaly case before the Cour d'Assises of Bobigny: the social actors of the trials

A few months later, in June 1991, Mrs Keita appeared before the Cour d'Assises of Bobigny for having excised 16 girls, one of whom died following the operation. Despite the number of young girls involved and the death of one of them, the punishment was clearly not as harsh as the one handed down in the trial before the Cour d'Assises of Paris. The *exciseuse* was sentenced to four years' imprisonment, with three in jail and a one-year suspended sentence, while three parents were released and the others given a one-year suspended sentence.[37]

The prosecutor's summation described parents as the victims of a binding obligation. It therefore implicitly emphasized their lack of autonomy with regard to excision. It did not characterize FGC as a lucrative practice but rather as a traditional one. Furthermore, it stressed that the accused had no intention of doing harm.[38]

In order to understand the output of this case, one must also consider the role played by the other social actors of the trials. The president of the Court, the experts, the interpreter,

34 'Réquisitoire de Mme Commaret' (1991) 21 *Droit et Culture: Revue semestrielle d'anthropologie et d'histoire* 193. The English translation is mine. Another English version can be found in 'The Summation of Prosecutor Commaret' (1992) *Passages* <http://quod.lib.umich.edu/p/passages/4761530.0003.004/—summation-of-prosecutor-commaret?rgn=main;view=fulltext> accessed 3 May 2017.

35 Traditionally, women who perform FGCs, the *exciseuses*, belong to the blacksmith caste (*forgerons*). The knowledge related to the operation is transmitted from generation to generation among the women of their families. In particular the Mandé (for example, Bambara, Diakhanké, Malinké, Mandingue, Nyominka, Socé, and Soninké) and Halpulaar peoples (Peul and Toucouleur) rely on *forgeronnes* to perform excisions.

36 'Réquisitoire de Mme Commaret' (n 34).

37 See M Lefeuvre-Déotte, *L'excision en procès: un différend culturel* (L'Harmattan 1997) 25.

38 See Verdier (1991) (n 28) 184; Rude-Antoine (n 32) 233; Verdier (1992) (n 28).

and the defending counsel had a crucial impact on the criminal proceedings. The trial before the Cour d'Assises of Bobigny lasted 10 days. During this time, the Court heard testimonies from a number of the accused as well as experts. With the approval of the presiding judge Yves Corneloup, ethnologists, anthropologists, doctors, and psychiatrists were heard. They explained excision and its cultural background, and the film by Jean-Pierre Zirn, *L'Afrique accusée?*, which does not contain explicit images of excision, was shown.

Throughout the entire Coulibaly trial before the Cour d'Assises of Bobigny, one woman of Malian origin, Mrs Tandia, acted as the interpreter.[39] Aramata Keita was defended by Xavier-Jean Keïta (Inchauspe co-counsel), an attorney of Senegalese origin. During the trial, Mrs Keita withdrew into silence and did not deny any accusations against her; in fact, she actually confessed.

The number and type of NGOs joining the proceedings as civil parties,[40] as well as the media attention surrounding the trials, were also key factors in the cases analysed. One can perhaps assume that they also weighed heavily upon the verdict.[41] In the case in question only one NGO, *Enfance et Partage*, which aims at defending children's rights, was admitted to the proceedings as a civil party. Furthermore, the case in Bobigny was tried before the Cour d'Assises des mineurs behind closed doors because not all of the accused had reached the age of majority. This case was therefore much less publicized.

FGC as an act of violence according to French courts and the European norms of the 2000s

None of the documents analysed in regard to the Coulibaly case make any explicit reference to the concept of autonomy or the like. The most recent ruling of the aforementioned Court of Appeal of Venice instead expressly refers to the concept of self-determination. As mentioned in the ruling, the rationale behind this reference is linked to the preparatory work leading up to the Italian law of 2006 and the explicit reference made therein to the 'European Parliament Resolution on Female Genital Mutilation' (2001/2035(INI)),[42] which, in paragraph F, declares that 'any form of female genital mutilation . . . is an act of violence against women.'

Certain terms used in European documents on FGC, as well as those used in the French legal system, clash with the fact that excision is practised with no intention to cause harm.[43] In most cases, in French rulings excisions are considered 'intentional acts of violence

39 By way of contrast, the translations provided in the Traore (Traoré, depending on the source), Doukoure case of 1993, which was tried before the Cour d'Assises of Paris, were inconsistent. On this case, see 'Procès de Mesdames Taky Traore et Oura Doucoure – Cour d'Assises de Paris (Ière section) (8–9 février 1993). Réquisitoire de Monsieur l'Avocat général Jean-Claude Thin' (1993) 25 *Droit et Cultures. Revue semestrielle d'anthropologie et d'histoire* 135; Lefeuvre-Déotte (n 37) 72, 75 and 76; Commission nationale consultative des droits de l'homme (CNCDH) (n 32) 72.

40 These can be, depending on the case, the NGOs *SOS Femmes Alternatives*, *CAMS*, *Ligue du Droit International des Femmes*, *Enfance et Partage*, *Planning Familial*, and *Femmes Solidaires*.

41 In this sense, see L Bellucci, 'Immigrazione, escissione e diritto in Francia' (2006) 33(3) *Sociologia del diritto* 183, 194–195.

42 In [2002] OJ C77E/126.

43 For details on the reasons given by immigrants to explain the perpetuation of this practice, see Bellucci (n 3) 77–92.

(*violences volontaires*) [or 'personal injuries' (*coups et blessures*)] causing mutilation (*ayant entraîné une mutilation*), perpetrated on a minor less than 15 years of age'.[44]

The notion that injury such as the cutting of an organ or part thereof is unequivocably and inevitably linked to the concept of violence is not, in fact, an obvious one. A man who cuts another man's arm on the job causes personal injury, but does not necessarily intend to commit an act of violence.

As a case in point, Article 582 of the Italian Penal Code, which punishes personal injuries, makes no mention of the concept of violence. Cases of FGC would be deemed in violation of this article if *ad hoc* incriminating norms did not exist in Italy. In fact, before the 2006 law was adopted, Italian judges applied this specific provision and in particular made reference to severe and very severe injuries.[45]

The idea that penal law should apply to excision cases only if FGC is deemed to be an act of violence is neither obvious nor inevitable. The link between excision and violence (or between excision and abuse/brutality) has been addressed in both European and international texts. My analysis will focus on the former since the issue of female genital mutilation (FGM) has gained considerable attention recently in the European Union and throughout Europe more generally.[46] Throughout the 2000s, EU institutions such as the European Parliament (hereinafter the Parliament), the European Commission (hereinafter the Commission), the Council of the European Union (hereinafter the Council), and the Council of Europe have intensified their focus on the issue of FGM. The result has been the consolidation of the link between excision and violence, and more particularly the pigeonholing of excision, because of its connection to mutilation, into the category of gender-based violence. A prime example of this is 'Directive 2012/29/EU of the European Parliament and of the Council of October 2012 establishing minimum standards on the rights, support and protection of victims of crime, and replacing Council Framework Decision 2001/220/JHA'.[47] It states that gender-based violence 'includes violence in close relationships, sexual violence (including rape, sexual assault and harassment), trafficking in human beings, slavery and different forms of harmful practices, such as forced marriages, female genital mutilation, and so-called "honour crimes" '.[48]

The 2013 *Female Genital Mutilation in the European Union and Croatia Report*, commissioned by the European Institute for Gender Equality, refers to FGM as a 'cruel form of gender-based violence'.[49] Furthermore, the *Strategy for Equality Between Women and Men 2010–2015*, adopted by the Commission in September 2010, considers FGM an act of violence, in particular gender-based violence.[50] The report of the Forum on the Future of Gender Equality in the European Union includes FGM among the acts of violence committed

44 See arts 222–9 and 222–10 of the new French Penal Code and art 312–3 of the former French Penal Code.

45 For an analysis of these cases, see F Basile, *Immigrazione e reati culturalmente motivati: Il diritto penale nelle società multiculturali* (Giuffrè 2010) 224–225.

46 See, for example, *Female Genital Mutilation in the European Union and Croatia Report* <http://eige.europa.eu/rdc/eige-publications/female-genital-mutilation-european-union-report> accessed 3 May 2017.

47 In [2012] OJ L315/57.

48 Ibid. para 17.

49 V Langbakk, 'Forward' in European Institute for Gender Equality (EIGE), *Female Genital Mutilation in the European Union and Croatia Report* (n 46) 3.

50 *Strategy for Equality Between Women and Men 2010–2015* (European Union 2011) 24 <http://ec.europa.eu/justice/gender-equality/files/strategy_equality_women_men_en.pdf> accessed 3 May 2017.

against women and therefore considers it 'a brutal manifestation of gender inequality'.[51] The binomial equation *FGM = violence*, with this latter term used in an utterly generic sense, can also be found in the European Parliament's resolutions on the subject matter.[52]

Among them, the 'European Parliament Resolution of 14 June 2012 on ending female genital mutilation' (2012/2684(RSP)), under paragraph C, compares excision with child abuse. The Council of the European Union (Justice and Home Affairs Council meeting) conclusions on 'Preventing and combating all forms of violence against women and girls, including female genital mutilation' (5 June 2014) refers to both violence and child abuse. Finally, the Commission's 'Joint Statement on the International Day against Female Genital Mutilation' refers to 'the brutal practice of female genital mutilation'.[53] The 'Communication from the Commission to the European Parliament and the Council: Towards the elimination of female genital mutilation' of 25 November 2013 recognizes 'FGM . . . as a form of child abuse'.[54] This stance was clearly inspired by the United Nations General Assembly Resolution 67/164 'Intensifying global efforts for the elimination of female genital mutilations', which was adopted on 20 December 2012 and likens FGM to 'an irreparable, irreversible abuse'[55] and a form of violence.[56]

As the inspiration underlying the 2013 Communication illustrates, international measures have strongly influenced the EU institutions' position on the issue of excision. However, it cannot be excluded, and in fact it is perhaps fair to assume, that this position has also been influenced by France's response to the custom in question, which took shape, in particular, through the actions of certain NGOs and the courts.

FGC and the Istanbul Convention

The Istanbul Convention considers 'genital mutilation [to be among the] serious forms of violence such as domestic violence, sexual harassment, rape, forced marriage, crimes committed in the name of so-called "honour" [to which] women and girls are often exposed',[57] and establishes that 'Parties shall ensure that culture, custom, religion, tradition or so-called "honour" shall not be considered as justification for any acts of violence covered by the scope' of the convention.[58]

51 European Commission, DG Justice and Consumers, Unit D.2 (Gender Equality) (Brussels 10 June 2015) 25 <http://ec.europa.eu/justice/events/future-of-gender-equality-2015/files/report_forum_gender_equality_en.pdf> accessed 3 May 2017.

52 See 'European Parliament Resolution of 6 February 2014 on the Commission communication entitled "Towards the Elimination of Female Genital Mutilation" ' (2014/2511 (RSP)), paras B, D, I and 3; 'European Parliament Resolution of 14 June 2012 on Ending Female Genital Mutilation' (2012/2684(RSP)), para E; 'European Parliament Resolution of 5 April 2011 on Priorities and Outline of a New EU Policy Framework to Fight Violence against Women' (2010/2209(INI)), para 3, in [2012] OJ C296E/26; 'European Parliament Resolution of 24 March 2009 on Combating Female Genital Mutilation in the EU' (2008/2071(INI)), para G), in [2010] OJ C117E/52; the aforementioned 'European Parliament Resolution on Female Genital Mutilation' (2001/20135(INI)), in [2002] OJ C77E/126.

53 European Commission, Memo/13/67 (Brussels 6 February 2013).

54 COM(2013) 833 final, para 1.

55 See ibid. para *Recalling*.

56 For the latter, see ibid. paras 4, 12, and 13.

57 Ibid. preamble.

58 Ibid. art 12, para 5.

France signed the Istanbul Convention on 11 May 2011. Chapter XII of Law no. 2013–711 of 5 August 2013[59] adapts French law to this convention, more specifically to Article 38 letter c), expressly devoted to FGM. Article 38 states:

> Parties shall take the necessary legislative or other measures to ensure that the following intentional conducts are criminalised: a) excising, infibulating or performing any other mutilation to the whole or any part of a woman's labia majora, labia minora or clitoris; b) coercing or procuring a woman to undergo any of the acts listed in point a; c) inciting, coercing or procuring a girl to undergo any of the acts listed in point a.

The 2013 law therefore bridges a gap in French legislation by creating a new *délit* that punishes the act of inciting someone to undergo or commit genital mutilation,[60] with the aim of criminalizing the conduct even if the injurious event never took place or, in this case, even if the excision has not yet been performed. Article 19 of the aforementioned law introduces Article 227–24–1 into the French Penal Code, which establishes that:

> The act of inciting a minor to undergo female genital mutilation in return for offers, promises, gifts, presents or other benefits, or through the application of pressures or coercions in whatever form, is punishable, when the mutilation has not been committed, by five years' imprisonment and by a fine of €75,000 [first paragraph]. The same punishment shall apply for the act of directly inciting, by any of the means set out in the first paragraph, a person to commit genital mutilation on a minor, when the mutilation has not been committed.[61]

It bears noting that the law's use of the word *mineur* in the masculine, which refers to both sexes, and not of the word *mineure* in the feminine, could in the future raise the issue of circumcision and spark debates on the freedom of religion.[62] This is not the place to develop this important topic. At this juncture, it will suffice to mention a point that emerged during the depositions of Mrs Christine Lazerges, professor of private law and criminal science at Université Paris I-Panthéon-Sorbonne and chairwoman of the Commission Nationale Consultative des Droits de l'Homme (CNCDH), and Mrs Fanny Benedetti, *chargée de mission*, before the Délégation aux droits des femmes et l'égalité des chances entre les hommes et les femmes. Mrs Benedetti pointed out that in the provision in question, 'making mention of "gifts, presents or other benefits" is completely artificial and was created by the French legislature (*le législateur*) to provide examples, albeit bad ones', because, as chairwoman Mrs Catherine Coutelle underlined, 'there are never any gifts, presents or benefits involved.' Mrs Lazerges and Mrs Coutelle thus requested that the words be eliminated and asked that the means of incitement not be specified. Mrs Benedetti noted that the legislature could

59 In JORF n. 0181, 6 August 2013, 13338.

60 See *LOI n° 2013–711 du 5 août 2013 portant diverses dispositions d'adaptation dans le domaine de la justice en application du droit de l'Union européenne et des engagements internationaux de la France* <www.legifrance.gouv.fr/affichTexte.do?cidTexte=JORFTEXT000027805521> accessed 3 May 2017.

61 Translated from French by the author.

62 See Délégation aux Droits des Femmes et àl'Égalité des Chances entre les Hommes et les Femmes, Assemblée Nationale, 'Compte rendu' (Paris, Wednesday 3 April 2013) 2–3 <www.assemblee-nationale.fr/14/cr-delf/12-13/c1213025.asp> accessed 3 May 2017.

have used a more appropriate 'by any means' (*par tout moyen*).[63] Clearly, this specific point on the wording of the law was raised in order to avoid limiting the punishability of acts of incitement, but it also draws attention to the fact that laws on this issue risk being disconnected from the reality of the custom that they set out to prevent.

Conclusion

Through the study of the response of the French criminal justice system to excision, my research has revealed that a conflict exists between the custom of FGC and the state legal system, and that this conflict has been exacerbated by the transfer of jurisdiction that occurred during the Coulibaly case.

This case is representative of the contesting narratives underpinning discussions around this issue, one of which argues that FCG violates fundamental rights as recognized by modern states and is incompatible with the widespread concept of autonomy in the 'Western' world, while the other maintains that FGC is passed down through the generations and rooted in tradition, and is, therefore, difficult to break away from.

The president of the Court, the prosecutor, the experts, the interpreter, the defending counsel, the members of the NGOs joining the proceedings as civil parties, and the media all play a major role in criminal proceedings. The Coulibaly case exemplifies the difficulty of reconciling modern interpretations of the notion of autonomy with the values of the community, which have an overwhelming influence with regard to the perpetuation of excision, in particular in the form of the extended family. The decision to perpetuate FGC could be made by grandparents, aunts, or older sisters[64] without a parent's knowledge, which contributes to making it even more difficult to determine an appropriate legal response to excision.

In French jurisprudence, there have been no cases of 'exemplary' punishments. Prosecutors, as well as NGO activists joining the proceedings as civil parties, have often requested that at least a part of the sentence be served in jail, citing the fact that the convicted, irrespective of their origins, do not understand the meaning of a suspended sentence. And yet suspended sentences have almost always been granted. Although the Penal Code allows for a maximum penalty of life in prison (downgraded following a reform to a 20-year prison sentence),[65] the accused tried before the Cour d'Assises have, in fact, received moderate punishments.

Among the cases analysed, the harshest punishment has been handed down to the *exciseuse* in the Graou (also Gréou or Grau, depending on the source) case, ruled on by the Cour d'Assises of Paris in 1999.[66] It consisted of eight years' imprisonment without

63 See ibid. 3–4; M Benillouche, 'L'interdiction des mutilations sexuelles: entre confirmation et révolution . . . ' (Revue des droits et libertés fondamentaux, chronique n. 6, 2014) <www.revuedlf.com/personnes-famille/linterdiction-des-mutilations-sexuelles-entre-confirmation-et-revolution-article/> accessed 3 May 2017.

64 See Raulin (n 14) 64.

65 See art 222–8 of the French Penal Code.

66 I received documentation on this trial, in particular on the hearing of Friday 12 February 1999, through GAMS (initially *Groupe femmes pour l'Abolition des Mutilations Sexuelles*, then *Groupe pour l'Abolition des Mutilations Sexuelles*; it is now part of the *Fédération nationale GAMS* [*Groupe pour l'Abolition des Mutilations Sexuelles, des Mariages Forcés et autres pratiques traditionnelles néfastes à la santé des femmes et des enfants*]). The documentation was given to GAMS activists by Marie-France Casalis, Préfecture d'Ile de

suspended sentence, but this was a case of recidivism in which a total of 48 excisions had been performed.[67]

The rulings analysed in my research are not detailed enough to offer any definite conclusions on the *modus decidendi* of judges and juries, or on the thought processes underlying the decisions expressed in the verdicts. Even the Coulibaly case, in relation to which a rich body of documentation is readily available, does not offer insights into this topic, which merits further exploration. Nevertheless, it may be that French courts have taken into consideration the complexity of both the conflict in question and the acculturation processes, all of which is accentuated by the social, cultural, and economic isolation of many of the accused. The notion of autonomy and its differing interpretations are at the heart of these processes and may be profoundly influenced by an absence of financial independence for the women who perpetuate excision. The difficulty in defining autonomy as a notion is related to the fact that its interpretations may vary not only among societies, but also among individuals. A community's understanding of the concept of autonomy can change over time. A woman's understanding of this concept can also change several times over the course of her life. Nevertheless, FGC and autonomy as a modern notion will always be in conflict. Since excision is usually performed on minors, mothers or members of the extended family are making a permanent decision over the bodies of young girls in their communities that freezes the aforementioned acculturation process at one point in time without any chance of physically rectifying the act later in life. The choice concerning FGC will already be made for that girl – and it is irreversible. That girl's diverging interpretations of the notion of autonomy may, however, be able to have an impact later, on future generations of girls and women within her community and beyond, although they will not be able to change her own circumstances.

The tensions and conflicts surrounding excision suggest that further research should be carried out to deepen our understandings of the theoretical and empirical knowledge about autonomy in contemporary, multicultural societies in order to overcome rigid conceptual categorizations and build new forms of intercultural dialogue. One can suggest that the lack of financial independence and social inclusion limits the chances of some women to shape alternative interpretations of the concept of autonomy that might differ from the one depicted within their group of origin. Nevertheless, the reinterpretation of the value of pain

France, Secrétariat Général-Délégation Régionale aux Droits des Femmes et à l'Egalité. On this case see also TH Atenga, 'Droits de l'homme: une Exciseuse Malienne Condamnée a Huit Ans de Prison' <www.ips.org/fr/droits-de-lhomme-une-exciseuse-malienne-condamnee-a-huit-ans-de-prison/> accessed 14 March 2015; TH Atenga, 'RIGHTS-FRANCE: Malian Immigrant Sent To Prison For Performing FGM' <www.ipsnews.net/1999/02/rights-france-malian-immigrant-sent-to-prison-for-performing-fgm/> accessed 3 May 2017; Commission nationale consultative des droits de l'homme (CNCDH) (n 32) 74; B Grosjean, 'Excision: une victime dénonce. Mariatou est la première à avoir porté plainte. Des dizaines d'accusés sont jugés aux assises', *Libération* (Paris, 2 February 1999) <www.liberation.fr/societe/1999/02/02/excision-une-victime-denonce-mariatou-est-la-premiere-a-avoir-porte-plainte-des-dizaines-d-accuses-s_263875#> accessed 3 May 2017.

67 The *exciseuse* continued to practise excision after being ordered to serve a one-year suspended sentence in 1994 in the Diarra, Traore, Greou (Traoré, depending on the source) case of 1994 before the Cour d'Assises, wherein the presiding judge was Yves Corneloup. See M Peyrot, 'Deux parents africains acquittés dans un procès d'excision', *Le Monde* (Paris, 17 September 1994) 15. On this case see also X-J Keïta, *Rapport France-Afrique. Le droit au respect de l'intégrité physique et la coutume: la pratique de l'excision en France* (Publications du Barreau du Val de Marne 1995) 14; P Gerin, 'L'exciseuse dénoncée par une de ses victimes', *Libération* (Paris, 17 May 1994) 12.

and the new space of autonomy that it creates, which is often ignored in traditional academic discussions of the subject, confirms that custom is much more flexible and adaptable than previously imagined. This, in turn, leaves room for future reinterpretations – among the populations that practise excision – not only about the notion of autonomy, but also about the perpetuation of FGC.

It should be evident from my writings on FGC that I do not belong to the category of scholars who believe that the law, and even penal law, should never interfere with the issue of excision. I am aware, too, of the fact that many NGOs, whose commitment to eradicating the custom of excision is commendable, have often put pressure on European institutions in an effort to guarantee greater protection for girls at risk of being subjected to FGC. However, I believe that automatically equating excision with a form of violence akin to rape or slavery, as the French legal system and the regulatory and non-regulatory texts of the European documents of the 2000s analysed here have done, is not inevitable. A line of reasoning such as this risks being interpreted by the populations involved as a post-colonial imposition and, consequently, unnecessarily strains relations between the so-called South and North of the world and complicates the already difficult social inclusion of migrants in Europe. It is possible for the law to intervene on the subject of FGC without ignoring or denying the social and cultural significations of excision and the intentions of those who perpetuate it. Paradoxically, spreading the message that excision equates to violence could prompt those who practise excision to hold on even more tightly to it as an act of defiance with regard to a 'West' that misunderstands their traditions, and simply have European resident girls excised in Africa without any publicity of the event in Europe. As can be seen from my analysis of the new French law, a disconnect could arise between the law and the reality in which a traditional rite is performed, and normative gates could be indirectly created that might give rise to complicated conflicts regarding religious freedom. These conflicts have nothing to do with the question of migration, and should be allocated to a debate within a more complex and constructive socio-political realm than can be encompassed by a single law.

14 The human rights dimensions of virginity restoration surgery

Alison Dundes Renteln

A woman's honor is like a match, it can only be lit once.[1]

Introduction

Although health is often treated as a neutral concept that can be analysed in objective terms, in reality cultural context shapes the interpretation of what constitute beneficial medical practices.[2] Women may sometimes find themselves at the mercy of medical professionals who question their motivations for seeking surgical procedures. This is particularly the case regarding 'elective' surgery not deemed necessary by 'cosmopolitan' medicine. One such operation is hymenoplasty (also known as hymenorraphy), a type of reconstructive or cosmetic procedure to repair a woman's hymen (the thin membrane that stretches across the vagina). While a number of activities can cause the hymen to break, it is most commonly ruptured when a girl or woman has sexual intercourse for the first time. A ruptured hymen is, therefore, often presumed to be evidence of past sexual activity, and for a variety of reasons some women want to avoid that presumption.

Taking the hymenoplasty debate as a starting point, in this chapter I consider whether physicians should have the power to refuse women access to surgery based on their possibly misguided concern for their patients' presumed lack of autonomy or the presumption that they suffer from 'false consciousness'.[3] Denying adult women access to elective procedures in the name of women's rights or on the basis of other justifications raises serious questions about whether they enjoy genuine autonomy in liberal democracies.

The anatomical status of unmarried girls is a concern across the globe. According to customary law in many societies, their condition affects family honour because premarital sex is often thought to bring shame on the family.[4] Sexual activity before marriage may be

1 K Shaheen, 'Hymenoplasty: Why Do Women Get Virginity Back?' *The Daily Star* (Beirut, 8 October 2013) <www.dailystar.com.lb/News/Lebanon-News/2013/Oct-08/233897-hymenplasty-why-do-women-get-virginity-back.ashx> accessed 24 April 2017.

2 CO Airhihenbuwa, *Health and Culture: Beyond the Western Paradigm* (Sage 1995); S Johnsdotter and B Essén, 'Genitals and Ethnicity: The Politics of Genital Modifications' (2010) 18 *Reproductive Health Matters* 29.

3 Some see this rather as a form of 'relational autonomy', whereby individuals willingly allow their choices and decision-making to be constrained by their social settings. See J Nedelsky, *Law's Relations: A Relational Theory of Self, Autonomy, and Law* (Oxford University Press 2011); in this volume see also Deveaux (Chapter 5), Johnson (Chapter 15), Benda-Beckmann (Chapter 16), and Ali and Kazmi (Chapter 19).

4 FH Stewart, *Honor* (University of Chicago Press 1994); A Agarwal, *Crimes of Honor: An International Human Rights Perspective on Violence Against Women in South Asia* (PhD dissertation, University of

DOI: 10.4324/9781315413617-17

dangerous for women in countries with strict codes of sexual morality, and the problem is exacerbated when women from these societies move to countries with more sexual freedom. Differing moral codes concerning sexual conduct inevitably complicate the lives of young women who move from Islamic polities to European countries.[5] Many have to manoeuvre in new social worlds where more liberal attitudes towards sexual activity exist while at the same time having to adhere to the more conservative rules of their families and communities. To function as required in both realms, some women ask surgeons to repair their hymens in order to conceal their past sexual activities.[6] While the question of whether a type of sexual behaviour alters virginity may appear to be relatively trivial, for these women it can be a matter of life and death.[7] They fear that if they do not appear to be virgins on their wedding night, they may become victims of honour killings.[8]

In this context, one asks whether women seeking hymen reconstruction should be legally guaranteed access to this surgical procedure, despite the well-intentioned objections of surgeons, especially when denial of 'revirgination' could result in death. In deciding how to formulate public policy regarding hymenoplasty, one should take into account the serious qualms doctors have about performing this surgery, including the commonly expressed view that hymen reconstruction perpetuates sexist attitudes towards women.[9] For surgeons, the basic question is whether performing a hymenoplasty is consistent with domestic law and international human rights standards; for women seeking the surgery, the question is whether the denial of the surgery violates their fundamental human rights.

In what follows, I assess the debate about hymen restoration. This study of a controversial surgical practice, complicated by cultural conflicts regarding its necessity, affords insight into biases inherent in the medical profession.[10] The analysis of this operation requires

---

Southern California 2008). Fatima Mernissi asserts that 'The concepts of honour and virginity locate the prestige of a man between the legs of a woman. It is not by subjugating nature or by conquering mountains and rivers that a man secures his status, but by controlling the women related to him by blood or by marriage, and forbidding them any contact with male strangers.' F Mernissi, 'Virginity and Patriarchy' (1982) 5 *Women's Studies International Forum* 183. See also R Husseini, *Murder in the Name of Honour: The True Story of One Woman's Heroic Fight Against an Unbelievable Crime* (Oneworld Publications 2009) 83.

5 A Steigrad, 'Muslim Women in France Regain Virginity in Clinics' *Reuters* (3 April 2007) <www.reuters.com/article/us-muslimwomen-europe-virginity-idUSL2532025120070430> accessed 24 April 2017; S Meichtry and M Colchester, 'Secular, Muslim Culture Clash Ensnares French Doctors. Hymenoplasty Spotlights Debate Over Repression' *Wall Street Journal* (New York, 10 June 2008) A11; E Sciolino and S Mekhennet, 'In Europe, Debate Over Islam and Virginity' *New York Times* (New York, 11 June 2008) <www.nytimes.com/2008/06/11/world/europe/11virgin.html> accessed 24 April 2017; 'More Women Becoming Virgins Again With Hymen Replacement Operations on the NHS' *Daily Mail* (London, 30 July 2010) <www.dailymail.co.uk/news/article-1298684/Surge-virginity-repair-operations-NHS.html> accessed 24 April 2017.

6 The status of this tissue is of such monumental significance that women in some societies worry about participating in athletic activities such as cycling, which can, in rare cases, result in the rupture of the hymen.

7 N Shalhoub-Kevorkian, 'Imposition of Virginity Testing: A Life-Saver or a License to Kill' (2005) 60 *Social Science & Medicine* 1187, 1190.

8 TT Pham, *Moroccan Immigrant Women in Spain: Honor and Marriage* (Lexington Books 2014) 113.

9 G Heinrichs, 'Is Hymenoplasty Anti-Feminist?' (2015) 26 *Journal of Clinical Ethics* 158.

10 Among important considerations of this practice, see, e.g., A Longmans et al., 'Ethical Dilemma: Should Doctors Reconstruct the Vaginal Introitus of Adolescent Girls to Mimic the Virginal State?' (1998) 361 *British Medical Journal* 459; RJ Cook and BM Dickens, 'Hymen Reconstruction: Ethical and Legal Issues' (2009) 107 *International Journal of Gynecology and Obstetrics* 266.

consideration of the motivations of those seeking it, as well as a brief assessment of the social value of virginity. Most importantly, this study demonstrates the necessity of having a realistic understanding of the consequences of defloration for women in particular cultural communities.

The cultural significance of virginity

In some societies women are expected to be virgins when they marry;[11] this is ostensibly to ensure the paternity of future offspring.[12] Although this expectation of virginity on the wedding night was prevalent in European countries and North America in the not-so-distant past, it has ceased to play as crucial a role since the mid-twentieth century and the advent of the sexual revolution.[13] Virginity continues to be an important requirement for individuals in some communities, including Islamic societies.[14] A study of South Asian women in Ontario, for instance, emphasizes the importance of the norm of virginity in the context of explaining the cultural motivation for domestic violence.[15]

Although many assume there is a single understanding of 'virginity', its meaning has changed over time and varies in different parts of the world. Scholarship about the historical

11 There is a double standard in that there is no such expectation for men.

12 D Holtzman and N Kulish, 'Nevermore: The Hymen and the Loss of Virginity' (1996) 44 (suppl) *Journal of the American Psychoanalytic Association* 303; H Blank, *Virgin: The Untouched History* (Bloomsbury 2007); TT Dao Jensen, 'Visions of Virginity in the Abstinence-Only Curriculum' (PhD dissertation, Arizona State University 2008). For rules governing how to evaluate paternity in light of the length of gestation, see I Ghanem, *Islamic Medical Jurisprudence* (Arthur Probsthain 1982) 30. DNA tests would provide a reliable method instead.

13 Evidence of continuing concern with virginity is reflected in U.S. practices such as abstinence and virginity pledges and the 'true love waits' movement. Controversies over 'slut walks' suggest that there continues to be a preoccupation with virginity in the United States; see A North, 'Should "Slut" be Retired?' *New York Times* (New York, 3 February 2015) <https://op-talk.blogs.nytimes.com/2015/02/03/should-slut-be-retired/?_r=0> accessed 24 April 2017. A sensational televised story of a few young women auctioning off their virginity for hundreds of thousands of dollars to pay for their college education and help support their families also suggests its enduring value in North America; see AB Wang, ' "It's My Decision." This Woman Is Auctioning Off Her Virginity to Help Her Family' *The Washington Post* (Washington, 25 October 2016) <www.washingtonpost.com/news/wonk/wp/2016/10/25/its-my-decision-this-woman-is-auctioning-off-her-virginity-to-help-her-family/?utm_term=.6c1caa84dc6d> accessed 24 April 2017.

14 BR van Moorst et al. contend that virginity is important in the religious ethics of many groups; see 'Backgrounds of Women Applying for Hymen Reconstruction, the Effects of Counselling on Myths and Misunderstandings About Virginity, and the Results of Hymen Reconstruction' (2012) 17 *The European Journal of Contraception and Reproductive Health Care* 93, 94. It also is used metaphorically to signify a lack of (business) experience, as with Richard Branson's Virgin Atlantic airlines, and high quality, as with extra virgin olive oil. For a famous essay analysing the trauma associated with the loss of virginity, see S Freud, 'The Virginity Taboo' in S. Whiteside (tr), *The Psychology of Love* (Penguin Classics 2006 [1918]) 262.

15 S Hunjan and S Towson, ' "Virginity Is Everything": Sexuality in the Context of Intimate Partner Violence in the South Asian Community' in SD Dasgupta (ed), *Body Violence: Intimate Violence Against South Asian Women in America* (Rutgers University Press 2007) 53, 59. See also Husseini (n 4) 83: 'So much of the problem of violence against women in general, and specifically in so-called honour crimes, revolves around the hymen – the proof of virginity; a literal seal of virtue. It represents the "honour" of the girl and, more importantly, of her family.'

significance of virginity usually associates it with an intact hymen.[16] For the purposes of this analysis, that definition is the relevant one, although it should be noted that relying on the hymen as the indicator of virginity is misleading. Not only can the appearance of an intact hymen vary considerably,[17] but as mentioned earlier, its rupture can occur for reasons other than sex. Moreover, the breaking of the hymen does not always result in bleeding. Indeed, studies indicate that only half of women observed blood during their first sexual experience.[18] This matters because traditionally, in societies in which the virginity of the bride had to be demonstrated, the presence of blood on the sheets was crucial. It is also erroneous to presume that virginity is necessarily related to what 'Westerners' might call chastity or purity. For instance, an ethnographic study of the sexual experience of young adults in Morocco noted that while young women accept the proposition that they should be virgins when they marry, they enjoy sexual intimacy without vaginal penetration.[19] The pressure to find alternative ways to have sexual experience without risking the loss of virginity, as understood in the community, has also intensified because the age of marriage has risen.

As virginity plays a significant role in marriage negotiations, families in many countries have been known to require virginity testing of their daughters. This practice has been strongly condemned by human rights organizations such as Human Rights Watch because it is regarded as an affront to women's dignity.[20] Moreover, as virginity testing is often compelled as a prerequisite to a forced marriage, it is considered even more reprehensible.[21]

In some societies rituals are performed to celebrate the virginal status of girls. For instance, regions in South Africa such as the province of KwaZulu Natal have experienced a revival of *umhlanga* – a Zulu reed dance ceremony celebrating virginity – despite vociferous protests against virginity testing.[22] To take part in *umhlanga*, girls must be 'certified'

16 J-J Amy provides a definition: '*Virginity* could be defined as the *absence of any prior sexual intercourse with penetration of the vagina that caused an identifiable lesion of the hymen.*' J-J Amy, 'Certificates of Virginity and Reconstruction of the Hymen' (2008) 12 *European Journal of Contraception and Reproductive Health Care* 111; see also D Pollack, 'Virginity Testing: International Law and Social Work Perspectives' (2008) 51 *International Social Work* 262–267; J Awwad et al., 'Attitudes of Lebanese University Students Towards Surgical Hymen Reconstruction' (2013) 42 *Archives of Sexual Behavior* 1627. In Christianity some struggle to explain the status of the Virgin Mary because although conceived through the Immaculate Conception, baby Jesus arrived through vaginal birth; see M Mayblin, 'People Like Us: Intimacy, Distance, and the Gender of Saints' (2014) 55 (suppl 10) *Current Anthropology S* 271.

17 Amy (n 16).

18 This fact is widely known (see, e.g., Pham [n 8] 100). Nevertheless, it seems not to have obviated the need for women to produce blood on their wedding night.

19 F Bakass, M Ferrand, and the ECAF team, 'Sexual Debut in Rabat: New "Arrangements" Between the Sexes' (2013) 68 *Population F* 37. Surprisingly, this empirical study makes no reference to hymenoplasty. Likewise, a study of Lebanon also mentioned that 'more than half of Lebanese female university students approved premarital sexual contact without vaginal penetration.' The researcher concludes: 'This finding underpins the fact that sexual taboos seem to relate more to the physical state of virginity than to the virtue of chastity.' See Awwad et al. (n 16) 1633.

20 Human Rights Watch, see <www.hrw.org/news/2014/12/01/un-who-condemns-virginity-tests> accessed 24 April 2017.

21 Parents sometimes take their minor daughters to doctors for testing and possible hymen restoration, if necessary, before marrying them off. L Kopelman, 'Make Her a Virgin Again: When Medical Disputes About Minors are Cultural Clashes' (2013) 39 *Journal of Medicine and Philosophy* 8.

22 L Vincent, 'Virginity Testing in South Africa: Re-Traditioning the Postcolony' (2006) 8 *Culture, Health & Sexuality* 17. For a comparative analysis of testing in Brazil and South Africa, see LB Brown, 'Abject Bodies: The Politics of the Vagina in Brazil and South Africa' (2009) 56 *Theoria* 1.

virgins. Although some fear the certification may put girls at risk because it may attract men who want a virgin in order to avoid contracting AIDS, others contend that the virginity testing is actually beneficial because it protects young girls. So, despite trenchant criticisms of virginity testing,[23] some commentators defend the practice because it is accepted by the communities.[24]

While many people assume that there is no longer a preoccupation with virginity in modern societies in the twenty-first century, wedding customs in modern societies reflect the continuing importance of this 'virtue', even though it is conveyed in symbolic terms. For instance, at American weddings the bride typically wears a white gown that ostensibly signifies her pure state. Before she departs for her honeymoon, it is customary for the bride to throw her bouquet, which symbolically represents her 'defloration'. Another wedding ritual that arguably reflects the cultural value attached to virginity is the breaking of glass. For example, at Jewish weddings after the bride and groom drink out of the same glass, the groom breaks it under his foot.[25] While it is unlikely that those participating in such rituals are deliberately perpetuating sexist or misogynistic attitudes requiring the purity of women at the time of marriage, they nevertheless reinforce these societal understandings.

The demand for hymenoplasty

One should not conflate virginity testing of young girls with the quite distinct debate about adult women requesting hymen restoration surgery to avoid honour-related violence.[26] An adult woman's decision to undergo a reconstructive surgery that does not involve any serious risk of physical harm has nothing to do with the question of the best interests of the child nor does it necessarily involve duress.

In Europe and North America women have been requesting hymenoplasty for the past few decades.[27] According to one study, 'hymenoplasty has proliferated in various parts of

23 For oppressive use of virginity tests, see, e.g., K Engelhart, 'Brides Forced to Take Tests for Virginity' *Maclean's* (Toronto, 27 July 2009) <www.macleans.ca/news/world/brides-forced-to-take-tests-for-virginity/> accessed 24 April 2017.

24 While Vincent concedes that some may object to the testing as a violation of the privacy rights of girls, her article (n 22) questions why it is treated differently from male circumcision under the Children's Rights Bill. For a defence of the testing as beneficial to girls, see A Wickström, 'Virginity Testing as a Local Public Health Initiative: A "Preventive Ritual" More than a "Diagnostic Measure" ' (2010) 16 *Journal of the Royal Anthropological Institute* 532.

25 For the association between unbroken glass and virginity, see A Dundes, 'The Psychoanalytic Study of Folklore' in A Dundes, *Parsing Through Customs: Essays by a Freudian Folklorist* (University of Wisconsin Press 1987) 32. It is probably no coincidence that the barrier to women's success in the workplace is usually called the 'glass ceiling'.

26 Although it is difficult to know whether the restoration surgery succeeds in protecting women from honour-related violence, there is some evidence in this direction. In Egypt hymen restoration was considered responsible for reducing the rate or honour killings by 80 per cent. See P Kandela, 'Egypt's Trade in Hymen Repair' (1996) 347 *Lancet* 1615; M O'Connor, 'Reconstructing the Hymen: Mutilation or Restoration? (2008) 16 *Journal of Law and Medicine* 164.

27 MHJ Bekker et al., 'Reconstructing Hymens or Constructing Sexual Inequality? Service Provision to Islamic Young Women Coping With the Demand to be a Virgin' (1996) 6 *Journal of Community & Applied Social Psychology* 329; A Chozick, 'Virgin Territory: U.S. Women Seek a Second First Time. Hymen Surgery Is On the Rise and Drawing Criticism' *Wall Street Journal* (New York, 15 December 2005) A1.

Europe,'[28] and the American Society of Plastic Surgeons says vaginal surgery, including hymenoplasty, is one of the industry's fastest-growing sectors.

The increase in demand for 'revirgination' surgeries in European countries and North America may be a consequence of increased migration, the reality that young women are caught between two cultures, and the fact that they marry at a later age. Underlying it all, however, is women's need to avoid honour-related violence or at least allay their fears that it might occur.

As hymen repair seems to be occurring more frequently, the medical profession is addressing the question of its legitimacy with a sense of urgency.[29] The pressure on surgeons to perform hymenoplasties led to an intense discussion about the ethical challenges they face: on one hand is the possibility that performing the surgery simply reinforces gender inequities in certain cultural milieus; on the other hand is women's fear that they will be subjected to honour-related violence and even death if the procedure is not performed.

Such ethical dilemmas regarding hymen restoration surgery are not limited to liberal Western countries. In Iran, for example, where hymenoplasty is illegal and doctors can be prosecuted for performing it, Ahmadi remarks that some doctors nevertheless went to great lengths to do the surgery in order to protect women from honour-related violence:

> The physicians seemed to assume the moral burden of protecting these women's welfare, suggesting they would have felt morally culpable if something were to happen to them, when knowing that performing a simple medical procedure may have prevented reprisal. Perceiving the risk of not performing hymenoplasty as too great, the physicians respect the autonomy of those requesting . . . the surgery.[30]

Social science supports the claim that adult women in Europe also seek hymen repair because they fear they will be victims of honour-related violence if they are discovered not to be virgins on their wedding night.[31] Research is available on the plight of young Muslim women in Spain, Sweden, and the Netherlands.[32] In light of past research on the importance of marriage traditions to immigrants, enforcement of norms regarding sexual morality may take on a special significance for migrants to ensure the maintenance of cultural identity.[33] Scholars contend that young women caught between Islamic and European norms concerning 'sexuality, virginity and marriage exposes these young women to very specific

28 Pham (n 8) 106; B Crumley, 'The Dilemma of "Virginity" Restoration' *Time* (New York, 13 July 2008) <http://content.time.com/time/world/article/0,8599,1822297,00.html> accessed 24 April 2017.

29 L Seng Khoo and V Senna-Fernandes, 'Hymenoplasty and Virginity – An Issue of Socio-Cultural Morality and Medical Ethics' (2015/2016) 3 *PMFA News* 1.

30 A Ahmadi, 'Ethical Issues in Hymenoplasty: Views from Tehran's Physicians' (2014) 40 *Journal of Medical Ethics* 430.

31 See Steigrad (n 5).

32 See especially B Essén, A Blomkvist, L Helström, and S Johnsdotter, 'The Experience and Responses of Swedish Health Professionals to Patients Requesting Virginity Restoration (Hymen Repair)' (2010) 18 *Reproductive Health Matters* 38; see also S Ayuandini, 'How Variability in Hymenoplasty Recommendations Leads to Contrasting Rates of Surgery in the Netherlands (2017) 19 *Culture, Health, & Sexuality*; Pham (n 8); Bekker et al. (n 27).

33 F Strijbosch, 'The Concept of the Pela and Its Social Significance in the Community of Immigrant Moluccans in The Netherlands' (1985) 17 *Journal of Legal Pluralism* 177.

and severe forms of acculturative stress'.[34] They also point out that keeping secrets from their families may result in 'feelings of guilt and anxiety'.[35]

Medical professionals, however, tend to handle questions of the proper nature of surgeries without adequate consideration of the consequences for their female patients, revealing the paternalism of medicine. Rather than allowing medical elites to decide a question on their own that affects the well-being of many women, it would be preferable to weigh the arguments for and against hymenoplasty.

Objections to hymenoplasty

The primary argument against hymen restoration is that it perpetuates sexist attitudes towards women. In essence, surgeons performing the procedure would be reinforcing the patriarchal notion that women must be virgins, or at least must appear to be, on their wedding night. Even though women are the ones requesting the surgery, its performance has the effect of undermining the dignity of women. Professor Jacques Lansac, president of the National College of Gynaecologists and Obstetricians of France, comments: 'The surgery is an attack on women's dignity . . . [and] liberty.'[36]

This argument is reminiscent of the position taken by the Human Rights Committee when it rejected the contention by Manuel Wackenheim, a man with dwarfism, that he had the right to employment in dwarf-tossing competitions.[37] France banned the contests because they allegedly undermined the dignity of persons with disabilities. According to this line of argument, a paternalistic approach to human rights is justifiable because the state has an obligation to protect the dignity of members of a group even if particular individuals fail to appreciate how their choices and actions undermine their own self-interest.[38]

A second objection is the 'virginity fraud' involved. As the purpose of the surgery is to deceive a future husband about the status of his wife's hymen and thereby create the illusion of virginity, some surgeons find the fraud involved objectionable; they regard their involvement as a form of complicity in the deceit.[39] According to this line of argument, they owe a duty not only to the woman who is the patient, but also to the husband and family.[40] This deceit is not new; for centuries women have used a number of circumvention techniques to fool their grooms on their wedding nights.[41] One trick was to ensure that the groom

34 Ibid. 331.

35 Ibid. 333.

36 Steigrad (n 5). A judgment in Lille where a judge annulled a marriage because a woman had lied about being a virgin sparked great controversy.

37 *Wackenheim v France*, Communication No 854/1999: France, 26/07/2002, CCPR/C/75/D/854/1999 (Jurisprudence).

38 For a thoughtful consideration of this decision, see E Stamatopoulou, *Cultural Rights in International Law* (Martinus Nijhoff 2007) 118.

39 Insofar as all cosmetic surgery involves deceit, taken to its logical extreme this argument would require rejection of all such procedures. P de Lora, 'Is Multiculturalism Bad for Health Care? The Case for Re-Virgination' (2015) *Theoretical Medicine and Bioethics* 141, 154.

40 DD Raphael, 'Commentary: The Ethical Issue is Deceit' (1998) 316 *British Medical Journal* 460.

41 C Addison, 'Enlightenment and Virginity' (2010) 2 *Inkanyiso: Journal of Humanities and Social Sciences* 71, 77; 'Virginity for Sale' *Marie Claire* (20 January 2010) <www.marieclaire.com/politics/a3809/fake-hymens-for-sale/> accessed 24 April 2017; see also R Evelth, 'Artificial Hymens Have Come a Long Way Since Blood-Filled Fish Bladders' *Smithsonian* (Washington, 12 August 2013) <www.

was sufficiently inebriated that he would not notice the difference in the bride's condition. Techniques discussed in the literature include having midwives repair the broken hymen with needle and thread and animal membrane;[42] using a vial (or sponge or capsule) of animal's blood and surreptitiously spreading it in the appropriate place; concealing a small blade in the wedding dress to make a small cut; and substituting already bloodied sheets. Another more contemporary option is the use of kits available online; some produced in China cost as little as $30. They involve the insertion of red substance that mimics blood. A company in Germany, VirginiaCare, also claims to sell artificial hymens that are basically pouches of bovine blood.[43]

But it is the relatively new use of surgery that implicates the medical profession in the wedding night schemes and may partly explain their reluctance to perform the surgery.[44] The fact that some physicians have conscientious objections to performing the procedure should not constitute a reason for disallowing the surgery altogether, provided another surgeon can be found to operate.

A number of professional associations have taken a position opposing the surgery on the grounds that 'refusal to do a hymenoplasty represented the best practice and current standard of medical care.'[45] Physicians opposed to the surgery referred to a policy statement from the American College of Obstetrics and Gynaecology, 'Vaginal Rejuvenation and Cosmetic Vaginal Procedures', which officially discouraged the procedure 'because of a paucity of information about their safety and efficacy'.[46]

The mostly consistent rejection of hymenoplasty by medical professional organizations – including the Royal College of Obstetricians and Gynaecologists and the National College of Obstetricians and Gynaecologists of France – reflects a genuine desire to undermine the patriarchal ideology that women must be virgins at the time of marriage.[47] The policy of the U.K.-based Royal College of Obstetricians and Gynaecologists states explicitly

smithsonianmag.com/smart-news/artificial-hymens-have-come-a-long-way-since-blood-filled-fish-bladders-27752278/> accessed 24 April 2017.

42 This is according to a former director of the Kinsey Institute for Research in Sex, Gender, and Reproduction, quoted in Chozick (n 27).

43 R Gert, 'Women Simulate Virginity With Artificial Hymens. German Company Sells Easy-to-Use Product Ensuring Blood on Wedding Sheets' (*The Times of Israel,* 18 December 2015) <www.timesofisrael.com/women-simulate-virginity-with-artificial-hymens/> accessed 24 April 2017.

44 People were concerned about fake or 'falsified' virginity in earlier centuries. Tassie Gwilliam provides an interesting analysis comparing faked virginity to counterfeit money, implying that the fraud devalues virginity just as 'fake money devalues coinage'. It also suggests women's bodies are comparable to commodities for exchange. Male authors have written at length in novels about virginity fraud or counterfeit maidenhead; see T Gwilliam, 'Counterfeit Maidenheads in the Eighteenth Century' (1996) 6 *Journal of the History of Sexuality* 518. In an influential essay, Fatima Mernissi refers to the phenomenon as 'artificial virginity' (n 4).

45 Kopelman (n 21) 10.

46 Despite the declared 'paucity of information', the committee that issued the policy warned that the surgery 'could cause scarring, pain, altered sensation, and sexual dysfunction'; see Kopelman (n 21) 10.

47 See Royal College of Obstetricians and Gynaecologists, Statement No. 6, 'Hymenoplasty and Labial Surgery' (July 2009) 1–3 and a subsequent position paper. This document lists the organizations in other countries such as France, New Zealand, and Malaysia opposed to hymenoplasty. But see the Swedish National Board of Health and Welfare's Ethical Committee's Protocol No. 43 (19 March 2004) (discussed in Essén et al. [n 32] 42–43) which allows the surgery if a woman's life is in danger.

> that cultural or religious norms which place women in positions of vulnerability or subservience are unacceptable. This includes cultures in which women fear for their safety if it is discovered that their hymen is perforated . . . .
>
> While the Standards Board supports the concept of patient and professional autonomy, it believes that any decision to provide cosmetic genital surgery should be based entirely on clinical grounds.[48]

While this position of trying to reject patriarchal logic by refusing to perform hymen repair is not without merit, it is an approach that may prove short-sighted if it winds up sacrificing the very individuals that the policy is designed to save.

Principles of biomedical ethics also enter into the debate. The key principle is non-maleficence, or do no harm. Some doctors consider the procedure unjustifiable because the women are not 'sick', the procedure is not 'medically necessary', and it appears to be a type of harm or mutilation.[49] Although hymenoplasty is usually a minor surgery lasting 30–45 minutes, performed under either local or general anesthesia, it does involve some risk, as do all surgical procedures.[50] The recovery may take four to six weeks, although innovations may reduce that.[51] As a matter of principle, there is a question as to whether doctors are required to perform surgeries that may be regarded as 'self-mutilation' or 'self-harm' when there is no medical reason for it.[52] On this basis, surgeons might decline to operate. Some doctors may also fear that 'performing the hymenoplasty will affect their stature among their peers.'[53]

Moreover, if the women who were their patients are attacked or killed and family members are prosecuted, the physicians worry that they might be required to testify in court, which may be another disincentive to performing the surgery. Even more worrisome may be the possibility that the doctors themselves could be subject to retaliation if the family members discover that they have performed the surgery. The experience of doctors running abortion clinics in the United States surely demonstrates the possibility that communities can show their extreme displeasure when they disagree with a specific type of surgery.

Another major concern of surgeons is the legal status of the practice. As various countries have enacted laws that ban genital surgeries, medical personnel have expressed concern about the legally ambiguous status of the procedure.[54] They contend that European laws

48 See Royal College of Obstetricians and Gynaecologists, Statement No. 6, 'Hymenoplasty and Labial Surgery' (July 2009) 1–3.

49 For a discussion of whether consent should be treated as a defense to self-harm, see AD Renteln, 'Cutting Edge Debates: A Cross-Cultural Consideration of Surgery' in W Teays et al. (eds), *Global Bioethics and Human Rights: Contemporary Issues* (Rowman & Littlefield 2014) 220, and DJ Baker, *The Right Not to Be Criminalized: Demarcating Criminal Law's Authority* (Ashgate 2011).

50 Amy (n 16) 112; Steigrad (n 5).

51 D Shaw and BM Dickens, 'A New Surgical Technique of Hymenoplasty: A Solution, but for Which Problem' (2015) 130 *International Journal of Gynecology and Obstetrics* 1.

52 For a discussion of the ethics of amputation for individuals who want to have certain body parts removed when there is no medical necessity, see D Patrone, 'Disfigured Anatomies and Imperfect Analogies: Body Integrity Identity Disorder and the Supposed Right to Self-Demanded Amputation of Healthy Body Parts' (2009) 35 *Journal of Medical Ethics* 541. This topic is beyond the scope of this analysis, and has little bearing on my argument inasmuch as the operation central here is *reconstructive* surgery.

53 LL Wynn, ' "Like a Virgin": Hymenoplasty and Secret Marriage in Egypt' (2016) 35 *Medical Anthropology* 547, 553.

54 O'Connor (n 26) 16.

that ban female genital mutilation (FGM) are broad in scope and appear to apply to genital cosmetic surgery and hymen repair. Although there may not yet exist a definitive interpretation of relevant statutes, the vagaries of the laws may also discourage surgeons from operating.

The high-profile prosecution of a physician in the United Kingdom suggests that this concern is not unfounded.[55] The doctor delivered a baby to a woman who had undergone female genital cutting in her homeland in Somalia. After the delivery, he stitched the area to repair tearing she had experienced during labour. To his surprise, he was prosecuted under the national law prohibiting surgery of the female genitalia. This charge was absurd insofar as the law was designed to prevent *removal* of parts of the female anatomy of little girls who lack legal capacity consent; it was not intended to prevent surgeons from performing reconstructive surgery on consenting adult women. Fortunately, the doctor was acquitted.[56]

This case indicates that legal officials may see fit to prosecute doctors for 'revirgination' under statutes that do not clearly distinguish among different types of surgeries. That surgeons must operate in the shadow of the vague laws may, in fact, discourage them from providing reconstructive surgery that adult women urgently request and actually need.

Arguments in favour of allowing hymenoplasty

The principle of patient autonomy

The most significant argument in favour of hymen repair is the autonomy interest of women. Simply put, women as patients should have the ability to decide what types of surgical procedures they wish to have, whether they are medically necessary or not. That patients who are in control of their mental faculties and have legal capacity should make decisions about surgery is hardly controversial. Patient autonomy, while admittedly not an absolute principle that should be limited in extreme cases of self-harm, is a well-established principle in medical ethics.

Even if one does not subscribe to full autonomy and supports the prohibition of some procedures, women should at least be able to have reconstructive surgery. The hymenoplasty debate emerged following heated public discussion of female genital mutilation, a surgery that has been designated as a criminal offence in many jurisdictions because it is considered a form of mutilation.[57] Yet it is unclear why some types of operations are condemned as 'mutilation' while others are accepted as elective procedures. Although many people in modern societies condone the pervasive trend towards 'flesh wounds',[58] FGM has usually been condemned as an extreme form of violence against women.

55 S Laville, 'First FGM Prosecution: How the Case Came to Court' *The Guardian* (London, 14 February 2015) <www.theguardian.com/society/2015/feb/04/first-female-genital-mutilation-prosecution-dhanuson-dharmasena-fgm> accessed 24 April 2017.

56 S Laville, 'Doctor Found Not Guilty of FGM on Patient at London Hospital' *The Guardian* (London, 4 February 2015) <www.theguardian.com/society/2015/feb/04/doctor-not-guilty-fgm-dhanuson-dharmasena> accessed 24 April 2017.

57 See, e.g., M Mabilia, 'FGM or FGMo? Cross-Cultural Dialogue in an Italian Minefield' (2013) 29 *Anthropology Today* 17.

58 See, e.g., V Blum, *Flesh Wounds: The Culture of Cosmetic Surgery* (University of California Press 2005).

A new double standard has emerged, which becomes particularly evident when one considers that certain types of genital surgeries are treated as permissible, while hymenoplasties to avoid 'honour'-related violence are not. In 'Western' societies adult women are increasingly opting for genital surgeries for aesthetic reasons,[59] giving rise to a new field called 'cosmetogynecology'. According to the American Society for Aesthetic Plastic Surgery, 400 girls 18 and younger had labiaplasty in 2015 – an 80 per cent increase over the previous year – and a 2013 British report noted a fivefold increase over 10 years.[60] These cosmetic genital surgeries have as of yet not been subject to regulation, nor have they generated much public debate about their legitimacy. This constitutes selective enforcement of laws that apply to female genitalia.

It is worth emphasizing here the major difference between FGM and hymenoplasty. Unlike female genital cutting, which involves the permanent removal of parts of the body, hymen restoration is a reconstructive surgery. Also, whereas female genital cutting is generally performed on very young girls, those seeking hymenoplasties are predominantly adult women. While some might question their judgement, it seems perfectly reasonable for the women to request the surgery when they face a credible threat of honour-related violence. Given that the surgery is restorative and requested by adults, women should be entitled to have it performed.

Human rights as a basis for hymenoplasty

Not only does the principle of patient autonomy support the argument in favour of hymenoplasty; the framework of human rights law also offers some basis for requiring that states ensure the availability of the procedure. A growing body of literature and global policies support the proposition that there is a right to health.[61] Even without such an explicit right, women arguably have a right of access to health care and medical services under existing instruments, particularly the international Covenant on Economic, Social and Cultural Rights. Article 12 stipulates that there is a human right to the highest attainable standard of health. This provision has been elaborated in General Comment Number 14 (2000), which calls for paying attention to women's right to health in particular.[62]

Although the right to health is considered a well-established human right, whether it applies to the right to surgery is not an entirely settled question. While some scholars regard it only as an 'emerging' norm, others support an expansive interpretation of the right to health that includes a right to essential surgery.[63] This logic is convincing: if the International Covenant of Economic, Social and Cultural Rights guarantees a right to the highest attainable standard of health, then this right should be construed as encompassing the right to surgery.

59 Johnsdotter and Essén (n 2); BJ Hill, *Supra-Natural: Genderventions and Genitalia* (PhD dissertation, Indiana University 2013) 101.

60 RC Rabin, 'A Baffling Trend in Surgery: More Teenage Girls are Seeking Cosmetic Changes to Genitalia' *New York Times* (New York, 26 April 2016) D4.

61 BCA Toebes, *The Right to Health as a Human Right in International Law* (Intersentia/Hart 1999). Toebes discusses women's health issues but makes no mention of hymenoplasty.

62 See <www.refworld.org/pdfid/4538838d0.pdf> accessed 24 April 2017.

63 See, e.g., KA McQueen et al., 'Essential Surgery: Integral to the Right to Health' (2010) 12 *Health and Human Rights* 137; Renteln (n 49).

If such a right to surgery is accepted, there would have to be further debate about whether hymenoplasty constitutes an essential surgery. It stands to reason that this relatively innocuous procedure should be covered as essential surgery if it can spare women from violence or death. In addition, the fact that women live in fear of honour-related violence serves as a mental health argument in favour of interpreting the surgery as essential.

Another relevant human right is the right to culture. Here the argument is that women may choose to remain a part of their cultural communities despite certain oppressive, patriarchal practices, and this choice is protected by international human rights law.[64] The right to culture guarantees the right to participate in the cultural life of the community, even if the relevant moral code is inconsistent with views of external observers. Hence, women should be guaranteed access to the surgery so they can continue to take part in the major activities of their communities. Although it may seem peculiar that deceit should be authorized as part of cultural rights, it may be a necessary means by which participation can be maintained.

The right to bodily integrity is another argument women could invoke in support of access to hymenoplasty. Although usually employed as part of campaigns against surgeries such as male circumcision and FGM, there is no reason why bodily integrity must necessarily be interpreted as *prohibiting* certain forms of surgery. After traumatic and disfiguring injuries, some people might argue that they have a right to reconstructive surgery in order to *restore* their bodily integrity. In a similar vein, women can justifiably argue that they want to restore the hymen because they consider it essential for their understanding of bodily integrity and their sense of well-being.

Feminists take differing positions on the propriety of this surgery. While some oppose it because it reflects patriarchal values, others champion it as an expression of autonomy. Although it would be preferable to live in a world that no longer valued virginity and used it as a cruel means of social control, the question is whether adult women should have the right to a reconstructive procedure in the interim.

Weighing the arguments

In the previous sections I considered arguments for and against hymenoplasty. Ultimately I conclude that women should have the right to undergo the procedure if they choose to do so.[65] Patient autonomy is important and should be recognized in legal systems as a general matter and certainly with regard to reconstructive surgery. If autonomous decision-making is to be protected, then the autonomy of physicians should be protected as well. If surgeons have objections to the surgery, whether based on feminist principles, a judgement that it is medically unnecessary, or other grounds, they ought to have the right to decline to do so.

The law as it is currently designed in some jurisdictions may not afford protection to doctors who perform the surgery. The fact that adult women elect to have the procedure may be insufficient to protect doctors again prosecution: the statutes may stipulate either that culture cannot justify the performance of the surgery or that consent is not a defence when the operation represents a form of mutilation.

Recognizing these risks, what policy changes should be implemented? For surgeons willing to perform hymen reconstruction, the question is whether the laws ought to be modified

64 LL Veazey, *A Woman's Right to Culture; Toward Gendered Cultural Rights* (Quid Pro, LLC 2015).
65 For an argument in favour, see de Lora (n 39) 141.

to address the ambiguous status of this procedure. That would at least avoid the worry that the surgery constituted a crime. For those who do not wish to perform the hymenoplasty, the code of medical ethics should permit an opt-out policy.

Questions also arise about whether doctors who do not wish to perform the procedure should be ethically required to refer women to other doctors or to other sources of counselling.[66] When young women migrate to new lands from countries that require virginity at the time of marriage, they often lack the mentoring of older women about how to handle their precarious situation. As a consequence, some medical professionals have suggested that counselling young immigrant women about possible alternatives to hymenoplasty might reduce the number of requests for this type of surgery.[67] According to one scholar, in the absence of mentors, surgeons in the Netherlands who declined to perform the surgery recommended use of the circumvention techniques mentioned earlier in the chapter.[68] Establishing more extensive counselling programmes with absolutely strict confidentiality could yield real benefits for both the young women and surgeons.

Autonomy in the medical context

In the field of biomedical ethics, the principle of autonomy is ordinarily of paramount importance. This means in practical terms that patients should be treated with dignity and that they are entitled to decide whether or not to accept medical treatment. Leading texts emphasize that as long as patients possess legal capacity and are informed of the potential risks of medical procedures, they should be able to make their own decisions about taking drugs, having surgeries, or making changes to their lifestyles.[69] With respect to surgical ethics, the conventional wisdom is that patients should be able to choose whether or not to undergo surgeries, even if the procedures are not medically necessary. Autonomy also requires that medical professionals operate in the best interests of their patients.[70]

Interestingly, recent studies of hymenoplasty regard the decision to undergo the surgery as an act of resistance. It demonstrates that women recognize the constraints of their social environment and cleverly find means to function within that reality. Those who conduct ethnographic research increasingly highlight the 'empowering' nature of the decision to 'medicalize' the procedure. One study concludes with the nuanced argument 'that women seeking HR [hymen reconstruction] are both victims and agents: they cannot realistically hope to be completely free of coercive patriarchal attempts to control their bodies, but they may resist such attempts by seeking HR'.[71] Nevertheless, it is still possible that by acting

66 S Bastami, 'When Bleeding Is Vital: Surgically Ensuring the "Virginal" State' (2015) 26 *Journal of Clinical Ethics* 154. In the U.S. a survey of 1,000 physicians showed they were divided over the question of referral.

67 S Ayuandini, 'Finger Pricks and Blood Vials: How Doctors Medicalize "Cultural" Solutions to Demedicalize the "Broken" Hymen in the Netherlands' (2017) 177 *Social Science & Medicine* 61, 64.

68 Ibid.

69 R Young, 'Informed Consent and Patient Autonomy' in H Kuhse and P Singer (eds), *A Companion to Bioethics* (2nd edn, Wiley-Blackwell 2009) 530; TL Beauchamp and JF Childress, *Principles of Biomedical Ethics* (6th ed, Oxford University Press 2009) 99.

70 A McLean, *Autonomy, Informed Consent and Medical Law: A Relational Challenge* (Cambridge University Press 2009).

71 V Wild et al., 'Hymen Reconstruction as Pragmatic Empowerment? Results of a Qualitative Study from Tunisia' (2015) 147 *Social Science & Medicine* 54, 60.

in this manner they reinforce patriarchal norms that demand 'purity' of women.[72] Future research will reveal whether this procedure serves the interests of women or not.

Conclusion

In an ideal world there would be no double standard regarding premarital sex for men and women, and women would not need to deceive their husbands. Until such time as women enjoy the same liberties as men, they will have to manoeuvre within patriarchal systems. As they strive to circumvent the sexist customs that limit their activities, the medical profession must reconsider its ill-conceived policies recommending that surgeons refuse to provide the 'revirgination'. Even if one wishes that women did not have to resort to surgery to avoid serious threats to their well-being, in democratic systems the possibility of requesting reconstructive surgery should be available to them.

The empowerment of patients should mean that they can choose to have elective surgeries whether physicians are eager to perform them or not. Surgeons' refusal to operate on women seeking hymenoplasty who believe it is necessary to save their lives clearly interferes with their autonomous decision-making. They should consider the possible consequences for their patients. Whether the state is obligated to fund the surgeries is another matter, but the absence of government financing would most likely result in the further victimization of poor women if they cannot obtain hymenoplasties.

While many types of cosmetic and reconstructive surgery could be condemned as reflecting self-hatred on the part of women,[73] only some types of surgical procedures seem to attract widespread condemnation. Despite the possible negative aspects of allowing hymenoplasty, it is ultimately better to empower women to make their own health care decisions. Instead of assuming that the choice to undergo the knife reflects a lack of agency, a feminist reconsideration could regard this choice as one that is strangely empowering.

72 M Kaivanara, 'Virginity Dilemma: Re-Creating Virginity Through Hymenoplasty in Iran' (2016) 18 *Culture, Health & Sexuality* 71, 81.

73 V Pitts-Taylor, *Surgery Junkies: Wellness and Pathology in Cosmetic Culture* (Rutgers University Press 2007) 20, 128.

Conclusion

Part II

Autonomy in context: empirical illustrations

B: Individual agency in situ

15 'It is better for me to agree when my guardian is here'

Consent and relational personhood in postcolonial Malawi

*Jessica Johnson**

In rural southern Malawi it is widely held that marriage ought to be consensual. Villagers, traditional authorities, police officers, and magistrates alike share a view that, in the words of a court clerk, 'You can't force it.' Such views were freely expressed during marital disputes, in the course of which divorce was often advocated on the grounds that, as one magistrate put it, 'It is dangerous to force an unwilling spouse to continue with the marriage.' The idea that forcing marriage or its continuation is dangerous was also shared by a police officer in a Victim Support Unit who counselled a male complainant against forcing his wife to remain with him: 'We'll hear that you have died, that she has poured poison in your food. It is better to leave her.' In accordance with such views, divorce rates are, and long have been, exceptionally high in matrilineal areas of the country.[1] Indeed, views such as those expressed by the police officer and clerk were not considered new, in the sense of having arrived with the transition to multiparty politics in the mid-1990s, nor were they influenced by religious renewal or overt opposition to traditional institutions and practices.[2] Rather they tended to be treated as statements of timeless and universal common sense. Nevertheless, I argue that attitudes towards marriage and consent in this context bear the imprint of local matrilineal norms while at the same time offering insight into relational understandings of personhood more generally.

Clearly, the situation described above does not fit easily with familiar media representations of, or popular assumptions about, African women as victims of forced marriage. Yet a view of marriage in Malawi as a relationship contracted between consenting, autonomous individuals tells only part of the story. The rhetorical question 'Do two people make a marriage?' (*Nanga banja ndi anthu awiri?*), to which the only possible answer is a resounding

* This chapter is based on 20 months of ethnographic fieldwork in southern Malawi, 2009–2010, including regular participant observation in magistrates' courts and a police-run victim support unit. The fieldwork was supported by the UK Economic and Social Research Council (ESRC).

1 JC Mitchell, *The Yao Village: A Study in the Social Structure of a Malawian People* (Manchester University Press 1956); A Kaler, ' "Many Divorces and Many Spinsters": Marriage as an Invented Tradition in Southern Malawi' (2001) 26 *Journal of Family History* 529; G Reniers, 'Divorce and Remarriage in Rural Malawi' (2003) S1 *Demographic Research* 175. Matriliny is best understood 'as a set of characteristics rather than a totality or "system" ' (PE Peters, 'Introduction: Revisiting the Puzzle of Matriliny in South-Central Africa' (1997) 17 *Critique of Anthropology* 125, 137). In the area of Malawi in which I worked, matriliny is expressed through female custodianship of land, which is inherited by daughters from their mothers, and the movement of men upon marriage to live in their wives' home compounds. Men do not inherit land and their own heirs are the children of their sisters. Sibling relationships and maternal uncles take on great significance in this context.

2 See MG Cattell, 'Praise the Lord and Say No to Men: Older Women Empowering Themselves in Samia, Kenya' (1992) 7 *Journal of Cross-Cultural Gerontology* 307; DL Hodgson, ' "My Daughter . . . Belongs to the Government Now": Marriage, Maasai and the Tanzanian State' (1996) 30 *Canadian Journal of African Studies* 106.

DOI: 10.4324/9781315413617-19

'No', signals that there is more to the matter of marital consent in this context, and raises questions pertinent to the discussion of personal autonomy. What does it mean to balance a sense that a marriage must be (and remain) agreeable to both parties with an understanding that marital relationships concern wider networks of kin who have a legitimate stake in the ongoing success of the marriage and the well-being of the spouses and their children? And how might we understand the involvement of aunts, uncles, and siblings in the marriages of their kins(wo)men where, in the absence of bridewealth or dowry, their own material interests do not provide a ready explanation?

The institution of *unkhoswe*, or marriage guardianship, is the most tangible instantiation of the important role assumed by matrilineal kin with respect to marital relationships in Malawi.[3] It is the assignment of *ankhoswe* (guardians; sing. *nkhoswe*) that marks a relationship as a marriage, making husbands and wives out of boyfriends and girlfriends (*zibwenzi*). At the point of marriage, the matrilineal kin of each spouse nominate a representative to serve as *nkhoswe*. The person selected may be either male or female and can be related to his or her charge in a number of ways – as maternal aunt or uncle, brother, sister, or grandmother, for example, but never as birth mother. The coming together of the respective *ankhoswe* in a *chinkhoswe* ceremony, no matter how low-key, marks the public recognition of the marriage and signals that the relationship has the blessing of the spouses' kin. In the absence of *ankhoswe*, a relationship would not generally be considered a marriage by rural residents, and might be characterized pejoratively as childish or puerile (*zibwana* or *za chibwanabwana*).[4] In legal terms, the institution of *unkhoswe* is the *sine qua non* of constitutionally recognized 'customary' marriage. In addition to customary marriages, which constitute by far the majority of marital relationships in rural Malawi, the national constitution recognizes marriages by repute, permanent cohabitation, and registration under the Marriage Act. This latter option is rarely taken up by rural citizens, and while relationships for which *ankhoswe* have not been assigned might meet the criteria of marriage by repute or cohabitation to the satisfaction of a magistrate, such unions would rarely gain the recognition of villagers or traditional authorities. In practice, then, marriage requires the cooperation and participation of matrilineal kin.

The vital importance of *unkhoswe* is related to the role of marriage guardians in marital dispute resolution. It is to their *ankhoswe* that disputing spouses are expected to turn in the first instance, and it is their responsibility to arrange discussions and attempt to bring about reconciliation. Should they fail and the dispute enter another forum – a traditional authority's court (*bwalo*), a religious setting, a non-governmental organization (NGO) office, a police Victim Support Unit (VSU), or a local magistrates' court – *ankhoswe* are expected to attend hearings and testify as to the veracity of the statements of their kin. In these forums, *ankhoswe* are held in high regard and are trusted to provide truthful, non-partisan accounts. Speaking of the importance of the presence of *ankhoswe* at the VSU, one police officer explained, 'Without *ankhoswe* things do not go well, they are our witnesses.' The non-attendance of *ankhoswe* at such hearings was liable to be taken as firm evidence of the unrepresented party's poor character or troublesome conduct, which were considered the most likely causes of such a palpable lack of familial support. Magistrates voiced such

3 JP Bruwer, 'Unkhoswe: The System of Guardianship in Chewa Matrilineal Society' (1955) 14 *African Studies* 113.

4 Indeed, these terms were used by police officers in the Victim Support Unit to chastise couples who had not formalized their relationship in this way.

assumptions on a number of occasions, remarking, for example, 'Let us not beat around the bush . . . . I am sure your advocate has not come because of your bad behaviour,' or 'It is my view that [the complainant] chose not to call his advocate because he was aware that the evidence could not be in his favour. . . . I therefore make a finding that his evidence lacks credibility.'[5]

Whether in the eyes of the state or those of kin and neighbours, then, *ankhoswe* are recognized as central to the establishment of marital unions in contemporary Malawi. Ethnographically speaking, it is interesting to consider the role of kin in making marriage in a matrilineal setting such as this, in which the absence of bridewealth negates the more directly material interests of elders that have been taken to explain their involvement in the marriages of junior kin elsewhere in Africa.[6] Moreover, the situation in Malawi does not entail a clash between a 'custom' of so-called forced marriage and a recently imported, human-rights based insistence on mutual consent in marriage.[7] Nobody with whom I spoke questioned the importance of marital consent, and yet, as we shall see, nor did an *nkhoswe*'s statement to the effect that he had a 'right' to direct his niece (to agree to a polygamous union) elicit rebuttal.

My objective in this chapter is to provide an ethnographic examination of the concept of consent to marriage in matrilineal southern Malawi. Two people do not make a marriage in this setting, yet marriage is also explicitly understood as something that 'you cannot force'. At the same time, marriage, customary or not, is an institution about which police officers, villagers, magistrates, and a progressive constitution have something to say, in the course of which they not uncommonly combine the language of human rights with that of custom. Marital dispute hearings thus provide a pertinent ethnographic window onto the intricate ways in which custom and rights, tradition, and liberal modernity intersect in postcolonial Africa.

In what follows, I present a detailed case study of a marital dispute heard in a police Victim Support Unit in a rural location. There is no better venue to explore legal and social plurality than a police-run VSU, which is staffed by officers from the Community Policing Services Branch with the help of selected local volunteers – in this instance a local sheikh (whose presence should not be taken as indicative of a Muslim majority).[8] The first VSUs

5 'Advocate' is a common translation of *nkhoswe*, 'guardian' is another. During court hearings magistrates speak in English, the official language of Malawi. Their words are translated by a clerk for the benefit of all present. Despite its status as the official language, proficiency in English is the preserve of very few Malawians, especially in rural areas.

6 Hodgson (n 2); M Mbilinyi, 'Runaway Wives in Colonial Tanganyika: Forced Labour and Forced Marriage in Rungwe District, 1919–1961' (1988) 16 *International Journal of the Sociology of Law* 1; BL Shadle, 'Bridewealth and Female Consent: Marriage Disputes in African Courts, Gusiiland, Kenya' (2003) 44 *The Journal of African History* 241; BL Shadle, *'Girl Cases': Marriage and Colonialism in Gusiiland, Kenya, 1890–1970* (Heinemann 2006).

7 Hodgson (n 2).

8 According to recent statistics, 13 per cent of the Malawian population is Muslim, 11 per cent of the population of Chiradzulu District where this research was carried out (*Population and Housing Census Main Report* (National Statistical Office 2008) <www.mw.one.un.org/wp-content/uploads/2014/04/Malawi-Population-and-Housing-Census-Main-Report-2008.pdf> accessed 3 May 2017; *Population Characteristics* (National Statistical Office 2008) <www.mw.one.un.org/wp-content/uploads/2014/04/Malawi-Population-and-Housing-Census-Main-Report-2008.pdf> accessed 3 May 2017). The sheikh tended to adopt an inclusive approach to religion, stressing to disputants that they all worship the same God and that the teachings of the different holy books reinforce each other in their calls for harmony and respect.

were established in 2001, and as such they constitute a relatively recent addition to the Malawian legal landscape, having been introduced during the restructuring of the Malawi Police Force in the wake of the transition to multi-party politics in the mid-1990s. By the time of my fieldwork (2009–2010), VSUs were a recognized and important institution in the district of Chiradzulu where I was based, and there is evidence to suggest that the same is true across much of the country.[9]

VSUs are one of several venues to which marital disputes may be brought in Chiradzulu. They are perceived as constituting an intermediary link in a 'loose chain' of dispute resolution forums, between *ankhoswe*, traditional authorities, and magistrates' courts. People can and do follow a wide variety of routes through these institutions, at times turning as well, or instead, to religious leaders or NGO representatives. During my fieldwork, I observed officers' efforts to 'counsel' disputants and to bring about reconciliation. Where that was not possible, they frequently referred cases on, usually to the magistrates' courts, *ankhoswe*, or village heads. Like the institution itself, discussions in the VSU were inherently plural, incorporating shared knowledge of custom, awareness of human rights as enshrined in the constitution, and the ever-present threat of arrest on criminal charges. Although I never witnessed a case brought to the VSU resulting in criminal proceedings, police officers frequently emphasized this possibility when parties to disputes were uncooperative or lacking in remorse.

Disputing marriage

I turn now to an account of a marital dispute heard in a VSU in 2010 by a sub-inspector and a local sheikh.[10] The complainant in this case, a woman named Anabanda, was joined in the office by Mr Phiri, who was her husband of nine years and the father of her three children, and Anambewe, the woman with whom Anabanda accused her husband of initiating an illegitimate second marriage – illegitimate because he had done so without Anabanda's consent. The case had been precipitated by a fight between the two women, following which Anambewe had made her way to Anabanda's home and smashed her belongings.

As the hearing got underway, Anabanda explained that she had first become aware of Anambewe's existence when Mr Phiri suggested that he bring her to their home for the two women to meet. Anabanda had refused, and she stressed that Mr Phiri's relatives did not support his endeavours to marry a second wife. When they had discussed the matter with their *ankhoswe*, she said, Mr Phiri had explained that he wanted to grow tomatoes for sale and thus that the gardens Anabanda's matrilineal kin had allocated to them were insufficient. Her relatives had agreed to provide them with additional land, and they had since farmed their extended gardens for two consecutive seasons:

> But he hasn't stopped. And his other wife, whenever we meet we fight . . . . Two days ago, we met on the path . . . and she provoked me, asking 'What are you staring at me for?' . . . I wouldn't have hit her if she hadn't provoked me. People around us stopped

9 FE Kanyongolo, *Malawi Justice Sector and the Rule of Law: A Review by AfriMAP and Open Society Initiative for Southern Africa* (Open Society Initiative for Southern Africa 2006); *2006 Executive Report on Human Rights Accountability in Malawi by the Three Arms of Government* (Malawi Human Rights Commission 2007).

10 The case was heard over two sittings. A sergeant was also present during the first of these, but he made no substantial contributions to the discussions.

> us fighting and she went and told my husband that I'd hit her. He reported to my uncle, and I explained that I wouldn't have hit her if she hadn't provoked me . . . . [Later that day she] smashed my things – plates, two pots, a plastic bucket, metal pails, and a basin.

Asked for his version of the events that had led them to the VSU, Mr Phiri pointed to both women in turn and declared that each was his wife. He did not show favour, he said; furthermore, their *ankhoswe* were aware of the situation and capable of verifying it. In answer to the sub-inspector's enquiry regarding the status of the *ndondomeko*, or proper programme, for contracting his marriage to Anambewe, Mr Phiri argued that it was his first wife, Anabanda, who was disrupting the *ndondomeko*. As far as he was concerned, she had agreed to the arrangement, and his younger brother had been witness to the decision.

The sub-inspector voiced his surprise that a woman would agree to polygamy (*mitala*) and then proceed to fight with her co-wife. Employing the language of human rights, he stressed that Anabanda had 'the freedom/right (*ufulu*) to refuse polygamy'.[11] Anabanda responded:

> Maybe he agreed with his brother when I wasn't there. When the *ankhoswe* were called they refused and he said, 'But I want a garden.' If things had been conducted properly, there would have been no cause for fighting.

At this point, the sheikh suggested that they hear from Anambewe, who had yet to speak. 'When he married you, what did he tell you? That he was married?' he asked. Anambewe explained that Mr Phiri had assured her that he would end his marriage to Anabanda because he did not want polygamy. 'So, what?' the sheikh demanded, refocusing his attention on Mr Phiri:

> You only told your first wife it was polygamy? You told your second wife that you would leave the first . . . . Do you know what polygamy is? Polygamy is to agree with your first wife; if she agrees, you go to the *ankhoswe* with your first wife to agree together. Then you look for a second wife. When you have found her, the two wives should be introduced to each other so that they won't fight. And there is *ndondomeko*: maybe you spend one week with each, maybe two days with one and two days with the other. But your wives are refusing, did you really arrange polygamy, or did you just arrange it on one side?

Mr Phiri insisted that he had followed the proper procedure in all respects. However, he acknowledged that he had promised Anambewe that he would end his first marriage, and that Anabanda's relatives had given him an extra garden so as to dissuade him from marrying a second wife.

When the sheikh put it to Mr Phiri that neither of his wives wanted polygamy, he replied angrily that, in that case, he would leave both women. Upon hearing this, Anabanda interjected: 'I cannot accept that. My mother is dead, how am I supposed to care for the children?' Anambewe, too, declared that she would not accept divorce, stating that

11 See H Englund, *Prisoners of Freedom: Human Rights and the African Poor* (University of California Press 2006) on the use and implications of the Chichewa word for freedom, *ufulu* (plural *maufulu*), to translate the English 'rights', and the dominant coinage *ufulu wachibadwidwe*, 'birth freedoms', for human rights.

Anabanda had caused her great hardship. Subsequently, the sheikh expressed his view that they could not overcome this impasse without the assistance of the *ankhoswe*, and the case was adjourned.

Reconvening a few days later, they were joined by Anabanda and Mr Phiri's *ankhoswe*. This time, when the sheikh asked if she would agree to polygamy, Anabanda acquiesced: 'I'll agree, provided that they give me my things [that were smashed],' she said. Unable to disguise his surprise, the sheikh remarked that this was not the same response he had received in the previous session: 'Were you lying then?' he asked. But Anabanda explained that that was before her husband had expressed his desire for polygamy and they had been given an opportunity to call their *ankhoswe*. 'It is better for me to agree when my uncle is here,' she said. 'It wasn't appropriate for me to agree in his absence.' Addressing their *ankhoswe*, the sheikh made clear that the first meeting had been somewhat different: 'That is why we called you as *ankhoswe*; please tell us if the marriage is acceptable.'

Speaking first, Mr Phiri's *nkhoswe* summarized the case as he saw it: Mr Phiri had been spending nights away from home because of the garden issue and he had announced his intention to leave Anabanda, but instead it had been agreed that he would marry Anambewe as a second wife. He had thus begun spending alternate weeks with each woman, but Anabanda had soon become dissatisfied and started fighting with her co-wife. Anabanda's *nkhoswe*'s account was somewhat different. The only marital difficulty he had been aware of, he said, was the matter of the garden and, following the allocation of additional land, there had been no further cause for disagreement. He was adamant that he knew nothing of the polygamous relationship with Anambewe.

Having listened carefully to the *ankhoswe*'s accounts, the sheikh did not hold back in chastising Mr Phiri for his behaviour, and he demanded to know 'which one is your wife?' However, Mr Phiri remained steadfast in his claim that he was married to both women. Invited to respond, Anabanda again assented: 'Seeing that he's agreed that we are both his wives, that's fine, we'll be two.' Seemingly reluctant to sanction this solution, the sheikh moved to distance the VSU from polygamous marriage while simultaneously demonstrating his knowledge of customary norms:

> Here we don't bring together polygamous unions . . . . If you are going to have polygamy, you should go home and agree with your *ankhoswe* there. Polygamy, how it works is that the wives help each other, send food to each other, share maize, send money when a child is in hospital, go to visit ill children, and so on.

The sub-inspector offered clarification: 'Polygamy is not unacceptable but it is also not to be forced; men have the right (*ufulu*) to marry twice, but the first wife also has the right to say that she does not want polygamy.' Continuing, he offered the following assessment of the case:

> It was not done properly, he came and said he wanted an extra garden but he had already found his second wife. Other men begin properly, announcing: 'I want to find a second wife for these reasons.' If you fail to resolve the issues, people agree. For example, if the first wife has not borne any children . . . . Mr Phiri, if you had behaved as other men do, you could have said openly that the garden was still inadequate, but you did not say that and that is the reason that they are fighting now. It is your fault. You didn't handle things as you ought to have. Now, Anabanda might agree because of the children, she does not want you to leave her. But if she were in a position to

choose freely (*pa ufulu, pa mtendere*), perhaps she would say that she does not want polygamy.[12]

Intervening before Mr Phiri could respond, Anabanda's *nkhoswe* explained that he had the right (*ufulu*) to tell his niece to accept. 'Mr Phiri should fail by himself,' he added, somewhat defiantly.

After a brief discussion of the smashed property, during which the sub-inspector insisted that it was Mr Phiri's responsibility to replace the damaged items, and following a warning to Anambewe that she was wasting her time with relationships with married men, the case was concluded. The sub-inspector's parting words served to remind Mr Phiri of his economic obligations as a polygamous husband and father: 'There are three adults and four children, a total of seven people, who must rely on you to share your resources. You should think about that with maturity.'

Custom, rights, and consent

Throughout this case, the matter of consent appeared in several guises. Most explicitly, perhaps, we have Anabanda's statement: 'It is better for me to agree when my uncle is here. It wasn't appropriate for me to agree in his absence.'[13] Anabanda clearly articulated her view that it was only proper, right, or appropriate (*kuyenera*) for her to consent to polygamy in the presence of her *nkhoswe* – a unilateral decision would not do. The sheikh was taken aback by her change of position, and he expressed his surprise before asking her *nkhoswe* whether the marriage was acceptable in this form to Anabanda's kin. Her *nkhoswe* made it clear that Mr Phiri had not informed him of his intention to seek a second wife. In other words, Mr Phiri had neglected customary procedure. It subsequently emerged that this *nkhoswe* was not opposed to polygamy in principle, and, moreover, he considered himself to have the 'right' to tell his niece to accept a polygamous marriage. This assertion went unquestioned, despite the fact that it represented a potentially controversial interpretation of the *nkhoswe's* responsibility to guide his kin, not to mention the consequent negation of Anabanda's stated 'right' to reject polygamy. However, the phrase 'he should fail by himself,' with which the *nkhoswe* followed up his remarks, articulated his concern to safeguard his niece's interests in the form of her reputation as a woman willing to persevere in marriage. His words conveyed a sense that the marriage might well fail in the future, but that any such failure ought to be seen to result from Mr Phiri's own inadequacies as a husband, and not from Anabanda's truculence or restiveness.

Divorce is not a source of shame in Malawi, where rates of divorce are, and long have been, remarkably high. But while no stigma is attached to the status of divorcée, women preferred to avoid seeming to desire separation, as this might suggest a lack of maturity or an appetite for multiple sexual partners, with the latter potentially inviting the derogatory label *hule* (whore). Neither impression would serve them well if they aspired to remarriage.

12 *Mtendere* is a possible synonym for freedom (*ufulu*), but with strong connotations of peace and harmony (see n 10).

13 Here, the verb employed for consent was *kuvomera*, which can also be translated as to agree, accept, acquiesce, or allow. Elsewhere the verb *kulola* (allow, permit, accept, consent) was employed to similar effect, or the idea of consent was expressed through phrases such as 'to say that she does or does not want'.

Similarly for men, a reputation for mistreating women, or for failing to meet the material expectations of wives and children, might undermine efforts to establish future relationships. Anabanda's *nkhoswe*'s remarks can be understood in this light as gesturing towards a desire to secure his niece's respectability by eschewing responsibility for marital breakdown, and thus to maintain the support of her kin and neighbours, which, in turn, was essential to the moral-material reproduction of her household.

Just as the sheikh and the sub-inspector oscillated between grounding their interventions in references to rights (*ufulu*) and to proper customary procedure (*ndondomeko*), the constitution also allows considerable ambiguity with regard to the legal status of polygamy. The constitution's explicit recognition of 'all marriages at law, custom and marriages by repute or permanent cohabitation'[14] might be taken to imply that parties to polygamous unions are entitled to the same constitutional protections as those engaged in monogamous marriages. However, Fidelis Edge Kanyongolo, Malawian expert in constitutional law, has asserted that it is (only) 'traditionalists and adherents of religious faiths that consider polygamy to be a right'.[15] Indeed, according to Lea Mwambene, Section 24(2) of the Constitution ought to be read as mandating the banning of polygamy, where it states that '[a]ny law that discriminates against women on the basis of gender or marital status shall be invalid and legislation shall be passed to eliminate customs and practices that discriminate against women.'[16] On the other hand, however, Section 26 establishes that '[e]very person shall have the right to use the language and to participate in the cultural life of his or her choice.' Plainly, the situation is far from clear-cut.

When the sub-inspector asserted that 'polygamy is not unacceptable but it is also not to be forced; men have the right to marry twice, but the first wife also has the right to say that she does not want polygamy,' he was not in fact referring to any particular legal provisions, despite his use of the language of human rights. Nevertheless, his statement drew its legitimacy from the plural sources of legal authority that he himself embodied: those of state law, of which he was a uniformed representative, and of custom, his extensive knowledge of which was demonstrated through his references to the *ndondomeko* that ought to be followed if things were to be carried out properly, according to custom. His words bring to mind Pnina Werbner's recent analysis of the ways in which judicial reasoning (in and beyond Africa) incorporates moral considerations of justice as fairness alongside rules and norms, and the related responsiveness of legal reasoning to changing circumstances and new idioms and ideas.[17]

Soon after he uttered this statement, the sub-inspector seemingly cast doubt on the position from which Anabanda had agreed to polygamy, pointing out that she had children to look after and thus did not want to be without a husband. Anabanda had made a similar point herself in the first hearing when she offered the fact that her mother had passed away as an explanation for why she could not accept divorce. In this matrilineal setting, mothers are an especially important source of support, both material and emotional, and could be expected to expend significant time and resources on the care and provisioning of their

14 The Constitution of the Republic of Malawi, sec. 22(5) (January 2004).

15 FE Kanyongolo, *Malawi Justice Sector and the Rule of Law* (Open Society Initiative for Southern Africa 2006) 48 (available at <www.opensocietyfoundations.org/sites/default/files/malawi_20060912.pdf> accessed 28 July 2017).

16 L Mwambene, 'Reconciling African Customary Law with Women's Rights in Malawi: The Proposed Marriage, Divorce and Family Relations Bill' (2007) 1 *Malawi Law Journal* 113.

17 P Werbner, ' "The Duty to Act Fairly": Ethics, Legal Anthropology, and Labor Justice in the Manual Workers Union of Botswana' (2014) 56 *Comparative Studies in Society and History* 479.

daughters' children. It is in this light that we can understand the sub-inspector's comments to the effect that, had Anabanda been in a position to choose freely or enjoy her rights (*pa ufulu, pa mtendere*), she might have rejected polygamy. Here the term *ufulu*, freedom/ right, is employed in all of its complex ambivalence, invoking simultaneously the spectre of human rights and an alternative sense of freedom as peace and harmony, summoned through its pairing with the possible synonym *mtendere* (peace, calm, freedom, liberty). The sub-inspector acknowledged restrictions on Anabanda's *ufulu*, signalling an understanding that her ability to consent to, or refuse, polygamy was inflected by her social and economic situation, not least the difficulties she would face bringing up her children with limited familial support.

The sub-inspector's words conveyed recognition that Anabanda did not act from a position of autonomous individuality, if that is taken to imply detachment from the relationships of matrilineal and affinal kinship in which she was inevitably enmeshed, or exemption from the significant economic constraints that characterize life for the vast majority of citizens in a country that consistently ranks among the poorest in the world. His statement also echoed a recent strand of Africanist anthropology that grapples with just these kinds of conundrums: What is the relationship between rights and social relations? How can we understand freedom or equality in conjunction with, rather than in opposition to, dependence and obligations? Much of this work is highly sophisticated and, taken seriously, it suggests that freedom and equality may be achieved through claims of hierarchical interdependence rather than autonomy.[18] These arguments are counter-intuitive to those steeped in a liberal discourse of freedom, equality, and rights, or what James Ferguson has called 'the emancipatory liberal mind'.[19] As Ferguson explains, 'the long, noble history of anti-slavery and anti-colonial struggles make it easy (perhaps too easy . . .) for us to equate human dignity and value with autonomy and independence.'[20] But anthropologists working in Africa have long held that personhood is inherently relational: persons do not exist prior to relations of dependence, they are constituted through them and in their efforts to discharge the obligations they entail.[21]

Such arguments owe a significant debt to the work of Marilyn Strathern, whose insights concerning the essential relationality of human life, while derived from rich Melanesian ethnography, establish what she terms 'a thoroughly trans-local social fact', namely, that '[p]eople are nowhere "free" to create relationships.'[22] Nevertheless, sociality and the inevitability of potentially constraining 'obligations embedded in the relationships one has with

18 Englund (n 11); H Englund, *Human Rights and African Airwaves: Mediating Equality on the Chichewa Radio* (Indiana University Press 2011); J Ferguson, *Give a Man a Fish: Reflections on the New Politics of Distribution* (Duke University Press 2015). African feminist scholars have engaged in similar debates; see especially NU Nzegwu, *Family Matters: Feminist Concepts in African Philosophy of Culture* (State University of New York 2006).

19 J Ferguson, 'Declarations of Dependence: Labour, Personhood, and Welfare in Southern Africa' (2013) 19 *Journal of the Royal Anthropological Institute* 223. It goes without saying, given liberalism's status as a 'broad and disputational philosophical tradition', that such arguments rely on a somewhat generalized characterization of liberalism's central tenets, including freedom, autonomy, and equality (J Laidlaw, *The Subject of Virtue: An Anthropology of Ethics and Freedom* (Cambridge University Press 2014) 142). Nevertheless, they remain faithful to dominant understandings of these concepts.

20 Ferguson (n 19) 224.

21 H Englund, 'Extreme Poverty and Existential Obligations: Beyond Morality in the Anthropology of Africa' (2008) 52 *Social Analysis* 33.

22 M Strathern, 'Losing (Out on) Intellectual Resources' in A Pottage and M Mundy (eds), *Law, Anthropology, and the Constitution of the Social: Making Persons and Things* (Cambridge University Press 2004) 232.

others' should not be interpreted as implying a lack of agency, for '[a]gency is evinced in the ability of people to (actively) orient themselves to or align themselves in particular relationships. This is not the same as free choice.'[23] In other words, an understanding of social relationships as somehow limiting a 'natural' state of 'freedom' or 'autonomy' is a red herring. Drawing explicitly on Strathern's insights, alongside her own research among sex workers in London, Sophie Day articulates a similar point: '[I]deologies of freedom', she suggests, 'seem to constitute an attempt to transcend social life altogether'.[24] The question, then, is whether in valorizing personal autonomy we ought to be careful what we wish for.

The sub-inspector recognized that Anabanda spoke not from a generic position of individual autonomy, but from within a particular configuration of relationships shaped by the matrilineal setting in which they lived. When she accepted polygamy, she was not bowing to coercion or buckling under the weight of custom; she was consenting as a woman who, in addition to being a wife, was also a mother, niece, and matrilineal kinswoman. In a setting in which marital instability and impermanence is the norm, she did so in the knowledge that this was unlikely to be the last time that she and Mr Phiri sat down with their *ankhoswe* to discuss the future of their relationship. Rather, this dispute hearing was but a single episode in the ongoing negotiation of her marriage and the wider web of kinship relations in which it was embedded. Unfinished and unfolding, her consent was secured for now, but by no means forever.

23 M Strathern, 'Resistance, Refusal and Global Moralities' (2005) 20 *Australian Feminist Studies* 181, 189 (original emphasis removed).

24 S Day, 'The Re-Emergence of "Trafficking": Sex Work Between Slavery and Freedom' (2010) 16 *Journal of the Royal Anthropological Institute* 816, 829.

16 The multiple search for autonomy among Moluccans in the Netherlands

A relational approach

Keebet von Benda-Beckmann

The concept of autonomy has been a subject of considerable interest in the literature on cultural rights, minority rights, and migration in general. Two sets of debates are particularly prominent. Political scientists have addressed the issue of multicultural citizenship and the recognition of cultural rights of individual migrants and migrant communities. Geoffrey Brahm Levey,[1] for example, shows in his discussion of the work of Will Kymlicka[2] that, at the core of this debate, is the question of whether and how recognition of cultural rights can be justified within the context of individual liberalism. This is primarily a debate about the political-philosophical underpinnings of a multicultural society. References to practices are often made mainly to illustrate the implications of the respective philosophical standpoints. Characteristic of this type of literature is that it takes the perspective of the side that either has to grant such rights or fails to do so. However, who exactly it is that has to grant the rights often remains implicit: is it the state, the dominant part of society that is accused of discrimination, or simply an indeterminate 'we'?

Related to these philosophical debates are the political debates concerning the autonomy of indigenous peoples or populations and of other types of minorities in the context of international organizations such as the International Labour Organization (ILO) and the United Nations. These debates focus on the characteristics social units should have in order to be able to claim legitimate autonomy, and on the extent of that autonomy.

Feminist theoreticians have criticized the overly individualistic connotations of the concept of autonomy in many of these writings. They do not object to the notion of personal autonomy as such, but insist that adopting an individualistic perspective on autonomy is fundamentally flawed because it abstracts from the social relations in which people are embedded. Such a concept is generally inadequate, but it is especially problematic for women in regard to the division of labour that assigns to them the provision of care for others as their core task. Authors like Nedelsky,[3] Mackenzie and Stoljar,[4] and others have argued that all persons are so deeply embedded in social relationships that individuals are shaped by or,

1 GB Levey, 'Equality, Autonomy, and Cultural Rights' (1997) 25 *Political Theory* 215; GB Levey, 'Liberal Autonomy as a Pluralist Value' (2012) 95 *The Monist* 103.

2 W Kymlicka, *Liberalism, Community, and Culture* (Oxford University Press 1989); W Kymlicka, *Multicultural Citizenship: A Liberal Theory or Minority Rights* (Clarendon Press 1995).

3 J Nedelsky (ed), *Law's Relations: A Relational Theory of Self, Autonomy, and Law* (Oxford University Press 2012).

4 C Mackenzie and N Stoljar (eds), *Relational Autonomy: Feminist Perspectives on Autonomy, Agency, and the Social Self* (Oxford University Press 2000).

DOI: 10.4324/9781315413617-20

according to some, constituted by their social environment.[5] Christman (Chapter 3 in this volume), from a different perspective, also emphasizes the importance of a person's history and social environment for her identity. These theorists argue that the concept of autonomy should accommodate this basic human condition. For that reason the term 'relational autonomy' has been coined to capture the socially and temporally embeddedness of persons.[6] Autonomy in this perspective is always a matter of degree. Such a relational perspective not only introduces more nuance to the philosophical debate, but it also helps to understand the dynamics of autonomy, including the role of law in shaping possibilities for autonomy, and as Nedelsky suggests in her 'Closing Reflections', that of participation in norm creation.[7] It can also help explicate the processes in which persons are searching for autonomy in a variety of relationships, which is the issue of this chapter.[8]

Efforts to gain greater autonomy, in the sense of reflectively being able to choose among various options, always concern autonomy in relation to specific persons, groups, or institutions. Most debates about autonomy concern autonomy from the state – often in connection with a particular state institution, or from the family, that is, autonomy in one particular set of relationships. They look at the hurdles that individuals encounter and how these hurdles might be overcome. The problems are often discussed from the perspective of the institutions that impede autonomy, as for example in discussions on the recognition of cultural rights. While it certainly is important to consider how the state maintains hurdles that inhibit the autonomy of its citizens, and to point out what legal and policy changes the state might make in order to eliminate the obstacles to autonomy, there is the danger that such a focus generates a one-sided view on the issue of autonomy. From a perspective of legal pluralism, the state is not the sole generator of law, however important state law may be in particular relationships. If the focus is not put on the perspective of the persons seeking autonomy in their various contexts and relationships, then some of the tensions and paradoxes remain underexposed. Individual persons may seek autonomy in a number of relationships at the same time. In each of these relationships the degree of autonomy and the problems people face in trying to enhance their level of autonomy may be different. What constitutes autonomy may even differ depending on the social setting and the relationship in which it is sought. Nedelsky rightly points out that autonomy is not only shaped by law but also by other social norms.[9] One should add that these 'other social norms' may comprise law of various provenance – religious law or, as in the case that is the focus of this chapter, customary law, each with its own conception of autonomy – which in certain contexts may have a greater impact than state law. The strategies that people use to seek (greater) autonomy and invoke law to do so may be appropriate in one setting, but may be quite inadequate in another set of relationships.

In the context of migration and calls for group autonomy by (leaders of) migrant communities, individual migrants typically have to fight for autonomy in a variety of relationships and in several arenas at the same time: individuals may fight for more autonomy for the migrant community vis-à-vis dominant and often conservative elites; the young generation

5 See H Baumann, 'Reconsidering Relational Autonomy: Personal Autonomy for Social Embedded and Temporally Extended Selves' (2008) 30 *Analyse und Kritik* 445, 447.

6 Ibid.

7 Nedelsky (n 3) 364–365.

8 On Moluccan personhood, see K von Benda-Beckmann, 'Social Security, Personhood, and the State' (2015) 2 *Asian Journal of Law and Society* 323.

9 Nedelsky (n 3) 2.

may request more autonomy within the family vis-à-vis the older generation(s); a community and its representatives may fight for autonomy vis-à-vis state institutions; individual migrants may attempt to acquire more autonomy as migrants vis-à-vis state institutions or employers. These fights usually have a specific gendered quality that renders them even more complex. This chapter uses examples of Dutch Moluccans to show that a relational notion of autonomy is particularly useful to understand the dilemmas and contradictions of these struggles, and to understand the degrees of autonomy that individual persons are attempting to achieve. They often find themselves in the paradoxical situation of having to underscore within the Moluccan community their integration into mainstream Dutch society while at the same time having to emphasize their difference in relation to Dutch state institutions or employers.

In some ways the Moluccan migrants constitute an exceptional community in the Netherlands. In contrast to the labour migrants from Turkey and Morocco, and in contrast to other groups from former Dutch colonies, the Moluccan community was established in 1951, when approximately 12,500 Moluccans arrived in the Netherlands and remained in relative isolation for two decades.[10] The intergenerational changes that occurred over time are perhaps more clearly visible than for other migrant populations within the Netherlands and elsewhere. However, I suggest that the problems and contradictions Moluccan migrants faced may be more generally valid, as the works of Anders and Rohregger on Malawi,[11] De Jong et al. on Burkina Faso and India,[12] and Thelen on Germany[13] demonstrate. In a similar vein, Baerends has pointed out the gendered ideologies underlying development cooperation, land, and family laws that have decreased women's autonomy in many sub-Saharan African countries.[14]

Moluccans in the Netherlands

In 1951 a group of 3,500 Moluccans, members of the Dutch colonial army (KNIL), arrived with their families in the Netherlands within a time span of a couple of months. These Moluccan men had fought on the Dutch side in the Indonesian war of independence. Fearing that these men would be subjected to retribution if they stayed on in Indonesia after the Dutch had withdrawn, the Dutch government ordered them to board the ships that

10 See D Bartels, *Moluccans in Exile, A Struggle for Ethnic Survival: Socialization, Identity Formation, and Emancipation Among an East-Indonesian Minority in the Netherlands* (Centrum voor Onderzoek naar Maatschappelijke Tegenstellingen 1989); D Bartels, *Ambon is op Schiphol*, vols 1 and 2 (Centrum voor Onderzoek naar Maatschappelijke Tegenstellingen 1990); K von Benda-Beckmann and F Leatemia-Tomatala, *De Emancipatie van Molukse Vrouwen in Nederland* (Jan van Arkel 1992); F Steijlen, *Moluks Nationalisme in Nederland 1951–1994: Van Ideaal tot Symbol* (Universiteit van Amsterdam 1996); H van Amersfoort, 'The Waxing and Waning of a Diaspora: Moluccans in the Netherlands, 1950–2002' (2004) 30 *Journal of Ethnic and Migration Studies* 151; H Smeets and F Steijlen, *In Nederland Gebleven: de Geschiedenis van Molukkers 1951–2006* (Bert Bakker 2006).

11 G Anders, *In the Shadow of Good Governance: An Ethnography of Civil Service Reform in Africa* (Brill 2010); BA Rohregger, *Shifting Boundaries: Social Security in the Urban Fringe of Lilongwe City, Malawi* (Shaker Verlag 2006).

12 W de Jong et al. (eds), *Ageing in Insecurity: Vieillir dans l'insécurité: Case Studies on Social Security and Gender in India and Burkina Faso* (LIT Verlag 2005).

13 T Thelen, 'Caring Grandfathers: Changes in Support between Generations in East Germany' in H Haukanes and F Pine (eds), *Generations, Kinship and Care: Gendered Provisions of Social Security in Central Eastern Europe* (University of Bergen Centre for Women's and Gender Research 2005) 163.

14 EA Baerends, 'Changing Kinship, Family and Gender Relations in Sub-Saharan Africa' in C Risseeuw and K Ganesh (eds), *Negotiation and Social Space: A Gendered Analysis of Changing Kin and Security Networks in South Asia and Sub-Saharan Africa* (Sage Altamira Press 1998) 47.

would repatriate the army to the Netherlands, where they would stay until a free Moluccan Republic had been established. Some disobeyed the orders and decided to remain within Indonesia, but most followed the command. On board they were demobilized, as a result of which they arrived in the Netherlands technically as civilians, a most unfortunate beginning of a strained relationship with the government. They were initially housed in camps where they would await their return to Indonesia. The powerful Dutch labour unions had strongly opposed the arrival of these former soldiers. Fearing that Moluccan ex-soldiers would take away scarce jobs, they only agreed on the condition that the government promise not to allow the Moluccans to enter the labour market. From proud members of the colonial army they were degraded to living in cramped camps with common kitchens and washrooms, virtually no privacy, no work, minimal educational facilities, and no status. Housing, food, clothing, health care, and a little pocket money to be spent in camp shops were provided by the government through the *Commissariaat Ambonezen Zorg* (Commissariat Care for Ambonese, CAZ) which, until 1954, provided their main connections with the outside world.[15] Life was characterized on the one hand by complete dependence on the government and, on the other hand, by a considerable degree of autonomy to run their internal affairs within the camps. Van Amersfoort characterizes the Moluccan community at that time as a true example of a diaspora because of its lack of integration in the social environment and the exclusive focus on the place of origin, dominated by a fierce yearning for a free South Moluccan Republic (RMS).[16]

Total dependence on the Dutch state only changed when it became clear that there would be neither a free RMS nor a return to Indonesia. Now that the Moluccans were to stay in the Netherlands, the Dutch government decided it would not continue this total care indefinitely. In 1956, it suddenly changed its policy and withdrew its general support. From then on Moluccan men had to look for jobs to earn a living and support their families. The few jobs that were available consisted of unskilled labour on farms and in factories. Many women also looked for jobs, usually a couple of hours on farms, or cleaning vegetables at home for farmers who brought the crates to the camps. Cleaning vegetables was popular because it allowed women to top up the meagre wages of their husbands while still being able to keep an eye on their children. From 1957 onwards, most Moluccan families were resettled from the camps to neighbourhoods that were specifically built for Moluccans, spread throughout the Netherlands on the fringes of small towns. Two such neighbourhoods were built for the small group of Muslim Moluccans; the other neighbourhoods were primarily populated by the Christian (mainly Protestant) majority. These neighbourhoods have continued to exist to the present day. They are still almost exclusively inhabited by Moluccan families, who resolutely defend their privilege to determine who may live there. However, many Moluccans nowadays live elsewhere.

For many years Moluccans living in the Netherlands were prohibited from entering Indonesia because they were suspected of supporting separatist movements within the Moluccas. From the late 1970s onwards, when political relations between the Netherlands and Indonesia had improved, they were allowed to travel to the Moluccas, but few could afford to pay for the trip, while others did not want to travel to Indonesia because Indonesia refused to establish an independent South Moluccan Republic. It was not until well into the 1980s that larger numbers actually had the means to travel to the Moluccas. Intensive personal

15 Van Amersfoort (n 10) 153.
16 Ibid.; see also Steijlen (n 10).

contact on a large scale, therefore, was only possible starting with the last decades of the twentieth century. This was painfully interrupted during the violent revolts around the fall of the Suharto regime in the late 1990s and could only be resumed years later.

The Moluccan community therefore has been more homogeneous, more locally concentrated, and more focused on a return to the place of origin; they have also maintained a more intensive relationship with government institutions over the years than other migrants. Due to the fact that they had been cut off from their place of origin and had maintained the dream of an RMS, they developed a strong Moluccan identity based on a nostalgic image of life on the Moluccas that even the first migrants had only known for a brief time in their youth. This image entailed closed village communities in which the customary law, called *adat*, stipulated that everybody take care of everybody else and in which there is little room for personal autonomy. While this exaggerated image had no correspondence to the actual situation on the Moluccas, it nevertheless was highly influential in the way Moluccans operated and understood their *adat* in the Netherlands. This strong corporate identity was set against an equally exaggerated notion, based on equally little experience, of a purely individualistic Dutch society in which the care for needy and elderly is the exclusive domain of the state.

The social background with which Moluccans grew up had both authoritarian and individualistic features. Younger persons were required to obey older ones, and women were expected to obey men. However, at the same time individualistic behaviour was also valued. From very early on, a person was expected to make his or her own decisions, and parents could not dispose of the property of their children without their consent. The colonial military setting and the early camp period in the Netherlands intensified the authoritarian side, which became more pronounced than it was on the Moluccas. Children were required to obey their parents without argument, and disobedience was harshly punished. However, if a child was disobedient and followed his or her own way, this was often also met with respect. Either way there was little discussion.

Autonomy

It is against this background that personal autonomy for Moluccans has to be understood. The concept of autonomy for many Moluccans had primarily a collective connotation of self-determination, both in the sense of the pursuit of an independent Moluccan Republic and, in the Dutch context, self-determination within the Moluccan community and neighbourhoods. Autonomy also had the connotation of emancipation and non-discrimination: in the case of Moluccan individuals, it was emancipation in relation to the Moluccan community; in the case of the Moluccan community (and people of colour in general), it was emancipation and non-discrimination in relation to white Dutch people; and in the case of women it was emancipation in relation to men.[17] Individual Moluccans therefore faced different kinds and degrees of autonomy or lack thereof: in relation to state institutions; in relation to relatives, especially with regard to care relationships; in relation to other Moluccans; and in relation to education and labour relationships.

In relation to state institutions the collective connotation of autonomy dominated in that the Moluccan community as a whole demanded special treatment because of their military service background. And indeed, within the neighbourhoods the Moluccan communities

17 Bartels (n 10) 526.

did have considerable autonomy in allocating housing, celebrating feasts and life cycle rituals, and organizing care. From 1976 onwards, the *Inspraakorgaan Welzijn Molukkers* (Participation Council for the Welfare of Moluccans) was the channel through which Moluccans secured this autonomy.[18] However, this autonomy also implied rather strict internal social control. Many women reported that as young girls they were caught between the demands of their parents and neighbours and those at school. Within the neighbourhood rather strict dress restrictions were maintained, and parents and older siblings, in particular brothers, saw to it that these were followed. In order not to be teased at school they secretly changed clothes on their way to school and back. This was the only way they could maintain themselves in school and still evade punishment at home. Often they had to secure the support of an older sibling or friend who attended the same school to avoid being betrayed.

Within the family, it was the task of the parents to take care of the members of their household. In the early times, daughters, especially older ones, were obliged to help in the household.[19] Often one or two daughters did all the work at home while their parents went out to work. Though children were required to go to school, many did not find the time to do their homework and dropped out as soon as possible because of the demands at home. This was primarily a result of insufficient means and financial constraints. The income of the father was rarely enough to provide for a decent living. Unmarried adults who had work were required to hand their wages over to their mothers, who controlled the family income and decided on how much pocket money each of the members of the household would get. This happened more out of necessity than out of a fundamental lack of autonomy of the children, though the effect was still a lack of autonomy. When the financial constraints relaxed, young adults with jobs were allowed to keep their wages, and parents took pride in being able to support the household without financial contributions from their children.

But dropping out of school early also had to do with parents' lack of interest in the education of their daughters. During the early days when the Moluccans were still expected to stay in the Netherlands only temporarily, Malay classes were organized to prepare the children for their return. Dutch education did not have great priority. When it became clear that they were to stay, attitudes towards education began to change slowly. However, with the exception of the children of the few Moluccan teachers, women were not expected to extend their education beyond the obligatory age, and schools in general tended to channel Moluccan children into lower-quality secondary schools that did not prepare students for higher education. Those who wanted a better education against all odds had to defy their parents and the opinion of the Moluccan neighbourhood, as well as overcome the prejudices of teachers. It was often an older sister who supported the wishes of her younger siblings to get the kind of education she herself lacked and to negotiate this with the school. From the 1970s onwards the attitude towards education changed, and it became more acceptable for both women and men to pursue higher education. Here, autonomy meant being able to determine independently and without discrimination the kind of education one would like to pursue.

18 Van Amersfoort (n 10) 166.

19 On caring relations among Moluccans, see K von Benda-Beckmann, 'Who Cares? And for Whom? Social Security as a Prism on Social Change' in W Kohte (ed), *Festschrift für Armin Höland* (Nomos Verlag 2015) 177; K von Benda-Beckmann, 'Social Security in Transnational Legal Space: Limitations and Opportunities' in S Köngeter and W Smith (eds), *Transnational Agency and Migration: Actors, Movements and Social Support* (Routledge 2015) 246.

The first generation of Moluccan men and women in the Netherlands had almost no autonomy in the choice of jobs and within labour relations due to their lack of language and other required skills, but especially due to a shortage of suitable jobs. This changed when they moved out of the neighbourhoods, when the idea that the government was responsible for their livelihood weakened, and when language skills, educational levels, and the job market improved. Autonomy here meant in the first place equal chances and non-discrimination on the labour market and in labour relations. However, the type of authoritarian command culture in which they had been raised posed some difficulties in relations with employers and colleagues. Paying respect to one's employer for Moluccans implied waiting for instructions rather than taking the initiative, but employers and colleagues often interpreted this attitude as a lack of interest. On the other hand, taking liberties 'behind their backs', as was customary within the Moluccan context to demonstrate autonomy, was unacceptable behaviour in the workplace.[20] Frequent requests for days off to attend Moluccan ceremonies also met with disapproval from employers and colleagues who did not share their understanding of (extended) kin obligations.

Insofar as women were allowed to work, it was understood that work should not interfere with their caregiver obligations within the family and the community. One of the most important tasks, bearing high symbolic and ideological value, was the care of ageing parents. Along with the obligation to participate in marriage and funeral rituals (and, especially in the early years, the struggle for the RMS) this was considered to be the core of being Moluccan. Such occasions take an enormous amount of time and resources, for marriage and funerals are big events that require a great deal of work because of a broad understanding of extended kin relationships that included foster parenthood, adoption, and 'boat brothers' – men who travelled to the Netherlands on the same boat where they became such close friends that they considered themselves kin.[21] There was yet another way in which kin relations were extended. During the period of warfare that characterized the sixteenth and seventeenth centuries, villages formed alliances (*pela*) with villages on different islands within the Moluccas so that people could safely travel and trade.[22] *Pela* were ritual kin to each other, and intermarriage was a strictly prohibited taboo. Moreover, *pela* relationships carried a strong obligation for mutual support. Both rules for marriage and for mutual support among *pela* became even stricter in the Netherlands.[23] While on the Moluccas *pela* relations were traced through the father's line only, in the Netherlands they were traced bilaterally. A request from a *pela* for help could not be denied. This was no problem on the Moluccas, because one's *pela* always lived far away. However, in the Netherlands *pela* might live within the same neighbourhood. *Pela* relations were considered a core characteristic of Moluccan identity, and children were taught never to refuse a request from a *pela* and to ask for support from a *pela* only if this was absolutely necessary.

These obligations for care and support to the extended kin relations could present a severe burden, especially for women who were expected to do the care work. Persons with

20 See J Veenman, *De Arbeidsmarkt van Allochtonen in Nederland, in het Bijzonder van Molukkers* (Wolters-Noordhoff 1990); J Veenman, *Molukse Jongeren in Nederland: Integratie met de Rem Erop* (Van Gorkum 2001).

21 F Strijbosch, 'Molukse Adopties in Nederland' (1988) 65 *Nederlands Juristenblad* 218.

22 Bartels (n 10).

23 F Strijbosch, 'The Concept of Pèla and Its Social Significance in the Community of Moluccan Immigrants in the Netherlands' (1985) 23 *Journal of Legal Pluralism* 177.

regular jobs were exempt from most of the work during rituals and much of the caring work, though some women managed to combine full-time jobs with the care of ageing parents. But if a more distant relative had an emergency and needed care, this was a different matter. This could cause problems with employers, who did not want to give their employees days off for emergencies involving people they did not consider close relatives. Occasionally this led to court procedures in which the court had to decide whether the care obligation for extended kin was sufficient reason for the employee to stay away from work, or whether the employee could be fired for doing so.

Pushing the boundaries of autonomy

Three important changes occurred that caused a great deal of conflict and friction. Over time, younger generations no longer found it acceptable to be ordered around by their parents or their husbands. The command ethos loosened and evolved into a more deliberative ethos. Like their Dutch age mates, young Moluccans wanted to participate in important decisions. Unmarried young men and women demanded and got full autonomy with regard to how they disposed of their wages. And, similar to what happened among the Dutch in general, it became common for married Moluccan couples to decide together how best to manage their household expenses. This did not mean that young persons no longer felt obliged to support their parents financially, but they wanted to do it their own way and on their terms. The obligation, in other words, could no longer be forced upon them by others; accepting such obligations was now considered a matter of one's own free will. Over and over again our interview partners emphasized that they put a lot of time and energy into caring for their relatives, but they did so because they felt 'obliged in their heart', not because they were forced to do so. They were very creative at finding ways to show that their help could not be taken for granted. Rather than making regular contributions to the household of their parents (with whom they still lived), which would be a sign of limited autonomy, they would pick up the bill for larger expenses, for instance when a washing machine or television needed to be replaced. Or they would every now and then pick up the tab for the large Saturday shopping. Contributions could be very substantial, but it was important to make them on an irregular basis because the irregularity underscored that it was their decision and not that of the parents. In this way they combined the quest for autonomy with the characteristic Moluccan obligation to care for their parents.

A second major change concerned care for children and care for the elderly. For parents in the oldest generation of Moluccans, caring for children primarily meant ensuring that they were fed and clothed. Even parents who considered education important did not think they had a role to play in it. Education was, rather, the exclusive domain of schools, an opinion that was supported by the schools, which often exhibited an extremely paternalistic attitude towards Moluccan pupils. The following generations began to absorb Dutch notions of proper care for children, which included intellectual and psychological care. But the time and energy that was put into this type of care for children left less time and energy for the care required by their ageing parents. Putting them in homes for the elderly, as was becoming fashionable among the Dutch, was an absolute taboo. There were some such homes for people with an Indonesian background, but Moluccans rarely made use of them. Many elderly people even refused professional care that would have been available, claiming that only daughters would understand their needs and were able to cook proper Moluccan food. Many elderly Moluccans did not know from personal experience what it took to take care of the elderly because they had been away since their early adulthood and therefore never had to care for their own parents. They maintained an idealized notion of care, and were often dissatisfied with their children who, in their eyes, did not pay due attention to them. Women who were facing the care needs of their ageing parents (or parents-in-law) at a time in their lives when their own children needed their full attention often were caught up in competing obligations. They could not live up to both the standards of care for ageing parents set by their Moluccan values and the standards of proper childcare that they had incorporated as they grew more acquainted with the broader Dutch society. Rather than seeking professional help for cleaning and care, they would leave their jobs and stay at home, negotiating their time allocation with their parents while trying to give their children the necessary attention. While they always emphasized that it was their autonomous decision to leave their jobs and care for their parents, they also insisted that the government should provide some kind of social services and health care that addressed the needs and wishes of Moluccans. This was a constant source of conflict with the social services. It was not until the last decade of the twentieth century that the government granted some financial compensation for women who took upon themselves the care for needy parents. Ageing parents today accept that their daughters have to devote much time to their children. Nevertheless, the dilemma of feeling the strong obligation to care for one's ageing parents and the limited time available is still an issue, as a recent film by Bartels and Huwaë shows.[24]

The third major change was that better financial circumstances and normalized political relations between the Netherlands and Indonesia allowed Moluccans to travel to the Moluccas. This happened shortly after a period of violence in which more extremist Moluccan groups tried to force the Dutch government to intensify its attempts to establish a free RMS. Indonesian visa regulations compelled many Moluccans to finally give up the stateless status that had been the hallmark of their struggle for an RMS. Despite a sense of betrayal to the cause, many eventually relinquished their dream of an independent RMS and adopted Dutch citizenship. This gave them a degree of autonomy to maintain and shape their relations with relatives on the Moluccas. Most Moluccans visited the Moluccas at least once, but many travelled there frequently and a few elderly even resettled there. But these very visits to the Moluccas made many realize that their *adat* was different from the *adat* on the Moluccas. This was one factor that made the majority decide that their future was definitely in the Netherlands, move out of their relative isolation, and quickly become a more integrated part of Dutch society, although as Van Amersfoort mentions, this movement lost some of its momentum towards the end of the century.[25]

Concluding remarks

What does a relational approach tell us about the Moluccan concept of personal autonomy? First, it shows that a strong corporate identity is not necessarily incompatible with a notion of personal autonomy, although it may be a source of tension in relations in which some seek more autonomy while others expect more obedience. Personal autonomy within the Moluccan context is not purely individualistic; it is relative in degree, bound by gendered obligations of support, care, and obedience. Put differently, autonomy is always situated within normative orders and enacted in relations that are differentially affected by these normative orders. The boundaries of autonomy are both contested and subject to change,

24 D Bartels and H Huwaë, *Maju Terus – Ervoor Gaan* (Nusasaku Ethnofilm 2011).
25 Van Amersfoort (n 10) 168, quoting J Veenman 2001 (n 20).

in response to developments that went on within Dutch society in general as well as within Indonesia. People from different generations hold different views on this. Though Moluccan social life has always been characterized by the coexistence of authority and personal autonomy, over time a more deliberative ethos evolved, though authority remained important. The oldest generation had felt the lack of autonomy in relation to the state most strongly, but had at the same time experienced a considerable degree of autonomy within the Moluccan camps, neighbourhoods, and families due to the Dutch policies and legal framework, which were predicated on an expected return to the Moluccas in the near future. While autonomy towards the state increased for all Moluccans, the deliberative ethos meant a greater degree of autonomy for the younger generations within the family vis-à-vis the older, and for women vis-à-vis men. Fulfilment of care obligations in the 1990s could no longer be simply commanded; rather, they had become a matter of overt or tacit negotiation. Young Moluccans carefully designed strategies to provide the care that their customary law required while emphasizing the autonomy of their decisions. Being able to decide autonomously how and when to fulfil these obligations was a matter of great pride for those providing the care, but it also generated a great deal of tension between the care providers and the elderly recipients, many of whom held on to their understanding of age-based autonomy. Within care relationships there had been a clear shift from a command relationship to a negotiated relationship in which the authority of the parents/recipients receded to make room for the increasing autonomy of the children/providers. Care obligations were still so strong in the 1990s that they prevented many women from entering the labour market in search of a career, or forced them to resign from their jobs. The state granted some autonomy by providing compensation to women who had given up their jobs to care for their parents. Moluccan persons living outside the neighbourhoods tended to have more autonomy to decide on the time and resources to devote to care outside their nuclear family than those within the Moluccan neighbourhoods. This was due in part to physical distance, but also in part to their greater exposure to Dutch society.

The total dependence on the government that characterized the early period of the Moluccans' stay in the Netherlands has given way to looser ties, less control, and a higher degree of collective and personal autonomy. By the 1990s the government had abandoned its group-specific policies for each of the migrant communities, meaning that Moluccans now fell under the generic policies that applied to all migrants. Yet, because of their colonial military background, they still felt entitled to special healthcare facilities and social services, and felt little inhibition in demanding special treatment. The high degree of autonomy granted to Moluccans within their neighbourhoods implied sustained exclusion of non-Moluccans. This kept the residents in relative isolation from their Dutch environment and allowed them to develop their Moluccan *adat*, or customary law, and modes of care and support. Intensified relations with relatives on the Moluccas made them realize that their Dutch Moluccan *adat* differed from that of the Moluccas. On the job market and in education, as well as in relations with government institutions, autonomy meant primarily non-discrimination. In relations with employers and fellow employees, the particular Moluccan combination of a command ethos and individual autonomy was a source of tension, especially for men, but the shift towards more deliberative relationships was taking the sharpest edges off these tensions, and the position of Moluccans on the labour market has greatly improved.

Finally, the analysis of the Moluccan examples presented here suggests that a relational approach that does not start out from the perspective of the state shows that the search for autonomy is not exclusively directed towards the state, but is in fact a far more complex process. Personal autonomy is constituted in many different but interdependent relationships, each with its own combination of normative demands and possibilities, based on a mix of different and at times contradictory normative orders of which state law is only one. For Moluccans their *adat* – which turned out to be different from the *adat* of their relatives on the Moluccas – was not only an important identity marker; it posed a strong normative influence on their behaviour within the neighbourhoods, among kin relations, and in relation to Dutch society and the government. In other words, the quest for autonomy in one relationship and in the context of one normative order often affects the quest for autonomy in other relationships and normative orders, creating dilemmas for which individuals creatively seek solutions.

17 An all but trivial abortion

Scrutinizing sex selection legislation in India through the lens of women's autonomy

Kalindi Kokal

Twenty-eight-year-old Manisha is a young mother of four daughters. Some months after I met Manisha, she disclosed that she was pregnant for the fifth time, even as her fourth child was just six months old. Manisha was trying to decide whether to have an abortion. Manisha works as a cleaning lady and cook in ten homes. She earns almost as much as her husband, but is still fearful that he would leave her if she were unable to have a son. 'He is pressured by his family,' explained Manisha when I asked her why, despite being economically independent and having her own parents living close by, she continued to live under the stress of her husband's demands. 'My grandmother-in-law threatened that she would find another wife for my husband if I couldn't have a son.'

This chapter takes Manisha's story as a case study to explore the concept of autonomy in a traditional and community-oriented context in Indian society. The first part presents the entire case study, explaining how Manisha finalized the decision she was struggling with. The second part focuses on understanding whether Manisha's decision actually was *or* could be perceived as autonomous. In the third part, in the context of the processes of autonomy described in the case study, I reflect on the relevance of the Pre-Conception and Pre-Natal Diagnostic Techniques (PC&PNDT) Act, introduced in 1994 to prohibit sex detection of the fetus through pre-natal diagnostic techniques. In this chapter I argue that when women like Manisha actively engage in processes of exercising agency, a blanket ban on fetal sex detection may actually be unfair and discriminatory, and hence unworkable in the reality of women's specific perspectives and circumstances.

Manisha's story: a case study

Over the months that I was in regular contact with Manisha, I observed her as shy and docile, always remaining attentive to her work and rarely laughing freely or even chatting with anyone after work hours. Manisha belongs to the Dhangar community, a nomadic tribe in Maharashtra with endogamous divisions. Some of these groups weave coarse woollen blankets, others rear buffaloes, and some are also nomadic shepherds.[1] But Manisha was brought up in more settled conditions. Having given up practising traditional occupations many years ago, some members of Manisha's family cultivate their own land or have migrated to larger cities in search of regular work. Manisha grew up in a village on the

1 G-D Sontheimer, 'The Danger: A Nomadic Pastoral Community in a Developing Agricultural Environment', *Nomadism in South Asia* (Oxford University Press 2003) 364–365.

DOI: 10.4324/9781315413617-21

outskirts of Pandharpur, a famous pilgrimage town in Maharashtra, where she was married at the age of 15. At the time, her community – a network of extended families – and the village where they lived was the only world Manisha knew. 'I didn't know that there was a choice to not be married at 15,' says Manisha, the same girl who, today at the age of 28 and the mother of four daughters, confidently confirms that education is her first priority with regard to her girls. 'All my cousins and my friends were married between the ages of 12 and 15. It would have been unusual if I wasn't.' When I asked Manisha about her plans for her own daughters and suggested that she should consider having them get married only after they are 18 years old, she smiled, nodded, and then confided that she would only have them marry after they are capable of earning their own living.

As the oldest sibling in her family, Manisha had to give up schooling the earliest, reaching only the fifth grade. But it was not long before she realized the power of basic literacy and higher education. After getting married Manisha moved to live with her husband in a big city (where she continues to live today). In the city Manisha was suddenly exposed to a world very different from the one she knew – a world intense with competition, a world where class asserted the power of caste, and a world where everybody had to help make a living – girls as well as boys.

Manisha had already lived in this big city for more than seven years when I met her. She was now pregnant for the fifth time and was only in the fifth week of this pregnancy. She had not yet revealed this to anyone in her family except her mother. Manisha was unable to decide whether she should keep the baby or terminate the pregnancy; her last born was still only an infant. At this point, Manisha knew that she and her husband would not be able to handle the increased financial burden a fifth child would bring; she also knew that it would be a challenge for her to run the house and at the same time manage five children, two of whom would be very young. An abortion, she understood, was the only sensible solution. But what weighed on her mind simultaneously was the knowledge that her husband and his family were keen for her to have a son. While she was pregnant once again too soon, she could not help but think that this child might be a boy; another girl, she was sure, would not be welcome. To aid her decision-making process, Manisha's mother suggested that Manisha should have the sex of the fetus detected and base her decision to retain or terminate the pregnancy on this knowledge. Though illegal, this was nevertheless a possible course of action for Manisha, but one that would come at an exorbitant price. According to the PC&PNDT Act, identifying the sex of the fetus through pre-natal diagnostic testing is prohibited in India. Despite this, pre-natal sex determination remains rampant in India, and for cases like those of Manisha it probably provides a realistic solution. There are women like Manisha throughout India, women whose identities are partly shaped by their deeper values, cares, and commitments. These factors are, therefore, necessarily central in their decision-making processes.[2] However, undergoing such a test is an expensive and risky affair: doctors charge extortionate amounts for carrying out these prohibited tests, and women put themselves and their families at risk of being penalized if caught for this act, which constitutes a criminal offence.

To learn more about the abortion procedure, Manisha visited the government-run family planning centre, where she was informed about the option of undergoing a reversible procedure whereby she could control child birth until she wished it. Since such family planning centres operate under strict codes of confidentiality, she was assured that knowledge of her treatment would not be shared under any circumstances. When Manisha told me about

2 M Friedman, *Autonomy, Gender, Politics* (Oxford University Press 2003).

the information she had received at the family planning centre, I thought it sounded like her best option in the present situation. The pregnancy had been her secret, so there was no reason for anyone to suspect an 'abortion'. Moreover, since the sterilization procedure would be short and simple, requiring no more than half a day, Manisha's absence from home – if she were to decide to undergo the procedure – would not even be noticed, let alone suspected. Like her pregnancy, she could have also kept the fact that she had undergone the reversible sterilization procedure to herself, deciding on her own whether and when she wanted to conceive again. Since none of the family members would have known about the pregnancy, the abortion, or the sterilization, there would be no reason for anyone to be upset or hurt.

But Manisha chose to do something very different. She decided to tell her parents and her husband about her pregnancy and her decision to terminate the pregnancy and undergo this reversible sterilization. By revealing her intentions, Manisha knew that she was running the risk of putting all her relationships at stake and challenging what are, in her social milieu, seen as culturally embedded power relations. But Manisha knew something more: her intimate knowledge of her family and community, the fabric of which she herself was an integral part, allowed her scope for speculation. The risk she took (as she may have speculated) proved fruitful; Manisha received support from what to an outsider – like me – seemed unexpected quarters. The same power relations now turned in her favour. The practical challenges of having a fifth child – even if it was to be a boy (an outcome of which no one could be sure without a sex detection test, which would have entailed paying an exorbitant amount of money and risking legal sanctions) – seemed tremendous not just to Manisha, but to her entire family. Her husband's family as well as her own left it to *her* to determine the best solution. Manisha's husband, as she had expected, was very upset at the beginning, but eventually came to terms with the reality of their economic situation and also of the fact that Manisha now had the support not only of her own family, but even of his entire family. With the backing of their families, Manisha too was more confident in her decision, which she now knew she could fully live up to.

This case study is an example of how the choice-making capacities of individuals, placed within a complex network of kinship relations the dynamics of which are largely determined by local cultures, are characterized by skilful negotiation.

Manisha and her husband live far away from her husband's family – his brothers, their families, and his grandmother – all of whom live in Manisha's husband's native village. Manisha, therefore, enjoys a fair deal of flexibility in deciding the terms of her family life – her relationship with her husband, the manner in which they use the money they earn, and the way in which they bring up their daughters. However, this flexibility does not undermine, as is evident from this case, the impact of power relationships, arising from the nature of kinship networks in Manisha's and her husband's communities, that continue to impose themselves despite the physical distance. However, the relationships that exert power do not do so arbitrarily. The power as Manisha articulates it arises out of a support system that this family constitutes and of which each of the members is a part. Against this background, Manisha's personal struggle to make a decision started seeming natural and understandable – she was going to put to the test these very same power relationships, as she decided whether to keep the child in the hope that it would be a boy and finally relieve her of the constant stress of her extended family's expectations *or* terminate the pregnancy, which would help her cope better with the practical challenges she was already faced with – carrying out the household chores, managing three young girls and an infant, and earning a living.

Manisha was confronted with a tug of war between practical and emotional realities – the pressure of economic constraints versus the possibility that her husband and his family would abandon her. Manisha knew that another child at this stage – even if it were a boy – meant increased financial expenditure for which, Manisha admitted, she and her husband were not yet prepared. But at the same time, could she run the risk of aborting a fetus that might be a boy? Would her husband and his family forgive her for this act? Could she herself afford to lose the chance of having a boy and finally freeing herself of this emotional burden and physical stress? Under these circumstances, pre-natal sex determination was a tempting option. But could she afford it financially?

When I look at the number of questions that Manisha was confronted with, I realize that the process of decision-making is in itself fraught with decision-making. It is almost like a tangled ball of yarn. There is one knot after another that a person must carefully undo so that the entire string of yarn can be straightened out. And at every stage the person must reflect on who he or she is and what matters most to him or her. The situation is best described by Christine Korsgaard's notion of 'practical identity', which she says is a necessary condition of agency.[3]

At no stage did Manisha wish to hide her decision from her family. The fact that she as an individual had the (human) right to make such a decision independently and without informing anyone else was nothing more than empty philosophy; had she done so, she would probably have lived in constant fear of the day her family found out what she had done. For Manisha, decision-making – even if it concerned her own body, her health, and her life – was not an individualistic process but a collective one in which negotiation was the key word.

This case gives rise to two questions that I propose to address:

a. Did Manisha exercise agency and was her decision autonomous?
b. What is the relevance of the Act in light of Manisha's decision?

The questions are interrelated. The manner in which exercise of agency is analysed will reveal how relevant the PC&PNDT legislation is in situations similar to those that Manisha found herself in.

The exercise of agency and processes of autonomy

Agency, if perceived in the sense of the capacity to act and reflect, is, as Phillips argues, a feature of pretty much anyone (and everyone) who is not bound and gagged;[4] therefore, the concept delivers too minimal a notion of what it is to exercise choice. The more relevant question, then, is whether Manisha's decision was marked by 'processes of autonomy', and I argue that, indeed, it was, and therefore her decision was autonomous. I believe this is true not so much on the basis of her final decision, but more so because of the manner in which she finalized it. For the purpose of understanding whether Manisha's decision was autonomous, I have relied, like Meyers, on an approach that views autonomy as dwelling in the process of deciding and not in the nature of the action decided upon.[5] Exploring the

3 C Korsgaard, *The Sources of Normativity* (Cambridge University Press 1996).

4 A Phillips, 'Does the Body Make a Difference?', *Gender, Agency and Coercion* (Palgrave Macmillan 2013) 143.

5 DT Meyers, 'Feminism and Women's Autonomy: The Challenge of Female Genital Cutting' (2000) 31 *Metaphilosophy* 469.

concept of autonomy in the context of female genital cutting among women in Asia and Africa, Meyers explains that autonomous individuals enact an introspective understanding of their true selves – one that is based on an understanding of what really matters to them, who they care deeply about, and what their capacities and limitations actually are.[6] In a context such as that of Manisha's, such an approach seems preferable to an individualistic notion of agency that often fails to account for the ways in which our lives, values, and commitments are shaped by a range of non-voluntary factors, from our social and material situations to some of our relationships with others.[7]

Naturally, in a community-oriented society like that in rural India, relationships – often defined by social institutions largely impacted by culture – are advantageous because of the support structure they provide. At the same time, however, they can also be restrictive, as in Manisha's situation. Interestingly, as a result of migration from rural to urban settings – the rate of which is only increasing[8] – cultural expectations are increasingly competing with economics. For many such migrating families, the extent to which an expectation with its roots in cultural traditions and customs can be realized is slowly being determined by the availability of financial resources.[9] I will delve briefly into some migration-related demographics to clarify this further. Based on the 2001 census, a report on rural-to-urban migration at the district level in India observed that the three primary reasons for urban-to-rural migration were employment, marriage, and education (in that order).[10] Interestingly, the same report further highlights macro-level data indicating that work participation rates of migrant women in the largest cities were higher than for non-migrant women.[11]

Manisha is one such woman who migrated to an urban setting because of marriage, but soon had to participate in the workforce out of financial necessity. Despite having four young children and being the sole person in charge of their upbringing and all household chores, Manisha knows that at present there is no alternative to her contributing to the household income. In contexts such as Manisha's, cultural expectations compete with financial constraints. Manisha chose to have an abortion because she and her husband were not ready for the financial exigencies a fifth child would bring. But does that mean that the cultural expectations that Manisha's family fostered were of no importance to her? I would perceive *this* as the turning point, a point from where the notion of autonomy practised by women like Manisha in India becomes evident. Even though Manisha's exercise of autonomy in some way – possibly because of economic pressures – involved critical reflection of her deepest attachments and commitments,[12] she did so without distancing herself from her values and concerns that were embedded in complex interpersonal, social, and cultural

6 Ibid. 476.

7 C Mackenzie, 'Relational Autonomy, Sexual Justice and Cultural Pluralism' in B Arneil et al. (eds), *Sexual Justice/Cultural Justice* (Routledge 2007) 110.

8 J Tulloch, 'India's Urban Migration Crisis' (*Open Knowledge*) <www.allianz.com/en/about_us/open-knowledge/topics/demography/articles/111018-indias-urban-migration-crisis.html/> accessed 3 May 2017.

9 These expectations may be related to the nature and composition of family structures, as well as (among other things) marriage, birth, and funeral ceremonies.

10 A Mitra and M Murayama, 'Rural to Urban Migration: A District Level Analysis for India' (Institute for Developing Economies, March 2008) <www.ide.go.jp/English/Publish/Download/Dp/pdf/137.pdf> accessed 3 May 2017.

11 Ibid. 15–16.

12 Mackenzie (n 7) 110.

contexts. The fact that she remained acutely aware of these contexts is evident from two actions: first, that *she decided to reveal and possibly discuss her decision with her family*; and second, that she chose to undergo a *medical procedure that provided temporary birth control*. In both of these actions Manisha left scope for deliberation, discussion, and negotiation. Perhaps Manisha feels that four children are enough and she would not want to have more, but her discretion told her that 'now' was not the time to debate this issue.

This analysis of Manisha's decision-making process brings to the forefront an important aspect. A woman, placed in a traditional socio-cultural situation, possesses immense knowledge about the nature of the intricate network of interpersonal relationships she is surrounded by and the dynamics of the manner in which such relationships play out through particular processes of interaction. Autonomy debates, particularly in the light of human rights, tend to undermine or ignore this reality. I would disagree with the claim that 'Manisha was plain lucky that her family supported her decision,' an argument many in the Dhangar community would make under the circumstances. Manisha did take a risk, but a calculated one.

When I asked Manisha what she felt about the gravity of the decision she had taken, she merely laughed it off. Unable to understand why I saw her decision-making process as crucial and an exceptional reflection of the process of autonomy, she remarked, 'It is like handling any other delicate situation. I have seen my sisters, my friends, and my sisters-in-law all go through such negotiations at several points in their married lives.'

That brings me to the second question I wish to discuss. If, as Manisha says, women in her position often exercise autonomy in the manner demonstrated above, then what exactly is the relevance of legislation that prohibits fetal sex detection for such women?

The PC&PNDT legislation and its impacts on processes of autonomy

The reasons why the PC&PNDT Act came into force and was implemented in 1994 can be found in the 'objects and reasons' of the bill preceding this act, which state that:

> Sex determination tests are being [*sic*] operative for the past so many years in the country. Many people have earned a lot of money by operating such centres. The tests are now increasingly used by parents and medical practitioners for pre-birth sex determination with the intention of aborting the female foetus. If this is allowed to continue, it will result in distorted male female ratio in the country. It is high time that such a legislation is brought forward to ban such tests in the country. Hence, this bill.[13]

The PC&PNDT Act was the central legislation that drew inspiration from similar state legislations, implemented first in Maharashtra in 1988 and then followed in three other states between 1988 and 1994. The act in Maharashtra arose from several years of campaigning by women's groups and health activists, who came together under the banner of Forum Against Sex Determination and Sex Preselection (FASDAP) with the aim of securing a legal ban on pre-birth sex determination in Maharashtra. Despite the evident failure of the Maharashtra Act,[14] the central legislation passed in 1994 was structured identically to the state legislations, except that the punishments and fines were set at a higher level in the former.

13 G Gangoli, 'Reproduction, Abortion and Women's Health' (1998) 26 *Social Scientist* 83, 100.
14 From 1988 to 1998, not even a single case was registered under the Act; see Gangoli (n 13).

The quote that encapsulates the intention of the central legislature to bring this act into force highlights two concerns on the part of the legislature:

a. a growing industry of pre-natal diagnostic techniques for sex determination; and
b. a distorted male-female sex ratio.

Through the enforcement of the PC&PNDT Act and its continued rigorous implementation, the legislature hoped to improve the male-female ratio in the country. Sex selection in preference of male fetuses was and is even today considered one of the primary factors resulting in a skewed sex ratio.

But figures regarding the number of convictions under the act and the undeterred distortion of the child sex ratio are indicators that this act has not had its intended impact. Between 1991 and 2011 the child sex ratio fell from 945 girls per 1000 boys to 914 girls per 1000 boys. Similarly, the figures for the number of convictions under this act are very low. Violations under the act include the non-registration of an ultrasound machine or a laboratory, non-maintenance of records, communication of the sex of the fetus, and failure to put up a notification concerning the 'prohibition of sex determination of fetus' by such laboratories. Figures that were included in affidavits filed as part of a writ petition seeking orders from the Supreme Court of India for rigorous implementation of the PC&PNDT Act reveal that as of June 2011, a total of only 874 cases had been lodged in various states under this act since its implementation.[15] According to these data provided by the Union of India, the defendants in this court case, in some states there had been no complaints filed at all! Moreover, the number of complaints actually filed under the act hardly reflects the real picture of how many clinics are actually conducting sex determination tests. Evidently, the punitive nature of this act has not deterred the practice of sex determination of the fetus, but merely pushed it underground.

But another troubling aspect of this act is the manner in which it interferes with women's autonomy. In light of Manisha's case and for many other women in India like her – what is the relevance of this Act and how does it impact on their decision-making process?

When the act came into force in 1994, under section 23(3), a woman undergoing a pre-natal diagnostic test to determine the sex of the fetus was also punishable with up to three years' imprisonment and a fine of 10,000 rupees. Therefore, under the earlier act, a woman like Manisha who had actually exercised agency and may have in light of her autonomy decided to undergo a test to determine the sex of the fetus could have faced imprisonment. In short, the law did not recognize the right of a woman to exercise such agency.

Later, this section was amended to explicitly state under section 23(4) that a woman who underwent such a test would not be punishable. However, what still remains is section 24, which continues to undermine women's capacity to make autonomous decisions. This section states that the court shall presume (unless the contrary is proven) that the pregnant woman was compelled by her husband (or any other relative, as the case may be) to undergo the pre-natal diagnostic test if it was for any purpose other than those that are allowed under the act. The husband or relative will be punished with imprisonment and/or a fine for abetting an offence under this act. What does this tell us? The act basically presumes that a woman is incapable of taking a decision to undergo a pre-natal diagnostic test for sex detection of the fetus; if she does undergo such a test, it is presumed that she did so under pressure from her husband or a relative. By this logic, Manisha's decision – had she decided to undergo a sex detection procedure – would not have been considered her decision at

15 *Voluntary Health Association of Punjab v Union of India and Ors* (2006) Writ Petition (Civil) 349.

all, but rather the result of coercion by her family. As is clear from the description of her decision-making process earlier in the chapter, had Manisha decided to undergo a fetal sex determination test, it would have been of her own accord.

Earlier, the Medical Termination of Pregnancy Act (MTP Act) of 1971 legalized abortions in India. While the act does not mandate the husband's consent, it does require every woman to give an explanation for wanting the abortion.[16] The MTP Act, read together with the PC&PNDT Act, clearly establishes that the results of a sex determination test cannot be a valid justification for abortion of a fetus. Let us look at Manisha's case study once again. Both the concern of a growing financial burden and fear of her family abandoning her were constraining concerns for Manisha. But why then is an abortion due to financial pressures more justified than one based on the sex of a fetus? How does the PC&PNDT Act, which criminalizes the latter type of abortion, explain the legislature's refusal to recognize the autonomy of women such as Manisha?

One can say that the spirit of the PC&PNDT Act is embedded in a human rights discourse supported by the state and a national educated elite. What is troubling, however, is that section 24 of the PC&PNDT Act echoes an aspect of the human rights discourse that is extremely paternalistic in nature. In presuming that a woman who undergoes a fetal sex detection test is surely being compelled to do so by her husband or a relative, the act falls in line with an understanding in human rights discourse that some acts are such extreme violations of personhood or bodily integrity that the 'victim' is simply incapable of freely choosing those acts or freely consenting to them. The PC&PNDT Act establishes a threshold beyond which the exercise of agency by a woman (in this case to carry out an abortion after a sex determination test) becomes irrelevant in deciding whether a particular act was actually an offence or not. That the woman was coerced is presumed to be undeniable.

Seen from the perspective of someone in Manisha's situation, this aspect of the human rights discourse seems to be engaged in fostering a particular type of subjectivity, a subjectivity of modernity where a person is expected to make 'self through choices based on utility and preference rather than on kinship obligations or the demands of custom'.[17] However, in matters where values concerning the family and community are involved, the process of exercising agency will rarely be perfectly autonomous, for any such choice is marked by an inner sense of one's own self. As in the case of Manisha and other women like her in India, who we are and how we perceive ourselves is not devoid of the impacts of the network of relationships we are placed within and our knowledge – both that we gain from our own experiences as well as that which we derive from what others tell us.[18]

Conclusions

Manisha's case highlights the nature of a situation in which it would be *possible* for a woman to take a decision – genuinely marked by processes of autonomy – to undergo a pre-natal diagnostic test to determine the sex of her fetus in order to decide whether to abort it or not.

16 Gangoli (n 13); N Menon, 'The Impossibility of "Justice": Female Foeticide and Feminist Discourse on Abortion' (1995) 29 *Contributions to Indian Sociology* 369.

17 SE Merry, 'Relating to the Subjects of Human Rights: The Culture of Agency in Human Rights Discourse' in N Freeman and D Napier (eds), *Law and Anthropology: Current Legal Issues* (Oxford 2009) 385.

18 A Phillips, *Multiculturalism Without Culture* (Princeton University Press 2007).

A feminist philosophical account of agency alone may not be helpful in making sense of such processes of autonomy, because when such conceptual accounts are applied within oppressive contexts they can be troubling. They rest upon unreconstructed models of universalist, ahistorical, acontextual liberal humanist agency that are almost always conceptualized in oppositional terms – as challenging or resisting power relations and articulating universalized models of emancipatory politics.[19]

Processes of autonomy such as those reflected in Manisha's decision-making pose an important question: Does exercising autonomy necessarily have to compel the person in question to make a choice between her community and 'distancing herself from particular cultural roles'[20] or, to put it another way, between 'modern' and 'traditional' conduct and ways of thinking? When a person's sense of herself is determined by a complex combination of all these factors, can the understanding of autonomy not be expanded to grasp this complexity? Restrictive value-saturated accounts of autonomy are disconcerting because they homogenize authentic selves and autonomous selves.[21]

A woman's decision to abort a female fetus (and, as we see from Manisha's case, perhaps even – inadvertently – a male) is not always only the result of being compelled by her family. Planning the size and sex composition of one's children is at the confluence of a range of processes, including stretching limited resources, wanting the 'best' for one's children with the effect of heightening the burden of having them, extreme socio-economic volatility, varying individual morality, the kinds of technology available, and the nature of gender disparities across classes in contemporary society.[22]

In the context of such processes of autonomy – in which women in India actively engage – the PC&PNDT Act begins to look like a draconian policy response, which as Phillips perfectly articulates, can catch within its net many individuals who are not being coerced but are simply going about their chosen business, trying to live autonomous lives.[23] Such policy measures are oddly indirect, for instead of targeting and assisting those who are subject to coercion, they ban certain practices for all.

The PC&PNDT Act, examined through the lens of a decision-making context like that of Manisha's, also compels us to dwell upon the relationship between processes of autonomy and coercion. The distinction between those practices that are 'freely' chosen and those that are adopted because they conform to everyday social practices will always remain blurry. Like Saharso,[24] I also find myself becoming extremely uncomfortable with this binary opposition between voluntary and coerced conduct. This opposition becomes even more vivid in light of what Madhok terms the 'action bias' in autonomy and agency formulations.[25] Madhok explains that this action bias is often characterized by 'act atomism' and 'value monism'. Here, I would like to emphasize the characteristic of act atomism, which, as Madhok explains, involves agency evaluations typically focusing on the coherence of a

19 S Madhok, 'Action, Agency, Coercion: Reformatting Agency for Oppressive Contexts' in S Madhok (ed), *Gender, Agency and Coercion* (Palgrave Macmillan 2013) 104.
20 Mackenzie (n 7).
21 Meyers (n 5).
22 ME John, 'Census 2011: Governing Populations and the Girl Child' (2011) 46 *Economic and Political Weekly* 10.
23 Phillips (n 18).
24 S Saharso, 'Feminist Ethics, Autonomy and the Politics of Multiculturalism' (2003) 4 *Feminist Theory* 199.
25 Madhok (n 19) 107.

single act which is then analysed independently of, and separate from, a particular sequence of related acts to which it belongs. However, persons do not perform acontextual, ahistorical, isolated acts, but instead engage in a stream or chain of acts that are linked to each other in certain ways. And whether a decision was marked by processes of autonomy can be determined only by observing the entire stream of actions holistically. As we saw, Manisha too did not have only one decision to make (whether or not to undergo an abortion). It was a tangled ball of yarn, and there were several knots to be undone before the ball would be finally undone. But the *manner* in which Manisha finally took the decision that she did explains that knots can be undone very strategically, such that they do not knot up again. Manisha made a decision that allowed scope for negotiation, giving relationships their due respect even as practicality steered the way. The reality is that so far as personhood is defined through relationships and life opportunities governed by kin, the obligation to behave in terms of these expectations is a fundamental feature of social life. Such perceived opposition fails to 'capture the complexities of women's agency in contexts of power and culture'.[26]

Documents such as this legislation based on paternalistic notions in the human rights discourse assume that they must protect vulnerable persons, who are presumed to be incapable of exercising their own agency. The PC&PNDT Act outlaws a situation in which a woman is likely to be placed under coercion. Yet, outlawing activities that are perceived externally as harmful[27] has evidently not provided a solution. Meanwhile, the female-male sex ratio, as we saw earlier, continues to drop.

The central government of India has made many attempts to redress the sex ratio of the country. Preference for male children has cultural as well as economic reasons.[28] The government recognizes this and has accordingly attempted to curtail the impact of traditional social and economic structures by introducing legislation to prohibit dowry, encourage registration of marriages, promote free education for girls, and establish quotas for women in higher education and public-sector employment opportunities. The PC&PNDT Act only adds to this list.

In a recent announcement following the latest population census, the Planning Commission revealed its proposal for a new strategy: it hopes to relax the ban on sex selection tests in the rural areas as part of a larger programme of 'adopting' female fetuses and generously incentivizing families and health workers to ensure the safe delivery of female babies.[29] What will happen to this proposal remains to be seen. Given the state of affairs in government-run children's homes, hospitals, and day-care centres, the government's idea to now 'adopt' female fetuses seems far too ambitious.

While the legislative efforts by the government are laudable, success rates in terms of effectiveness, impact, and implementation are marginal. The 66th round of the National Sample Survey (2009–2010) reveals that even after 20 years of unprecedented economic

26 B Baum, 'Feminism, Liberalism and Cultural Pluralism: J. S. Mill on Mormon Polygyny' (1997) 5 *Journal of Political Philosophy* 230, 243.

27 Merry (n 17).

28 Traditional social structures and economic arrangements bestow upon sons important ritualistic rights in marriages and funerals and the responsibility to financially support their parents when the need arises. Daughters, however, will become economically and socially part of their husbands' families after marriage, a ceremony for which the parents must ensure a reasonable dowry.

29 A Dhar, 'Should Ban on Sex Determination Tests Be Relaxed?' *The Hindu* (New Delhi, 8 October 2011) <www.thehindu.com/news/national/should-ban-on-sex-determination-tests-be-relaxed/article2518757.ece> accessed 3 May 2017.

growth, the total proportion of women in any kind of paid work is no more than 15 per cent.[30] In other words, this means that 85 per cent of all women in India are destined to find their future through structural forms of dependency.

What is required is a nuanced approach towards holistically understanding and addressing the reasons for male-child preference in contemporary Indian society. Experiments with increasing education and employment opportunities for women must be coupled with efforts to improve women's capacities in order to enable them to take full advantage of the opportunities made available for them.[31] Encouraging, empowering, and enriching the present generation of women to recognize and be confident of their own self-worth must become a crucial part of the campaign to save the girl child of tomorrow. As demonstrated here, punitive legislation such as the PC&PNDT Act merely undermines processes of autonomy and fails to tackle the root causes of female feticide; the official law is woefully unaware of the realities of the complex processes of decision-making among Indian women about birth-related matters.

30 Figures from the 68th round of the National Sample Survey are not any better. In general female participation in the labour force has been low and is falling. A Shaw, 'Employment Trends in India' (2013) 48 *Economic and Political Weekly* 23.

31 MC Nussbaum, 'Human Capabilities, Female Human Beings' in Pogge Thomas and Darrel Moellendorf (eds), *Global Justice: Seminal Essays*, vol 1 (Paragon House 2008).

18 Rethinking social norms

Contraceptive use and women's right to choose in Senegal

Chiara Quagliariello

Introduction

To what extent are women in Senegal guaranteed the possibility to choose if, when, and how to access the experience of being a mother? Answering this question requires an analysis that takes into account different normative systems governing reproductive behaviour in Senegal. In the first part of this chapter, I focus on the rules suggested by the legal and social systems: according to state law, women have the right to use contraceptive methods; by contrast, social norms promote the importance of having children. To bridge this gap, Senegalese legislation permits the use of contraceptive measures, but only with the husband's consent *and* only to facilitate family planning in cases where women have one or more children already. In the second part of the chapter, I will focus on how some women have resisted these laws and continue to use contraception without their husbands' consent and without already having children. On the one hand, I explore how in the Senegalese context – where in order to be considered a proper woman one must be a mother – social expectations limit women's ability to choose for themselves when to have children. On the other hand, I examine some of the strategies women use to assert their reproductive rights. Highlighting experiences I have come across in the course of fieldwork, I focus on the choices women make to fulfil their personal desires, as well as on some of the difficulties and the risks related to these choices. The overarching aim of the chapter is to determine whether this assertion of reproductive rights can be understood as a form of agency whereby women, creatively using contraceptive methods allowed by law, not only manage to avoid overtly opposing the social norms, but even to actively adapt them to their personal desires.[1]

Research and methods

This chapter is based on findings from seven months of ethnographic fieldwork (January to July 2011) carried out at 15 public medical facilities offering family planning services in Senegal. Nine of the facilities were located in urban areas (Parcelles Assainises district in Dakar), while the other six were in rural areas (Mbacké Department, in the region of Diourbel). The aim was to understand if (and to what extent) women's reproductive behaviour varied over the two contexts. The research primarily involved qualitative research methods,

1 Throughout this article I use the generic expression 'Senegalese women'; however, I am referring more specifically to women belonging to the Wolof ethnic group, which comprises 40 per cent of the population of Senegal. See Makhtar Diouf, *Sénégal. Les ethnies et la Nation* (Éditions L'Harmattan 1994).

DOI: 10.4324/9781315413617-22

including direct observation of activities within the medical facilities; 'shadowing' of medical staff during women's visits and consultations; and some 50 interviews, 15 with medical staff (midwives) and 35 with female clients of the public facilities. In addition, I analysed statistics regarding the use of contraception in Senegal, as well as the demographic profiles of women attending family planning facilities over the preceding five years.

Governing reproduction in Senegal

Two main systems govern women's reproductive behaviour in Senegal: the first is the set of principles established by the national law on reproductive rights (Les droits en matière de Santé de la Reproduction, hereinafter Law No. 18), approved by the Senegalese government on 5 August 2005; the second comprises popular attitudes informed by social norms.

The legal system

Unlike the situation in other West African countries, article IV of Law No. 18 establishes the right to contraception for all Senegalese citizens, although in practice it mainly affects women. As noted in the anthropological literature, in most West African contexts the domain of reproduction is primarily associated with women.[2] Law No. 18 reinforces this bias towards women in the area of reproduction. The general provisions of article IV state that the right to contraception in Senegal aims to achieve the development of public health via the implementation of women's health services. According to the law, in fact, because women contain the reproductive function within their bodies, they constitute the main 'pillar' of Senegalese society upon which the future of the country rests. Hence, in order to have a healthy society, it is necessary to have healthy women.

Similarly, state-promoted discourses insist that the use of contraception may provide a solution to three problems related to public health. The first problem is the rate of HIV. Statistical data from the last Demographic and Health Survey (DHS) indicate that this disease still affects 2.5 per cent of children and 1 per cent of the adult population in Senegal.[3] The second problem is childbirth-related female mortality. According to statistics from the World Health Organization (WHO), Senegal had a maternal mortality ratio of 320 in 2013.[4] This problem both encourages and is exacerbated by high fertility rates. As shown by the DHS data, the fertility rate in Senegal is more than four children per mother in urban areas and six per mother in the rural context. These figures are consistent with my own research in the district of Parcelles Assainises (Dakar) and Mbacké (Diourbel region), where the average number of children per woman is at least four in the first case and five in the second. The age at first birth is usually between 20 and 22 years in urban areas and under 20 years in the rural context. The demographic profiles of the women I met in Senegal, such as level of education and occupation, indicate that these fertility rates are not limited to certain groups only. They represent, on the contrary, a *structural phenomenon*. As pointed out by promoters

2 See, e.g., CP MacCormack (ed), *The Ethnography of Fertility and Birth* (Academic Press 1982); F Héritier, *Masculin, Féminin. La pensée de la différence* (Éditions Jacob 1996).

3 See <http://dhsprogram.com/publications/publication-FR320-DHS-Final-Reports.cfm> accessed 31 March 2017.

4 Per 100,000 live births. See <www.who.int/maternal_child_adolescent/epidemiology/profiles/maternal/sen.pdf> accessed 31 March 2017.

of Law No. 18, such as Macky Sall (who is currently the president of Senegal and served as prime minister from 2004 to 2007), increased access to and use of contraception would lead to later first pregnancies and a decrease in average number of births per woman, ultimately improving women's well-being and alleviating a third health problem: the high infant mortality rate. According to demographic studies,[5] infant mortality is directly linked to high fertility rates and the accompanying difficulties families experience in providing the necessary material support to their children. This is reflected in the neonatal mortality rate in Senegal (23 per 1,000 live births), which is mostly due to mothers' and children's malnutrition.[6]

While the transmission of HIV clearly cannot be solved solely by legislating women's access to and use of contraception, women's access to contraception could indeed play an important role in the improvement of both their own health and their children's health. As stated by Abdou Fall, the former minister of health, during a debate prior to the passage of Law No. 18 in 2005, women's access to contraception should be viewed as a tool for the achievement of at least two of the 10 Millennium Development Goals supported by the WHO since 2000, namely, the reduction of maternal mortality and child mortality rates throughout Africa.[7]

The social system

Social and cultural norms, on the other hand, emphasize the importance of having children. Social anthropological studies have identified two main cultural factors leading to the valorization of motherhood.[8] The first factor is the formal correlation between sexuality and reproduction as expressed in religious precepts, in this case represented by the values of Islam, a religion that 93 per cent of the population of Senegal follow. The second factor is the social obligation to continue the lineage of the ancestors, as required by the traditional marriage system in Senegal.[9] The separation of sexuality from reproduction, as well as having children outside of marriage, both of which are more or less accepted in most contemporary Western societies, clash with the shared system of values in Senegal. Moreover, the legitimation of sexual activity only within the matrimonial union is a social norm that, although it formally involves both sexes, 'weighs' more heavily on women. The *de facto* social condemnation of women's sexual activity (and hence pregnancies) outside of marriage is clear from the value attributed to a woman's virginity (*ndaw* in Wolof) – a condition that even today is 'checked' on the wedding night.

Similarly, the importance of having children is reflected in the widely shared idea that a childless marriage is a failed marriage, and the responsibility for having children (and hence the blame for not having them) generally falls on the women. To be appreciated by their families-in-law, women must not only be good wives, but they must also invest in a 'mother career'.[10] This expectation is more understandable in light of the traditional marriage system that is still common in Senegal – and in West Africa more generally – which is based on

5 FD Ginsburg and R Rapp (eds), *Conceiving the New World Order: The Global Politics of Reproduction* (University of California Press 1995).

6 See <www.who.int/maternal_child_adolescent/epidemiology/profiles/maternal/sen.pdf> accessed 31 March 2017.

7 Y Jaffré, 'Towards an Anthropology of Public Health Priorities: Maternal Mortality in Four Obstetric Emergency Services in West Africa' (2012) 20 *Anthropologie Sociale* 3.

8 See, e.g., AB Diop, *La société wolof* (Éditions Karthala 1981).

9 Recall that I am referring in particular to the Wolof people (see n 1).

10 S Gojard, *Le métier de mère* (Éditions La Dispute 2010).

the husband's family (*jekker* in Wolof) offering compensation (*ndagaan* in Wolof) to the bride's parents (*jabar* in Wolof).[11] Marriage in Senegal does not involve only two persons; it is a union between two families and lineages who join together to guarantee the social reproduction of the husband's group. The payment of the so-called bride price is, according to Levi-Strauss, the first sign of an alliance between the two families.[12] As Jack Goody observed, the price paid by the husband is related to the reproductive potential of the bride, and the principal way for women to prove their value is by giving birth.[13] In such a system it would be inconceivable for a woman to choose not to have children.

The expectations of motherhood accordingly give rise to different forms of control over women's reproductive behaviour. This control is usually exercised by mothers-in-law and sisters-in-law, who are socially recognized as being responsible for the 'success' of the marriage.[14] In this sense, the obligations that come with inscription of the subject into the social group run counter to the idea of a person as a completely autonomous individual who is entitled to act according to his or her personal wishes.[15] In Senegal, the family system is one in which a woman's right to determine her own reproductive behaviour is mediated by her social roles and the expectations of the community. This contrasts sharply with the aspirations of Western feminist theorists, who have hoped and predicted that women worldwide will someday be socially accepted as women even if they are not mothers.[16] In Senegal, not only is the primary function assigned to women a reproductive one, but women are usually not even the ones who decide when it is the 'right time' for them to have children. Social anthropological and demographic studies have underlined how Senegalese motherhood is an experience managed by the social group and not an individual project.[17]

Between the legal and social systems

The tension between the rights granted by Law No. 18 – such as the possibility of using contraception – and the values suggested by the social norms – such as the importance of having children within the frame of marriage – have resulted in a compromise: official permission to use contraceptive methods, but only with the husband's consent and only

11 C Levi-Strauss, *Les Structures élémentaires de la parenté* (Presses Universitaires de France 1949); J Goody, *Production and Reproduction: A Comparative Study of the Domestic Domain* (Cambridge University Press 1976).

12 Levi-Strauss (n 11).

13 Goody (n 11).

14 AB Diop, *La famille wolof: tradition et changement* (Éditions Karthala 1985).

15 L Dumont, *Essai sur l'individualisme. Une perspective anthropologique sur l'idéologie moderne* (Éditions Seuil 1983); B Purkayastha and M Subramaniam, *The Power of Women's Informal Networks: Lessons in Social Change From South Asia and West Africa* (Lexington Books 2004); P Descola, *Par-delà Nature et Culture* (Éditions Gallimard 2005); S Fainzang, 'La culture, entre représentations de la personne et politiques de santé. Mises en perspective avec quelques données occidentales' in M Godelier (ed), *Maladie et santé selon les sociétés et les cultures* (Presses Universitaires de France 2011) 111.

16 S Beauvoir, *Le deuxième sexe* (Éditions Gallimard 1949); A Rich, *On Women Born: Motherhood as Experience and Institution* (Norton 1976); A Oakley, *Women Confined: Toward a Sociology of Childbirth* (Martin Robertson 1980); N-C Mathieu (ed), *L'arraisonnement des femmes. Essais en anthropologie de sexe* (Éditions de l'École des Hautes Etudes en Sciences Sociales 1985); F Descarries and C Corbeil, 'Entre discours et pratiques: l'évolution de la pensée féministe sur la maternité depuis 1960' (1994) 15 *Nouvelles Questions Féministes* 80–82.

17 A Andro, 'Projets de fécondité en Afrique de l'Ouest. Quelles négociations entre hommes et femmes?' in T Locoh (ed), *Genre, population et développement* (Les Cahiers de l'INED 2007) 373.

in cases where women have one or more children already. Art. 1 of the law makes it quite clear that the purpose of promoting contraception in Senegal is to allow families to space pregnancies within the framework of marriage. Contraception is not intended to be a right for women who have not yet had children or, even less, for women who are not yet married. Access to contraception is functional; it is an instrument to facilitate family planning. As such, the law represents a compromise, not a conflict, between the legal and the social systems: the principles defended by the law are oriented in the same direction as the values established by social norms. Unlike the legal instruments in some other national contexts that conform to internationally agreed upon fundamental individual rights, the law in Senegal does not defend access to contraception as an individual choice or outside the framework of marriage.[18]

What is missing is the implementation of a margin of choice regarding reproduction, or how to make use of one's own individual body more generally. The DHS data reveal that in 2014, 12 per cent of the population used contraception in Senegal. Of those who acknowledged using contraceptives, more than 90 per cent were women and fewer than 10 per cent were men. Together with this significant discrepancy in contraceptive use, two more noteworthy facts emerged during fieldwork that affect both the urban and the rural areas of the country equally. The first is that all women who attended the family planning services were married. Although this finding is not sufficient to assert that unmarried women do not use contraception, it does allow us to highlight the formal absence of unmarried women in the services officially devoted to this purpose. Second, 90 per cent of the women attending the family planning services had already given birth to one or more children.

Furthermore, it is interesting to note the close correspondence between three factors: the number of children a woman has before using contraception, her age, and the contraceptive method chosen. On this basis I can identify three categories of women who are interested in contraception in Senegal: women between 40 and 45 years of age who have already had four or five children constitute the first group. For them, the contraceptive method of choice is the intrauterine device (IUD), whose efficacy is undiminished over time. Women between 35 and 40 years of age who have already had at least three children make up the second group. They tend to prefer a subcutaneous implant (JADELLE) that is activated by the release of hormones. This method lasts for about five years. Finally, the third group is composed of women between 30 and 35 years of age who have already had two or three children and whose main contraceptive method is the pill. These profiles strongly suggest a connection between the 'mother careers' achieved by women and the use of a short-, medium-, or long-term contraceptive method. These data allow me to hypothesize that husbands (and the rest of the family group) are more tolerant of contraceptive use among women who have already experienced mothering. My claim was confirmed during the conversations I had with women who have at least three children. Sixteen women interviewed (seven with three children and nine with more than three children) told me that their husbands were aware of the contraceptive method used by their wives and consented to it. On the contrary, of 10 women without children, only one told me that her husband was aware that she was using contraception. In the rest of the cases, women underlined how husbands and other family members, such as mothers-in-law and sisters-in-law, strongly

18 N Bajos, 'Tensions normatives et rapport des femmes à la contraception dans 4 pays africains' (2013) 68 *Population* 17.

opposed contraception.[19] In sum, for women with an extended 'mother career', the use of contraception is more acceptable than for women without previous mothering experiences.

Women's resistance

Despite these findings, my fieldwork revealed that more and more Senegalese women are choosing to use contraception without their husbands' consent or without having already become mothers. These women, who are usually between 25 and 30 years old and whose social profiles vary significantly between, and within, the urban and the rural areas, share two common characteristics. First, they have the opportunity to go to a hospital service located far from their district of residence. According to some of the midwives who work in the services, this strategy aims to limit the risk of running into a member or close acquaintance of their family or their husband's family.

The second commonality between these women is the preference for hormonal injections (DEPO), the effective duration of which is approximately three months after receiving the injection. According to midwives, the choice of hormonal injections is not only related to their cost. The price of this method (about 50 cents per injection) is lower than the cost of the pill (about 50 cents for a one-month supply). Another reason behind women's preference of hormonal injections over the pill is their perception that an injection is a *more discreet* or *less perceptible* method of birth control because it does not require daily intake of the drug. The aim, then, is to ensure that their decision remains 'invisible' to other members of the social group, and especially to their husbands, who presumably oppose the choice. This method also seems to attract women for a third reason: it gives them the possibility to re-enter the 'reproductive circuit' whenever they choose, unlike the medium-term and long-term contraceptive methods. In other words, the women say that the hormonal injections allow them not only to discreetly control *whether* they get pregnant or not, but also to determine for themselves on a finer time scale *when* they do or do not become pregnant.

In addition to these shared elements, there are also some important differences in the experiences of women who choose to use contraception. One example is the women's relationships to midwives, who are primarily responsible for the medical services that provide contraception in Senegal. These relationships can differ depending on the individual situation of the women, especially whether they have already had children before accessing family planning services. Fieldwork data show that midwives often experience a conflict between three different principles governing their work: the ethical code of their profession, which dictates that they act in the best interests of the health and well-being of all women; the tenets laid out in the national law on contraception in Senegal; and the society's values and norms. The difficulty of reconciling these principles emerges during midwives' consultations both with women who have already had children and are seeking contraception without their husbands' consent and with women who have not yet had children and are nevertheless seeking contraception without their husbands' consent. Midwives' interpretation of women's right to choose seems to differ depending on which of these two situations they encounter. In the first case they tend to assume the role of women's allies, helping them to pursue their personal choice. Many midwives, for example, agree to keep the women's *carnet de santé* (the booklet in which the women's medical history is recorded) in the facility rather than having the women bring them home, where they would risk being

19 N Bajos and M Ferrand, 'La contraception, levier réel ou symbolique de la domination masculine' (2004) 22 *Sciences Sociales et Santé* 117.

discovered by the husbands. Others give advice on how to avoid the suspicions of mothers-in-law and sisters-in-law. Some provide their phone number so that women can call them if they are in trouble. The midwives justify giving such support on the grounds that the use of contraception after one or more pregnancies may be beneficial to the health of women and their children. In the second case, by contrast, one can observe a greater distance between women and midwives. The different climate during the meetings is evidenced by, for example, the critical attitude of midwives, who persistently enquire into the motivations behind the women's personal choice to use contraception. Many of the midwives with whom I talked explained that the problem is not that women do not have their husbands' consent (as required by the law), but the fact that they do not yet have any children.

Looking for *mothering autonomy*: challenges and risks

The difficulties faced by the latter category of women are not limited to their relationships to midwives. Their reproductive behaviour often exacerbates other problems within the social group. Aida's story is exemplary in this respect.[20] When I met her in Italy in 2012,[21] Aida was 29 years old and had been married to Moustapha for seven years. However, it was only in the fourth year of their marriage that they started living together. Moustapha, in fact, immigrated to Italy in 1996, when he was 23. He is 10 years older than Aida. Moustapha comes to Senegal once a year for about a month. It was during one of these trips that he met Aida and the two decided to marry. After the wedding Aida moved in with her husband's family, which is usual in the traditional marriage system. During the first three years of marriage, however, Mustapha's family began to frown upon Aida because she had not yet become pregnant. They were not aware that she had unilaterally decided to prevent pregnancy by having hormonal injections during her husband's stays in Senegal. Aida very much wanted to join Moustapha in Italy, but was afraid that being pregnant or having a child would make it more difficult for her to migrate to Italy. Her decision to use birth control, however, exposed her to the same risks faced by most of the women encountered in Senegal who choose to use contraception despite the social expectations of the group.

The first risk is divorce. According to Fatou Binetou Dial,[22] one main cause of divorce in Senegal is childlessness. In Islam and within the Senegalese legal system, the primary proof of a successful marriage is children. Moreover, the percentage of divorces that are demanded by husbands because of their wives' non-compliance with marital obligations (17 per cent per year) shows that in Senegal the lack of children is still usually blamed on women.[23]

The second risk, which is related to the first, is the possibility that the husband will take another wife.[24] The probability of this occurrence, which affects all women whether they have children or not, increases in the case of childless marriages and helps explain the high fertility rates in Senegal.[25] In the polygamist model, the absence of one wife's monopoly over the husband implies the division of the inheritance among the different wives according to

20 All names are pseudonyms.

21 The research I carried out in Senegal is part of my PhD project, which also included long-term fieldwork (13 months) in Italy (Val d'Elsa area) among Senegalese migrant women.

22 FB Dial, *Mariage et divorce à Dakar: itinéraires féminins* (Éditions Karthala 2008).

23 Héritier (n 2).

24 S Fainzang and O Journet, *La femme de mon mari. Anthropologie du mariage polygamique en Afrique et en France* (Éditions L'Harmattan 1988).

25 N Mondain, 'L'évolution de la polygamie en milieu rural sénégalais: Institution en crise ou en mutation?' (2004) 33 *Cahiers Québécois de Démographie* 273.

the number of children each has.[26] This helps explain why women are more willing to invest in a 'mother career' than to choose not to have children.

The third risk is the suspicion on the part of other members of the group that the woman is sterile. In Senegalese culture, sterility or even the suspicion of sterility is a *social stigma*. Childless women, in fact, are not considered real women, and their behaviour is often associated with witchcraft (*dëmm* in Wolof). In this sense, the cultural imaginary contributes to the negative representation of these women but, at the same time, offers a number of traditional medical remedies for this social anomaly.[27]

All these risks are present in Aida's story. The lack of children, despite the regular meetings with her husband in Senegal, increasingly became the focus of criticism from her in-laws. On the one hand, they strongly urged Moustapha to 'change' his wife or, at least, to take a second wife in order to secure a descendent for himself. On the other hand, the presumed sterility of Aida led Moustapha's mother and sisters to search for a solution. At first they solicited the help of a traditional healer. The sacrifices to the ancestors suggested by the healer, however, did not have the desired effect of helping Aida become pregnant. Then they decided to consult a local priest (*marabout* in Wolof). This time the advice was to make an offering to the mosque and to intensify their prayers. Faced with the failure of this second attempt, the criticism against Aida increased. Ever more tired of these accusations, Aida chose to undergo a medical fertility test as suggested by a midwife to whom she explained her personal situation. It was only after 'proving' her fertility that Aida could convince her mother-in-law that the best solution for having children would be to spend more time with Moustapha by joining him in Italy. At the same time, Aida's family started to insinuate that the absence of children was caused by Moustapha and proposed that he also undergo a fertility test. This proposal produced a conflict between the two families and an increase in the pressure on Moustapha who, following the solution *strategically* proposed by Aida, decided to take her to Italy. This was how Aida's dream of migrating was realized.

Despite the geographical distance, however, the social pressure from the families continued and became ever more insistent right up to the moment when Aida finally became pregnant. After the birth of her first child, Aida decided to tell the truth to her husband, confessing her decision to use contraception during his stays in Senegal. As a result of this confession, Aida's family had to repay the costs of the traditional remedies that Moustapha's mother and sisters had undertaken to help Aida become pregnant. Despite this act of reconciliation, Moustapha's family continued to nurture hatred against Aida because they felt betrayed and deceived. It was only after three years, when Aida chose to name her twins born in Italy after Moustapha's mother and father, that the conflict between the two families came to an end.

Conclusion

Women's reproductive behaviour in Senegal is subject to several systems of norms: legal, social, and cultural. Within this context, more and more women are trying to reflect upon and reconcile the normative systems, as is demonstrated by their increasing use of contraception. In the experiences of these women, however, using contraception does not appear

26 Diop (n 13).

27 A Barry, *Le corps, la mort et l'esprit du lignage. L'ancêtre et le sorcier en clinique africaine* (Éditions L'Harmattan 2001).

to be a rejection of the local system of values nor a form of 'liberation' from motherhood.[28] They are not opposing the linkage between being a woman and being a mother, but rather trying to find a balance between social expectations and their personal life projects. The intention is not to emancipate themselves from the traditions of the group, but to join these traditions in a *new individual form*. Similarly, the creative use of the possibilities offered by the law as well as the attempt to act *tactically*[29] to find a balance between their personal desires and the expectations of the group can be understood as a form of agency that guarantees them a greater level of autonomy within the legal and social systems. In conclusion, what emerges from the experiences of women who choose to use contraception in Senegal, with or without the support of midwives and the consent of their husbands, is an example of *mothering autonomy*, whereby women take advantage of the rights allowed by law in order to adapt the social norms to their personal wishes.

28 Héritier (n 2).

29 M de Certeau, *L'invention du quotidien, 1. Arts de faire* (Éditions Gallimard 1980).

19 Autonomous aspirations? Re-reading the CEDAW drafting process and examining Muslim women's contributions

Shaheen Sardar Ali and Arjumand Bano Kazmi

Introduction

The ratification process of the United Nations Convention on the Elimination of All Forms of Discrimination Against Women (CEDAW) brought into sharp relief the chasm between the rhetoric and the reality of women's rights worldwide. This treaty, adopted by the General Assembly of the United Nations on 18 December 1979,[1] has been hailed as an international bill of women's rights and is the most comprehensive treaty in the field,[2] with 188 ratifications.[3] But it is also the treaty that, upon signature and ratification, generated the largest number of reservations from states.[4] Among those states entering reservations, some Muslim states specifically mentioned Islam and Islamic law as their reasons,[5] while others did not invoke religious grounds.[6] A third group of Muslim states ratified CEDAW without entering any reservations at all, or to Article 29 alone,[7] while a fourth group (Iran and Somalia) has neither signed nor ratified the treaty.[8]

1 Adopted by UN General Assembly Resolution 34/180 (1979).

2 EY Krivenko, *Women, Islam and International Law Within the Context of the Convention on the Elimination of All Forms of Discrimination Against Women* (Martinus Nijhoff Publishers 2009) 43 describes CEDAW as 'the most progressive and comprehensive among existing international treaties dealing with women's human rights'. That is not to say that CEDAW has not been critiqued for its 'silences', including the omission of violence against women.

3 As of April 2014, the latest state party being Palestine.

4 A list of reservations is available at <www.un.org/womenwatch/daw/cedaw/reservations-country.htm> accessed 28 July 2016.

5 Bahrain, Bangladesh, Brunei, Egypt, Iraq, Kuwait, Libya, Malaysia, the Maldives, Mauritania, Morocco, Oman, Pakistan, Saudi Arabia, Syria, and the UAE have expressly mentioned Islamic law and sharia as reasons for entering reservations to substantive provisions. We have used membership in the OIC at the time of the drafting of CEDAW as the criterion for inclusion as a Muslim state. Israel too reserved on the basis of religion, specifically 'concerning the appointment of women to serve as judges of religious courts where this is prohibited by the laws of any of the religious communities in Israel', and 'to the extent that the laws on personal status which are binding on the various religious communities in Israel do not conform with the provisions' of one article (see <www.un.org/womenwatch/daw/cedaw/reservations-country.htm> accessed 9 September 2016).

6 Algeria, Jordan, Niger, Tunisia, and Turkey have entered reservations on the basis of national laws.

7 Indonesia, Mauritius, and Yemen have reserved on Article 29 (on dispute resolution), but not on any of the substantive provisions. Afghanistan, Albania, Azerbaijan, Benin, Bosnia Herzegovina, Burkina Faso, Chad, the Comoros, Cote d'Ivoire, Djibouti, Gabon, Gambia, Guyana, Guinea, Guinea-Bissau, Kyrgyzstan, Lebanon, Mozambique, Mali, Palestine, Senegal, Sierra Leone, Sudan, Surinam, Tajikistan, Togo, Turkmenistan, Uzbekistan, and Uganda have not entered reservations.

8 Texts of all reservations are available at <www.un.org/womenwatch/daw/cedaw/reservations-country.htm> accessed 9 September 2016.

DOI: 10.4324/9781315413617-23

Literature on CEDAW in relation to Muslim states has focused almost entirely on their reservations which, as stated earlier, are neither similar nor homogeneous.[9] The plurality of positions and interpretations adopted by these states demonstrates the complexity of Islamic legal traditions as well as the political nature of the reservations.[10] In addition, there are widely held assumptions as to why reservations were rendered. For example, it is often assumed that Muslim states' delegates perhaps did not actively participate in the discussions and drafting of CEDAW, and/or failed to articulate the nuances of their national laws and religious and cultural practices, hence the subsequent state reservations were expected. It is also inferred that even if Muslim delegates did participate, they belonged to the elite of their respective societies and could only represent a minority of women in their countries; therefore, their participation was bound to clash with the religious and cultural practices of the majority. By the same token, a third assumption considers women delegates from Muslim states to be merely diplomatic 'window-dressing', whereas the ultimate decision-making remains in the hands of state bureaucracy.

These assumptions obscure the contribution of women delegates from Muslim states to the making of CEDAW and other human rights treaties. They also characterize the 'nature' of participation as *weak* and *subservient* to a number of political and cultural factors. Surprisingly, even in academic discussions, there has been sparse critical engagement with the drafting processes of CEDAW and interventions made by representatives of Muslim states during the deliberations. Little is made of the positive role played by delegates from Muslim states, which includes ensuring a developmental perspective on women's human rights in collaboration with other states from the developing South. This has led to the impression that, as Waltz states with reference to the drafting processes of the Universal Declaration on Human Rights, the International Covenant on Civil and Political Rights, and the International Covenant on Economic, Social and Cultural Rights, 'Frequently, it is supposed

9 N Burrows, 'The 1979 Convention on the Elimination of All Forms of Discrimination Against Women' (1985) 32 *Netherlands International Law Review* 419; B Clark, 'The Vienna Convention Reservations Regime and the Convention on Discrimination Against Women' (1991) 85 *American Journal of International Law* 281; CE Welch, 'Human Rights and African Women: A Comparison of Protection Under Two Major Treaties' (1993) 15 *Human Rights Quarterly* 853; AE Mayer, *Islam and Human Rights: Tradition and Politics* (3rd edn, Westview Press 1999); J Resnik, 'Comparative Inequalities: CEDAW, the Jurisdiction of Gender, and the Heterogeneity of Transnational Law Production' (2012) 10(2) *International Journal of Constitutional Law* 531; LR Pruitt, 'Migration, Development, and the Promise of CEDAW for Rural Women' (2009) 30 *Michigan Journal of International Law* 707 (this article does refer to some discussions in the drafting process, but it does not focus on Muslim states); F Raday, 'Gender and Democratic Citizenship: The Impact of CEDAW' (2012) 10(2) *International Journal of Constitutional Law* 512; MA Freeman, C Chinkin, and B Rudolf (eds), *The UN Convention on the Elimination of All Forms of Discrimination Against Women: A Commentary* (Oxford University Press 2013); E Sepper, 'Confronting the "Sacred and Unchangeable": The Obligation to Modify Cultural Patterns under the Women's Discrimination Treaty' in S Kouvo and Z Pearson (eds), *Gender and International Law* (Routledge 2014). SS Ali's doctoral research and some subsequent work also focuses on this aspect of CEDAW and reservations of Muslim states: see SS Ali, *Gender and Human Rights in Islam and International Law: Equal Before Allah, Unequal Before Man?* (Kluwer Law International 2000); SS Ali (ed) *Conceptualising Islamic Law, CEDAW and Women's Human Rights in Plural Legal Settings: A Comparative Analysis of Application of CEDAW in Bangladesh, India and Pakistan* (UNIFEM Regional Office 2006) 245; SS Ali, 'Women's Rights, CEDAW and International Human Rights Debates: Toward Empowerment?' in J Parpart, S Rai, and K Staudt (eds), *Rethinking Empowerment: Gender and Development in a Global/Local World* (Routledge 2002) 61.

10 SS Ali's *Modern Challenges to Islamic Law* (Cambridge University Press 2016) argues that the plurality of understandings and interpretations of sharia among Muslim countries results in diverse responses to CEDAW and their reservations to the Convention.

that Muslim states were either absent, fundamentally contested the process and project, or played no significant role. That is not the case.'[11]

In response to the gap in the literature and to the widely held assumptions, this chapter has a dual aim. First, it highlights the inputs of delegates from Muslim states during the drafting process of CEDAW. It critically engages with the archival records of the CEDAW drafting processes to demonstrate that not only did the delegates of Muslim states actively participate, their contributions were pragmatic as well as aspirational. Muslim women delegates were present not simply as 'passive witnesses' but as active participants – negotiating, challenging, and contributing. Despite their ideological, political, cultural, and religious diversity, their role was part of a complex and multi-layered process of diplomacy, alliance making, and consensus building.

The second aim of this chapter is to take a step further to examine the 'complex' and 'multi-layered' *nature* of the participation of Muslim women delegates. In so doing, it goes beyond existing explanations behind reservations and questions the widely held assumptions that consider the participation of Muslim women delegates 'weak' or 'subservient' to political and cultural factors. By using a lens of 'relational autonomy', the chapter *analyses the nature of participation by examining the participants.* It explores and brings to the fore the profiles of Muslim women delegates who led their national delegations at the UN Commission on the Status of Women (CSW). It enquires into their political standpoints and develops an understanding of the extent to which their contributions could be labelled 'autonomous' or 'subservient' to the demands of political diplomacy. This exploration has tremendous relevance to the academic debates that explore the lawmaking process by examining the lawmakers.

The chapter is presented in four parts: after this introduction, the second part analyses the nature of the participation and contribution of Muslim women in the making of CEDAW. In so doing, it engages with the archival records and presents the evidence of active and aspirational participation of Muslim women delegates. Thus, part two sets the context in which a theoretical understanding of the participation and contribution of Muslim women delegates will be supported. Part three briefly discusses the notion of 'relational autonomy' and develops critical insights into how and why Muslim women delegates participated and contributed in the manner in which they did. In response to the assumptions of their participation as 'weak' or 'subservient' to political and cultural factors, the key inquiry in this part is to investigate whether these delegates participated 'autonomously'. It does so by engaging with the profiles of a few Muslim women who led their countries in the drafting processes.[12] Finally, part four concludes with an informed assertion that Muslim women

11 S Waltz, 'Universal Human Rights: The Contribution of Muslim States' (2004) *Human Rights Quarterly* 799, 801. The exception to this statement is in the form of a book on the *travaux preparatoires* of CEDAW, which is not the same as an analytical account of Muslim states' interventions. See LA Rehof, *Guide to the* Travaux Preparatoires *of the United Nations Convention on the Elimination of All Forms of Discrimination Against Women* (Martinus Nijhoff Publishers 1993); see also Freeman, Chinkin, and Rudolf (eds) (n 9), in which commentary on each article refers to the *travaux* of that particular provision. There is literature available on the contribution of Muslim states in the drafting of the Universal Declaration of Human Rights, of which the most prominent is S Waltz (n 11). There are synergies between Waltz's work and the present chapter, which takes forward her suggestion to look into records of other human rights treaty drafting processes.

12 The profiles of only a few Muslim women delegates are discussed here by way of illustration and to strengthen the argument. The brevity and scope of this chapter do not allow the authors to bring in a large number of profiles.

delegates to the CSW were not only proactive in negotiating the treaty, they did so as fully autonomous beings, where autonomy is understood in its 'relational' sense.

The CEDAW drafting process and the contribution of Muslim women delegates

Lawmaking as a process speaks to its times and is born of multiple narratives, and the drafting of CEDAW was no exception. Socio-economic, religious, political, and ideological posturing at the global level evidently contribute to a treaty during its drafting as well as after its adoption, and in the context of the present inquiry this was manifested through the wider capitalist–socialist polarity, since CEDAW was drafted at the height of the Cold War. Divisions were also visible in those developed and developing countries' concerns and priorities under the umbrella of the burgeoning 'non-aligned' movement, as well as in the positions adopted by Muslim states. Krivenko has noted that the process and circumstances of the adoption of CEDAW were characterized by two main tendencies:

> Firstly, when the idea about a convention on women appeared, there were many voices arguing that such a convention would be unnecessary and superfluous. When it nevertheless came to the negotiation of such a convention this tendency had been transformed into an ideological and religious confrontation and, therefore, a need to use 'constructive ambiguity' in formulating the terms of the future convention.[13]

The second tendency came to the fore when the Economic and Social Council (ECOSOC) declared 1975 to be International Women's Year and the General Assembly declared the 'UN Decade for Women: Equality, Development and Peace 1976–1985', raising the pressure to draft and adopt CEDAW. As a consequence, some controversial questions were put aside or left ambiguous in the text.

With this external political context in the background, the CSW was the UN body tasked with responding to women's rights issues, including taking the lead in drafting women's rights treaties. In 1972, a CSW resolution requested the Secretary-General of the UN to call upon member states to transmit their views on or proposals for a possible international convention on women's rights.[14] A working paper on a new instrument was consequently developed, and included views and comments from governments. A working group based on 'equitable geographical distribution' was set up to look at the draft treaty.[15] In all, four working groups were set up during the drafting process, starting in 1973 and ending with the adoption of CEDAW in December 1979. In all these forums, delegates from Muslim states were active participants in the drafting process, as is obvious from the records. In 1976, the CSW presented its draft to the General Assembly. This draft was discussed article by article in the Third Committee of the General Assembly, after which it was adopted.

13 Krivenko (n 2) 22. At footnote 77 on the same page she perceptively observes that 'two lines of confrontation existed at the time of elaboration of CEDAW: firstly between socialist and Western States and, secondly, between Islamic and Western and socialist States. Nowadays, the former line of confrontation has disappeared almost completely thereby reinforcing the latter line of confrontation.'

14 Resolution 5 (XXIV) of the Commission on the Status of Women.

15 At its 1856th and 1877th meetings, the ECOSOC elected 15 members: Canada, Chile, Colombia, the Dominican Republic, Egypt, Finland, Hungary, Indonesia, Liberia, Nigeria, the Philippines, the USSR, the USA, the UK, and Zaire (E/CN.6/573).

Drafting treaties is a complex and time-consuming process, not least due to the effort and perseverance required to arrive at a consensus. Especially demanding is the effort needed to instil certain aspirational and standard-setting norms within human rights treaties beyond what delegates believe their respective governments will sign up to. Thus they consciously strive for a forward-looking model of human rights 'without prejudice to national positions', and this approach indeed comes across in the records of the various drafting meetings of CEDAW. However, in the interests of full disclosure, we should note that while we were working with the archives for the purposes of this chapter, we were informed by the librarians that some of the physical records of the drafting process had been lost in transit from New York to Geneva. The records of what was said are, unfortunately, not verbatim, but are instead condensed and rather sanitized. Tone of voice, facial expression, and body language are of course all lacking, yet some statements nevertheless spring to life on the page, offering insights into the atmosphere and environment within which the drafting took place.

A notable and possibly surprising aspect of the CEDAW drafting process is that, with the exception of the occasional male delegate stepping in to cover a meeting, all the delegates to the CSW, including all those hailing from Muslim states, were themselves women.[16] Given that these were nations spread across several continents, it must be more than coincidental that their delegates were all female, yet it must be assumed that there was no formal prior agreement that this would be the case. Much more likely is that these were the most suitable candidates for the roles, chosen for their competence, expertise, and passion for human rights and women's rights.

In the records of the many meetings of the drafting committees and working groups, the interventions of some Muslim women in particular stand out. These include Mrs Haleh Esfandiari of Iran, Begum Tazeen Faridi of Pakistan, Mrs M. Tallawy and Mrs Aziza Hussein of Egypt, Mrs Lena Gueye of Senegal, and Ms Suwarni Salyo of Indonesia.[17] The contributions of Ms Kamila Tyabji of India were striking and counterintuitive on three counts: she was a Muslim representing a nation where Muslims only formed around 10 per cent of the population; her interventions did not invoke Islam or Islamic law; and she adopted a position based on secular women's rights activism. Her presence and interventions on such a public platform reflected the various possibilities of what it might mean to be 'a Muslim woman'. The same is true of Senegal's Mrs Lena Gueye, who made some highly perceptive interventions during the drafting process that were guided primarily by her desire to draft a strong treaty to advance women's rights, and who also did not allude to Islam or Islamic law.[18]

16 See Waltz (n 11) 829. Susan Waltz is quite right when she states that UN delegates hailing from Muslim states, including those assigned to the drafting processes of human rights treaties, were mostly women. These were: Mrs Shaista Ikramullah and Mrs Aziz Ahmed (Pakistan), Bedia Afnan (Iraq), and Halima Embarek Warzazi (Morocco), whose names appear in the summary records of drafting meetings of the Universal Declaration of Human Rights, the International Covenant on Civil and Political Rights, and the International Covenant on Economic, Social and Cultural Rights.

17 For the sake of consistency, we are using the terms of address for these actors as noted in the records of the drafting meetings.

18 A paper based on this chapter was presented as a keynote address at the Annual Conference of the British Association of Islamic Studies in London, April 2015, and I was asked why I was only referring to a few Muslim delegates. The reason is that the Working Groups set up to draft CEDAW were composed of representatives of various regions and legal systems, and at any given time only around one-third of delegates were from Muslim countries. These were predominantly delegates from Pakistan, Egypt, Iran, Iraq, Indonesia, and Senegal.

Despite the acknowledged gaps in the records, a fairly detailed picture of the discussions nevertheless emerges. As touched upon earlier, to judge from the subsequent academic literature on the reservations entered by states, it would seem as if most of the discussions in the drafting sessions had been generated by Muslim delegates arguing against provisions on the basis of their incompatibility with Islamic laws.[19] Furthermore, if we were to judge solely on the objections of Western states to reservations entered by Muslim states, it would appear as if those Western states were a homogeneous entity, in complete agreement with CEDAW's substantive provisions and keen advocates of them. The archival records, however, tell a far more complex story and show that such a narrow focus fails to capture the true nature of the process. As we will see in the following discussion, the drafting of CEDAW was certainly not a matter of secular, Western human rights values pitted against the entrenched religious traditions and laws of Muslim nations desperate to uphold patriarchal norms. In fact, the nations of the non-Muslim world were more than capable of bringing their own entrenched positions, legal hierarchies, and global alliances to the table, while Muslim delegates were more than capable of pressing for women's rights.

The archival records also show that there was not one sole, pre-determined script with which delegates drafting CEDAW were engaged. Rather, a number of drafts were submitted by different states or groups of states: a draft presented by the Philippines,[20] followed by a second prepared by the USSR, were based mainly upon the Declaration on the Elimination of Discrimination Against Women.[21] A third draft emerged, jointly prepared by the Philippines and the USSR,[22] followed by a draft that became known as the 'alternative' text, based on amendments to that third draft. This alternative text was put together by representatives of Egypt, Finland, the United Kingdom, the United States, and a representative of the International Labour Organization. There was also the working paper prepared by the UN Secretary-General on the basis of inputs and replies received from states, NGOs, international organizations, and specialized UN agencies.[23] Other drafts and working papers were also floated, reflective of amendments suggested at various meetings. Delegates to the drafting process did not feel restrained by one single text and proposed a variety of formulations, illustrating another fascinating fact: the delegates from Muslim states, true to their backgrounds in feminist activism, moved well beyond any pre-determined 'script' as initially placed on the negotiating table. This they did on two levels: first, by challenging traditional conceptions of Islamic family law and, second, by presenting counter-proposals reflecting the particularities of their own cultural contexts. These included proposals regarding family planning, setting a minimum age for marriage, and women's rights to education.

The first challenge came in the form of robust interventions to ensure that Article 16 expressly prohibited child marriages in the strongest possible terms. Muslim women delegates proposed that states be required to set a minimum age for marriage and that, as a protective measure, registration of marriage be made compulsory. Within traditional conceptions of Islamic family law, as well as in Muslim cultural contexts, the onset of puberty has long determined the minimum age for marriage, and this has led to an acceptance of what

19 Cold War politics and the capitalist-socialist divide are also mentioned, but the existing literature does not go into any great depth regarding the impact of the Cold War divisions on the drafting of CEDAW.
20 UN Doc. E/CN.6/573/Annex 1 of 6 November 1973.
21 UN Doc. E/CN.6/AC.1/L.2 of 7 January 1974.
22 UN Doc. E/CN.6-/AC.1/L.4 of 8 January 1974.
23 UN Doc. E.CN.6/591 of 21 July 1976.

can reasonably be classified as child marriage. Spurred on by cultural practices in Asia, the Middle East and Africa, child marriages remain one of the major hindrances to women's personal development and empowerment. Colonial rulers attempted to eliminate the practice through legislation, but with minimal success.[24] Local reformers and human rights activists later adopted a different perspective and raised it as a health issue, but popular perceptions of its permissibility on cultural and religious grounds meant that the practice continued.

Yet during the drafting of CEDAW, and especially in the CSW, all delegates from Muslim states adopted a unified stance against child marriages. Mrs Aziza Hussein stated forcefully that she 'should make clear that child marriages were prohibited' in Egypt.[25] Mrs Tazeen Faridi of Pakistan was likewise firm in her position:

> In tropical countries where puberty often occurred at an early age, it was of the greatest importance to set a minimum legal age for marriage. Pakistan had had great difficulty in introducing such a minimum and now wished to raise it.[26]

Delegates who were not shy in using Islamic law to defend positions on certain formulations during the drafting process displayed vigour and enthusiasm for moving beyond traditional understandings of the minimum age for marriage by seeking to raise it. Interestingly, the unanimity among the delegates from Muslim states on this point was not replicated in their respective national laws, where the minimum age of marriage varied with the ideological position of the regime in power.[27]

The next challenge regarded family planning, which according to some interpretations is not permitted in Islam.[28] The delegates from Muslim states supported the proposal made by the Indian delegate. Ms Kamila Tyabji (herself a Muslim woman, though not speaking from an Islamic perspective) called for '[t]he equal rights of men and women to decide freely and responsibly on the number and spacing of their children and to have access to the information, education and means to enable them to exercise this right'.[29] Mrs Aziza Hussein (who, to judge from the record, made the greatest number of interventions invoking Islamic law) gave her unequivocal support to Ms Kamila Tyabji's proposals on women's reproductive

24 For instance, in India British colonial rule adopted the Child Marriages Restraint Act 1929.

25 E/CN.6.SR.651, para 50.

26 E/CN.6/SR.651 at para 55.

27 Prior to the 1979 revolution, Article 1049 of the Civil Code of Iran prescribed a minimum age for marriage of 15 for girls and 18 for boys. This was amended in 1991 thus: 'Marriage before reaching the age of puberty is prohibited. Note: A contract of marriage before reaching puberty is valid if authorized by the natural guardian provided that the interest of the ward has been taken into consideration.' By an amendment to Article 1210 in 1991, the age of puberty was stated as nine full lunar years for girls and 15 full lunar years for boys. By an amendment in the Civil Code, minimum age for marriage has been set at 13 and 15 respectively (MAR Taleghany (tr), *The Civil Code of Iran, Translated From the Persian* (Fred B Rothman & Co 1995). In Pakistan, the Child Marriages Restraint Act 1929 and the Muslim Family Laws Ordinance 1961 prescribe 16 as the minimum age of marriage for girls, and the same is prescribed by Egyptian law. Saudi Arabian law sets 17 as the minimum age for the marriage of girls.

28 There is no clear Qur'anic injunction in this regard, and those arguing that Islam permits contraception as well as those who believe it prohibits it tease out meanings to support their stances. Those who argue in favour cite the permission of the Prophet Muhammad for coitus interruptus, while those against believe that the duty to increase the Muslim population and therefore to not prevent a human being from coming into the world militates against family planning.

29 E/CN.6/SR.650 para 104.

rights, stating that she 'approved the text proposed by the representative of India, which filled a gap in the Declaration on the Elimination of Discrimination Against Women'.[30] The records indicate similar support from delegates from all other Muslim states.[31]

The focus thus far has been on inputs to the 'script' by delegates from Muslim states as either a challenge to or an invocation of Islamic legal traditions. But alongside this observation, it is also important to report those moments when Islamic law was *not* invoked, so as to demonstrate the broader worldview of Muslim women delegates. This is critical if we are to break the stereotypical perception that the delegates from Muslim states always adopted positions by invoking 'Islamic' perspectives. The evidence from the drafting process provides a far more complex picture, testifying to active participation without reference to Islam.

For example, women from diverse backgrounds rallied to ensure a wide range of rights in areas such as political and public life and representation (Articles 7–8). In Part III of CEDAW, women's rights to education, employment, health, and economic and social benefits (Articles 10–13) and the application of these to rural women in particular (Article 14) met with significant support from most delegates. Records show that delegates from all geographical regions were enthusiastic about including such rights, some of which were clearly aspirational in nature. In deliberations on education, delegates from the Muslim states of Indonesia, Pakistan, Egypt, Guinea, Iran, Senegal, and Morocco all supported a comprehensive article.[32] The Iranian delegate's suggestion went so far as to include 'the elimination of any stereotyped concept of masculine and feminine roles at all levels and in all forms of education, in particular by revising textbooks and school curricula accordingly and by encouraging co-education'.[33] Guinea and Indonesia were concerned about the knowledge gap between men and women and suggested a specific mention in the article to address this, whereas Egypt, Indonesia, Iran, and Pakistan wanted reference to a guarantee giving rural women adequate 'family planning advice and services'. The Pakistani delegate also wanted the phrase 'all appropriate measures shall be taken to ensure women equal opportunity at all levels' to be included.[34]

The solidarity among women and their desire to share perceptions and experiences informing their interventions was clear from the manner in which both Western and non-Western delegates spoke. Thus Mrs Marcelle Devaud of France observed that the Belgian intervention

> sought to ensure that girls had the same length of schooling as boys. Indeed, in countries like France, and particularly in the rural areas, girls often had to leave school if their mother died in order to bring up their brothers and sisters. In large families, the eldest girl was often obliged to discontinue her studies at an early age to help her mother at home. It was never the boy but always the girl, and in most cases, the eldest girl, who was sacrificed in that way.[35]

This statement resonated with Mrs Lena Gueye from Senegal, who responded by saying that 'in her country too, particularly in the rural areas, girls left school at an earlier age than

30 E/CN.6/SR.650 para 106.

31 Ibid. It is interesting that, this point having been agreed on, a reversal was sought at the 1994 International Conference on Population and Development through an alliance of self-proclaimed Muslim clergy and the Catholic Church! My thanks to Shirin Rai for highlighting this.

32 See UN Doc. E/CN.6/SR.642.

33 Ibid.

34 Ibid.

35 Ibid. 2.

boys to help their mothers at home or to get married.'[36] France's intervention is quite revealing, as one might not have expected such an admission from a country in the heart of Europe, and it is a good example of the openness of the debating environment and of delegates' eagerness to share their experiences in order to draft a comprehensive text. The important point to be learned here is that the discussion was far from being a matter of Muslim nations holding patriarchal positions based in Islamic law pitted against Western nations arguing from a position of presumed equality.

Like all legal instruments, CEDAW reflected the dominant discourse and contemporary issues in human rights of the day. The 1970s was the era of the Women in Development (WID) model for women's inclusion into development processes worldwide.[37] CEDAW delegates from the non-Western states (including Muslim states) were well aware of the limitations on the ground in their own countries regarding women's access to basic needs, yet still they grasped the opportunity provided by CEDAW to lay claim to basic rights such as health, education, and employment.[38] One example of this strategy was the proposal to include a new paragraph in the preamble, as sponsored by three Muslim states – Bangladesh, Pakistan, and Somalia – and Singapore:[39]

> Concerned also that in situations of abject poverty where basic needs of the majority of the population are not provided for, women have the least access to basic needs of life such as food, education and training for employment.[40]

In a similar vein, Morocco proposed a formulation for Article 13, which was adopted by the working group at its 33rd session:

> Each State Party shall take all appropriate measures to eliminate discrimination against women in the field of economic and social life and to ensure for women on the basis of equality the same rights as men.

Several states, including Pakistan, Benin, and Syria, made interventions proposing an equal right to participate in politics and to have leadership roles. On women's voting rights, the Pakistani delegate supported taking all appropriate measures to ensure women the right to vote without discrimination, to be eligible for election to all publicly elected bodies, to hold public office, and to exercise public functions. It is particularly interesting to note that a number of Muslim countries did not at the time allow women to vote or run for office, yet there was no note of dissent from any of the Muslim delegates in affirming their support for the drafting of this article.

One of the most ground-breaking articles in this regard is Article 14, which explicitly asserts the rights of rural women, a provision that is not included in any other human rights instrument.[41] It represents an example of delegates across geographical regions and ideological

36 Ibid.

37 See S Rai, *Gender and the Political Economy of Development* (Polity Press 2002), in particular 56–69.

38 Ibid.; see generally M Saward, *The Representative Claim* (Oxford University Press 2010).

39 A/C.3/32/WG.1/CRP.2.

40 After deliberations, the working group adopted this paragraph by consensus with minor amendments and the text now reads: 'Concerned also that in situations of poverty, women have the least access to food, health, education, training, and opportunities for employment and other needs.'

41 For a comprehensive analysis of the drafting process of Article 14, see Pruitt (n 9) and LR Pruitt, 'CEDAW and Rural Development: Empowering Women With Law from the Top Down, Activism from the Bottom Up' (2011) 41 *Baltimore Law Review* 263.

perspectives extending significant support to formulating a right that has an impact on vast segments of the world's population. In their commentary on CEDAW, Freeman et al. note that:

> The drafting of article 14 was noncontroversial. Initially, rural women had only been considered in provisions on employment and education. It was at the 26th session of the Commission on the Status of Women (CSW) in 1976 that a representative of the FAO raised the plight of rural women. She suggested that the existing drafts of the Convention did not take adequate notice of the challenges faced by rural women. The FAO representative reminded delegates about the concerns expressed at the Mexico Conference and beyond. Following the Mexico Conference, States were keen to emphasise the importance of engaging rural women in development, exemplifying the WID analysis.[42]

The working group formed to draft Article 14 comprised Egypt, India, Indonesia, Iran, Pakistan, Thailand, and the United States (four of which are Muslim states).[43] Drafts were presented to the CSW by India, which noted that two-thirds of the world's women lived in rural areas and deserved special attention. The aim of proposing a separate article was to enable rural women 'to participate, equally with men, in agricultural and rural development and to enjoy all benefits such as planning, health, training, community activities, credit, agricultural credit, agricultural reform, etc.'

The archival records clearly show the active and engaged participation of Muslim women delegates in all aspects of the making of the treaty and in all areas that the treaty touches upon, from development to educational and reproductive rights. However, arguably the most pronounced discrepancy between our analysis of the archival records and the existing CEDAW narrative is the fact that there was minimal discussion of Islamic law and sharia during the drafting process. Where the delegates did mention religion, it was in the context of the national laws of their respective states. This leads to a further important observation regarding the process: the conflation of the terms 'Islamic law', 'national law', and 'sharia'.[44] This is critical to an understanding of the broader picture of the reservations entered subsequently by Muslim states, where a similar conflation is visible. That national laws are 'based upon' Islamic law does not imply that national laws are sacrosanct or coterminous with either sharia or Islamic law, but simply that national laws may be informed by both. The outcome of this conflation had led to confusion both within Muslim communities and in the wider world. The withdrawal of reservations initially based upon 'Islamic law' by some Muslim states is an example of this confusion. If Islamic law and sharia are immutable, how can these suddenly become open to change? How can a provision of CEDAW be un-Islamic today but Islamic tomorrow, as the withdrawal of reservations would suggest? To appreciate what is happening, we must remember always to look through the lens of the interpretative plurality of Islamic legal traditions when reading the interventions of the delegates from Muslim states, and pay attention to how understandings of Islam vary with cultures, traditions, and national laws and constitutions.[45]

42 Freeman, Chinkin, and Rudolf (eds) (n 9) 361. FAO here refers to the Food and Agriculture Organization of the United Nations.

43 The Byelorussian SSR, Kenya, and France also participated in the general discussion of Article 14.

44 In *Modern Challenges to Islamic law* (Cambridge University Press 2016), Shaheen Ali has argued that sharia is the overarching umbrella of norms and principles, based on the Qur'an and Sunna, informing all aspects of life for Muslims. Islamic law is but one element of sharia, and it has historically drawn upon more than just the religious text; in other words, factors extraneous to religion inform Islamic law.

45 Ibid.

Autonomous aspirations?

Just as it is generally assumed that Muslim women delegates may have participated only on occasions where the discussions involved the (in)compatibility of the provisions of CEDAW with Islamic laws, there also appear to be other widely held assumptions that assess Muslim women delegates' participation as 'weak' or 'subservient' to political and cultural factors. The delegates are often charged with being 'elites' of their societies and therefore not truly representative of the majority of women in their respective states. They are also dismissed as diplomatic 'window-dressing' with little or no authority to make decisions on international human rights platforms.

In the preceding section we dealt with the first assumption, showing that in fact there was minimal discussion of Islamic law and sharia during the drafting process, and that Muslim women delegates were actively engaged in all discussions leading to the final treaty. They brought in contextual insights on matters beyond religion, including provisions for advancing women's rights in political and public spheres as well as their developmental rights to health, education, and employment. In this section, we argue that the Muslim women delegates were not only steeped in feminist activism and upheld equal women's rights as a universal value, they were also deeply rooted in the political, cultural, and religious local contexts that they represented. Indeed, they strove for a more nuanced approach to diplomacy without compromising either their principles and beliefs or their national laws. Furthermore, their participation and contribution must not be understood as 'weak' or 'subservient'. Rather, it should be characterized as 'autonomous', where autonomy is understood in its 'relational' sense.[46] We believe it is imperative to examine and reveal the intentions of Muslim women delegates behind the making of CEDAW. CEDAW is regarded as aspirational lawmaking, and rightly so. But it is essential to determine the factors that contributed to making it aspirational, including the participation of its Muslim member states.

There is no consensus on what constitutes the concept of 'relational autonomy'. In their anthology, MacKenzie and Stoljar (2000) attempt to 'reconceptualize and refigure' the concept of individual autonomy from a feminist perspective.[47] From this perspective, relational autonomy is an 'umbrella term' that loosely ties together a collection of views that share the conviction that autonomous selves are socially embedded and that their 'identities are formed within the context of social relationships and shaped by a complex of intersecting social determinants, such as race, class, gender, and ethnicity.'[48]

Challenging liberal conceptions of autonomy that stand on the values of self-determination or self-government and free will of people, feminist perspectives regarding autonomy are concerned with oppressive social contexts and their effects on people's choices and political will. MacKenzie and Stoljar bring together feminist perspectives on what constitutes oppressive social contexts and how they shape individuals' autonomy.

Relational theories of autonomy are broadly divided into 'procedural' and 'substantive' conceptions. Additionally, 'causal' and 'constitutive' conceptions are also being discussed. Procedural conceptions of relational autonomy are regarded as 'content neutral'. Here autonomy is not concerned with any moral values or set of preferences for what constitutes the

46 See C Mackenzie and N Stoljar, 'Introduction: Autonomy Refigured' in C Mackenzie and N Stoljar (eds), *Relational Autonomy: Feminist Perspectives on Autonomy, Agency, and the Social Self* (Oxford University Press 2000).

47 Ibid. 4.

48 Ibid. 4.

good life. In other words, autonomy is not concerned with what is morally 'right' or 'wrong'. So long as choices are made with critical self-reflection and, in that process, the person has acquired a 'capacity' that enables her to critically assess the social, structural, and historical environment in which she has come to make these choices, she is 'autonomous'.[49] Procedural theorists further argue that autonomy also requires the skills and competence necessary for self-direction, self-definition, and self-discovery.[50] Autonomy in this sense is 'integrated' and 'dynamic', as a person with these skills, competence, and the capacity to self-reflect may exercise autonomous choice against a particular oppressive environment, but she might choose not do so in another oppressive social situation. For procedural theorists, 'there can be no blueprint to what constitutes an autonomous life.' It is essentially dynamic in nature.[51]

Substantive theories of relational autonomy maintain that critical reflection alone is not enough; an autonomous person must also have 'normative competence', that is, the capacity to identify right and wrong.[52] For substantive theorists, some oppressive social conditions hinder this competence, thereby preventing people from being autonomous and 'morally responsible' for their actions.[53] Furthermore, a strong 'sense of self-worth',[54] which enables a person to put her will into action, is a key factor in exercising autonomy.

Causal and constitutive approaches to relational autonomy maintain that both social relationships and socio-historical circumstances influence people's capacities to reflect critically and make autonomous choices. Relationships with people such as parents, friends, and teachers, as well as a person's social and historical background (for example, her education and domestic culture), shape her choices and develop or hinder her capacity for autonomy.

This brief sketch of approaches to relational autonomy situates the present examination of the extent to which Muslim women delegates were autonomous in their participation and contributions to developing CEDAW. It helps us investigate their intentions and develop a narrative about 'where they were coming from', their 'standpoint', and what guided their approaches to CEDAW.

As mentioned earlier, the archival material is incomplete, which leaves certain gaps when one tries to piece together a complete story. Yet, as we have shown in part two, Muslim women's contributions to various aspirational features of the treaty are evident. There can be no doubt that these women were outstanding, well informed, vocal, and competent to inform the international lawmaking processes, bringing in the knowledge and understanding of their national laws, history, culture, and politics. For example, Mrs Aziza Hussein of Egypt, who forcefully supported Article 16 of CEDAW requiring the states to set a minimum age for marriage, was a well-educated Egyptian women's rights activist whose work was of paramount importance in creating awareness of Egypt's population problem. She set up a centre for rural women and established women's clinics that later helped in developing a formal population policy for Egypt in 1966, a family planning association in

49 J Christman, 'Relational Autonomy, Liberal Individualism, and the Social Constitution of Selves' (2004) 117(1–2) *Philosophical Studies* 143.

50 DT Meyers, *Self, Society and Personal Choice* (Columbia University Press 1989).

51 Mackenzie and Stoljar (n 46) 17.

52 Ibid. 19. See discussion on substantive theories of autonomy.

53 Ibid. Susan Wolf likewise defends substantive accounts of autonomy. See 'Sanity and the Metaphysics of Responsibility' in F Schoeman (ed) *Responsibility, Character and the Emotions* (Cambridge University Press 1987).

54 Ibid. 20. See also Paul Benson's normative competence theory in 'Free Agency and Self-Worth' (1994) 9112 *Journal of Philosophy* 650–658.

1967, and changes in family law in 1979. Born in 1919 in Zefta, Gharbia Governorate, and having graduated from the American University of Cairo, she was the first female Egyptian member of the UN to address the General Assembly. Knowing the traditional conceptions of Islamic family law as well as the local social and cultural contexts of Muslim states, where child marriages remained one of the most significant obstacles to women's personal development, health, and empowerment, Mrs Aziza Hussein's approach to Islamic legal traditions was plural and dynamic. Recognizing the shortcomings of the Egyptian national legislation with regard to Article 16 of CEDAW on setting a minimum age for marriage, Mrs Hussein stated that

> under current Egyptian legislation women did not have equal rights let alone equal duties with men in the matter of marriage and the dissolution of marriage. But measures to improve the situation were under consideration . . . [and] time would be needed to develop a system ensuring equality of rights to men and women without undermining the unity and concord of the family and its legitimate interests from the legal point of view.[55]

Mrs Hussein had exceeded the mandate of her official position by expressing frustration at the unequal status of women and men in Egyptian society, but proceeded on a more positive note to say that all was not lost – they were aware of this undesirable situation but needed time to improve matters.

It may be argued that Mrs Aziza Hussein led the Egyptian delegation at CSW as an individual who not only had the 'capacities' and 'skills' for critical reflection, but also had a positive and aspirational approach to what any women's rights treaty must achieve both in Egypt and globally. She was indeed not neutral to the content of Article 16 and ensured that her contribution to its development raised the bar for Egyptian governments to protect women's rights in their national legislations. Thus she meets the conditions of being an autonomous contributor to CEDAW, sensitive to the demands of her diplomatic and activist roles and taking firm positions on approaches to advancing women's rights where most needed.

It must not have been easy to challenge traditional conceptions of Islamic legal traditions and, in so doing, implicitly accept the plurality of interpretations among Muslim states. What Muslim women delegates notably also achieved was a willingness and ability to agree on common values across representative Muslim states and with non-Muslim state partners to CEDAW. On the right to education, delegates from the Muslim states of Indonesia, Pakistan, Egypt, Guinea, Iran, Senegal, and Morocco all supported a comprehensive article.[56] Mrs Aziza Hussein of Egypt expressed concern about France's proposed wording of Article 10, stating that equal access to real professional training must not be restricted to 'young' people only, but was important to people of all ages.[57]

One of the most pronounced themes to emerge during the CEDAW drafting process was the sense of solidarity among delegates across religious, cultural, ideological, and political divides with the common aim of adopting a robust women's rights treaty. CEDAW's long preamble is one example,[58] distinctive in that it recalls the broad historical, economic,

55 E/CN.6/SR.650 para 74.
56 See (n 32).
57 Ibid., art 10.
58 It is twice the length of the preamble to the Universal Declaration of Human Rights.

political, and social factors contributing to discrimination against women, with mention of colonialism, apartheid, imperialism, and other factors one would not necessarily expect to find in a women's rights treaty. For example, the preamble speaks eloquently to the alliances fostered among former colonized states, irrespective of the ideological, political, or religious differences between and among them, despite the opposition of Western states to the inclusion of such references. This was possible because, in addition to the Cold War alignment of nations into capitalist and socialist camps, during the 1970s the developing South was positioning itself under the umbrella of the non-aligned movement. The combination of socialist, developing, and non-aligned states outnumbered the capitalist Western bloc, allowing this contested preamble to be included in the treaty.[59]

In the drafting of CEDAW's preamble, Muslim women delegates, the majority of whom were also representing the developing South, ensured that the political inequalities of the past and the present that contribute to structural inequalities facing women in their states were acknowledged. For example, in a moment of exasperation at some delegates' insistence that the CSW was a political body rather than one dedicated solely to advancing women's rights, Mrs Tazeen Faridi of the Pakistani delegation, an outspoken women's rights activist, declared that she was

> astonished to hear that the Commission was a political body. The Commission had been established as a result of the steady pressure exerted by women's organizations in the world in order to promote the cause of women. It was above any political considerations. It endeavoured to ascertain what was good or bad for women, and not for countries. It was composed of women experts who placed women's interests before everything else, and she expressed the hope that it would continue to work in that spirit.[60]

Ms Kamila Tyabji, representing India, and Mrs Tazeen Faridi were both brought up by politically active parents during and soon after the independence of India and Pakistan; they had the best education available and exceptional careers; and they shared a conviction for advancing women's rights, which is evident from their voluntary and professional engagements. Being Muslim women delegates to CEDAW, their presence and contribution cannot be overlooked. The choices they made while helping to develop CEDAW into a robust and contextually relevant treaty that speaks to their beliefs and is sensitive to their domestic legal, political, cultural, social, and religious particularities must be considered 'autonomous', and their aspirations were supported by their deep knowledge of and ability to reflect on local domestic situations.

Such examples also reflect the delegates' strong sense of rootedness in their national and local contexts and their acute awareness of the issues facing women in their respective jurisdictions. Their inputs into the drafting process also resonate with their profiles as autonomous activists. Mrs Tazeen Faridi, while working on a health and education project in the most deprived areas of Karachi, often rode in a donkey cart, an act that 'horrified other company wives'. Ms Kamila Tyabji, a daughter of India's elite who had lived on London's Park Lane, left her comfortable life as an insurance lawyer and walked through rural India to support famine victims. Mrs Aziza Hussein set up Egypt's first women's rural health centre and

59 T Meron, *Human Rights Law-Making in the United Nations: A Critique of Instruments and Process* (Oxford Scholarship Online March 2012).

60 E/CN.6/SR.667, point 6, p 2.

worked with rural women in family planning and in campaigning against female genital mutilation. While the records suggest that Mrs Hussein did not appear to support the equality of men and women within the family, her 'real' self nevertheless came to light in one statement:

> The draft convention had good legal provisions and she generally accepted its broad lines, but could not agree to the provisions concerning measures to ensure protection for women in absolute and general terms. Although recognizing the need for protective measures, especially for working women, who had suffered the worst discrimination, any idea that women were the weaker sex, must be avoided.[61]

In deliberations on Article 11 (on employment), Mrs Hussein expressed wariness of governments that might take advantage of the phrase 'equal treatment with men as regards working conditions' in order to deny women the special attention they deserved.[62]

Relationally autonomous conceptions also emphasize that external social situations must be conducive to the exercise of autonomous choices. Reaching agreements and developing consensus on fundamental values and principles of women's rights was a shared conviction among the delegates. Once again, Muslim women delegates were active supporters of deliberation and consensus-based decision-making. For example, Mrs Tazeen Faridi

> welcomed the fact that the Commission had been able to work out the essential elements which would serve as a basis for amending the legislation of countries throughout the world in the area with which the draft Convention was concerned. Her delegation had entered a few reservations; however, they did not relate to the Convention as a whole but only some of its minor aspects. The draft was of course not perfect and could be improved, but the fact that many countries had approved it indicated that, despite differences in their systems and ways of life, they had much in common.[63]

And the view of the Egyptian delegate meanwhile was that

> [o]wing to differences of views in the Commission, it had been difficult to reach agreement. The Commission should therefore take pride in the fact that the draft Convention had been adopted by consensus, which showed that women from different regions of the world had a great number of interests in common.[64]

In reading accounts of their interventions, it is striking to note the degree to which the delegates from the Western Hemisphere and the developed world come across as lukewarm towards what was undeniably a great achievement – the drafting of an international bill of women's rights – whereas the delegates from Muslim states took the opportunity to point out the core common universal values that had been agreed upon.[65] Yet the focus of

61 E/CN.6/SR.615, para 25.
62 E/CN.6/SR.646, para 55.
63 E/CN.6.SR.679, para 29.
64 E/CN.6.SR.679, para 35.
65 As mentioned earlier, one-sixth of the CEDAW Working Group consisted of representatives from Muslim states. The interventions of the Egyptian and Pakistani delegates are presented as examples of the viewpoint of the Muslim delegates in general.

academic literature on reservations and on objections entered by Western states to the reservations of Muslim states suggests a different angle is being taken.[66] Almost by default, and ignoring the drafting process, the literature makes it appear as if it was the delegates from *Western* states who were the most enthusiastic supporters of women's rights, with *Muslim* delegates holding them back.

Concluding remarks

The discussion in this chapter leaves little doubt that Muslim women delegates were outstanding, well-informed, vocal, and competent women, steeped in their own cultural and religious contexts as well as in issues of international law. They came across as astute professionals, realistic as well as aspirational in their inputs, prepared to defend their corner but also to leave doors open for future developments. They demonstrated an admirable rootedness in their local contexts and were prepared to voice their concerns regarding formulations of CEDAW that they believed would endanger ratification and acceptance within their communities. They sought to express the diverse positions and contexts of women as well as the constraints under which they operated in their respective societies. The CEDAW drafting processes witnessed robust interventions from all the delegates from Muslim states. These interventions aimed at protecting their ideological, political, and national interests and their national constitutions and laws, and expressed their support for women's rights. Their participation and contribution as relationally autonomous persons who were nevertheless unavoidably bound by their gender, culture, tradition, and politics is a fascinating example of gendered discourse in international lawmaking.

This autonomous participation offers another possible reason for the number of reservations entered by Muslim states. In weaving together a counter-narrative of the drafting process, we must acknowledge that Muslim women delegates came together in solidarity to consciously subvert the status quo. They certainly accomplished this by raising the bar of women's rights, despite the knowledge that some provisions would be unacceptable to their respective states and governments.

However, their struggle for recognition as activists for women rights rooted in local contexts still continues. To this day, Muslim women representatives to the Committee on the Elimination of All Forms of Discrimination against Women are often accused of being distant and ignorant of the realities facing local 'women on the ground'. Their contributions to advancing women's rights are seen as limited to their 'Western' 'liberal' ideals of human rights, and their intentions are questioned by none other than officials from their own countries. Yet we know that CEDAW was a product of years of effort by women's organizations and women activists around the world, including Muslim women activists and their organizations. The implementation of CEDAW and representation at its

66 Besides the works cited above, the following have focused on Muslim states' reservations: J Connors, 'The Women's Convention in the Muslim World' in M Yamani (ed) *Feminism and Islam: Legal and Literary Perspectives* (Ithaca 1996); A Haugestad, 'Reservations to the United Nations Women's Convention, with Special Focus on Reservations Submitted by Muslim Countries' (1995) 39 *Studies in Women's Law* 39; L Lijnzaad, *Reservations to UN Human Rights Treaties: Ratify and Ruin?* (Martinus Nijhoff Publishers 1995); C Chinkin, 'Reservations and Objections to the Convention on the Elimination of All Forms of Discrimination Against Women' in JP Gardner (ed), *Human Rights as General Norms and a State's Right to Opt Out: Reservations and Objections to Human Rights Conventions* (British Institute of International and Comparative Law 1997).

committee are still supported by women's voluntary organizations through advocacy and shadow reporting parallel to the official reports published by the states. Collectively, these efforts have brought numerous changes to the domestic legislation of many countries.[67] National policy frameworks have been informed by CEDAW and its requirements. And in all this, it is women activists across the world who – with shared conviction for women's human rights, gender equality, and justice – are continuing to ensure that aspirations are transformed into actions.

67 A Stewart, 'Aspirations to Action: 25 Years of the Women's Convention (CEDAW)' (British Council Report 2004).

20 'That's not our culture'

Paradoxes of personal property in indigenous self-governance

Ian Kalman

If you cannot govern yourselves to your own satisfaction, there are always those who are willing to govern *you* to *their* own satisfaction.

—Ernest Benedict, Mohawk elder (1941)[1]

Introduction

'Self-governance' is on a lot of people's minds in Akwesasne, a single indigenous community of roughly 14,000 members that straddles the borders of Quebec and Ontario in Canada and New York State in the United States. Akwesasne is the largest community in the Mohawk Nation, one of the six nations of the Haudenosaunee, or Iroquois, confederacy. By some measures, Akwesasne has long been self-governing; by others, it is under the strict control of Canadian and American authorities.

As members of the Haudenosaunee (Iroquois) confederacy, Akwesasronon (people of Akwesasne) have produced and travelled on their own passports since the 1920s. They have their own justice department, their own police departments and traffic court, their own licensing for local fishing, and their own schools, emergency services, and medical centre with a substantial traditional medicine clinic. While the buildings on the reserve are mostly indistinguishable from those in the surrounding region of upstate New York, various signs proclaim 'You are on Indian land,' as stores such as Three Feathers and The Bear's Den celebrate Mohawk clans, symbols, and other traditions. Most American and Canadian government officers do not set foot within the community without invitation, especially when doing so would involve traversing an international border. By many measures, Akwesasne is more autonomous than most other indigenous communities in North America.

At the same time, like other indigenous North American communities, Akwesasne's governing structures are mandated by the United States and Canada, as are their budgets for many essential services. There are also some restrictions particular to Akwesasne that are not shared elsewhere. Many in Akwesasne are not free to travel far beyond their homes without having to present themselves to US or Canadian customs and immigration officers. US Border Patrol officers covertly and blatantly patrol the areas around the territory, often stopping people many dozens of miles away from the borderline. The community, long referred to as a 'jurisdictional nightmare',[2] is answerable to two federal governments (the

1 Cited in LM Hauptman, *Seven Generations of Iroquois Leadership: The Six Nations Since 1800* (Syracuse University Press 2008) 164, emphasis in original.

2 See <www.akwesasne.ca> accessed 3 May 2017.

DOI: 10.4324/9781315413617-24

United States and Canada), two provincial governments (Quebec and Ontario), and one state (New York), as well as two Mohawk governments (an 'American' government south of the border and a 'Canadian' government to the north), not to mention several institutions describing themselves as the community's traditional governing body. In a nutshell, Akwesasne is often beholden to all, and often beholden to none.

Whereas among most indigenous nations the eventual attainment of 'self-determination' is seen as the ultimate objective, in Akwesasne the dialogue is more often about the ongoing exercise of sovereignty. Sovereignty, in this view, is something Akwesasne and other Haudenosaunee peoples have always held, even if unrecognized by settler states. 'Self-governance' is, depending on to whom one talks and the context of the conversation, either something Akwesasne has already had for more than a century or a pipe-dream, or something in between.

These days, 'self-governance' has a specific meaning for officers in the Mohawk Council of Akwesasne (MCA), the elected Mohawk government charged with administering portions of the community north of the borderline. Self-governance, in this context, means extrication from the Indian Act of Canada, which is the main piece of legislation that delimits the rights and restrictions of First Nations in Canada, as well as everything from membership to governance to funding. The MCA is one of several indigenous political organizations undergoing the multi-year process of designing its own governing and legislative structure, and vacating those that Canada has imposed under the Indian Act.

These efforts were the topic of a presentation entitled 'The Indian Act and You', which I attended on 1 November 2012 in a recreation hall in Akwesasne. The presentation was one of several in a multi-year community consultation process organized by the MCA's *Entwetatha:wi* ('nation-building') programme. Translated literally, *entwetatha:wi* means 'we will govern,' and several meetings such as this one had been held to apprise community members of the advantages of self-governance and of the ways in which their lives are restricted under Canada's Indian Act. As a packed meeting room enjoyed pasta, salad, cake, and bread rolls provided by the MCA, a presenter talked about the Indian Act and its history, followed by a Q&A session led by the director of the *Entwetatha:wi* programme.

It was from an exchange during this Q&A that I extracted the title of this chapter. The discussion transitioned, as discussions often do in Akwesasne, to the topic of land. A contentious facet of indigenous self-governance is the fact that it makes it possible for communities to render their lands alienable. While under the Indian Act reserve lands cannot be sold to people outside the reserve, a self-governing reserve can change that rule, a matter I return to later in this chapter. Akwesasne's self-governance initiative maintains the inalienability of native lands – even with self-governance, residents would not be able to sell their land. One community member stood up to argue against this. He said that he felt he should have the right to do whatever he wanted with the land he and his family had held and worked for generations. It was, after all, in his eyes, 'his land'.

The presenter's response to his statement was respectful, but unwavering. She said that Mohawk people had long been a collective more than an individual culture, and that any new laws would have to reflect that fact. Lands would remain in the community, for the collective good. In this way, the discussion of land and law was also a discussion of culture, and the Mohawk programme director suggested politely to another Mohawk resident, 'That's not our culture.'

It reminded me of the scene from Monty Python's *Life of Brian*, in which Brian tells a crowd, 'You're all individuals,' and the crowd responds, in sync, 'Yes, we're all individuals,' with a lone dissenter shushed after saying, 'I'm not.' I felt I was watching that scene in reverse, as a Mohawk member of government stated 'We're all collective,' contradicting a shushed Mohawk citizen proclaiming 'I'm not.'

Is the man 'less' Mohawk for taking such an individualist stance? If not, how can I reconcile these two seemingly self-contradictory yet nevertheless coexistent facets of Akwesasne's attitudes towards self-governance and their culture – the valuing of personal autonomy and the valuing of collective determination?

In the remainder of this chapter I wish to unpack this exchange and the tensions that indigenous self-governance reveals between two different sorts of autonomy: personal and collective. I do so through the lens of 'paradox', a titular concept within this volume, albeit one that is largely underexamined in social and legal studies. In looking at the paradoxes of personal autonomy in indigenous self-governance, we can illuminate broader concerns over the way 'paradox' is employed as a concept in legal reasoning.

There are multiple paradoxes inherent in indigenous self-governance. It is built upon an appreciation of pluralism and autonomy which, in order to be viable, it must reject. It involves the coexistence of both Western and indigenous notions of what it means to be autonomous. It is at the same time a move away from state control of local affairs, and a step towards subjugation to state laws. Perhaps most strikingly, self-governance, in Akwesasne, requires simultaneously protecting a collective right to autonomy while limiting individual rights to claim autonomy from that collective.

Indigenous self-governance in Canada may be paradoxical, but it nevertheless works, and has become ever more popular among Canadian indigenous populations. It serves as a useful case study of Peter Fitzpatrick's assertion that law (as myth) both produces and resolves paradoxes. The paradoxes of personal autonomy in indigenous self-governance are both produced and resolved (or if not resolved, 'mediated') by Canadian law, traditional law, and Akwesasne's own emergent codified legal system.

On paradox

Before looking to the particularities of indigenous self-governance in Canada, I wish to address the question, 'What is paradox?' The title of this volume is *Personal Autonomy in Plural Societies: A Principle and Its Paradoxes.* Many of the contributions, this one included, critically address key terms from the title: 'autonomy', 'plurality', 'society'. Yet I want to take an opportunity to begin with a consideration of 'paradox'. This discussion may seem to be a digression, as I introduce paradox through anthropological engagement with the term, particularly in the study of myth. Nevertheless, after introducing myth in this light, I draw on legal theorist Peter Fitzpatrick to show, in the next section, the ways in which law, often seen as myth's opposite, may actually be seen as 'mythic' in its production and resolution of paradox.

What do we mean when we use the word 'paradox'? A lot of thinkers incorporate the term in their writings, but simply use it as shorthand for 'a problem'. Yet 'paradox' has historically referred to a particular logical permutation, a very distinct type of problem. Claude Levi-Strauss stands out as a thinker who addressed paradox systematically. According to Wendy Doniger, 'Paradoxes are to Levi-Strauss what whales were to Captain Ahab.'[3] It is perhaps unsurprising that Levi-Strauss would use his structural approach to tackle the

3 W Doniger, 'Foreword' in C Levi-Strauss, *Myth and Meaning* (Schocken Books 1979) x.

relationship between human beings and paradox. By seeing human thought in terms of binary oppositions, his theories required an understanding of the ways in which human beings deal with the coexistence of seemingly irreconcilable binaries.

My definition of paradox, for the purposes of this chapter, may not be universal, but I believe it meshes well with Levi-Strauss's uses of the term. As I employ it, paradox involves the coexistence of two mutually exclusive and at the same time mutually constitutive concepts. Take, for instance, the statement, 'I am lying to you right now.' In a particularly well-known episode of *Star Trek*, Captain Kirk uses this utterance to shut down the logical processors of a robot. There is no way the statement can make sense, yet it can still be uttered. Paradoxes are often about reconciling the world that we find ourselves in with the concepts and structures that we use to interpret that world.

Levi-Strauss, like Kirk, recognized that paradox is something fundamentally human. He argued that 'pre-modern' societies used myth not so much to resolve paradoxes as to 'mediate' them.[4] This is a useful distinction, as it suggests that paradoxes do not occur 'out there' in the world, but rather in the human mind. It is also important to note that myth, in Levi-Strauss's terms, is not the colloquial 'something that is commonly believed to be false', but rather an oral narrative explaining something's origins.

For Levi-Strauss, the basic paradox underlying myth is anthropogenesis – the origins of human beings. Humans are at the same time 'natural' and 'cultural' beings, even if in practice we view the two as mutually exclusive categories.[5] We are simultaneously born of the earth and born of already existent human societies, and we are aware of this inconsistency. We are from people and we are from nature. This paradox, incapable of logical resolution (we cannot be both at the same time, yet nevertheless we clearly are), is mediated through myth by creating a world in which beings can be both natural and cultural at the same time. Myths contain demi-gods, beings jointly sired by humans and deities (or totemic spirits). *These* beings can be simultaneously natural and cultural. Because the realm of myth lies both within and outside the realm of humanity – it is our world but, at the same time, a world outside our own – paradoxes that cannot be resolved elsewhere become solvable in myth. In this way, myth, like law, can be viewed as 'a problem solver'.[6]

On law and paradox

Peter Fitzpatrick's *The Mythology of Modern Law* suggests that while law positions itself as the antithesis of myth, it is actually myth's modern counterpart.[7] Law, Fitzpatrick argues, like myth, both produces and mediates paradoxes. For Fitzpatrick, the basic underlying paradox of law is 'the opposition between law as autonomous doctrine and law as dependent on society'.[8] I'd like to take a moment to unpack that assertion.

Law is frequently understood as 'autonomous', meaning it produces and responds to its own norms. Statements such as 'the law says this' and 'according to the law' often work

4 C Levi-Strauss, *Myth and Meaning* (Schocken Books 1979).

5 C Levi-Strauss, 'The Structural Study of Myth' (1955) 270 *The Journal of American Folklore* 428.

6 S Falk Moore, 'Certainties Undone: Fifty Turbulent Years of Legal Anthropology, 1949–1999' (2001) 7(1) *The Journal of the Royal Anthropological Institute* 97.

7 P Fitzpatrick, *The Mythology of Modern Law* (Routledge 1992).

8 Ibid. 3.

on the assumption that the law is an internally coherent system. Both positivist[9] and autopoietic[10] understandings of legal systems emphasize law's autonomy as a self-referential, self-sustaining system that lies distinctly outside the societies that implement law. Law is at the same time frequently recognized as socially contingent. Law is a reflection of societal norms and is created and enforced in reference to those norms. Rather than being internally self-sustaining, law is contingent upon socially delineated concepts and ideals, and changes when those concepts and ideals change.

As Fitzpatrick saw it, although people argue as to whether law is, in practice, social or autonomous, it is generally understood as both at the same time. This should not be possible, yet it is demonstrably the way people talk about law. Law, according to Fitzpatrick, is able to mediate the paradox of its own existence because law, like myth, is at the same time within the realm of society and outside of it. Law not only permits and resolves paradox; it both produces and is born from it.

When Fitzpatrick is talking about 'law', he is responding to a particular notion of the term linked to contemporary Western models. This meshes with my current use of the term 'law' as well, but should not be assumed to be universal. In fact, this is one of the reasons why the installation of self-governance in Akwesasne is problematic, as Akwesasne attempts to overlay Canadian understandings of law and autonomy on its own.

Much as Western models of 'law' are by no means universal, the same can be said of 'autonomy'. The Comaroffs have gone so far as to (re)ask, 'Is the idea of "the autonomous person" a European invention?'[11] Indeed, my ethnographic illustration seeks to demonstrate that Akwesasronon are actively involved in the self-conscious assertion and development of non-Western models of autonomy in their own pursuit of sovereignty.

Putting aside for the moment Fitzpatrick's notion of 'the law as autonomous', Akwesasne's self-governance efforts, and arguably those of any indigenous government, involve at least two distinct sorts of autonomy. Collective autonomy is typically understood as the capacity of groups to self-determine, and individual autonomy is typically understood as the capacity of individuals within a given group to self-determine.[12]

In the context of the 'that's not our culture' exchange, the representative of the Mohawk government, in articulating a plan for Akwesasne's collective autonomy, clashed with an Akwesasronon's claims to personal autonomy. I elaborate upon this issue in the next section. For now, it is useful simply to recognize the coexistence of these two sorts of autonomy and their precarious and often mutually contradictory application.

In trying to develop a body of law and governance that simultaneously reflects their culture and is legible within a Western legal framework, Akwesasronon are engaging with the debate Fitzpatrick sees at the core of law as myth. Yet whereas Fitzpatrick is focused on already existent legal systems in a sort of 'just-so' story, Akwesasne could be said to be undergoing 'jurisgenesis' – the production of new law and legal meanings.[13] In observing

9 J Donovan, *Legal Anthropology: An Introduction* (Almira Press 2007).

10 H Baxter, 'Niklas Luhmann's Theory of Autopoietic Legal Systems' (2013) 9 *Annual Review of Law and Science* 167.

11 Jean Comaroff and John Comaroff, *Theory From the South: Or, How Euro-America Is Evolving Toward Africa* (Paradigm Publishers 2012) 51.

12 See W Kymlicka, *The Rights of Minority Cultures* (Oxford University Press 1995).

13 R Cover, 'Nomos and Narrative' in M Minow, M Ryan, and A Sarat (eds), *Narrative, Violence, and the Law: The Essays of Robert Cover* (University of Michigan Press 1992) 95.

Akwesasne conceptualize, articulate, ratify, and enforce its own law, those paradoxes are not relegated to an imagined past, but are part of the ongoing present.

Paradox in indigenous self-governance

Indigenous self-governance in Akwesasne and elsewhere is, therefore, a sort of cosmology – the creation of something new. As predicted by Fitzpatrick, this creation involves the coexistence of multiple seemingly contradictory yet nevertheless mutually contingent concepts – in other words, paradox. Below, I wish to highlight the origins of Akwesasne's call for self-governance and a legal system 'autonomous' from that of Canada. In doing so, I suggest that this self-governance both produces and seeks to resolve paradox.

Though it has grown well beyond its initial goals, Akwesasne's self-governance initiative originated in efforts to simplify land dispute resolution in the community. This was explained by Akwesasne policy analyst Gilbert Terrance in a film disseminated within the community titled *Indian Act and You: Our Path to Entewatatha:wi*:

> Currently, there's a blame game going on. Canada, through Indian Affairs, devolved some of the management to the council, but when the council goes to make a decision regarding a land dispute, the decision does not hold water in the [Canadian] court of law. So what you find is winners and losers. The losers go to the outside court and create more of a mess, the dispute goes on unsettled, and it just multiplies upon itself to the point where we're at today, where you've got thousands of disputes, some of them haven't been settled for generations.[14]

In the context of our present discussion, one can understand Akwesasne's self-governance initiative as spurred by efforts to reduce what legal theorists refer to as 'forum shopping'.[15] The Mohawk government wishes to claim exclusive judicial authority over land claims and thereby diminish the possibilities for individual tribal members to seek out external legal forums where they can find a more favourable verdict. According to this view, in order to uphold the collective autonomy of Akwesasne as a sovereign entity, the personal autonomy of members to access multiple forums must be circumscribed. A question emerges as to who the holder of Akwesasne's rights is: is it the individual members of the tribe, or the tribe as a collective unit?

It is ironic (though not surprising) that Canadian popular support for indigenous self-governance is largely tied to the values of pluralism at a national level, which Akwesasne must refute at a local level in order to activate and take full advantage of. Let me unpack that: the popular discourse among proponents of self-governance suggests that minority peoples have the right to self-determine, and therefore their laws should be recognized and accommodated. Canadian multiculturalism discourse draws heavily upon this assumption. However, in order for that self-determination to hold meaning, to have 'teeth', individual members of a minority group cannot simply look towards state intervention whenever they are dissatisfied with the outcome of a judicial intervention. Pluralism justifies the sovereignty

14 The Mohawk Council of Akwesasne, *Indian Act and You, Part 2: Entewatatha:wi & You* (2009) <www.akwesasne.ca/node/122> accessed 3 May 2017.

15 The Harvard Law Review Association, 'Forum Shopping Reconsidered' (1990) 103(7) *Harvard Law Review* 1677.

of indigenous polities, but has the potential to negate it. It is, to use the words of Scott Matter in his discussion of indigenous land rights in Kenya, a 'shield and a double-edged sword'.[16] As long as national and indigenous authorities overlap, autonomy both constitutes and contests indigenous self-governance.

Making the law

Community responses to the self-governance project are mixed. Proponents see it as an important step towards the articulation of Mohawk sovereignty. Antagonists suggest that it is merely another effort by the Canada-recognized Mohawk Council of Akwesasne (MCA) to consolidate its authority locally. One online commentator remarked that self-governance was simply another power play by the 'old boys' club'. Another saw this active collaboration with the Canadian government as 'the road to assimilation'.[17] The critics suggest that, rather than taking a step away from Canadian control, by buying into a Canadian model of self-governance the MCA is diminishing Akwesasne's own sovereignty.

Architects of the Mohawk Council's new laws shared some ambivalence regarding the extent to which self-governance could successfully reflect true autonomy. Several mentioned feeling pressure, if not the necessity, to frame their laws in a way that would be recognizable and acceptable to Canada. In other words, they made intentional efforts to 'Canadianize' their own laws, to bolster their 'legibility'[18] and efficacy, and to distinguish them, in form if not in substance, from 'traditional' laws. Both supporters and detractors of the self-governance initiative had the sense that Akwesasne's autonomy and sovereignty are important, and that the administration of the territories should reflect these ideals. At the same time, opinions differed as to how best to achieve these aims.

The MCA's decision to maintain lands as inalienable communal properties demonstrates one effort at producing culturally contingent albeit universally legible by-laws. Akwesasne's decision to keep lands in the community is also a reaction against historical notions of land distribution and 'civilization' that settlers of North America brought with them and tried to impose.

At present, reserve lands are held in trust by the Canadian government and are inalienable – they can be transferred within the band (tribe), but not sold outside of it. Self-governance initiatives make it possible to change this institution, and have done so with varying degrees of success. Conservative proponents of aboriginal self-governance in Canada feel that the ability to borrow money against tribal land makes it possible for native communities to access the capital necessary for self-governance.[19] Popular critics say that this is just another means for settler states to take land away from Indians.

Indeed, one can draw parallels between the potential privatization and alienation of land under aboriginal self-governance and previous efforts in North America to 'civilize'

16 S Matter, 'The Title Deed as Shield and Double-Edged Sword: Land Adjudication and Titling at Enoosupukia, Kenya' (108th Annual Meeting of the American Anthropological Association, Philadelphia, November 2009).

17 LA Baker, 'Going their Own Way on Cornwall Island?' *Cornwall Standard-Freeholder* (18 January 2014) <www.standard-freeholder.com/2014/01/16/going-their-own-way-on-cornwall-island> accessed 3 May 2017.

18 J Scott, *Seeing Like a State: How Certain Schemes to Improve the Human Condition Have Failed* (Yale University Press 1998).

19 T Flanagan et al., *Beyond the Indian Act: Restoring Aboriginal Property Rights* (McGill-Queen's University Press 2010).

indigenous peoples by transforming communally held tribal lands into privately held plots. The Dawes Act of 1887 attempted to do just that in the United States and defined America's 'Indian Policy' for nearly half a century. It inspired similar legislation by colonial powers as far away as Japan's Ainu territories.[20] The presumed connection between private property ownership and civilization was deeply embedded in the evolutionist assumptions in the social sciences of the late nineteenth century which (ironically) were built largely upon ethnological studies of Haudenosaunee peoples.[21]

Whereas settler states historically forced privatization on indigenous peoples with the stated intention of bringing them into the folds of 'Western civilization', contemporary efforts place the decision to privatize in the hands of indigenous polities in an effort to support their distinctiveness. One could say that whereas the Dawes Act privileged individual autonomy as the hallmark of civilization, contemporary measures privilege collective autonomy. Whether this is an effort to support indigenous sovereignty or merely the continuation of colonization by other means remains a subject of debate.

While the MCA wants to change the way land claims are handled, its current proposal for self-governance maintains the provision that land cannot be sold off reserve. This was the cause of the discussion between the community member and the MCA representative over Akwesasne as a collective culture.

What fascinated me about the exchange was not the debate over land use, but rather the framing of that debate in terms of a definition of Akwesasne's culture. Whereas for well over a century legal conceptions of indigenous 'culture' in Canada have been decided largely by non-native elites within the courtroom,[22] Akwesasne's self-governance initiative has inverted this model. It demands a community-level consultation in the development of new laws by consensus. In other words, self-governance requires turning culture into law at the local rather than the state level. Whether or not it is a good idea to bring law in Akwesasne closer to Mohawk culture is not the issue – most everyone agrees that is a good idea. The issue is what constitutes that culture, and how best to formalize it into a juridical structure.

The question of 'our culture' can be interrogated both in terms of what constitutes 'culture' and in terms of what constitutes 'our'. It is of little surprise, then, that much of the North American media attention to indigenous self-governance has focused on 'the membership issue', that is, the question of who is granted access to tribal membership. This issue is controversial, in part because after writing their own constitutions some native North American tribes disenfranchised particular groups of members.

Perhaps the most notable case involved the Seminole Nation of Oklahoma's decision to remove members of African descent from the rolls.[23] When newly disenfranchised 'black Seminoles' appealed to the United States government, the courts ruled that they had no right to interfere with native sovereignty. Legislators found another solution by refusing to provide aid to the tribe, saying that the Seminoles with whom they signed treaties included

20 DF Medak-Saltzman, *Staging Empire: The Display and Erasure of Indigenous Peoples in Japanese and American Nation Building Projects (1860–1904)* (ProQuest 2008) 104.

21 LH Morgan, *Ancient Society: Or, Researches in the Lines of Human Progress From Savagery Through Barbarism to Civilization* (Charles H. Kerr & Company 1878).

22 R Niezen, 'Culture and the Judiciary: The Meaning of the Culture Concept as a Source of Aboriginal Rights in Canada' (2003) 18(2) *Canadian Journal of Law and Society* 1.

23 K Mulroy, *The Seminole Freedmen: A History* (University of Oklahoma Press 2007).

black members, and once the membership was altered, so too was the status of those treaties. The Seminole Nation quickly reversed its policy and readmitted those members.

I see these debates as related to, albeit distinct from, what Ronald Niezen has called 'the law's legal anthropology'.[24] Niezen has pointed to the fact that human rights discourses 'have also produced their own distinct legal anthropology, a body of rights-oriented knowledge that includes an understanding of the essence of humanity and the legitimate forms and categories of human belonging'.[25] Indigenous self-governance similarly involves the interrogation and definition of cultural values in service of the law.

This engagement with culture is explicit. At the beginning of the *Entwetatha:wi* video (quoted earlier), a voiceover states, 'As Onkwehonwe [indigenous] people, our relationship with the land is an integral part of our identity. This idea is taken into account while negotiating the land sectoral agreement.'[26] This remark was made in a video designed for Akwesasronon, not academics or other publics. Contrary to Vine Deloria's remark that 'tribal identity is assumed, not defined by reservation people,'[27] the identity of reservation people in Akwesasne is, and in fact *must* be, both assumed and defined. Tribal identity must be assumed in order to justify self-governance, but it must be defined in order to write the laws.

By linking rights claims to a distinct notion of 'traditional' culture that is bound to the past but constituted in the present, the juridification of indigenous culture raises some difficult questions. If a member of an indigenous group chooses to dissent from majoritarian notions of culture, is he or she to be viewed as an outsider within that group? Or disenfranchised entirely?

Resolving paradox

How can we resolve these paradoxes? Fitzpatrick's argument suggests that the law itself resolves or, if not resolves, mediates those paradoxes that it has created. Though it has not been finalized, self-governance will likely mean the adoption of a legal code in Akwesasne that will take these concerns into account, even if it cannot 'solve' them. And like other legal systems, it will 'work' in spite of any intrinsic paradoxes.

In the context of Akwesasne's self-governance, we can also look beyond the new law to traditional governance principles, which dealt with similar questions in the past. Haudenosaunee traditional practices sit both within contemporary self-governing principles, as they are undeniably a facet of Mohawk culture, and outside those principles, as they draw upon a largely oral, frequently metaphorical, and narrative structure that cannot easily be translated into codified laws recognizable by the Canadian state. It is myth, drawing on narratives and metaphors, and it is law, articulating prescribed practices and accepted norms. These narratives take place in a world where what may seem impossible is possible, and as such, are useful to draw upon in resolving paradox. Here I highlight two principles of Haudenosaunee governance: the 'two-row *wampum*' and the deposition of chiefs. While these traditions are unique to Haudenosaunee peoples, if we assume that all law, not only Western law, must produce and mediate paradox, then we can expect to find corollaries in other indigenous legal traditions.

24 R Niezen, 'The Law's Legal Anthropology' in M Goodale (ed), *Human Rights at the Crossroads* (Oxford University Press 2012) 185.

25 Ibid. 186.

26 Mohawk Council of Akwesasne (n 14).

27 V Deloria Jr, *Custer Died for Your Sins: An Indian Manifesto* (University of Oklahoma Press 1988) 84.

The two-row *wampum* (*kaswentha*) symbolizes the proposed relationship between Haudenosaunee (Iroquois) nations and settler states. The word *wampum* refers to purple and white shell beads that Haudenosaunee people have long tied together to form belts or strings communicating ideas and information. The *wampum* depicts two vessels travelling side by side along a single stream. One is a European-style ship; the other, a Haudenosaunee canoe. Three rows of beads separate the two vessels: two parallel rows of purple *wampum* symbolizing peace and friendship, separated by a single row of white *wampum*. The *wampum* is meant to demonstrate a relationship that respects the autonomy of indigenous peoples and European settlers. Neither party should try to steer the other's ship, nor should one set foot in the other's vessel.

Wampum is understood by Haudenosaunee peoples as a political and legal document, and not a mythical or religious one; it offers a solution to the problem of two sovereign powers occupying the same land. It does so, much like myth or law, through narrative, symbolism, and metaphor. The two-row *wampum* stands out as the most frequently cited *wampum* in court cases and international political forums. While many indigenous rights claimants refer to it as a treaty, Kathryn Muller suggests it is, perhaps, best understood as the articulation of a particular 'ethic' of non-interference.[28]

The *wampum* encapsulates Haudenosaunee sovereignty by depicting a nation-to-nation relationship, and is a defining expression of the way sovereignty is enacted among Haudenosaunee peoples.[29] For this reason many Haudenosaunee, especially Mohawk people, have long refrained from voting or otherwise participating in the political affairs of Canadian or American states. There is a general sentiment that voting for governments installed by those states would serve as de facto recognition of their authority, a notion that is rejected by Haudenosaunee.

The two-row *wampum*, in the words of Jon Parmenter, 'makes manifest the joint decision by two parties to remain independent together'.[30] It suggests the confluence of a plurality of autonomies. To extend the two-row metaphor, we can say that legal pluralism seeks to create multiple sections on the same ship, whereas indigenous self-governance (at least in the case of Akwesasne) tries to get all its citizens onto one boat and maintain a safe distance from the other boats. Such a narrative helps mediate the paradoxes of multiple authorities occupying the same territories. Whereas multiple polities may have trouble maintaining sovereignty in one space, multiple ships can steer their own courses along the same river. In this regard, the Mohawk Council of Akwesasne's self-governance programme seeks to define its vessel and get everyone on board.

Darlene Johnston suggests the latter in 'The Quest of the Six Nations Confederacy for Self Determination'.[31] Drawing on oral histories, she states that any chief who sold land to someone outside the community would, by virtue of his actions, be 'de-horned' and effectively removed from the confederacy. The dehorning of chiefs is built into the visual

28 K Muller, *Holding Hands With Wampum: Haudenosaunee Council Fires From the Great Law of Peace to Contemporary Relationships With the Canadian State* (DPhil thesis, Queen's University 2009).

29 J Rickard, 'Visualizing Sovereignty in the Time of Biometric Sensors' (2012) 110(2) *South Atlantic Quarterly* 465.

30 J Parmenter, 'The Meaning of *Kaswentha* and the Two Row Wampum Belt in Haudenosaunee (Iroquois) History: Can Indigenous Oral Tradition be Reconciled With the Documentary Record?' (2013) 3 *Journal of Early American History* 82, 85.

31 D Johnston, 'The Quest of the Six Nations Confederacy for Self-Determination' (1986) 1 *University of Toronto Faculty of Law Review* 44.

representation of the great law: male chiefs holding hands within a circle facing inward while clan mothers hold hands in a larger circle facing outward. Horns – the signs of chiefly authority – are worn on the chiefs' heads. According to one elder I interviewed, they represent a keen awareness of danger, much like antennae on a TV set pick up signals. While someone could bend down to step under conjoined hands and go outside the circle, in doing so his horns would fall off and, as a result, he would no longer be a chief. The horns remain in the circle, even if the wearer tries to step outside.

In other words, it is impossible to dissent (at least in some regards) and retain status. According to Johnston's reading of the underlying logics of Haudenosaunee governance, if the man who stood up in the meeting sold his land, he would no longer be considered Haudenosaunee, and therefore would (in the eyes of many, though certainly not himself) have had no right to sell land which belongs only to Haudenosaunee peoples. The land, like the horns, must remain inside the circle. In this way, the exercise of autonomy may result in disenfranchisement from the regime that grants the possibility of autonomy.

Conclusion

Whereas Jo Carillo has suggested that the collectivist 'symbolic Indian' is ultimately a legal fiction, a device created by the courts for their own purposes,[32] ongoing discussions about collective land ownership suggest that, symbolic or not, the 'image' of indigenous peoples as collective societies is being reflected in internal political considerations. This image is no less complete, no less critical, and no less vibrant than 'the concept of humanity at the foundation of human rights'.[33] It differs in that it is being articulated and formalized *within* rather than outside community voices.

Indeed, these legal conceptions of culture *must* be integrated into an indigenous self-governance regime that is based upon culture and seeks to integrate it into law. While social scientists (native and non-native alike) have long criticized lawyers for not taking an extensive, nonessential, empirical, and critical notion of identity into account, the mechanisms of indigenous self-governance demonstrate that efforts to address indigenous difference in the judiciary, even if by native people themselves, invoke particular and limited notions of culture.

I want to lay my cards on the table and say that I feel self-governance in Akwesasne is a good thing – simply because it is paradoxical does not mean it should be rejected. Rather, one can benefit from looking at the ways in which the articulation and resolution of paradoxes involve new applications of law and contribute to long-standing debates about the relationships between collectivity and individuality.

Carillo, echoing Fitzpatrick (though not citing him), suggests that there is a mythic quality to law; that law, like myth, 'is itself a narrative tradition . . . meant to illuminate the mystery we find ourselves in'.[34] Law, like myth, involves 'the stories that we tell ourselves about ourselves'.[35] Law, like myth, involves the resolution of paradoxes about ourselves, the most fundamental involving who 'we' are and how 'we' came to be. Indigenous self-governance requires re-asking these questions, and also requires answers compatible with

32 J Carillo, 'Getting to Survivance: An Essay About the Role of Mythologies in Law' (2002) 25(1) *PoLAR: Political and Legal Anthropology Review* 37.

33 Niezen (n 24) 186.

34 Carillo (n 31) 38.

35 C Geertz, *The Interpretation of Cultures* (Basic Books 1973) 448.

a legal framework. In this context, the establishment of a new legal system involves the formalization of locally pertinent definitions of autonomy and collectivity, which it must then reconcile.

Indigenous self-governance programmes such as Akwesasne's create, and indeed necessitate, the assertion of legal/mythical narratives concerning the fundamental qualities of a particular group of people. Paradoxes of personal autonomy in a plural society are one expression of paradoxes of both humanity and law as at the same time autonomous and social.

Index

For Product Safety Concerns and Information please contact our EU representative GPSR@taylorandfrancis.com Taylor & Francis Verlag GmbH, Kaufingerstraße 24, 80331 München, Germany